Spotlight on Comprehension

From the Beginning

From the beginning, we seek meaning
We look
We wonder
We learn

From the beginning, we want our world to make sense
We make connections
We ask questions
We focus on what is important to us

From the beginning, reading can make sense, too
We use sounds and make words
But that isn't enough
We need more

From the beginning

—Linda Hoyt

Spotlight on Comprehension

Building a Literacy of Thoughtfulness

LINDA HOYT
with other leading experts

HEINEMANN
Portsmouth, NH

KH

Heinemann
A division of Reed Elsevier Inc.
361 Hanover Street
Portsmouth, NH 03801–3912
www.heinemann.com

Offices and agents throughout the world

The author and publisher wish to thank those who have generously given permission to reprint borrowed material:

Book covers from *Windows on Literacy* and *Reading Expeditions* reprinted by permission from National Geographic School Publishing.

Screenshots from iMovie Tutorial reprinted by permission from Apple Computer, Inc.

Library of Congress Cataloging-in-Publication Data
    Spotlight on comprehension : building a literacy of thoughtfulness / [edited by] Linda Hoyt.
        p.   cm.
    Includes bibliographical references and index.
    ISBN 0-325-00719-5
    1. Reading comprehension.   2. Reading (Elementary).   I. Hoyt, Linda.
LB1573.7.S66   2004
372.47—dc22   2004021034

Editor: Lois Bridges
Production coordinators: Abigail M. Heim and Elizabeth Valway
Production service: Patricia Adams
Typesetter: Technologies 'N Typography, Inc.
Cover design coordinator: Renée Le Verrier
Cover design: Jenny Jensen Greenleaf
Cover photography: Megan Hoyt (front middle photo and back), Carol Updegraff (front top photo), Gloria Jarrell (front bottom photo)
Manufacturing: Louise Richardson

Printed in the United States of America on acid-free paper
09 08 07 06 05 04 ML 1 2 3 4 5

8/26/05

To Steve

My friend, my partner . . .
for so many reasons.

Contents

ACKNOWLEDGMENTS   xii

DEAR READER   xiii

PART ONE   LAYING THE GROUNDWORK FOR EFFECTIVE INSTRUCTION

1   LINDA HOYT
Building a Literacy of Thoughtfulness   2

2   NELL K. DUKE and JULIA MOORHEAD REYNOLDS
Learning from Comprehension Research: Critical
Understandings to Guide Our Practices   9

3   ELLIN OLIVER KEENE
To Understand   22

4   DONA MCILVAIN
Building a Context for Strategy Instruction   40

5   KEVLYNN ANNANDALE
Comprehension Instruction: Explicit and
Multifaceted   46

6   LINDA HOYT
Many Ways of Knowing   58

PART TWO   CRAFTING ENVIRONMENTS THAT FOSTER COMPREHENSION

7   LINDA HOYT
An Environment for Thoughtful Literacy   66

8   KATHLEEN FRANCESCANI
The Intimate Classroom: Establishing an
Emotional Environment That Encourages
Thoughtful Literacy Learning   76

9   JANE RAMBO
The Comprehension Classroom   85

10   MARGE COLLINS, MARION ODELL, and
SUSANNE C. SCOTT
Check It Out   92

11   V. SUSAN BENNETT-ARMISTEAD
Helping Parents Help Us: Promoting
Comprehension Through Parent
Involvement   97

Contents

• **PART THREE** Comprehending Strategically:
  Questioning, Inferring, Summarizing

12 Alison Maloney
  Guiding Comprehension Through Questioning
    and Coaching   108

13 Joy Scurlock
  The Ease of Questioning   117

14 Linda Hoyt
  Partner Think Alouds   125

15 Franki Sibberson
  Read It Again, Differently   130

16 Judy Wallis
  Inference: A Partnership with the Author   138

• **PART FOUR** Getting at Language: Words, Writing,
  and Reading Like a Writer

17 Linda Hoyt
  Comprehending at the Word Level   150

18 Linda Hoyt
  Building a Robust Vocabulary   161

19 Molly House
  Alphaboxes and the Two-Word Strategy . . . Not
    Just for Little Kids   174

20 Mary Monroe
  Language Banks, Imagery, and Poetry: Reading
    from a Writer's Point of View   185

21 Pat Adkisson and Joyce Price
  Strategies Authors Use to Aid
    Comprehension   194

22 Linda Hoyt
  Interactive Paragraphs   209

23 Marissa Ochoa
  Text to Tunes: Extending Understanding by
    Writing Songs   217

• **PART FIVE** Comprehension Instruction: Read
  Alouds, Guided Reading, and
  Independent Reading

24 Teresa Therriault
  Building Comprehension Through Read Alouds
    with Picture Books   226

25 Michael F. Opitz and Matthew D. Zbaracki
  Listening Is Comprehension Too!   236

26 Linda Hoyt
  Making Connections: Building Companion
    Collections for Guided Reading   243

27   TONY STEAD
     Comprehending Nonfiction: Using Guided
       Reading to Deepen Understandings   264

28   JANE RAMBO
     Guided Reading: More Than Just Decoding and
       Retelling   275

29   CAROL UPDEGRAFF
     From Doubt to Celebration: Strategy Instruction
       in Independent Reading   283

30   STACI MONREAL and JENNIFER WHITE
     Reading Partnerships: Grasping Deeper Layers of
       Meaning   291

PART SIX   TACKLING TEXTS (AND TESTS) ACROSS THE
           CURRICULUM

31   LINDA HOYT
     The Power of Rereading Informational
       Texts   308

32   JODI SNYDER
     A Recipe for Success: Comprehension Strategies
       Across the Curriculum   314

33   MARLEE WRIGHT
     A Teachable Moment for a Teacher: Nonfiction for
       Emergent Readers   320

34   RACHEL JORDAN
     Science Notebooks: Developing Understanding
       and Strategies   326

35   MARY LEE HAHN
     I See What You Mean: Using iMovie in the
       Reading Workshop   333

36   BARBARA COLEMAN
     Paint Pots of Poetry: Deepening Comprehension
       Through Cooperative Poetry Discussion   340

37   CATHY BERNHARD
     Math + Literature = Comprehension and
       Concepts!   347

38   CATHY TOWER
     Is Pluto a Planet? How Inquiry Curriculum
       Supports Comprehension   356

39   LINDA HOYT
     Comprehending Standardized Tests   363

40   BARBARA COLEMAN
     Puzzled About Comprehension and Standardized
       Testing?   374

PART SEVEN   UNDERSTANDING COMPREHENSION AND THE
EMERGENT READER

41   LINDA HOYT
Comprehension for Emergent Readers   386

42   GRETCHEN OWOCKI and CAMILLE CAMMACK
Comprehending the Cereal Box   397

43   CAROLE IMUS
Making Thinking Come Alive in the Early
Childhood Classroom   406

44   JILL HAUSER
"You Are My Sunshine" Is Not About the Sun!
Teaching Comprehension to Young Children
Through Song Lyrics   414

45   CATE HILL
Read Alouds and Retells: Building Early Text
Comprehension   425

46   KAREN LOKTING
Searching for a Comprehension Game-
Plan? . . . Just Follow the Yellow Brick
Road!   434

PART EIGHT   SUPPORTING COMPREHENSION FOR ENGLISH
LANGUAGE LEARNERS

47   JAN McCALL
Frontloading for ELL's: Building Concepts and
Vocabulary Before Reading   444

48   YVONNE and DAVID FREEMAN
Preview, View, Review: Giving Multilingual
Learners Access to the Curriculum   453

49   ALICIA J. BOLT
Three for the Road: Strategies for Success with
Bilingual Learners!   460

50   DENISE REA and SANDRA MERCURI
Scaffolding and Contextualizing: Reading for Real
with English Learners   470

51   LESLIE MARICLE-BARKLEY
Expanding the World Through Read Alouds:
Unlocking Comprehension for English
Language Learners   479

PART NINE   CONSIDERING INSTRUCTION THAT WORKS

52   TERESA THERRIAULT
      A Veteran Teacher Reflects on
          Comprehension   490

53   AMY GOODMAN
      Aligning Strategy Instruction Across Classrooms:
          The Middle School High Five   499

54   KELLI KESLER
      "Can I Tell You a Secret?" Lessons from a Resistant
          Middle School Reader   511

55   ADRIA F. KLEIN
      Finding Our Way Through Diverse Perspectives:
          Comprehending Points of View and
          Language   520

56   BRUCE MORGAN
      Boys Will Be Boys   527

      CLOSING THOUGHTS   534
      INDEX   535

Acknowledgments

The contributors to this book are amazing. They have willingly shared their work with children and their thinking on our profession, and in many cases, worked exhaustively to squeeze a bit of writing into overcrowded lives. I thank them, sincerely, and hope that their thinking and their stories bring you insight into your own work with learners.

A number of individuals were key players in the photographs that appear on the cover and within the pages. My daughter, Megan, was instrumental in photos taken at Boeckman Creek Elementary in Wilsonville, Oregon. At Boeckman Creek, Charlotte Morris and her team make wonderful things happen for children and have generously opened their doors to me. Many more photos can be credited to Hopland Elementary in Ukiah, California, where Gloria Jarrell, principal-cum-photographer, captured the essence of quality instruction in her school. Carol Updegraff, multiage primary teacher at Hopland, also took many photos of her students in action.

Team Heinemann. What can I say? They are my friends, my anchors in stressful times, and visionaries who help turn dreams into reality. Lois Bridges, editor extraordinaire, loves to say she doesn't do anything for me but the reality is that she holds up a mirror and gives me the same support that a writing coach provides children in writers workshop. Her questions, her suggestions, and her praise are treasured. Abby Heim is the magician who turns a shapeless manuscript into visually inviting pages where readers can explore their own thinking. Renée Le Verrier worked with designers to create the beautiful front cover. I am delighted to work again with Patty Adams, whose copyediting brings clarity and precision to my work.

There are never enough thanks for Lesa Scott, Leigh Peake, and the rest of the Heinemann crew.

Dear Reader

Welcome to *Spotlight on Comprehension*! The voices you hear in this book represent passion about teaching, deep knowledge of the teaching and learning process, and a commitment to the unending learning journey that professional educators undertake in their effort to bring the highest-quality instruction to children.

The authors represented in this book invite you to share with them a belief that quality instruction is always "under construction" as we strive to reach greater levels of expertise in our efforts to best support learners. It is both our obligation and our challenge to never stop learning professionally . . . to never stop seeing children as the center of our work . . . and to resist being fearful of growth and change. The authors of this book share a belief that no one set of practices, no one set of materials will meet the needs of all children. We believe that it is the knowledgeable teacher who makes the difference.

As you enter this book, we invite you to interact with our thinking, ask questions of the authors, yourself, and your colleagues . . . to wonder with us how we might bring all learners to a place where the goals of thoughtful reflection and deep understanding are built and nurtured.

This book is organized to support book study groups or individual teachers working independently. The sections can be read in any order that suits you or your book study partners. Each article includes a "Meet the Author" section that presents the author's background and spotlights a "Focus Quote." The end of each article will support continued reflection through the Key Questions and the array of "tools" that are provided for your consideration. The Key Questions could be used for personal reflection as you consider your own practices and reflect upon the unique learning needs of your students and the curriculum of your district. If you are part of a book study group, the Key Questions might be used to stimulate discussion and dialogue about current practices and enticements for new practice offered in each article. The "tools" are a resource that you might consider as stimulus for writing on plain paper, as an idea that you could modify to fit your own thinking, or as reproducibles that are ready to use.

As you weave your way through the articles, it is our sincere hope that, in addition to new perspectives, you will also find affirmations for your current practices. . . . Isn't it powerful to learn that other educators have found the same or similar practices to empower readers?

These articles, while spotlighting comprehension and the environments that support deeper thinking, are not meant to represent everything there is to know about reading comprehension. Rather, they are a tapestry of relevant classroom research, effective instructional strategies, and opportunities for you to extend and refine your professional understandings.

There is no need to read these articles in order. You are encouraged to weave in and out of the sections, selecting articles and tools of interest to you and then making your own connections to the comprehension instruction you strive to create for your students.

Welcome to *Spotlight on Comprehension.* A world of possibility awaits.

Part One

Laying the
Groundwork for
Effective Instruction

1 Building a Literacy of Thoughtfulness

LINDA HOYT

MEET THE AUTHOR

LINDA HOYT *lives in Wilsonville, Oregon, with her husband, Steve, and their dog, Oakley. She finds great personal joy in spending time at the Oregon coast walking on the beach, spending time outdoors, or curling up by the fire with a good book.*

FOCUS QUOTE

Decoding and fluency are important. There is no question about it. But, we know too much to allow them to be blown out of proportion. We know too much to tolerate having any reader engaging with text without a well-developed toolbelt of strategies that include decoding, fluency, and comprehension.

I am passionate about my work as an educator. I am passionate about the joy of seeing a child's eyes light up with excitement about a topic or a reading selection. Most of all, I am passionate about the importance of comprehension. I believe that reading is making meaning, that it is the construction of images in our minds, the fervent generation of questions as we read, and the ability to determine what is important that separates "reading" from "decoding."

A literacy of thoughtfulness requires that *teachers are thoughtful* about their practices and the environments they create for learning. That they look with open eyes at what is happening and how time is used, that they look reflectively and objectively at the resources they offer children, and that they take time to wonder if demonstrations and student interactions are bringing deep thinking into every dimension of the curriculum. A literacy of thoughtfulness occurs when teachers engage in explicit demonstrations of meaning-seeking strategies in every subject area, giving learners time and support as they focus on deeper levels of meaning.

FIGURE 1–1 Readers need to bring strategy use to a conscious level.

A literacy of thoughtfulness requires that *learners become conscious about their strategy use.* That they focus on monitoring their own comprehension and make conscious decisions about ways to help themselves understand. A literacy of thoughtfulness is a literacy in which learners bring their behavior with text to a conscious level where they can analyze it, understand it, and become a deliberate participant in their own growth.

When Balance Is Lost

On occasion, I have walked into classrooms where children are reading lists of nonsense or pseudowords, or building fluency by reading passages for speed rather than expression of meaning and author style. In these moments I have to wonder, "What definition of reading are these children developing?" "Will these children understand that the absence of understanding that is inherent in nonsense words must be set aside when reading the real texts of our world?" "Will children whose goal is reading as fast as possible understand that pacing is something that shifts according to the kind of reading we are doing, our purpose as a reader, and the mood or tone of the piece we are reading?" "Will learners who emerge from these experiences develop strategies for self-monitoring their comprehension and find passion in reading for pleasure and for savoring well-crafted language?"

This issue was brought painfully to mind recently when I was in a fourth grade classroom as a visiting educator. After I did a demonstration lesson on finding key words in text (Hoyt 2003), a young reader asked me to listen to her read. I had noticed her paying careful attention during the demonstration and fully expected her to read a bit and then show me how she could apply the key word strategy that I had modeled.

With a sweet smile, she began to read from an article about conflict in the Middle East. As she read, she tracked with her finger across the line of print moving from the left side of the page completely across to the right side. This particular text was an article with a three column structure. But she didn't notice the columns running down the page and she didn't think about the meaning as she hopscotched across the page.

As she ran her finger in a straight line from left to right straight across all three columns, she read: "As the tension in the Middle spread. In many towns, schools such danger from rock . . ."

"As the tension in the Middle ‑‑➤ spread. In many towns, schools ‑➤ such danger from rock throwers East continues to escalate, con‑ have closed and children are and snipers. cerns about the safety of the not allowed to go on the street children in the area is wide‑ or into their yards as there is

She read each word accurately. She was fluent. Yet she made absolutely no sense! By completely ignoring the column structure of the page, she missed the meaning of the text and the vital importance of this world issue. Indeed, she seemed unaware of the very foundation of language . . . meaningful communication.

I was again treated to that big smile as she looked at me with pride. This student had read in a way that she thought was going to earn her praise. She had used decoding strategies well and she was grinning from ear to ear. She had read the passage on the Middle East with the very same strategies she had been taught to use in lists of nonsense words.

The reading teacher in me wanted to scoop her up and show her so many things about the act of reading . . . to help her become thoughtful and focused on reading. The researcher in me wanted to know, "why?" HOW could a child reach fourth grade and have so little sense of the essence of being a reader? What kind of instruction, or absence of it, could have brought this bright little girl to a definition of reading that did not include understanding the text? What kind of assessment practices could have enabled this reader to travel unnoticed through the system? What can be done now, quickly, to help this learner create a definition of reading that includes comprehension . . . a literacy of thoughtfulness that includes conscious, effective strategy use?

Decoding and fluency are important—there is no question about it. But, we know too much to allow them to be blown out of proportion. We know too much to tolerate having any reader engaging with books without a well-developed toolbelt of strategies that include decoding, fluency, and comprehension.

A Metaphor for Reading Instruction

I am reminded of a time after a serious wind storm in Oregon. The wind had ripped away a good many of the shingles on our house and left us with massive water leaks and freezing cold interior temperatures. I called roofer after roofer, asking them to come and help us with repairs. One at a time, they arrived, looked at the very steep pitch of our roof, the dramatic winds that were still blowing, and one at a time, they climbed in their vehicles and left. When I finally found a roofer who was willing to climb on our roof despite its steep incline, he wired two tall ladders together to reach the top, strapped on a toolbelt that was absolutely banging and clanging with tools, and hoisted a stack of shingles on his shoulder. Now, it was my turn to worry. Fighting the wind to even stay on my feet, I asked this roofer if he would like to leave some of the tools on the ground? He looked at me calmly and said: "Mrs. Hoyt, once I climb on that roof, I want every tool I might need right here with me. Having you hand me tools will not make me safer and I will never get this job done with just a hammer."

I realized that this was a metaphor for reading! Don't we want every reader to climb into books with a toolbelt banging and clanging with tools for getting the most out of their reading? Don't we want them to have a toolbelt that is ready at hand, easy to draw from, and representing the range of challenges a reader might encounter with a text? Don't we want that toolbelt to be loaded with multiple comprehension strategies that will empower them for understanding, for questioning, for making connections, and for finding pleasure in the texts of their world?

Teach Comprehension with a Sense of Urgency

Regie Routman reminds us to "teach with a sense of urgency" (Routman 2003). To build a literacy of thoughtfulness, we need that sense of urgency as we focus on comprehension instruction.

We need to engage a sense of urgency as we look at the learning day to ensure that comprehension instruction is being taught with expertise and being practiced in many settings. We need that sense of urgency as we examine the quality of texts and the quality of comprehension instruction proposed by programs. That sense of urgency will help us to determine if we might follow the guidance in a program or choose to engage learners with comprehension strategies that can be flexibly applied across the curriculum.

We need that sense of urgency as we consider the strategies being used by our students. Our children deserve a literacy that is filled with meaning, with questioning, with relevant connections, and with the ability to self-monitor understanding. A sense of urgency may help us to set aside nonessential activities to make more room for deep conversation and to focus instruction on how to create understanding as we read.

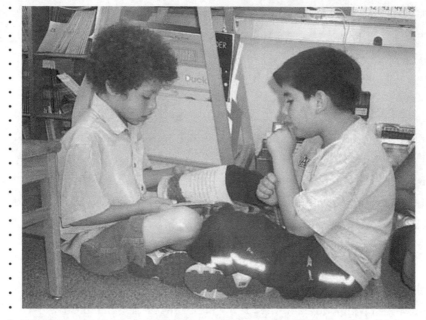

FIGURE 1–2 Second graders discuss the story and the comprehension strategies they used.

We need that sense of urgency to remind us that when students talk with partners about their reading strategies and the content being learned, their partner learning can be just as powerful as teacher-directed conversation.

We need that sense of urgency to guide conversations with colleagues so we can create a school culture that is focused on well-crafted comprehension instruction.

With a sense of urgency, comprehension instruction can reach greater heights. When there is balance between word knowledge and comprehension instruction, readers can not only wear but can use a toolbelt that is bristling with strategies and empowering in its ability to guide them into a literacy of thoughtfulness.

References

Hoyt, Linda. 2002. *Make It Real: Strategies for Success with Informational Texts.* Portsmouth, NH: Heinemann.

Routman, Regie. 2003. *Reading Essentials: The Specifics You Need to Teach Reading Well.* Portsmouth, NH: Heinemann.

KEY QUESTIONS

1. How can we ensure word study does not crowd out comprehension instruction?

2. Which strategies are most important for the readers' toolbelt?

3. Assessment for every lesson is essential. What kinds of assessments gather the most information about comprehension strategy use?

4. How can we convey the message to students that they must think about comprehension?

5. How might you create a schoolwide culture of comprehension instruction? How could you share with colleagues? How would you get the conversations started?

Questions to Ponder: Creating a Literacy of Thoughtfulness

- Is every minute used as wisely as possible to get the greatest gain for the learner?

- Is there a careful balance in instruction for word knowledge and comprehension?

- Are learners engaged in authentic reading tasks for real purposes and real audiences?

- Are the texts being offered to learners engaging and do they invite deep thinking?

- Is adequate value placed on conversations about meaning, diversity of opinions, and student-generated questions?

- Are comprehension strategies being modeled every day in every content area? Do you have discussions about reading strategies in math, science, health, and so on?

- Do we give our students enough *time* to talk to each other about their learning?

- Are our students spending enough time reading so they can build deep understanding?

- Are reading-related tasks such as worksheets, acrostics, and fill-in-the-blank being set aside to make more time for authentic comprehension moments?

- Do learners have ongoing experiences in applying strategies across all curricular areas?

- Is vocabulary being enriched by working with relationships between words and their meanings versus dictionary and rote level work?

- Does the environment invite conversation, collaboration, and deeper thought, or is it focused on the front of the room giving an impression that understanding resides with the teacher?

- Are performance assessments a part of every lesson to ensure that we know our learners well and can plan instruction to match their needs?

- Are assessments focused on comprehension strategies as well as the content learned?

- Can learners tell you which comprehension strategies they are using well and which ones they are trying to get better at?

- Would you describe your classroom as a place where thoughtful literacy is the focus?

Learning from Comprehension Research

Critical Understandings to Guide Our Practices

2

NELL K. DUKE AND
JULIA MOORHEAD REYNOLDS

MEET THE AUTHORS

NELL K. DUKE *is an associate professor of teacher education and learning, technology, and culture at Michigan State University. Her work focuses on early literacy development, especially the development of informational literacies in young children, comprehension teaching and learning in early schooling, approaches to addressing the needs of struggling reader-writers, and issues of equity in literacy education. She is co-author of the book* Reading and Writing Informational Text in the Primary Grades: Research-based Practices *(Scholastic, 2003).*

JULIA MOORHEAD REYNOLDS *is a doctoral student from Michigan State University and she works at Aquinas College in Grand Rapids, Michigan. She is a former high school English teacher and a language arts curriculum coordinator. Her research interests include secondary literacy, comprehension, and content-area literacy.*

FOCUS QUOTES

Comprehension instruction and instruction in word recognition and decoding can occur side by side, and even work synergistically.

Research on comprehension should guide the changes in instruction to improve reading comprehension of students throughout schooling.

Can you remember reading something that made you stop because you were so unclear about what was written on the page? All of us have become confused when reading at one time or another, possibly even resorting to giving up, feeling frustrated, and putting the passage down. Also, can you remember reading something that made you jump into the pages, being able to visualize the characters, the setting, and the emotions? Hopefully, there have been times when we could easily understand what we have read, even to the point of embracing it. What is it about comprehension that has enabled us to construct meaning while reading, and also to realize when meaning breaks down? How did we come to learn about this? Research on comprehension sheds light on these and other critical questions. In this chapter we summarize seven critical understandings from research on comprehension.

1. What Good Readers Do When They Read

Research has shown that good readers are active readers. From the outset, they have clear goals in mind for their reading. They constantly evaluate whether the text, and their reading of it, is meeting their goals. Good readers typically look over the text before they read, noting such things as the structure of the text and text sections that might be most relevant to their reading goals. As they read, good readers frequently make predictions about what is to come. They read selectively, continually making decisions about their reading—what to read carefully, what to read quickly, what not to read, what to re-read, and so on. Good readers construct, revise, and question the meanings they make as they read. They draw upon, compare, and integrate their prior knowledge with material in the text. For instance, they think about the authors of the text, their style, beliefs, intentions, and historical milieu. They monitor their understanding of the text, making adjustments in their reading as necessary. Good readers try to determine the meaning of unfamiliar words and concepts in the text, and they deal with inconsistencies or gaps as needed. They evaluate the text's quality and value, and react to the text in a range of ways, both intellectually and emotionally. Good readers read different kinds of text differently. For example, when reading narrative, good readers attend closely to the setting and characters; when reading expository text, these readers frequently construct and revise summaries of what they have read. For good readers, text processing occurs not only during reading as we have traditionally defined it, but also during short breaks taken during reading, even before the reading has commenced, and even after the reading has ceased. Comprehension is a consuming, continuous, and complex activity, but one that, for good readers, is both satisfying and productive. (Adapted from Duke and Pearson 2002.)

2. The Importance of Related Skills and Dispositions

Comprehension entails a complex web of skills and dispositions. Basic understandings entailed include *concepts of print* (the direction in which print is read, parts of a book, etc.), *phonemic awareness* (the understanding that the speech stream is composed of phonemes), the *alphabetic principle* (that these sounds or phonemes map onto letters), and *graphophonic knowledge* (specific sound-letter relationships). Skilled word recognition and decoding and fluent reading are critical in comprehension, and indeed, problems in these areas are a common cause of comprehension difficulties (Duke, Pressley, and Hilden 2004, Pressley 2000). Importantly, however, research does *not* suggest that these things should be in place *before* comprehension instruction occurs. On the contrary, comprehension instruction and instruction in word recognition and decoding can occur side by side, and even work synergistically (Pearson and Duke 2002, Pressley and Wharton-McDonald 2002, Stahl 2004).

The Link Between Vocabulary and Comprehension

Special note should be made of the relationship between vocabulary and comprehension. This relationship is unparalleled in strength and importance. One's knowledge of vocabulary relevant to a text is integrally related to comprehension of that text. Overall vocabulary knowledge is an excellent predictor of how strong a comprehender one is, and vice versa. And most importantly, at least some approaches to teaching vocabulary result not only in gains in vocabulary but in gains in comprehension as well. (See Beck and McKeown 1991, Blachowicz and Fisher 2000 for reviews.)

Effective Vocabulary Instruction

Good vocabulary instruction includes at its base a great deal of time spent reading and rich conversations about text. Good vocabulary instruction focuses on important words, and usually involves teaching conceptually related words rather than individual words unrelated to one another. The maxim to "relate the new to the known" is highly applicable in vocabulary instruction—students must make connections between words they already know and words they are learning. Exposure to words multiple times in multiple meaningful contexts is important. And most elusively, but perhaps most importantly, good vocabulary instruction raises word consciousness (Graves and Watts-Taffe 2002). Students think about words as words, notice when they hear or read words they don't know, and remember when they hear or read words they've just recently learned. They have an interest in words, in playing with words, in multiple meanings of words. This picture of good vocabulary instruction could not contrast more sharply with the classroom in which students are handed a list of unrelated words, write the dictionary definition, and use the word in a sentence. That kind of vocabulary instruction does not appear to work. (For further reading about effective vocabulary instruction, see Beck, McKeown, and Kucan 2002, Blachowicz and Fisher 2001, Stahl 1999.)

Reader Engagement

Many dispositions are integrally related to comprehension as well. For example, the disposition to read like a writer (and write like a reader) likely leads to stronger comprehension (Shanahan 1988). And being motivated and engaged in reading is absolutely central. As John Guthrie and Allan Wigfield (2000) remind us:

> Within a given school at a given time, some students are intent on reading and writing to understand. They focus on text meaning and avoid distractions. These engaged readers exchange ideas and interpretations of text with peers. Their devotion to reading spans across time, transfers to a variety of genre, and culminates in valued learning outcomes. In contrast, disengaged readers are inactive and inert. They tend to avoid reading and minimize effort. Rarely do they enjoy reading during free time or become absorbed in literature. (403)

Studies of exemplary teachers indicate that there are myriad things they do to promote literacy engagement in classrooms (Pressley *et al.* 2003). There are also specific instructional approaches, tested in research, designed to promote comprehension and engagement (Guthrie, Wigfield, and Perencevich 2004).

3. The Importance of Volume Reading

No one ever improved at playing the piano without practicing on a piano. Athletes do not make better basketball shots, hit more home runs, or score more hockey goals without practicing. The same goes for comprehension. Students need to read often and practice the comprehension skills and strategies that they are learning in real contexts. And reading provides benefits well beyond an opportunity to practice. Through reading, students learn new words and encounter new meanings or connotations for previously known words. As students read they also learn more about text itself—text structures, authors, devices, and so on. And through reading, students are able to learn about the world around them; for example, learning about what is happening in the world through events recounted in newspapers or developing a deeper understanding of an issue by reading multiple sources and points of view. Indeed, wide reading is associated with greater vocabulary, textual knowledge, and world knowledge (Stanovich and Cunningham 1993). And, of course, greater vocabulary, textual knowledge, and world knowledge enable stronger comprehension. For example, research indicates that good comprehenders have stronger knowledge of text structures than do poor comprehenders (e.g., Meyer, Brandt, and Bluth 1980). The student who does not read often and widely will almost surely stagnate in comprehension development.

4. The Potential in Discussion of Text

Discussion of text clearly has the potential to deepen comprehension (Gaskins *et al.* 1993, Van den Branden 2000). In fact, simply asking students questions about what they read, and creating situations in which students ask each other questions about what they read, has been shown to improve comprehension (Duke and Pearson 2002). A caution here, however. It is critical to ask a range of questions, including many higher level questions—questions that get at important content or issues, that do not have an answer right there in the text, that do not have just one answer in any case.

Think Alouds

Another important form of talk about text is the think aloud. Through think alouds, teachers model their thought processes (Davey 1983, Olshavsky 1976–77), showing students, through oral presentation, what is going on in their (the teacher's) mind while reading. Students can also engage in think alouds with one another or by themselves. This can spark interesting discussion, as students begin to think aloud to each other and talk about their thinking.

Instructional Conversations

Some specific approaches to structuring and conducting discussion of text have been tested in previous research. One approach shown to improve comprehension (not just of the texts discussed but of future texts to be read) is instructional conversations (Goldenberg 1993, Saunders and Goldenberg 1999).

Discussion is planned in advance   In this approach, teachers plan discussions in advance: selecting a text, identifying a thematic focus of the discussion, anticipating possible difficulties students may have (for example a lack of relevant background knowledge), and considering ways to address them, (thinking through directions the conversation may take, and contemplating possible ways of following up the discussion). The discussion itself then has a thematic focus, involves activating relevant background schemata, and includes, as needed, direct teaching and modeling by the teacher of knowledge or strategies that might aid comprehension. The teacher works to promote complex language and expression, for example, by recasting students' contributions or asking students to elaborate on their statements.

Questions to encourage connections and explanations   In this approach, few questions are asked in which the answer is simple and already known. Many questions are asked that require students to connect their prior knowledge to the reading or to explain the basis of their statements (e.g., "What makes you say that?"). Teacher and student build upon one another's contributions to the discussion, though the teacher also works to maintain a thematic focus and coherence of the discussion.

Connected discourse   The result with this approach is connected discourse rather than the old pattern in which the teacher asks a question, a student responds, the teacher evaluates the response, a teacher asks a new, unrelated question, the student responds, the teacher evaluates, and so on (known as the I–R–E (Initiation–Response–Evaluation) pattern; Cazden 1988). The atmosphere for Instructional Conversations is described as "challenging but nonthreatening" (Goldenberg 1993). Instructional Conversations are the kinds of rich conversations about text that many of us revel in.

5. The Effectiveness of Explicit Instruction in Comprehension Strategies

Perhaps the most critical understanding about building comprehension is the effectiveness of explicit instruction in comprehension strategies. Study after study has revealed that **explicitly** teaching students even one strategy for comprehending text can improve their comprehension (National Reading Panel 2000, Pearson *et al.* 1992, Pressley 2000). Lists of which strategies are worth teaching, with respect to research-proven gains in comprehension, vary somewhat, but usually include:

- generating questions
- thinking aloud
- monitoring comprehension and adjusting reading as needed
- attending to and uncovering text structure
- activating and applying relevant background knowledge, including making predictions
- drawing inferences
- constructing visual representations
- summarizing (Duke and Pearson 2002)

Many studies of these strategies include the following components in their instructional model:

1. An explicit description of the strategy, including when and how it should be used
2. Teacher and/or student modeling of the strategy in action
3. Collaborative use of the strategy in action (e.g., students and teacher making and justifying predictions together)
4. Guided practice using the strategy
5. Independent use of the strategy (Duke and Pearson 2002)

This reflects a gradual release of responsibility model, in which the teacher increasingly hands over control for use of the strategy to the student (Pearson and Gallagher 1983). Of course, one cycles through this release of responsibility over and over as texts become more difficult, new genres or situations are encountered, and so on.

6. The Particular Value of Multiple Strategy Instruction

As much as we have emphasized the impact of teaching even a single comprehension strategy, it seems that teaching multiple comprehension strategies simultaneously is particularly powerful (Duke and Pearson 2002, National Reading Panel 2000, Pressley 2000), including for students with learning disabilities (Gersten *et al.* 2001). One multiple strategy instruction approach is Collaborative Strategic Reading (Klingner and Vaughn 1999). In this approach, which draws from past work on reciprocal teaching and on cooperative learning, students work in small, cooperative groups while applying four comprehension strategies: *Preview* (think about what they already know, predict what the passage might be about), *"Click and Clunk"* (monitor comprehension, use fix-up strategies as needed), *Get the Gist* (glean and restate the most important idea), and *Wrap-Up* (summarize, ask questions). Students in the group have specific roles, such as leader, clunk expert, gist expert, and encourager, to assist in application of the strategies and, of course, understanding the text. Cue cards may be used to remind students of strategies, such as a clunk card that says: "Reread the sentences before and after the clunk looking for cues" or a student leader cue card that says: "Did everyone understand what we read? If you did not, write your clunks in your learning log." Students also complete learning logs before and after reading; this can both support their comprehension as well as provide valuable assessment information to the teacher. This approach has been tested in several studies and is shown to be effective at improving comprehension in upper-grades students. (See Vaughn, Klingner, and Bryant 2001 for a review of research on this approach; see Klingner *et al.* 2001, for a book on implementing the approach; see Duke and Bennett-Armistead 2003 for a discussion of use of this approach with primary grade students.)

7. The Importance of Authenticity

Relatively recent research suggests the importance of authenticity in developing comprehension. Briefly, as defined by Purcell-Gates and Duke (not yet published), authentic literacy events replicate or reflect reading and writing purposes and texts outside of a schooling context. For example, in authentic literacy events with informational text, students read not solely for the purpose of learning to read and write or satisfying a teacher's requirement, but because they actually want or need to know something—the reason people read informational text outside of schools. Students write informational text not simply to complete a report and hand it in to the teacher, but because they have information to convey to someone who wants or needs to know that information. Texts involved in authentic literacy events are rarely worksheets, textbooks, or short passages followed by multiple choice questions, but rather actual trade books, pamphlets, letters, magazine articles, and other types of texts commonly found outside of schools. In one study, teachers who included more authentic literacy events with informational and procedural text in science had students who showed more growth in comprehension (and writing) (Purcell-Gates and Duke, not yet published).

Teachers used many strategies to establish authentic literacy events. For example, they would use hands-on experiences to elicit children's questions about a topic, then setting the purpose for their reading and writing to answer these questions. Or they would establish outside audiences for children's writing—the class down the hall, pen pals, a community group, a local museum or nature center, and so on.

Concept-Oriented Reading Instruction (CORI)

One research-tested instructional approach that lends itself to authentic literacy events is Concept-Oriented Reading Instruction (CORI) (e.g., Guthrie, Wigfield, and Perencevich 2004). CORI centers on a conceptual theme in science, which is usually a big idea or universal concept. Students are engaged in hands-on experiences related to this theme, and also consult a wide variety of interesting, often student-selected texts. Students work in groups toward conceptual goals; for example, one group of students might work to learn about wetland habitats and to share what they've learned with another group of students (perhaps one working on desert habitats, who would in turn share what they've learned). Students are explicitly taught comprehension strategies, but it is done while meeting their conceptual goals. For example, they might be taught a summarizing strategy to help in summarizing material for their presentation. Evaluation of students focuses on the comprehension, conceptual knowledge, as well as their engagement.

Looking to the Future

We believe that these seven critical understandings from research on comprehension should be reflected in every classroom, in every content area, and with students of all ages. But we worry that they are not, and even recent research provides reason for our worry (Pressley and Wharton-McDonald 2002). You are reading this book, which suggests this is probably not the case in your classroom, but outside of your own classroom, how many students are still handed worksheets with literal questions to answer after reading a passage? How many discussions about text mirror the I-R-E format? How many teachers still give students a list of words on Monday to memorize and to spit back definitions on Friday? Comprehension is too important for us to continue ineffective practices. Comprehension is too important for us to neglect the practices that research has shown to be effective. Research on comprehension should guide the changes in instruction to improve the comprehension of students throughout schooling.

References

Beck, I. L., and M. McKeown. 1991. "Conditions of Vocabulary Acquisition." In *Handbook of Reading Research: Volume II,* edited by R. Barr, M. L. Kamil, P. Mosenthal, and P. D. Pearson, 789–814. White Plains, NY: Longman.

Beck, I. L., M. McKeown, and L. Kucan. 2002. *Bringing Words to Life: Robust Vocabulary Instruction.* New York: Guilford Press.

Blachowicz, C., and P. Fisher. 2001. *Teaching Vocabulary in All Classrooms, Second Edition.* Upper Saddle River, NJ: Prentice Hall.

——— 2000. "Vocabulary Instruction." In *Handbook of Reading Research: Volume III,* edited by M. L. Kamil, P. B. Mosenthal, P. D. Pearson, and R. Barr, 545–61. Mahwah NJ: Erlbaum.

Cazden, C. B. 1988. *Classroom Discourse: The Language of Teaching and Learning.* Portsmouth, NH: Heinemann.

Davey, B. 1983. "Think-Aloud: Modeling the Cognitive Processes of Reading Comprehension." *Journal of Reading* 27. 44–47.

Duke, N. K., and V. S. Bennett-Armistead, with A. Huxley, M. Johnson, D. McLurkin, E. Roberts, C. Rosen, E. Vogel. 2003. *Reading and Writing Informational Text in the Primary Grades: Research-Based Practices.* New York: Scholastic.

Duke, N. K., and P. D. Pearson. 2002. "Effective Practices for Developing Reading Comprehension." In *What Research Has to Say About Reading Instruction* (3rd edition), edited by A. E. Farstrup and S. J. Samuels, 205–42. Newark, DE: International Reading Association.

Duke, N. K., M. Pressley, and K. Hilden. 2004. "Difficulties with Reading Comprehension." In *Handbook of Language and Literacy Development and Disorders,* edited by C. A. Stone, E. R. Silliman, B. J. Ehren, and K. Apel, 501–20. New York: Guilford Press.

Gaskins, I. W., R. C. Anderson, M. Pressley, E. A. Cunicelli, and E. Satlow. 1993. "Six Teachers' Dialogue During Cognitive Process Instruction." *Elementary School Journal* 93: 277–304.

Gersten, R., L. S. Fuchs, J. P. Williams, and S. Baker. 2001. "Teaching Reading Comprehension Strategies to Students with Learning Disabilities: A Review of Research." *Review of Educational Research* 71: 279–320.

Goldenberg, C. 1993. "Instructional Conversations: Promoting Comprehension Through Discussion." *The Reading Teacher* 46: 316–26.

Graves, M. F., and S. M. Watts-Taffe. 2002. "The Place of Word Consciousness in a Research-Based Vocabulary Program," In *What Research Has to Say About Reading Instruction* (3rd edition), edited by A. E. Farstrup and S. J. Samuels, 140–165. Newark, DE: International Reading Association.

Guthrie, J. T., and A. Wigfield. 2000. "Engagement and Motivation in Reading. In *Handbook of Reading Research: Volume III,* edited by M. L. Kamil, P. B. Mosenthal, P. D. Pearson, and R. Barr, 403–24. Mahwah, NJ: Erlbaum.

Guthrie, J. T., A. Wigfield, and K. C. Perencevich. 2004. *Motivating Reading Comprehension: Concept-Oriented Reading Instruction.* Mahwah, NJ: Erlbaum.

Klingner, J. K., and S. Vaughn. 1999. "Promoting Reading Comprehension, Content Learning, and English Acquisition Through Collaborative Strategic Reading (CSR)." *Reading Teacher* 52: 738–47.

Klingner, J. K., S. Vaughn, J. Dimino, J. S. Schumm, and D. Bryant. 2001. *From Clunk to Click: Collaborative Strategic Reading.* Longmont, CO: Sopris West.

Meyer, B. J. F., D. M. Brandt, and G. J. Bluth. 1980. "Use of Top-Level Structure in Text: Key for Reading Comprehension of Ninth-Grade Students." *Reading Research Quarterly* 16: 72–103.

National Reading Panel. 2000. "Teaching Children to Read: An Evidence-Based Assessment of the Scientific Research Literature on Reading and Its Implications for Reading Instruction: Reports of the Subgroups." Washington, DC: National Institute of Child Health and Human Development. NIH Publication No. 00–4754.

Olshavsky, J. E. 1976–77. "Reading as Problem-Solving: An Investigation of Strategies." *Reading Research Quarterly* 12: 654–74.

Pearson, P. D., and N. K. Duke. 2002. "Comprehension Instruction in the Primary Grades." In *Comprehension Instruction: Research-Based Best Practices,* edited by C. C. Block and G. M. Pressley, 247–58. New York: Guilford Press.

Pearson, P. D., and M. C. Gallagher. 1983. "The Instruction of Reading Comprehension." *Contemporary Educational Psychology* 8: 317–44.

Pearson, P. D., L. R. Roehler, J. A. Dole, and G. G. Duffy. 1992. "Developing Expertise in Reading Comprehension." In *What Research Has to Say About Reading Instruction,* edited by J. Samuels and A. Farstrup, 145–99. Newark, DE: International Reading Association.

Pressley, M. 2000. "What Should Comprehension Instruction Be the Instruction Of? In *Handbook of Reading Research: Volume III,* edited by M. L. Kamil, P. B. Mosenthal, P. D. Pearson, and R. Barr, 545–61. Mahwah, NJ: Erlbaum.

Pressley, M., and R. Wharton-McDonald. 2002. "The Need for Increased Comprehension Instruction." In *Reading Instruction That Works,* edited by M. Pressley, 236–88. New York: Guilford Press.

Pressley, M., S. E. Dolezal, L. M. Raphael, L. Mohan, A. D. Roehrig, and K. Bogner. 2003. *Motivating Primary-Grade Students.* New York: Guilford Press.

Purcell-Gates, V. and N. K. Duke (in preparation). Explicit Explanation of Genre Within Authentic Literacy Activities in Science: Does It Facilitate Development and Achievement?

Saunders, W., and C. Goldenberg. 1999. "Effects of Instructional Conversations and Literature Logs on Limited and Fluent-English-Proficient Students' Story Comprehension and Thematic Understanding." *Elementary School Journal* 99: 277–301.

Shanahan, T. 1988. "The Reading-Writing Relationship: Seven Instructional Principles." *The Reading Teacher* 23: 636–47.

Stahl, K. A. D. 2004. "Proof, Practice, and Promise: Comprehension Strategy Instruction in the Primary Grades." *The Reading Teacher* 57: 598–609.

Stahl, S. A. 1999. *Vocabulary Development (from Reading Research to Practice. Vol. 2).* Brookline, MA: Brookline Books.

Stanovich, K. E., and A. E. Cunningham. 1993. "Where Does Knowledge Come From? Specific Associations Between Print Exposure and Information Acquisition." *Journal of Educational Psychology* 85: 211–29.

Van den Branden, K. 2000. Does Negotiation of Meaning Promote Reading Comprehension? A Study of Multilingual Primary School Classes." *Reading Research Quarterly* 35: 426–43.

Vaughn, S., J. K. Klingner, and D. Bryant. 2001. "Collaborative Strategic Reading as a Means to Enhance Peer-Mediated Instruction for Reading Comprehension and Content-Area Learning." *Remedial and Special Education* 22: 66–74.

KEY QUESTIONS

1. Of the seven critical understandings, which do you see reflected in things you are already doing in your classroom? Which need more attention?

2. Consider trying one of the instructional approaches identified in this chapter, such as Collaborative Strategic Reading or CORI, during a unit of study in your classroom. What happens? How do students respond? What type of feedback do they give you based on their experience?

3. What do you do with vocabulary instruction? Consider ramping up your vocabulary instruction and/or trying some new things. What could you do to enhance or further enhance word consciousness in your classroom?

4. Authentic literacy events appear to have an impact on comprehension. How might we ensure more authenticity with real purposes and real resources for our students?

5. Focus on the discussions you have with your students. Are the discussions teacher dominated (possibly even reflecting the I-R-E pattern)? Or do your students take a more active role in the discussions?

What Good Readers Do

- Are active

- Set goals

- Evaluate whether the text and their reading of it is meeting their goals

- Look over the text

- Notice the text's structure

- Make predictions

- Read selectively

- Adjust reading to their purpose and the style of text

- Read some things carefully while skimming others

- Build and revise meaning as they read

- Ask questions

- Use prior knowledge to understand text

- Think about characteristics and intentions of the author

- Monitor their understanding

- Try to determine the meaning of unfamiliar words in the text

- Evaluate the text's quality and value

- Respond intellectually and emotionally

- Read different kinds of text differently

- Process text before, during, and after reading
  (adapted from Duke and Pearson 2002)

Reflecting on Your Practice

Critical Understanding from Research	Things I Do	Ways to Integrate This into Classroom Instruction
What Good Readers Do When They Read		
The Importance of Related Skills and Dispositions		
The Importance of Volume Reading		
The Potential in Discussion of Text		
The Effectiveness of Explicit Instruction in Comprehension Strategies		
The Particular Value of Multiple Strategy Instruction		
The Importance of Authenticity		

3 To Understand

I should like to do portraits which will appear as revelations to people in a hundred years' time.
—Vincent Van Gogh

ELLIN OLIVER KEENE

MEET THE AUTHOR

ELLIN OLIVER KEENE *has been a classroom teacher, staff developer, and adjunct professor of reading and writing. For sixteen years she directed staff development initiatives at the Denver-based Public Education & Business Coalition. Currently, she is Deputy Director of Cornerstone, a National Literacy Initiative at the University of Pennsylvania. She consults with schools and districts around the country in all aspects of literacy learning. Ellin is co-author of* Mosaic of Thought: Teaching Comprehension in a Reader's Workshop *(Heinemann, 1997).*

FOCUS QUOTE

We all have hundreds of these experiences and memories that, if we study them carefully, help us create a definition for comprehension that goes well beyond traditional definitions to encompass understanding in all areas of our own and children's lives. If we take the time to scrutinize those memories, we can generate a common language in our classrooms, and beyond that, help children manage and maximize their own thinking.

Elizabeth, my daughter, and I stand in line at the National Gallery, holding our 12:10 P.M. tickets to the Van Gogh exhibit. We each have a notebook and we're planning our approach. She wants to go it alone, wander around the exhibit at her pace, not mine, and sketch as she roams. I want to linger for long periods with the paintings that are most magnetic to me, recording thoughts I hope will later evoke images of the paintings. I want to guard against forgetting. I want to *understand* Van Gogh. I want Elizabeth to understand Van Gogh.

We agree on a time to meet and begin a game we have designed. Toward the end of our visit, I will have written about several paintings, she will have sketched a half dozen. We will trade notebooks and search for the paintings depicted in our tablets, write the title next to the entry, and reconvene to see if we found the painting the other wrote about or sketched. Her drawings make the pieces easier to identify than the notes I take. I know I begin this challenge with a strong advantage.

"Do they ever kick you out, Mom?" Elizabeth wants to know. "How long will they let us stay in here?"

"I don't think they'll kick us out until the museum closes at 5:00."

It is early November in Washington, D.C. When we emerge the air is cool and dry and the light drains over the Potomac highlighting the sky in pale orange. Planes lift out of National with staggering frequency. I hope this is one of those times Elizabeth just wants to walk along in silence. The exhibit is still too overwhelming to talk about. I take her hand. We are almost to the Metro station before I ask her what she thought of it. Beauty and pathos, color and movement, a crushing sense of loss, or was it madness, I can't find words, but feel sure she will. It's likely she understood far more than I.

"Mom," she finally says, "did you see the quote where he said, 'I want to get to the point where people say of my work: that man feels deeply'?"

"It's amazing you should say that! I'll show you something in a minute." In the crush of rush hour, we are lucky enough to find seats on the Metro. I rustle in my bag and pull out my notebook to show her where I recorded the same quote.

"I liked that because it made Van Gogh seem like a regular person. I want other people to understand that I feel deeply too. When he said that, it was like I could understand him. I just want to understand him, but he's dead, so we can't really."

Her words roll out as a question. It's hard for me to respond. I, too, want to feel some shred of connection to a person capable of such creation. I want to discover if I am capable of creating beauty. Dare I presume to understand what he felt or how he used his brush to define those emotions? We want so much to understand and do our best to try. Elizabeth used her sketches to better understand the paintings she was most attracted to; I used my pen to make sense of others. I'm not sure we did understand fully, but I am certain that we tried.

I turn the pages in my notebook. Under the title, *An Old Woman from Arles,* I wrote:

Another woman of no historical import. Van Gogh confronts us
from close range, his subject stares directly at us. She is cloaked in
strong but faded blue. Her scarf is knotted tightly about her head.
She has tied it exactly the same way for how many days of her
long life. Some color remains in her cheeks but it is doing open
battle with her mortality. The bed, only a corner of headboard
and a triangle of white linen in the left center, reminds us of her

age. Is she an invalid? Is her direct but absent stare focused on a mirror or into the distance as she tries to imagine a way she will feed her family for the day, the week? A tiny line of a mouth bespeaks her silence, even solitude. Though she has much to say, she will not. I feel a sad resignation but a clear sense of reality. Do I understand? What should I try to remember?

The Metro streaks toward Virginia as we huddle over our notebooks. A thousand fragments of sound reach my conscious thought but are easily put aside. I tell Elizabeth that I don't know if what I wrote has anything to do with what Van Gogh intended when he painted that portrait; but I was trying, like she, to understand him and his subject, to feel what he felt, to give my concentrated attention to something worthy of remembering, worthy of understanding.

"The best I can do is write in my notebook until I figure it out." She laughs. "Don't try to draw it, Mom."

"Nope," I say. "That's for you to do! But, you know what? Sometimes when I'm writing, words just come out of my mind and onto the paper and I smile and think to myself, 'yeah, that's what that painting is about.' I feel like all the writing was worth it because finally I understand better. I really want to remember what I wrote about the color in her cheeks doing open battle with her mortality because I think the conflict in that painting is about her impending death. Yet she still has energy and much left to say." I so want to understand her.

We pull out the exhibition catalogue to find the painting, but quickly have to stash it away. It would be just like us to miss our stop.

· · · · ·

The conversation Elizabeth and I had that day comes back to me as I write this chapter. I remember hoping she would begin to enjoy the search for understanding and give thoughtful attention to what was most worthy of remembering. Some things are worth immersing oneself passionately in, in order to understand, I'm sure of that. I wonder, as an educator and a mother, what are they? How will she determine what matters most to her? How do I decide what matters most to me? How old was I when those decisions became conscious? What *does* matter enough to me that I will lose myself in study in order to understand? My eyes leave the screen as I write those last lines; I mull over the questions. What matters enough that I will work hard to understand it? *What does it really mean to understand something?*

I think about the ways in which we have always defined comprehension in American classrooms. Our operating definition of comprehension is clearly visible in the classroom materials we consume. I recently attended a large literacy conference and, as I browsed the exhibits, it became clear to me that many children are barraged with tasks and activities whose stated purpose is to enhance their comprehension. The publishers of those materials certainly have an operating definition of comprehension. Are we comfortable with it? In nearly any workbook, basal anthology, unit of study, activity packet, literature unit, or visual organizer one picks up, we see three elements we are led to believe enhance children's comprehension:

- Retelling, summarizing, or restating key events in the piece by filling in story maps, advanced organizers, etc.
- Answering questions, both literal and inferential
- Vocabulary development

If one scrutinizes commercially available materials and even "tried and true" classroom practices, much of what we call comprehension instruction fits into one of those three categories. Is that how you would define comprehension, if given the chance? Is that how we want the children with whom we work to think about comprehension? If they can only answer the questions, fill in the maps, complete the double entry journal forms or story pyramids correctly, if they can only define the vocabulary from a story in their own words, surely they must comprehend, right?

When Elizabeth and I were trying to understand Van Gogh's motivation, passion, color, shape, composition, and form, were we answering some pre-formulated questions, defining vocabulary words we learned or completing a story map about our time in the National Gallery? A ridiculous thought, but weren't we trying to understand? How was our "real-life" experience different from the process of comprehending in America's classrooms?

The sticky problem is that real understanding isn't limited to the hours we call reader's workshop and real comprehension doesn't fit neatly into forms that require children to record two words about the main character, three words about the setting, four words about the conflict, and five words about the resolution. Real understanding is sloppy, difficult work that transcends our arbitrary time constraints and the inauthentic activities we ask children to complete in the name of improving comprehension. Real understanding is huddling over scratches in a notebook on a subway and *generating* rather than answering questions.

I began to realize that, to the degree that we can devote time to speculating about what it really means to understand, in any area of human endeavor, we can become better teachers of comprehension, in all content areas. Consider your own experiences as a learner. What do you work hard to understand? When you achieve insight, what were the circumstances that permitted you to understand deeply? Is there a way we might help children work harder to truly understand, not just what they read and hear, not just what they write and speak, but deeply understand ideas throughout their days with us? Might this new look at the comprehension strategies help us achieve those goals?

When I reconsider my own learning experiences, I recall moments in which I was confronted with an intellectual challenge that went, I believed, beyond my limits. I recall as a sophomore in college, in the early weeks of an Irish Literature course, receiving a B on a paper. I was incensed and stormed into the professor's office demanding an explanation. (Yes, for a B, I should have been thrilled!) I pointed out to him, in no uncertain terms, that my bibliographic citations were correct, down to the commas and colons, the length of the paper was exactly what he had suggested, and that I had met all the syllabus requirements. He studied me and, from behind his red beard looked at me and spoke words I've never forgotten. "Yes," he said slowly, gaining speed as he went, "your bibliography is fine, the length is fine, and you've met the syllabus requirements." Here he paused as if reading my thoughts, which were, "Then what the heck is the problem?" He leaned forward toward me and said, "But, Miss Oliver, there is no original thinking in this paper. I don't give A's to papers without original thought. You haven't shown me any evidence that you know how to think, Miss Oliver."

I trudged back to my dorm room painfully aware that my professor was absolutely right. I hadn't included an original thought in that paper and furthermore, I wasn't sure how to *get* an original thought.

I realize now that I was confronted with a problem of synthesis. The Irish Literature professor was challenging me to take what I had learned in my readings and from his lectures, combine them with my existing knowledge, opinions, beliefs, and emotions to create a *synthesis*. My professor spoke of having original thought—I know now that thoughts original to the reader are inferences and that, when combined with many inferences and background knowledge from many sources, the resulting ideas are syntheses. Had I understood the concept of synthesis, I could have returned to my dorm room and, instead of producing a summary, which is what my original paper was, I could have coalesced all the information I had, infused my own ideas and opinions and produced—*voila*—original thought.

We all have hundreds of these experiences and memories that, if we study them carefully, will help us create a definition for comprehension that goes well beyond traditional definitions to encompass understanding in all areas of our own and children's lives. If we take the time to scrutinize those memories, we can generate a common language in our classrooms, and beyond that, help children manage and maximize their own thinking in a way I was unable to do as a sophomore in college.

Take a moment to consider a learning experience that presented, for you at the time, an almost insurmountable challenge. Put this book down for three quick minutes and write about the experience, taking care to consider the particular qualities and characteristics of the experience such as:

- What helped you gradually comprehend the ideas that were, at first, so challenging?
- What conditions did you require in order to understand the intellectual challenge with which you were faced?
- When you experienced an insight—an aha moment—how did you use the insight to help you understand more?

My guess is that, in your short piece of writing, you'll find many insights about your own comprehension that extend your definition of what it means to understand far beyond the traditional notions of summarizing, answering questions, and learning a few new vocabulary words. If you consider the factors that influenced your understanding, you are simultaneously identifying the elements of real comprehension—the elements we need to teach our children explicitly.

For example, if you found that your intellectual challenge required generating dozens of questions that you systematically went about studying and answering, that is real comprehension! If you noticed that you needed to talk through your emerging ideas and insights with others who had more expertise than you, that's what you need to discuss with the children in your classroom! If you found that you became so immersed in your learning that everything around you became less important, talk to your students about the power of real concentration, of fervent learning! If you realized that you had to struggle for a long period of time before sorting out a knotty problem or if you needed to work in silence in order to understand, work with your class to figure out how you can create similar conditions in your classroom! You are well on your way to defining comprehension in a way that is compelling and meaningful for all learners, all day.

Now ask the children to take a short period of time to write about a time when learning was particularly challenging for them. What characterized their experiences? How can those factors be recorded so that your class has its own emerging definition of what it means to understand in the world. Kids will tell us what it means if we listen carefully . . .

A dear friend and colleague, Colleen Buddy, once told me a story that froze me in my tracks. Kevin, a second grader in her first–second grade classroom, brought her up short one morning as she was teaching a lesson on predicting. She was presenting the concept of predicting as one type of inference, one of the comprehension strategies. Apparently, Kevin raised his hand and politely asked, "Mrs. Buddy, how come when we're in reading you teach us about *predicting,* and when we're in math you teach us *estimating,* and when we're in science, you call it *hypothesizing,* aren't they all sort of the same thing?"

When Colleen recounted that story, I realized that I had missed a fundamental piece of the puzzle we call comprehension. Comprehension is about *understanding ideas,* not just in text, but throughout the day. The term *comprehension* is, for teachers, so often associated with reading that we had failed to consider the implications for learning outside reading. Until Kevin. Kevin's profound inquiry was a way of saying, "Hey, guys, what you're really talking about is thinking into the future. When you call it estimating, hypothesizing, and predicting, it confuses the help! Why don't you use some consistent language here so we have a chance to figure out what you're saying?" Certainly, there are subtle differences between predicting, estimating, and hypothesizing that children will need to explore as they engage in more discipline-specific study in later years, but Kevin's question was of great consequence.

Kevin's profound question made me realize that, not only must we rework our definition of comprehension, we must extend the comprehension strategies we know are useful tools for enhancing reading comprehension and extend them until they become *tools for understanding* across the curriculum.

Along with my colleagues at the Public Education & Business Coalition in Denver, I created a new set of defining statements for each of the seven comprehension strategies about which we had written in *Mosaic of Thought.* (See below.) We considered what we already knew and were implementing in classrooms with respect to teaching reading comprehension strategies and imagined what children would be able to do if they used those strategies across the curriculum as cognitive tools for understanding.

We considered, for example, how a writer might use sensory images to create compelling detail or select particular details that would cause her readers to infer; we thought about how a mathematician would ask questions or relate an algorithm she was learning to one already well understood; or how a researcher in social studies or science would synthesize or determine importance as he contemplated an experiment or research study he was planning to undertake. Kevin's insightful question helped us transform *reading* comprehension strategies into *thinking* strategies that crossed all areas of learning.

When we are studying how readers ask questions to enhance their understanding of the various texts they read, for example, we should also take the opportunity to discuss and model ways in which writers, mathematicians, and researchers, perhaps in the social sciences and sciences, might also be guided by questions. When teachers integrate their instruction using *strategies,* children make connections and learn in ways that transcend curricular boundaries.

I was visiting a school in Bridgeport, Connecticut, when a seventh grader approached me during an English class I was observing and asked if I was a teacher. I said that I had been but that my job now was to help teachers. He motioned for me to follow him to a back corner in the room. He was clearly eager to tell me something that he didn't want his teacher to hear. "Do you know what a conspiracy is?" he asked. I smiled and said I believed I was familiar with the concept. "Well, there's one in this school," he whispered. When I inquired about the nature of this insidious conspiracy, he said, "Well, you just saw Ms. B teaching us about determining importance in books, right? I have to go to math next hour and in there, Mr. P is teaching us how you determine importance in math, and when I go to social studies sixth hour and science seventh hour, those two [teachers] are doing determining importance, too. Do you see the conspiracy?" I had a quick visual image of some poor hostage writing HELP in the frost on a window! "Honey, I gotta tell you," I said, "that's actually called planning."

Of course, this story becomes part of the lore that I'll retell hundreds of times in my work, but there is a very serious message underlying my young friend's conspiracy theory. Students are so unaccustomed, particularly as they get older, to being asked to *think in the same ways* from class to class, day to day, they may even think we're engaged in a dastardly plot to make them think when we take the time to plan with our colleagues and use the same language of thought in our instruction.

· · · · ·

During and after the extraordinary exhibit at the National Gallery those many years ago, Elizabeth and I struggled to understand Van Gogh's painting and his life. Surely, we never came close to truly comprehending the mystery of his life and work but I would argue that our verbal, written, and artistic struggle to understand better represented what it is to understand than any packet the museum might have created to guide us. I would argue that the conversation, our writing, her art, and the content of the exhibit—so worthy of our struggle to understand—helped us develop insights that influence our thinking to this day in ways seen and unseen.

As an educator, I am determined to continue to focus on a definition of understanding that came to me first as a mom. And, I'm determined to listen to our children, in and out of the classroom, when they tell me that the *ways in which we talk to them about the nature of understanding* matter very much. I'm determined to operate with a definition of comprehension and a language defining thought that extends across the curriculum.

I offer, therefore, a working set of outcomes for readers, writers, mathematicians, and researchers in all content areas, that we can use in a conspiratorial manner (or not!) with our colleagues and within our own classrooms. Part of considering what it means to understand includes helping children learn that to understand is to utilize the same thinking tools or strategies to enhance understanding in any class, in any learning process in their lives.

KEY QUESTIONS

1. What is your operating definition of comprehension? In your classroom? Your school? Your district?

2. In what ways would you revise that definition based on your own, most intellectually challenging, experiences?

3. In what ways might you engage students in re-defining comprehension?

4. In what ways will you know if your new (and evolving) definition of comprehension is helping your students to think more deeply about what they read?

5. What are the advantages/disadvantages of integrating across content areas based on thinking strategies rather than more conventional tools for integration such as themes/authors/topics? In what ways might you and your colleagues plan curriculum and engage students around a common language that extends comprehension strategies across the curriculum?

Determining What Is Important in Text

Readers
- Identify key ideas or themes as they read.
- Distinguish important from unimportant information in relation to key ideas or themes in text. They can distinguish important information at the word, sentence, and text level.
- Utilize text structure and text features (such as bold or italicized print, figures, and photographs) to help them distinguish important from unimportant information.
- Use their knowledge of important and relevant parts of text to prioritize in long-term memory and synthesize text for others.

Writers
- Observe their world and record what they believe is significant.
- Make decisions about the most important ideas to include in the pieces they write. They make decisions about the best genre and structure to communicate their ideas.
- Reveal their biases by emphasizing some elements over others.
- Provide only essential detail to reveal the meaning and produce the effect desired.
- Delete information irrelevant to their larger purpose.

Mathematicians
- Look for patterns and relationships.
- Identify and use key words to build an understanding of the problem.
- Gather text information from graphs, charts, and tables.
- Decide what information is relevant to a problem and what information is irrelevant.

Researchers
- Evaluate and think critically about information.
- Sort and analyze information to better understand it.
- Make decisions about the quality and usefulness of information.
- Decide what's important to remember and what isn't.
- Choose the most effective reporting platform.

Contributed by E. Keene © 2005 by Linda Hoyt from *Spotlight on Comprehension*. Portsmouth, NH: Heinemann.

Drawing Inferences

Readers
- Use their schema and textual information to draw conclusions and form unique interpretations from text.
- Make predictions about text, confirm their predictions, and test their developing meaning as they read on.
- Know when and how to use text in combination with their own background knowledge to seek answers to questions.
- Create interpretations to enrich and deepen their experience in a text.

Writers
- Make decisions about content inclusions/exclusions and genre/text structure that permit or encourage inference on the part of the reader.
- Carefully consider their audience in making decisions about what to describe explicitly and what to leave to the reader's interpretation
- Particularly fiction and poetry writers, are aware of far more detail than they reveal in the texts they compose. This encourages inferences such as drawing conclusions, making critical judgments, making predictions, and making connections to other texts and experiences possible for their readers.

Mathematicians
- Predict, generalize, and estimate.
- As mathematicians read a problem, they make problem-solving decisions based on their conceptual understanding of math concepts (i.e. operations, fractions, etc.).
- Compose (like a writer) by drawing pictures, using charts, and creating equations.
- Solve problems in different ways and support their methods through proof, number sentences, pictures, charts, and graphs.
- Use reasoning and make connections throughout the problem-solving process.
- Conjecture (infer based on evidence).
- Use patterns (consistencies) and relationships to generalize and infer what comes next in the problem-solving process.

Researchers
- Think about the value and reliability of their sources.
- Consider what is important to a reader or audience.

 Contributed by E. Keene © 2005 by Linda Hoyt from *Spotlight on Comprehension*. Portsmouth, NH: Heinemann.

Using Prior Knowledge—Schema

Readers
- Spontaneously activate relevant, prior knowledge before, during, and after reading.
- Assimilate information from text into their schemata and make changes in those schemata to accommodate the new information.
- Use schema to relate text to their world knowledge, text knowledge, and personal experience.
- Use their schema to enhance their understanding of text and to store text information in long-term memory.
- Use their schema for authors and their style to better understand text.
- Recognize when they have inadequate background information and know how to create it—to build schema—to get the information they need.

Writers
- Frequently choose their own topics and write about subjects they care about.
- Use content that comes from and builds on his/her experiences.
- Think about and use what they know about genre, text structure, and conventions as they write.
- Seek to better recognize and capitalize on their own voice for specific effects in their compositions.
- Know when their schema for a topic or text format is inadequate, and they create the necessary background knowledge.
- Use knowledge of audience to make decisions about content inclusions/exclusions.

Mathematicians
- Use current understandings as first steps in the problem-solving process.
- Use their number sense to understand a problem.
- Add to schema by trying more challenging problems and hearing from others about different problem-solving methods.
- Build understanding based on prior knowledge of math concepts.
- Develop purpose based on prior knowledge.
- Use their prior knowledge to generalize about similar problems and to choose problem-solving strategies.
- Develop their own problems.

Researchers
- Frequently choose topics they know and care about.
- Use prior knowledge and experience to launch investigations and ask questions.
- Consider what they already know to decide what they need to find out and self-evaluate according to background knowledge of what quality products look like.

Asking Questions

Readers
- Spontaneously generate questions before, during, and after reading.
- Ask questions for different purposes including clarification of meaning, making predictions, determining an author's style, content, or format, and to locate a specific answer in text or consider rhetorical questions inspired by the text.
- Use questions to focus their attention on important components of the text.
- Are aware that other readers' questions may inspire new questions for them.

Writers
- Compose in a way that causes the reader to form questions as they read.
- Monitor their progress by asking questions about their choices as they write.
- Ask questions of other writers in order to confirm their choices and make revisions.
- Have questions that lead to revision in their own pieces and in the pieces to which they respond for other writers.

Mathematicians
- Ask questions before, during, and after doing a math problem.
    - Could it be this?
    - What happens if?
    - How else could I do this?
    - Have I seen this problem before?
    - What does this mean?
- Test theories/answers/their hypothesis by using different approaches to a problem.
- Question others to understand their own process and to clarify problems.
- Extend their own thinking by asking themselves questions they don't have an answer to.

Researchers
- Ask questions to narrow a search and find a topic.
- Ask questions to clarify meaning and purpose.
- Ask themselves:
    - What are the most effective resources and how will I access them?
    - Do I have enough information?
    - Have I used a variety of sources?
    - What more do I need?
    - Does it make sense?
    - Have I told enough?
    - Is it interesting and original thinking and does my writing have voice?

   Contributed by E. Keene © 2005 by Linda Hoyt from *Spotlight on Comprehension*. Portsmouth, NH: Heinemann.

Monitoring Meaning and Comprehension

Readers

- Monitor their comprehension during reading—they know when the text they are reading or listening to makes sense, when it does not, what does not make sense, and whether the unclear portions are critical to overall understanding of the piece.

- Can identify when text is comprehensible and the degree to which they understand it. They can identify ways in which a text becomes gradually more understandable by reading past an unclear portion and/or by rereading parts or the whole text.

- Are aware of the processes they can use to make meaning clear. They check, evaluate, and make revisions to their evolving interpretation of the text while reading.

- Can identify confusing ideas, themes, and/or surface elements (words, sentence or text structures, graphs, tables, etc.) and can suggest a variety of different means to solve the problems they have.

- Are aware of what they **need** to comprehend in relation to their purpose for reading.

- Must **learn** how to pause, consider the meanings in text, reflect on their understandings, and use different strategies to enhance their understanding. This process is best learned by watching proficient models "think aloud" and gradually taking responsibility for monitoring their own comprehension as they read independently.

Writers

- Monitor during their composition process to ensure that their text makes sense for their intended audience at the word, sentence, and text level.

- Read their work aloud to find and hear their voice.

- Share their work so others can help them monitor the clarity and impact of the work.

- Pay attention to their style and purpose. They purposefully write with clarity and honesty. They strive to write boldly, simply, and concisely by keeping those standards alive in their minds during the writing process.

- Pause to consider the impact of their work and make conscious decisions about when to turn a small piece into a larger project, when revisions are complete, or when to abandon a piece.

Mathematicians
- Check to make sure answers are reasonable.
- Use manipulatives/charts/diagrams to help themselves make sense of the problem.
- Understand that others will build meaning in different ways and solve problems with different problem-solving strategies.
- Write what makes sense to them.
- Check their work in many ways: working backwards, redoing problems, etc.
- Agree/disagree with solutions and ideas.
- Express in "think alouds" what's going on in their head as they work through a problem. They are metacognitive.
- Continually ask themselves if each step makes sense.
- Discuss problems with others and write about their problem-solving process to clarify their thinking and make problems clearer.
- Use accurate math vocabulary and show their work in clear, concise forms so others can follow their thinking without asking questions.

Researchers
- Are aware of what they need to find out and learn about.
- Can identify when they comprehend and take steps to repair comprehension when they don't.
- Pause to reflect and evaluate information.
- Choose effective ways of organizing information—note-taking, webbing, outlining, etc.
- Use several sources to validate information and check for accuracy.
- Revise and edit for clarity, accuracy, and interest.
- Check sources for appropriate references and copyrights.

    Contributed by E. Keene © 2005 by Linda Hoyt from *Spotlight on Comprehension*. Portsmouth, NH: Heinemann.

Fix-Up Strategies

Readers
- Use the six major systems of language (graphophonic, lexical, syntactic, semantic, schematic, and pragmatic) to solve reading problems. When not comprehending, they ask themselves questions such as: does this make sense, does the word I'm pronouncing sound like language, do the letters in the word match the sounds I'm pronouncing, have I seen this word before, is there another reader who can help me make sense of this, what do I already know from my experience and the context of this text that can help me solve this problem?
- Have and select a wide range of problem-solving strategies and can make appropriate choices in a given reading situation (i.e., skip ahead or reread, use the context and syntax, or sound it out, speak to another reader, consider relevant prior knowledge, read the passage aloud, etc.).

Writers
- Revise (add, delete, and reorganize) and edit (apply correct conventions), continually seeking clarity and impact for the reader. They experiment with and make changes in overall meaning, content, wording, text organization, punctuation, and spelling.
- Capitalize on their knowledge of writers' tools (i.e., character, setting, conflict, theme, plot structure, leads, style, etc.) to enhance their meaning.

Mathematicians
- Listen to others' strategies and adjust their own.
- Use estimation to determine if their answer is reasonable.
- Use trial and error to build thinking.
- Cross-check by using more than one way to do a problem. (i.e., check subtraction by adding).
- Use tools (i.e., manipulatives, graphs, calculators, etc.) to enhance meaning.

Researchers
- Revise and edit for clarity and accuracy.
- Check sources for updated copyrights and legitimate reliable sources.

Synthesizing Information

Readers
- Maintain a cognitive synthesis as they read. They monitor the overall meaning, important concepts, and themes in the text as they read and are aware of ways text elements "fit together" to create that overall meaning and theme. They use their knowledge of these elements to make decisions about the overall meaning of a passage, chapter, or book.
- Retell or synthesize what they have read. They attend to the most important information and to the clarity or the synthesis itself. Readers synthesize in order to better understand what they have read.
- Capitalize on opportunities to share, recommend, and criticize books they have read.
- May respond to text in a variety or ways either independently or in groups of other readers. These include written, oral, dramatic, and artistic responses and interpretations of text.
- Using a proficient reader's synthesis, are likely to extend the literal meaning of a text to the inferential level.

Writers
- Make global and focal plans for their writing before and during the drafting process. They use their knowledge of text elements such as character, setting, conflict, sequence of events, and resolution to create a structure for their writing.
- Study other writers and draw conclusions about what makes good writing. They work to replicate the style of authors they find compelling.
- Reveal themes in a way that suggests their importance to readers. Readers can create a cogent synthesis from well-written material.

Mathematicians
- Generalize from patterns they observe.
- Generalize in words, equations, charts, and graphs to retell or synthesize.
- Synthesize math concepts when they use them in real-life applications.
- Use deductive reasoning (e.g., reach conclusions based on knowns).

Researchers
- Develop insight about a topic to create new knowledge or understanding.
- Utilize information from a variety of resources.
- Enhance their understanding of a topic by considering different perspectives, opinions, and sources.

Contributed by E. Keene © 2005 by Linda Hoyt from *Spotlight on Comprehension*. Portsmouth, NH: Heinemann.

Using Sensory and Emotional Images

Readers

- Create sensory and emotional images during and after reading. These images may include visual, auditory, and other sensory (as well as emotional) connections to the text, and are rooted in prior knowledge.
- Use sensory and emotional images to draw conclusions and to create unique interpretations of the text. Images from reading frequently become part of the reader's writing. Images from a reader's personal experience frequently become part of their comprehension.
- Use images to clarify and enhance comprehension.
- Use sensory and emotional images to immerse themselves in rich detail as they read. The detail gives depth and dimension to the reading, engaging the reader more deeply, and making the text more memorable.
- Adapt their images in response to the shared images of other readers.
- Adapt their images as they continue to read. Images are revised to incorporate new information revealed through the text and new interpretations as they are developed by the reader.

Writers

- Consciously attempt to create strong images in their compositions using strategically placed detail.
- Create impact through the use of strong nouns and verbs whenever possible.
- Use images to explore their own ideas. They consciously study their mental images for direction in their pieces.
- Learn from the images created in their minds as they read. They study other authors' use of images as a way to improve their own.

Mathematicians

- Use mental pictures/models of shapes, numbers, and processes to build understanding of concepts and problems and to experiment with ideas.
- Use concrete models/manipulatives to build understanding and visualize problems.
- Visually represent thinking through drawings, pictures, graphs, and charts.
- Picture story problems like a movie in the mind to help understand the problem.
- Visualize concepts in their head (i.e., parallel lines, fractions, etc.).

Researchers

- Create rich mental pictures to better understand text.
- Interweave written images with multisensory (auditory, visual, kinesthetic) components to enhance comprehension.
- Use words, visual images, sounds, and other sensory experiences to communicate understanding of a topic (that can lead to further questions for research).

4 Building a Context for Strategy Instruction

DONA MCILVAIN

MEET THE AUTHOR

Dona McIlvain *is a literacy specialist serving schools in Williamson County, Tennessee. She serves as a staff developer as well as a teacher. She spends many hours self-reflecting as she trains for Ironman triathalons.*

FOCUS QUOTE

Four major factors can be extrapolated from the research and are essential to the teaching of reading comprehension and strategy development.

The importance of comprehension strategy development and metacognition is well researched. Teaching them, therefore, ought to be cut and dried. But is it? As an educator, I tackled the massive amounts of information and research on the topic. I taught lesson after lesson and observed to see how well my students could apply the learning in multiple contexts. I had the research behind me but was not always guaranteed success.

I have, finally, come to realize that it is the effective teacher who takes the research and then gently molds those understandings within a rich context for learning. I have now come to the belief that it isn't enough to teach comprehension strategies. I have come to the belief that comprehension strategies must be taught within the presence of four important elements that are the underpinnings of one's strategy instruction. These four elements are extrapolated from research and are essential to the teaching of reading comprehension and strategy development. They include:

- gradual release of responsibility
- strong sense of community (a safe haven)
- engagement in self-reflection and awareness
- thought-provoking conversations

Gradual Release of Responsibility

Key elements for this release of responsibility include an abundance of teacher modeling using a rich variety of diverse texts drawn from real life, plus time for practice and response, and finally, independence with the strategy. The richness of repeated think alouds by the teacher showing the strategy applied to a wide range of sources sets the standard for students to achieve. Practice and response in guided and independent settings gives learners the opportunity to truly own the strategy, ultimately leading to self-extension.

A Strong Sense of Community

Establishing a strong sense of community within the classroom, a safe haven that cares, nurtures, and sustains its members, is a crucial foundation for strategy development. Students need a classroom in which they are free to take risks. Learners need to be comfortable, taking risks with the understanding that error is part of the learning process. Teachers and learners who view error as a part of growth build community together.

Within the context of a stable and literate community, students become empowered to share themselves and their life experiences. An environment

FIGURE 4–1 As responsibility is released, learners begin to apply strategies independently, noticing their own thinking and monitoring understanding.

that is designed to promote thinking and inquiry provides a purpose and vision for future development.

Self-Reflection and Awareness

Megacognition, "thinking about my thinking," helps learners become aware of their strategy use and develops a conscious level of awareness that can make the difference between comprehension and word calling. When students become aware of what they are doing while reading, they consciously monitor their learning. Readers who have developed metacognitive strategy use can pause midstream and think:

- I am really visualizing this! The sensory images I am getting are clear and understandable. I am going to focus on adding to my visualization

FIGURE 4–2 and 4–3 Learners may engage in self-reflection privately or with a partner before sharing with a larger group.

as I continue reading . . . Or, my visual images are so clear, I am going to decrease my focus on visualizing and pay closer attention to the myriad of questions that are evolving as I read.

• Is this strategy working for me? Would another one help me reach deeper as a learner?

• I am inferring that _____. I am going to reread a bit and confirm that there is justification for that inference.

• This is a point I want to bring up in our conversation today. I think this is important because _____.

Deep Conversations

Conversation helps us to search for meaning, to view it through a variety of lenses reflected by the others in the discussion, and to synthesize our understandings. As students engage in conversations about content, authors' craft, or the message an author is extending, they explain their thinking while reaching for deeper understanding. It is from this social interaction that heightened understanding often emerges. Conversations that take learners from surface recall to deeper explorations can create inspiration, motivation, and insight.

References

Gambrell, Linda, and Janice Almasi. 1996. *Lively Discussions! Fostering Engaged Reading*. Newark, DE: International Reading Association.

Keene, Ellin, and Susan Zimmerman. 1997. *Mosaic of Thought: Teaching Comprehension in a Reader's Workshop*. Portsmouth, NH: Heinemann.

McLaughlin, Maureen, and Mary Beth Allen. 2002 *Guided Comprehension: A Teaching Model for Grades 3–8*. Newark, DE: International Reading Association.

Miller, Debbie. 2002. *Reading with Meaning: Teaching Comprehension in the Primary Grades*. York, ME: Stenhouse.

KEY QUESTIONS

1. Teaching is not enough. The environment must support learning. What do you think are the key environmental factors required as we incubate deeper thinking and strategy use?

2. Is it possible to think we can create a risk-free environment for all? How?

3. Can we model self-awareness and reflection for our students as we do with the other metacognitive strategies?

4. How can we encourage more consistent and deeper conversation amongst our students?

Factors for Success

Gradually release responsibility

- Include an abundance of think alouds; model, model, model—explicitly teach
- Expose students to a variety of cognitive strategies
- Allow ample time for practice and response in small group settings and with a variety of texts
- Focus on independence; students using the comprehension strategies *on their own* is key

Establish a strong sense of community (safe haven)

- Build community in a risk-free environment
- Emphasize inquiry
- Create a culture and climate for thinking
- Initiate and sustain the idea that *all* thoughts, feelings, and ideas are valued

Provide time for self-reflection and awareness techniques

- Encourage self-monitoring
- Enable students to become aware of themselves as readers
- Guide individuals to set goals and analyze their progress
- Provide time to ponder and reflect

Promote deep conversations

- Make conversation a routine part of the day
- Inspire students to share their insights
- Foster engagement through discourse
- Allow opportunity for choice in selection of the text and in discussion partners

Contributed by D. McIlvain © 2005 by Linda Hoyt from *Spotlight on Comprehension*. Portsmouth, NH: Heinemann.

Self-Assessment: Building a Context for Strategy Instruction

	Help! What do I do?	OK, I'm getting it now.	This is working well.	Aha! I've got it!
Gradually Releases Responsibility	I am just beginning to model my thinking but have not given students an opportunity to share.	I continue to think aloud and have begun to include students in the discussion. They are showing signs of engagement.	We are thinking aloud as a whole group, charting responses and having discussions in small group settings. My students are beginning to think about their thinking on their own.	Modeling and think alouds are happening daily and are fostering high levels of engagement. Students are applying and grasping skills across a variety of genres with teacher support and independent work shows evidence that students are using all strategies.
Designs Community	A community has been established but most children continue to only answer questions when asked.	We have become respectful of one another and make every effort to listen to what others have to say.	In addition to feeling safe in their environment, students are beginning to know the terminology and are anxious to share their thoughts. They are taking greater risks.	My classroom is a place where inquiry, intimacy, and rigor are abundant. We share a common language and children's oral responses are heard daily and written responses are displayed everywhere. We are a community of learners and have a literate climate of thinking.
Builds Self-Awareness	My students look to me to prompt them in discussion. They are very unaware of what they need to do as good readers and are unable to express themselves when they do begin to use good strategies.	Students have begun to think about how they are constructing meaning. They are aware as they reread, make connections, or don't understand what the author is trying to say.	Self-awareness is surfacing. Students are beginning to reflect on the whole process. They are piecing together how these strategies are helping them to comprehend.	Responsibility is transferred to students to keep track of their thinking. They reflect on their learning by the self-selection of books and are thinking deeply about what they are doing.
Allows for Conversation	Most classroom discussions are led by the teacher. My students seem to think they have little to share.	Several students have shared in discussions; however, the teacher is still leading the conversation.	Almost all students are interacting on a daily basis. They are beginning to piggyback off one another's responses.	Students have many opportunities to talk about books, share their thoughts, ideas, and opinions. They talk and write in response to their reading. Time is built in to talk informally and naturally. They are gaining insight from each other.

Contributed by D. McIlvain © 2005 by Linda Hoyt from *Spotlight on Comprehension*. Portsmouth, NH: Heinemann.

5 Comprehension Instruction
Explicit and Multifaceted*

KEVLYNN ANNANDALE

MEET THE AUTHOR

Over the past twelve years **KEVLYNN ANNANDALE** *has been actively involved in all phases of development, review, and implementation of* First Steps *professional development and materials for local, national, and international markets. After working in the United States for six years, Kevlynn recently returned to Western Australia and is currently overseeing the development of the second edition of* First Steps.

FOCUS QUOTE

These teachers understand the importance of providing explicit instruction in multiple comprehension strategies then supporting learners as they apply their fledgling strategies in many contexts . . . adding new layers and much more substance.

The teaching of comprehension was once viewed as the simple task of providing students with ample opportunities to read a piece of text and respond to a variety of questions. The number of correct responses provided by the student was then taken as an indication of their level of understanding of the text. Comprehension instruction, once viewed as a black or white proposition, is now regarded as a complex challenge for many classroom teachers. Effective teachers now know that reading passages and answering questions is far too shallow. These teachers understand the importance of providing explicit instruction in multiple comprehension strategies then supporting learners as they apply their fledgling strategies in many contexts . . . adding new layers and much more substance.

---

* From *First Steps,* Second Edition, Reading Resource Book, Chapter Four, "Processes and Strategies." Rigby Harcourt: Melbourne, Australia. 2004.

Reading Strategies: The Substance of the Cake

The work of Keene and Zimmerman (1997) provides important insights into the identification of the processes and strategies most commonly used by skilled or efficient readers. This work, based on previous research done by Pearson (1976) and Pearson and Gallagher (1983) provides a springboard for teachers as they design explicit instruction of reading strategies.

The following table identifies and defines eighteen key reading strategies that support comprehension. The strategies are not hierarchical or age/grade related, and certainly not a definitive list of what needs to be taught. The selection of what strategies to teach when will be determined by student needs and the type of text being introduced.

Teaching the Strategies

The use of a reading strategy rarely happens in isolation, but often involves the interaction of a number of strategies simultaneously. A reader might make a *connection* within a text and at the same time make *predictions* about what will happen, as well as make an *inference* using implicit information presented.

It is important that, over time, students be introduced to a variety of strategies and understand how different strategies can work together. However, it is also appropriate to explicitly teach and have students practice an individual reading strategy. A unit of study focusing on one strategy may consist of a combination of demonstrations, think alouds, opportunities for practice and application across several texts and multiple curriculum areas. A variety of authentic literary and informational texts can be selected to support the instruction of a particular strategy.

The Gradual Release of Responsibility Model, originally presented by Pearson and Gallagher (1983) helps teachers plan for the effective introduction of reading strategies. The framework involves moving students from a supportive context where the teacher has a high degree of control (modeling) to a more independent context where the student has more control (independent application).

The sequential and recursive use of four effective teaching practices—modeling, sharing, guiding, and applying—helps to facilitate the gradual release of responsibility for the use of reading strategies. Using a balance of these practices helps students to:

- become aware of and talk about their strategy use
- monitor their effectiveness
- use strategies flexibly and independently during any reading event

Reading Strategies

Reading Strategy	Definition
Predicting	Using prior knowledge to anticipate what is going to occur in text before or during reading. Readers also use predicting to identify unknown words using surrounding context clues.
Connecting	Making links between what is read to other texts, to oneself, or to personal knowledge about the world.
Comparing	Thinking about similarities and differences between what is known and what is portrayed in texts.
Inferring	Combining what is read in the text with one's own ideas to create a unique interpretation of the text.
Synthesizing	Bringing together pieces of information within a text during or after reading for a specific purpose.
Creating Images	Using all five senses to create images before, during, and after reading.
Self-Questioning	Generating one's own questions before, during, and after reading.
Skimming	Quickly glancing through a text to get a general impression or overview of the content.
Scanning	Glancing through material to locate specific information.
Determining Importance	Making decisions about what is and is not important in a text.
Summarizing/Paraphrasing	Condensing information in a text to the most important ideas.
Rereading	Going back over parts of or whole texts to clarify meaning or assist with word identification.
Reading On	Continuing to read when encountering difficulties or unknown words.
Adjusting Reading Rate	Speeding up or slowing down reading depending on the purpose and/or text difficulty.
Sounding Out	Saying the sound represented by individual letters or letter combinations, blending them together, and arriving at a pronunciation.
Chunking	Identifying unknown words by breaking them into larger units than phonemes and then attaching sounds to the units.
Using Analogy	Thinking about what is known about familiar words and transferring it to an unknown word.
Consulting a Reference	Using a variety of sources to unlock word meaning.

Contributed by K. Annandale © 2005 by Linda Hoyt from *Spotlight on Comprehension*. Portsmouth, NH: Heinemann.

	Modeling	Sharing	Guiding	Applying
Role of the Teacher	The teacher demonstrates and explains the reading strategy being introduced. This is achieved by thinking aloud the mental processes used when using the strategy.	The teacher continues to demonstrate the use of the strategy with a range of texts inviting students to contribute ideas and information.	The teacher provides scaffolds for students to use the strategy. Teacher provides feedback.	The teacher offers support and encouragement as necessary.
Role of the Students	The students participate by actively attending to the demonstrations.	Students contribute ideas and begin to practice the use of the strategy in whole class situations.	Students work with help from the teacher and peers to practice the use of the strategy using a variety of texts.	The students work independently to apply the strategy in contexts across the curriculum.

Degree of Control

Through the use of modeling, sharing, guiding, and applying teachers can provide opportunities for students to:

- attend actively to a variety of "strategy" demonstrations
- hear the thinking behind the use of each strategy
- contribute ideas about the use of strategies in supportive, whole group situations
- work with others to practice the use of strategies
- receive feedback and support from the teacher and peers about the use of strategies
- read and independently practice the use of the strategies with a range of texts
- apply the strategies in authentic reading situations

The following information provides ideas about how to plan and use each of the four practices to explicitly teach reading strategies.

Modeling

Modeling is the most significant step when teaching any reading strategy. It is often overlooked or deemed unnecessary by some teachers. It is essential that teachers conduct regular, short modeling sessions that involve thinking aloud and demonstrations of how an effective reader makes use of a particular strategy.

By using the practice of modeling to introduce new reading strategies, teachers are able to articulate all that is happening inside their head, making the reading processes evident. This thinking aloud is a vital part of the modelling process. When introducing a new strategy, it is necessary to plan for multiple demonstrations.

Modeling sessions also need to be well planned and thought out. Thinking through what needs to be modeled and where in the text that might happen is more effective than making spontaneous comments as a text is being read.

Planning Modeling Sessions

Consideration of the following questions will help teachers conduct effective modeling sessions.

1. How do I use this strategy in my own reading?
2. How does this strategy help me become a more efficient reader?
3. What is important for students to know about this strategy?
4. Which texts might be the most appropriate to model this strategy?
5. Where in this text will it be possible to demonstrate the use of the strategy?
6. What language can I use to best describe what I am doing and my thinking?

Following a Strategy Demonstration Plan fomat allows teachers to consider the previous questions and to record pre-planned thoughts, language to be used, and key points to be modeled. Completion of a plan helps to ensure that modeling sessions are focused and successful.

FIGURE 5–1 Modeling occurs throughout the day during whole class and small group instruction.

Conducting Modeling Sessions

- Introduce the name of the strategy and what it means.
- Explain why the strategy is useful and how efficient readers use it.
- Explain to students that modeling involves times when the text is being read and times when thinking is being described. Alert students to how they will know what is happening, e.g., "*When I look up, I will be thinking about the text.*"
- Begin reading the text to students, stopping at selected places to think aloud. Use precise, accurate language to describe the thinking while demonstrating the use of the selected strategy.

First Steps: Second Edition   Reading Strand

Name: **Ms Annandale**   Date: **May 04**

Strategy Demonstration Plan

Strategy to be Introduced: **Connecting**

When and Why it's Useful:
- Making connections helps us to understand the choices that characters make.
- Helps us to make predictions about what might happen.

Key Points to Model:

- Make connections before, during and after reading
- Can make connections to things that have happened to you
- Can make connections to other texts you have read.
-

Text Selected: Wanda-Linda goes Berserk - Kaz Cooke

Pages to be Used:	Language to describe my Thinking
Cover	I've read another book by Kaz Cooke, it was also about Wanda-Linda. She was quite naughty. I wonder if she is in this text?
Page 1	The connection I'm making here is . . .
Page 2	This character reminds me of a friend . . .
Page 7	This is reminding me of a time when I . . .
Page 11	I remember when . . .

FIGURE 5–2 Strategy Demonstration Plan.

- Invite students to discuss their observations of the demonstration, e.g., *"What did you notice?" "What did you hear me say?"*
- If appropriate, jointly construct a chart with the students listing any key points or associated language with the use of the strategy.

Sharing

Sharing sessions provide the opportunity for students and teacher to think through texts together. The major difference between the modeling sessions and sharing sessions is that students are now invited to contribute ideas and information during these demonstrations.

Thinking aloud during sharing sessions is an opportunity for the teacher to continue to demonstrate the use of a selected strategy and also provides time when individual students are invited to "have-a-go." For example, while the text is being read and a strategy is demonstrated, students can be asked to share how they are using the strategy, e.g. *"What connections are you making?"* By inviting different students to share, other students will hear a range of ideas.

It is beneficial to use a variety of informational and literary texts for continuing demonstrations during sharing sessions. As students begin sharing their use of the strategy, jointly constructed strategy charts can be refined by adding or deleting ideas.

Planning Sharing Sessions

Consideration of the following questions will help teachers to conduct effective sharing sessions.

1. What aspects of the strategy do I need to demonstrate further?
2. Which texts might be the most appropriate to reinforce this aspect of the strategy?
3. What language associated with this strategy do I want to review?
4. How can I best encourage students to contribute to the demonstrations?
5. Can I create an opportunity to add to a cumulative strategy chart?

Conducting Sharing Sessions

- Reintroduce the strategy. Invite students to explain what it means.
- Elicit from the students why the strategy is useful and how effective readers use it.
- Begin reading the text to students, stopping at selected places to think aloud and demonstrate the use of the strategy. Use precise, accurate language to describe the thinking involved.
- Invite students to make use of the strategy throughout the demonstration and to share their thinking.

- Provide constructive feedback and positive comments about students' use of the strategy.
- Summarize different ways that individuals made use of the strategy and add them to the class chart if appropriate.

Guiding

Guiding sessions provide students with the opportunity to practice the strategies in meaningful reading contexts with a variety of texts. Guiding sessions involve the teacher providing scaffolds as students practice the strategy. It is important to provide ongoing feedback and support as students move toward taking responsibility for the use of the new strategy.

Activities linked to particular strategies can be selected and completed by students in oral or written forms. Students can work in small groups or in pairs to share a text and complete selected activities.

Planning Guiding Sessions

Consideration of the following questions will help teachers to conduct effective guiding sessions.

1. Which strategy do my students need to practice?
2. Have I provided multiple demonstrations of thinking aloud about the use of the strategy?
3. Have I provided many opportunities for sharing where students and I have discussed and used the strategy?
4. What texts do I want the students to use to practice the strategy?
5. Which activity might I use to provide a scaffold for the practice session?
6. What is the most effective way for the students to record their work?
7. What grouping arrangements will be most suitable for the students?
8. How will I provide feedback to the students during the activity?
9. How will I provide the opportunity for students to reflect on and share their learning after completing the activity?

Conducting Guiding Sessions

- Select texts to be used for both demonstration and independent student use.
- Reintroduce and discuss the strategy
- Model the use of the strategy using a selected practice activity.
- Provide time for students to work in partners or in small groups to read an allocated text.
- Provide time for students to complete the selected activity.
- Provide constructive feedback and support where necessary.

- Encourage students to share completed activities.
- Encourage students to reflect on the use of the reading strategy being practiced.

Applying

After participating in multiple demonstrations, sharing sessions, and scaffolded practice activities, students will benefit from opportunities to apply the use of the new strategy during independent reading. It is also important to encourage students to make use of the strategy when reading across other curriculum areas.

Teachers can and should continue to talk about and demonstrate the application of any strategies when sharing texts in other curriculum areas such as during science, math, or social science. Ongoing modeling of how and when strategies can be applied and how they assist readers to identify unknown words and comprehend text, will encourage students to use strategies beyond planned classroom reading events.

Comprehension Instruction: A Piece of Cake?

Comprehension instruction is not a piece of cake! However, the identification of the strategies efficient readers use, coupled with the recursive use of four powerful teaching practices of modeling, sharing, guiding, and applying are a first step to simplifying the complex challenge for classroom teachers. Providing explicit and multifaceted instruction will support readers to achieve the long-term goal of successfully comprehending a wide range of texts.

References

Booth, D., ed. 1996. *Literacy Techniques for Building Successful Readers and Writers.* York, ME: Stenhouse Publishers.

Cole, A. D. 2003. *Knee to Knee, Eye to Eye—Circling In on Comprehension.* Portsmouth, NH: Heinemann.

Education Department of Western Australia. 2001 *Success for All—Selecting Appropriate Learning Strategies.* Curriculum Corporation, Carlton Sth, Victoria, Australia.

Goodman, K. 1996. *On Reading: A Common-Sense Look at the Nature of Language and the Science of Reading.* Portsmouth, NH: Heinemann.

Harvey, S., and A. Goudvis. 2000. *Strategies That Work—Teaching Comprehension to Enhance Understanding.* York, ME: Stenhouse Publishers.

Kajder, S. B. 2003. *The Tech-Savvy English Classroom,* Portland, ME: Stenhouse Publishers.

Keene, E. O., and S. Zimmerman. 1997. *Mosaic of Thought: Teaching Comprehension in a Reader's Workshop,* Portsmouth, NH: Heinemann.

Meyer B. J. F., D. M. Brandt, and G. J. Bluth. 1978. *Use of Author's Schema: Key to Ninth Grade's Comprehension.* Paper presented at meeting of the American Educational Research Association, Toronto, Canada.

Pearson, P. D. 1976. "A Psycholinguistic Model of Reading." *Language Arts* 53: 309–14.

Pearson, P. D., and M. C. Gallagher. 1983. "The Instruction of Reading Comprehension," *Contemporary Educational Psychology* 8: 317–44.

KEY QUESTIONS

1. Which of the reading strategies in the Reading Strategy list are your students already using well? Which might you target as next steps for your learners?

2. Are your students applying comprehension strategies in informational texts as effectively as in fiction?

3. How might we ensure that students are generalizing the strategies and applying them in all the texts of their lives?

4. The gradual release of responsibility model provides extensive opportunity for modeling and think aloud. Some teachers, however, find it difficult to craft experiences that move learners to personal application. How is this going for you?

Strategy Demonstration Plan

Strategy to be Introduced: _____

When and Why It's Useful: _____

_____

Key Points to Model:

- _____

- _____

- _____

- _____

Text Selected: _____

Pages to be used:	Language to describe my thinking

Texts/experiences to be used for: _____

Sharing

_____

Guiding

_____

Applying

Contributed by K. Annadale © 2005 by Linda Hoyt from *Spotlight on Comprehension*. Portsmouth, NH: Heinemann.

Literature Log

Reading Strategy	Literature Selections to Use while Modeling, Sharing, Guiding, and Applying the Strategy	
	Fiction Selections	Nonfiction Selections
Predicting		
Connecting		
Comparing		
Inferring		
Synthesizing		
Creating Images		
Self-Questioning		
Skimming		
Scanning		
Determining Importance		
Summarizing/Paraphrasing		
Rereading		
Reading On		
Adjusting Reading Rate		
Sounding Out		
Chunking		
Using Analogy		
Consulting a Reference		

6 Many Ways of Knowing

LINDA HOYT

MEET THE AUTHOR

LINDA HOYT *freely admits that she can't sing or create artistic products that look like the images she is trying to represent, but she celebrates the need of learners to use many forms of expression to comprehend. She believes that drawing, singing, and talking are all important tools for learning. It isn't about making something "perfect," it is about stretching our thinking and using the arts to deepen comprehension.*

FOCUS QUOTE

As we strive to support comprehension, it is vital to remember that there are many ways of coming to understandings.

Kyle frowned and leaned closer to the clay he was molding. He seemed mesmerized by the challenge of creating wrinkles in the trunk of an elephant that was emerging from the gray blob before him. Kyle had been involved in reading about elephants in a variety of guided reading selections with his third grade group. These readers had compared the way different authors presented information on elephants and considered the validity of elephant poetry in light of the research they had done. These students could expound about the difference between African and Asian elephants, explain the social nature of an elephant herd, and dramatize the lumbering gait of a baby elephant. Perhaps best of all, they were very conscious of the comprehension strategies they had used during this study. They could explain how *visualization* had helped them understand the poetry, how *questioning* got them through places where the author's meaning had been unclear, and how *determining importance* helped them to seek out the most important words and ideas in the selections they were comparing.

Transferring Learning

Transmediation is a process of moving information from one communication system to another (Short, Harste, and Burke 1996). This process encourages learners to generate new meanings and expand existing ones. For Kyle to show what he knew about elephants through the medium of clay, he had had to determine the most important information and then develop a new perspective toward that information as he took on the role of the artist. To integrate his elephant knowledge into the lump of clay, he had to think deeply about what he knew and engage in a lively interplay that had him repeatedly moving from a book to clay, and back to a book again.

For Kyle, the creation of the clay elephant was a powerful way of solidifying and synthesizing his learning about elephants. It became a symbol of a study that had energized him as a reader and brought new knowledge into his life.

Transmediation Takes Many Forms

When a reader talks to a partner before writing, he is moving information into another communication system as he shifts from talk to writing. When a reader dramatizes the behavior of a character in a book, then talks and writes about the development of that character, transmediation has occurred in each of the steps. As we seek to move learners toward synthesizing what they know, transmediation of information can make a difference.

The Importance of Time with Text

As I use opportunities for transmediation, I want to be cautious in two ways:

1. We must be sensitive to the amount of reading and writing that learners are doing. If transmediation begins to take substantial time away from or to even replace reading, it needs to be reduced.

2. Transmediation cannot take the place of reading. It is not enough to have a learner listen to a book read aloud, draw a picture of the story line, and then talk about it. This learner must also have time to hold a book in his or her hands and read. One of my greatest concerns is the amount of reading-related activity which occurs during so-called "reading time." With an array of worksheets and activities and listening centers, it is entirely possible that a child could go an entire day without taking responsibility for personally reading a book. We cannot allow that to happen.

Many Ways of Understanding

As we strive to support comprehension, it is vital to remember that there are many ways of coming to understandings. Some people need to talk to think. These learners often don't seek a response but find that the act of telling someone what they are thinking helps to clarify personal understandings. Some learners need to sketch, to doodle while thinking and building understanding; others need to move physically, to use their body while thinking. Many learners find that music in the background sooths them and opens the door to creative thinking. The range of learners we support in our classrooms is great. Understanding that there are many ways of knowing can help us to provide lessons that support comprehension through diverse ways of processing and learning. A few suggestions:

• Writing about reading. Research has made it clear that when writers write about reading, they show better comprehension and better overall achievement. (Taylor and Pearson 2004). It is important that they write about the content they are learning and about the strategies they are employing while they learn.

• Writing about cross-curricular experiences. If learners write after a manipulative experience in math, after a science experiment, after a read aloud, they must translate their understandings into writing that will help to retain the information.

• Talking about reading. When we talk about our learning, we are using a communication system that is different from the one in which we took in the information. Talking about learning is transmediation.

• Drama. Jeff Wilhelm (2002) has reminded us of the power of action strategies to deepen comprehension. Strategies such as Tableaux and

FIGURE 6–1 A first grader writes about learning to solidify understanding.

FIGURE 6–2 A third grader writes to wonder and to question.

FIGURE 6–3 Detailed drawings support detail-level thinking.

FIGURE 6–4 Quick draw and sketching support main ideas and symbolism.

Active Dramatization allow learners to use their physical self to express meaning.

• The visual arts, as in the clay elephant, are powerful motivators for children. Drawing, painting, clay, or collage can offer alternative ways to express understanding. Learners who have difficulty with written and oral language may find that artistic expression can help them to organize thinking and rehearse for writing. Strategies such as Sketch to Stretch (Seigel 1984), Quick Draw (Hoyt 2003), Sketch Around the Text (Hoyt 2003) all focus learners on sketching before writing to help them solidify their thinking before committing ideas to print.

• Pausing to think, exploring your own inner voice. A moment of reflection when there is no talk and no need to listen can allow an internal transmediation to occur. Moments of quiet reflection in which students simply think about what they have learned increase the likelihood that there will be connections made between prior knowledge and the new learning. Moments of reflection after or during a learning experience can improve comprehension (Anderson, March, and Harvey, 1999). These pauses are a time when the brain goes into alpha state and when insights and creative thinking are best achieved.

• Use kinesthetic responses to learning. When you are active through touch, physical sensation, feelings, and movements your brain is intensely active (Jensen 1998). If students pace off the length of a whale's body, use their physical self to demonstrate changing angles in triangles, physically move vocabulary cards around until they are grouped in categories, or dramatize, kinesthetic action is assisting comprehension. A favorite thought from Eric Jensen: "Motion Equals Memory." (Jensen 1998).

• Play quiet, classical music during learning and reflecting times. Slow Baroque movements at 55–70 beats per minute support deep thinking and increase movement of information into long-term memory (Anderson, March, and Harvey 1999). Select your personal favorites or go to *<relaxwiththeclassics.com>* where they specialize in music for comprehending and thinking.

FIGURE 6–5 Learners can deepen understanding with physical action.

FIGURE 6–6 Partners physically sort pictures to reflect on the life cycle of a butterfly.

- Engage learners in Readers' Theater using their voices and expressive abilities to communicate meaning.

- Have students write poetry and songs about their units of study.

Celebrate all the ways we have of knowing. Open the door to physical movement, language, writing, art, drama, and expressive oral reading as sources of interpretation and comprehension will occur.

References

Anderson, Ole, Nancy March, and Dr. Arthur Harvey. 1999. *Learn with the Classics: Using Music to Study Smart at Any Age.* San Francisco, CA: Lind Institute.

Hoyt, Linda. 2002. *Make It Real: Strategies for Success with Informational Texts.* Portsmouth, NH: Heinemann.

———. 1992. "Many Ways of Knowing: Using Drama, Oral Interactions and the Visual Arts to Enhance Reading Comprehension." *The Reading Teacher* 45 (8): 580–5.

Jensen, Eric. 1998. *Teaching with the Brain in Mind.* Alexandria, VA: Association for Supervision and Curriculum Development

Short, Kathy G., Jerome Harste, with Carolyn Burke. 1996. *Creating Classrooms for Authors and Inquirers* (2nd ed). Portsmouth, NH: Heinemann.

Taylor, Barbara, and P. David Pearson. 2004. *"Schools That Beat the Odds Study."* Presentation at International Reading Association Conference, San Francisco, California.

Wilhelm, Jeff. 2002. *Action Strategies for Deepening Comprehension.* New York, NY: Scholastic.

KEY QUESTIONS

1. In what ways do you see transmediation already in place in your classroom?

2. How might many ways of knowing be integrated into your existing practices with whole class and small group lessons?

3. How might music be part of your comprehension classroom?

4. In what ways are you having learners write across the curriculum? Do they write poems in science, reflections about strategies in social studies, and combine sketching and writing in language arts?

5. How might more kinesthetic learning be brought forward to support learning?

Engaging Learning: Using Many Ways of Knowing

Thoughts to ponder:

- Are you playing music in the background while students are writing, reading, and talking? Is it at about 55–70 beats per minute, the rate that best supports thinking?

- Do you provide reflections at the end of each learning segment in the day? A few moments to reflect personally, to ponder what has been learned, and to have freedom from stress?

- Are learners using physical action to show what they know, representing their learning with kinesthetic movement, or engaging with manipulatives across the curriculum?

- Are talking and writing an element of every part of the curriculum?

- Do students sketch or draw to represent what they know? Is writing linked to the sketch or drawing?

- Is drama being used to interpret and further understanding?

- Do students have opportunities to express understanding by writing poetry and lyrics to songs?

- Is time with text being consciously monitored to ensure that interpretations and extensions are not diminishing actual reading time?

Part Two

. . . .

Crafting Environments That Foster Comprehension

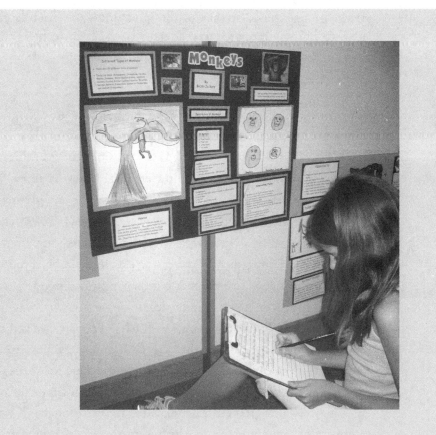

7 An Environment for Thoughtful Literacy

LINDA HOYT

MEET THE AUTHOR

LINDA HOYT *started teaching in a small town in Oregon. Her first experiences were in kindergarten, first, and second grade. She was fortunate to have a mentor teacher who showed her that when children don't learn, it is the teacher's job to change strategies and adjust to meet the needs of the learner. Susan Ulbricht, mentor teacher, will always be high on Linda's List of Heroes.*

FOCUS QUOTE

If we are to build a literacy of thoughtfulness in which learners are held to higher standards as readers, writers, and thinkers then we must hold ourselves to higher standards in the environments we craft for that learning.

If we are to hold high standards for student achievement and high standards for instruction, I believe that we have reached a time when we must also hold high standards for the environments in which the teaching and learning occur. Shelley Harwayne (1999) discusses the importance of creating a "literary landscape" where literature, literacy, and living are all woven together. We have reached a time in our profession where teachers must know their content but they must also know how to build community and create classrooms that are interesting, inviting, and a model of organization. Sterile classrooms with piles of papers, stacked boxes of stored resources, overflowing shelving, and commercial posters on the walls need to become places of the past. Classrooms where the focus is on the teacher with desks all facing forward and no space reserved for community meetings or small group interactions need to be rethought. If we are to build a literacy of thoughtfulness in which learners are held to higher standards as readers, writers, and thinkers then we must hold ourselves to higher standards in the environments we craft for that learning. Comprehension develops when there is a spirit of inquiry, deep thinking, and open attitudes about new ideas. It is time that our thinking about literate environments be brought to a conscious level. We cannot excuse messy, uncared for classrooms to lack of time and space. We are professionals. We wouldn't feel good about going to a dentist with an uninviting waiting area and a messy, cluttered treatment room. We wouldn't want to go to a restaurant that had failed to decorate, organize, and provide for our comfort and dining pleasure. Our learners deserve the best possible environment if they are to give us their best thinking and move forward as comprehenders.

Attractive Learning Spaces

As we strive to create attractive learning environments in which comprehension can flourish, it is often the small touches that make a difference. The small touches that make a home, a home, do wonders in a classroom. Instead of filling every shelf to the max with supplies, try leaving a small area clear for an artistic display of flowers, framed photos of students, or a statue to give a more home-like atmosphere. Many of our learners today come from environments where they do not see high quality models of organized living, feel the soothing presence of background music, or have the sense of peace that comes from soft lighting and carefully chosen decorations.

We have all been in settings where overly bright lights, crowded conditions, disorganization, and loud noise add stress and reduce our capacity for thinking. We can also identify with that marvellous feeling of, "Wow. I'm home . . . as you start to relax and unwind." Environment does affect thinking.

The nationally recognized Arkansas Literacy Model (Dorn and Soffos 2002) takes environments for achievement so seriously that criteria for environmental beauty are included in classroom evaluation. In these classrooms you can expect to see organization at its best. Storage boxes are removed and art or silk flowers put in their place. Children have a clear understanding of how resources are to be used and returned to storage so everything looks neat and tidy. Shelves are artfully arranged and furniture is clustered as you might see in a home with lamps and area rugs. The overall tone is one of peace and comfort. It is no wonder that the Arkansas model is also producing amazing achievement gains in all dimensions of literacy!

Learning from Retail Stores

If we want students to become deeply engaged with books, we have to become the best book *sellers* ever. Like a high quality commercial, we need to make books look and sound irresistible. While our think alouds and discussions will certainly play a key role in building passion for books, the way we display books is a key factor as well. If you go into any major bookseller and look at their displays, there is a lot to be learned. Which books catch your

FIGURE 7–1a, b Books arranged in an inviting format with a bit of colorful fabric underneath create an invitation to comprehension and extensive reading.

eye? Which areas draw you in, make you feel you want to sit, read, and become engaged with text? In looking at the efforts of commercial booksellers, I particularly notice the number of books that are displayed face out, how books are clustered by author as well as by topic, and how there are so many inviting spots to sit and browse. Can we accomplish that in our classrooms? You bet!

The Power of Partner-to-Partner Conversation

As we lift the organizational and visual quality of our environment, we also need to lift the quality of the conversations within that environment. Historically, conversations in classrooms have been teacher controlled with students being called on one at a time to share. This type of interaction results in very few learners getting to speak and produces a sluggish attitude about comprehension as struggling learners quickly learn that if they are quiet long enough, a more verbal peer will speak out and let them off the hook.

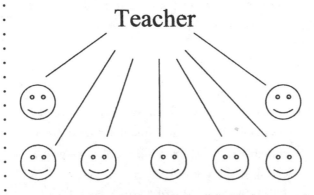

FIGURE 7–2 Teacher controlled talk limits learner thinking and volume of language production as well.

When partner-to-partner talks punctuate whole class discussions, comprehension and conversation both increase. To take advantage of this scaffold for thinking, students turn to a partner or gather in prearranged triads for focused talk on a topic. These miniconversations can occur as part of an interactive read aloud, during a science or social studies lesson, during guided reading, or after independent reading. Partner talks don't need to last very long. During a read aloud, I might have students turn to their partners four or five times during the read aloud/think aloud session. While partners converse, I can quickly circulate and listen in to acquire important assessment information. After a few moments, I call the students back together and we resume the read aloud/think aloud. A bit further into the story, it is time for another round of partner-to-partner. The important issue is to resist allowing any one student to speak out before he or she has had a chance to process the content with a partner.

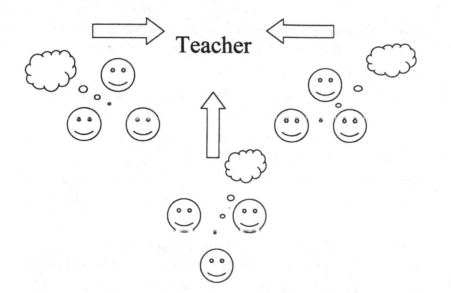

FIGURE 7–3 Partner conversations, when explicitly taught, can improve comprehension and language development.

When partner-to-partner pairs or "elbow partners" (Wilson 2003) look each other in the eye and converse about the learning, they are talking, thinking, and stretching their understanding. This kind of knee-to-knee and eye-to-eye conversation (Cole 2003) empowers thinking, expands English language proficiency, and offers high levels of motivation.

A few ideas for stimulating richer conversation:

- Model knee-to-knee and eye-to-eye conversations. Create a fishbowl by gathering the class in a circle with two students in the middle. As they carry on a conversation, the class will see active listening in action.

- Practice active listening when your students talk to you during class discussions. Consciously give them eye contact, lean a bit toward

FIGURE 7–4 Knee-to-knee conversations increase comprehension and expand oral language proficiency.

them, and say something that piggybacks on their statement. Then, talk to them about what they noticed you doing.

• Encourage students to link up or piggyback on statements: "Is there anyone who could link up to what Alia just said?" "Who can piggyback on Jonah's comment?" "Can anyone extend the idea we have started?" (This teaches how to conduct responsive conversation rather than just a miniversion of show and tell.)

• Take notes while your students are talking. Then, you can refer to your notes and make statements like, "I heard _____ say that _____." Or, "I am noticing a connection here, a minute ago, Juan said _____ and yesterday I see in my notes that Alicia said _____." Quoting your students and using their names affirms deeper thinking and reminds the students that you place value on their thoughts.

• Teach the students to label statements as deep or surface level thoughts. Students can then make statements like, "At first I was thinking on the surface level and I noticed that Sylvester was a donkey. Now, I am thinking more deeply and I realize that what is important is that he is in a family and his parents love him very much."

Time Is Precious

As we craft environments for thoughtfulness, it is also important to consider time and how it is used. Curricular demands are greater than ever and teachers feel pressured to cover content and cover it quickly. I am concerned, however, that in the classrooms of the very teachers who have told me there isn't enough time for silent reading, students can be found doing acrostics, fill-in-the-blank activity sheets, and in one kindergarten, using crayons to color in a photocopied page!

Shelley Harwayne (2002) reminds us to treat every minute in the classroom as though it were a precious pearl. With that metaphor as a guide, I find that it is easier to let go of projects and activities that are fun, were perhaps enjoyed by students, but have little credibility as a learning tool. For example, kindergarten teachers have for years conducted leprechaun hunts for St. Patrick's day and had special celebrations for Zero the Hero. With the precious pearl metaphor in hand, we need to look at those kind of activities and wonder: Is this the best, most meaningful way I can spend this pearl for this learner today? Would this learner be better served by more reading, more writing, a small group strategy lesson, or a hands-on experience with science? Is there anything in my assessment data to suggest that these students do not understand the concept of zero and therefore need a whole day to think about it? With this metaphor, we can more easily look at workbook pages and reproducibles and be selective consumers, using only those pages that are truly targeted to learner need; things that could not be done on plain paper. We can look at acrostics and time fillers and again wonder: If this time is a precious pearl, how will I spend it to create comprehension and meaning in the lives of these students?

Think Deeply

As we continue to reach for higher levels of attainment in our profession and in the comprehension of the learners we serve, conversations about environment can guide us in making a bigger difference for learners.

I invite you to consider time, space, and methods of instruction in light of your own environment and your own students; consider additions you would make or points that you could omit. Personalize and adjust. But most of all, take the importance of environment seriously.

References

Cole, Ardith Davis. 2003. *Knee to Knee, Eye to Eye: Circling in on Comprehension.* Portsmouth, NH: Heinemann.

Dorn, Linda, and Carla Soffos. 2002. *Building Literate Minds.* York, ME: Stenhouse.

Elias, Maurice, *et al.* 1997. *Promoting Social and Emotional Learning: Guidelines for Educators.* Alexandra, VA: Association for Supervision and Curriculum Development.

Harwayne, Shelley. 2002. "Non-Negotiables in Teaching Reading." Presentation at the Beaverton Literacy Conference, Beaverton, Oregon.

———. 1999. *Going Public: Priorities and Practice at the Manhattan New School.* Portsmouth, NH: Heinemann.

Routman, Regie. 2003. *Reading Essentials: The Specifics You Need to Teach Reading Well.* Portsmouth, NH: Heinemann.

Wilson, Jodi. 2003. "Raising the Quality of Our Instruction." Presentation at NCTE, San Francisco.

KEY QUESTIONS

1. What are the strengths of your environment? What are the challenges?

2. How are you doing at embedding partner conversations into whole class conversations? What is going well? What are the challenges?

3. In what ways have you created an inviting, home-like feel to your learning space? Do you have lamps, a rug, soft pillows or furniture? Do you have spaces for art and beautiful things on shelves and in easily viewed areas?

4. How are you doing with clutter? What could be done to remove materials that are simply "stored" or excess textbooks that are not used regularly?

5. Does your environment show what you believe about learning? Could a visitor immediately tell which strategies and content your students are learning?

What You See in a Thoughtful Classroom

- Teacher talk is focused on modeling and demonstrating, showing rather than telling. Purposeful learner talk is encouraged and expanded. Each lesson is analysed to monitor the amount of student talk and the level of learner engagement. Learning is extended through discussion of how the target strategy can be applied in other books and other content areas.

- The teacher is a partner in the learning, actively engaged and assertively teaching. The teacher uses moments of learner independence to meet with individuals or small groups rather than focus on paperwork.

- The walls in the room reflect the learning being accomplished. Bulletin boards are created by students for purposes related to their learning. Charts showing strategies and content being studied are evident. Strategy instruction is "visible." Tools for thinking and learning are posted in a clear and visible way. The walls are tools for learning, rather than just for display. There are few commercially developed posters.

- There is an atmosphere of trust and caring. Each learner knows he is cared about but also knows there are high expectations for engagement and quality thinking.

- In the primary grades, personal alphabet strips are on each desk and the class alphabet is at children's eye level along the wall. There is an interactive word wall that changes to reflect reader development.

- Phonics is taught explicitly and is based on ongoing assessment, not just prescribed order in a program. Word study lessons are integrated into language arts time as well as content area studies. The lessons are targeted to observed learner needs and practice is immediately provided in real-life contexts.

- There is a strong sense of purpose to the learning. Students can tell you what they are doing, what they are learning, and what progress they are making toward their goals. They can tell you what they are doing today, why they are doing it, and what they will be likely to be working on tomorrow.

- Concept development and language are encouraged through hands-on experiences related to the learning. Real experiences that widen the children's knowledge of the world around them are linked to experiences with reading and writing.

What You See in a Thoughtful Classroom, *continued*

- Standards are woven into each lesson rather than addressed as additional curriculum.

- The teacher reads to students from diverse sources. Read alouds occur more than once during the day and include fiction, informational sources, and poetry. At least one read aloud each day features a think aloud and a minilesson. Read aloud selections are made available for readers to reread and compare to other texts.

- The teacher shares his or her personal reading with students and shares the way comprehension strategies are used by adult readers too.

- Desks are arranged in groups to encourage collaborative work. There is a meeting area for whole class discussions, read alouds, and group explorations. Partner talk is encouraged in all grouping formats.

- A variety of grouping patterns are used throughout the day. These include individual, small group, and large group activities. Structures such as guided reading, one to one conferences, literature circles, reciprocal teaching, and cooperative learning are evident.

- There are many books in the room reflecting the full range of text forms. Many are displayed face out. The classroom library reflects a careful balance between fiction and inviting informational texts. Informational texts include directions, descriptions, persuasive writings, and other informational genre. Books are sorted and re-sorted by students to match current studies of text and writers craft.

- Independent reading, from a variety of reading materials that the students select themselves, is set up for blocks of 20–60 minutes. At least one day a week, the reading time is 60 minutes long to build stamina for sustaining attention. Independent reading is opened with a minilesson and closed with a sharing session to encourage conversation about content and strategies used. Each student has a personal collection of books at hand that may include familiar favorites or books that are waiting to be read. The personal collections include fiction and nonfiction.

- Content-area lessons for math, science, social studies, and health are seen with dual purposes: teaching content and teaching reading. Conversely, content-area texts are often used for guided reading lessons during the language arts block. Comprehension is taught in all areas.

What You See in a Thoughtful Classroom, *continued*

- Students develop fluency through choral reading, readers' theater, partner reading, or with tape-recorded books. Reading in the round is avoided as it diminishes interactions with the text and reduces comprehension.

- Multiple systems of communication are emphasized by writing about reading, drawing during science, using drama to act out a mathematical equation, and integrating music across the curriculum.

- Writing is developed across the curriculum. Students write as a response to every subject studied. The writing process is clearly in place and students understand that some writing (lists, notes, journal entries) will stay in draft form. Other pieces, meant for an audience, will move through all stages of the process and be published. Writers have opportunities to write on topics of personal interest as well as assigned topics. A culture of minilessons and hands-on practice are facilitated by writing conferences and guided writing groups which might meet during writers workshop or during the same time blocks as guided reading groups.

- Explicit attention is given to the amount of *time* spent reading and writing. The reading time is filled with reading. Writing time is filled with writing. Reading-related behaviors such as acrostics and other busy work are minimized.

- Assessments are ongoing. They are a natural extension of daily reading/writing experiences and are used to inform daily instruction. These assessments may include running records, phonic writing analyses, retells, anecdotal records, short reading miscue inventories, checklists of good reader strategies, and so on. Decisions about next steps in instruction are based upon observable learner need.

- The environment is highly organized and conscious attention has been paid to making it beautiful. Storage boxes, random piles of paper, and unattractive piles are removed to establish the classroom as a model of beautiful and organized living. There is space on the floor for learners of all ages to gather in a learning community . . . close proximity stimulates language and bonding. Teacher space is minimized to ensure learning spaces are maximized. (Teacher desks, storage areas, etc., are created *after* the learning spaces have been arranged to maximize learner's spaces.)

The Intimate Classroom

Establishing an Emotional Environment That Encourages Thoughtful Literacy Learning

8

KATHLEEN FRANCESCANI

Happy, relaxed, stimulating relationships between children and between the child and teacher promote growth of personality which in turn advances achievement.
—Marie Clay, *Becoming Literate*

MEET THE AUTHOR

KATHLEEN FRANCESCANI *has taught in primary classrooms in the Cleveland Municipal School District for several years. Currently, she facilitates professional development in the Cleveland School District, as a literacy coach through Cornerstone. Cornerstone is a national literacy initiative that serves children in impoverished rural and urban communities across the country.*

FOCUS QUOTE

When children think aloud about, question, respond to, and enjoy their literacy experiences, their voices resonate, their smiles broaden, and learning happens!

Schools today go to great lengths to increase student achievement. Teachers participate in workshops featuring the latest trends in instructional strategies. New texts are adopted that promise higher test scores. Assessments are routinely administered and the results carefully analyzed. Still we struggle with advancing student achievement. Marie Clay's suggestion that we can promote higher levels of learning by establishing a rapport with and among our students seems too good to be true, but it is.

Trusting Relationships

Connecting with others on a personal level seems to thaw intellectual inhibitions. This past year I joined a book club with a group of women. Although all of the women didn't know each other, we each shared a desire to engage in thoughtful conversations about books. When I reflect on the depth of the discussions during our book club meetings, I realize that the most passionate, honest discussions occurred when we shared our innermost thoughts and personal connections to the literature. This didn't come about easily. In order for this to happen, each of the women in the book group had to feel comfortable enough to open up and know that although her viewpoint may be challenged, it would always be treated with respect. Over the year, trustful relationships formed and consequently deeper discussions have ensued. We felt happy and relaxed and our capacity for insightful discourse soared.

Trusting Relationships in Our Classrooms

Trusting, intimate classrooms can be developed to encourage this same level of dialogue. Once children feel free to express themselves, conversations about literature become limitless, and comprehension deepens. A learning community that nurtures trusting relationships and celebrates individual differences is essential. When students feel supported and know that their background experiences are valued, they will feel more inclined to express their thoughts and ideas with their classmates and the teacher. Through this exchange of ideas, thinking is clarified, questions are raised, and a profound joy of learning occurs.

FIGURE 8–1 Students need to feel secure in order
to comfortably express themselves.

FIGURE 8–2 Students in our classroom take responsibility for their words and actions.

Risk-Free Learning Environment

A risk-free learning environment is carefully fostered. When my second grade students enter the classroom, they know they are accountable not only for their actions but also for their words. We have one absolute rule in our classroom: *No Put Downs*. At the beginning of the school year we work together to determine what this rule means for our classroom.

Through the process of defining this rule, we have come to understand that everything we say to each other has an impact, and that we are all responsible for choosing our words carefully. As we negotiate our understanding of this rule, the students have astutely decided that "No Put Downs" transcends defining, yet has significance in a variety of situations. Some of the comments made during our discussions include:

- "Look at someone when they are talking. If you don't look at the person talking, they won't know if you're listening, and when you don't listen to someone who's talking to you, it's a put down."
- "Don't interrupt someone who is talking. Wait until they're finished because if you interrupt them, it seems like you aren't listening."
- "Don't laugh at someone when they're wrong. Everyone makes mistakes."
- "Use your manners."
- "Don't tell someone their idea is stupid. Ask them to explain. It might hurt their feelings if you say that their idea is stupid, and it's a put down to hurt someone's feelings."
- "Tell someone when you don't agree using kind words."
- "Don't raise your hand when someone else is talking. If you have your hand up, then maybe they won't think you're listening and that's a put down when you don't listen. We should give our friends time to think."

As the students generated this list, awareness developed that led to a genuine respect for one another. We realized the importance of listening to one another attentively and responding thoughtfully, careful not to "put anyone down." Students learned how to disagree and how to express their likes and dislikes, and feelings and opinions. Trust developed as a result of our class rule, and vital conversations were promoted where students felt free to take risks and share their deepest thoughts.

Quality Discussions

Quality discussions occur when children feel comfortable enough to take risks. During the course of these discussions, students question and support each other's thinking. The following conversation illustrates how one student felt uninhibited enough to express an original idea and how another student respectfully challenged his reasoning after listening to *Because You're Lucky* by Irene Smalls, a story about a boy who must unwillingly share his room, and ultimately his family, with an orphaned boy his age. The class was wondering aloud about questions they had about the text.

Teacher: We know that asking questions can help us better understand what we are reading. Did you wonder about anything while you listened to the story, *Because You're Lucky?*

Tyrone: I was wondering why the mother likes Kevin better than Jonathan.

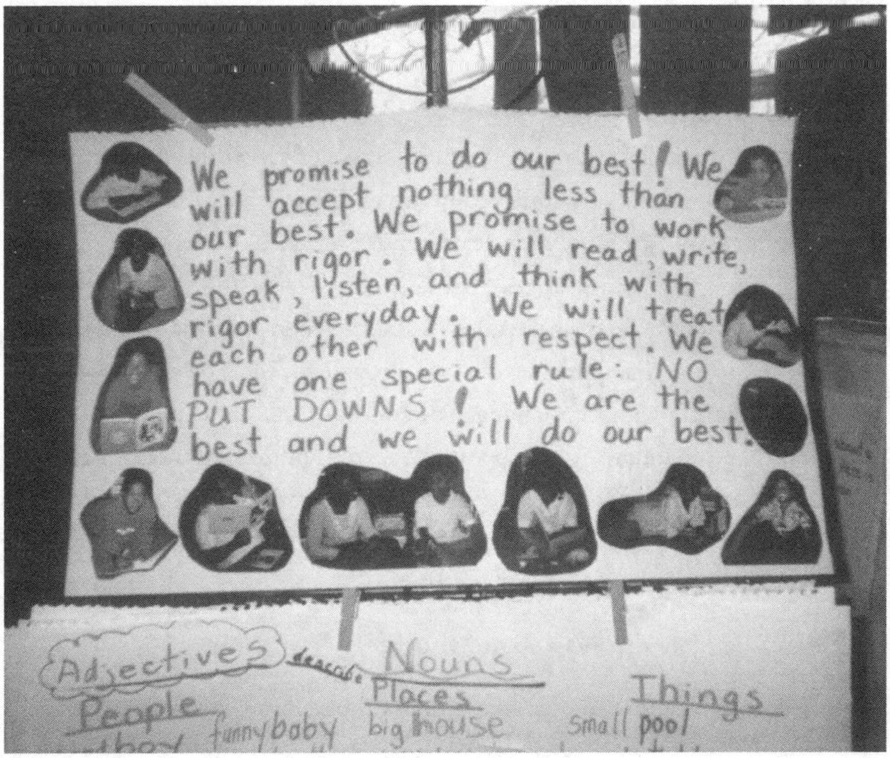

FIGURE 8–3 Our class-generated list.

Felix: I disagree. I don't think she does. Why do you think she likes him more?

Tyrone: Because she was nicer to him. She always talked nice to him. She was mean to Jonathan.

Felix: Where did you see that in the book?

Tyrone: When she pushed Jonathan's toys and stuff out of the way and told Kevin to stay in his room.

Teacher: Felix, why do you think Jonathan's mother did that?

Felix: I think she's trying to help him.

Tyrone: Why is she just helping him and not Jonathan?

Felix: Because he doesn't have a mom and she thinks he's sad.

Tyrone: Oh. I know, like when my brother got a skateboard and I thought my mom liked him better. I was jealous. I wonder if Jonathan is just jealous like I was . . .

This level of discourse made all of us more reflective about the text, and encouraged other students to contribute their ideas. If Tyrone and Felix hadn't felt as if it was okay to challenge each other I may not have known what they were thinking. Eventually the rest of the group began to voice their opinions and the chatter of students questioning the text and one another filled the classroom.

Talk Can Be Inspiring

Traditionally, quiet classrooms were upheld as orderly well-disciplined environments where learning unequivocally occurred. However, learning in silence to many children is equal to learning in a vacuum. Talk can be inspiring. Often the conversations that take place when students are learning to employ new comprehension strategies scaffold their learning by giving language to their thoughts that they couldn't provide on their own. Choosing poetry or literature with rich language often leads to thought-provoking conversations like the following one between Aleecia and Marcus about the language in Eloise Greenfield's poem, "Neighborhood Street."

Aleecia: I like how it says "soft sugar-names."

Teacher: What does that help you to visualize?

Aleecia: I don't know. It sounds like candy. I think about candy . . . what it taste like.

Teacher: How does thinking about the sweetness of candy help you understand the part of the poem when the poet says, "morning mamas and daddies roused the children with soft sugar-names"?

Aleecia: Uhmmm. I don't know.

Marcus: My mom calls me sweetie but not like I'm candy. I think the mom in the poem might call them sweetie cause she love them.

Aleecia: Candy is sweet and so are the children to their momma and daddies?

Reaching for Expression

Aleecia knew that the language in the poem helped her visualize the sweetness of candy, but she wasn't able to articulate how that image helped her understand the poem better. When she heard Marcus explain how his sensory images enhanced the poem for him, she had a realization about how her idea helped her better comprehend the poem. I had the feeling that Aleecia was reluctant to respond because she felt she didn't know the "right answer." It wasn't until she heard Marcus relate his thinking that she tentatively took a chance and expressed a thought that she wasn't decidedly sure about. Through the discussion that ensued students began to realize that there are many answers and that these answers are viable if they can be substantiated.

Authentic conversations between students and between the teacher and students can generate thoughts and ideas that may not germinate if students are always reading and writing in isolation. Just as talk is essential in stimulating thinking, solitude too, has its place. In my classroom, quietness is rare, but when it does occur it is a comforting silence, a purposeful interlude for

FIGURE 8–4 A supportive emotional environment fosters authentic conversations.

thoughtful reflection. Balancing time for conversations and opportunities for working quietly gives consideration to the needs of all students.

Thoughtful Conversations

A supportive emotional environment encourages individuality and intellectual challenges. Classrooms that encourage students to express themselves are places where students confidently engage in thoughtful discussions about literacy, and motivate one another to think more deeply. When children think aloud about, question, respond to, and enjoy their literacy experiences, their voices resonate, their smiles broaden, and learning happens!

References

Clay, M. M. 1991. *Becoming Literate: The Construction of Inner Control.* Portsmouth, NH: Heinemann.

KEY QUESTIONS

1. How can children in a classroom be provided with opportunities to talk to each other and share ideas?

2. What kinds of things can a teacher do to establish a learning environment that fosters cooperation and collaboration among students?

3. Why should students be included in determining rules and procedures?

4. Does the choice of literature used in a classroom impact thoughtful discussions? What are some books that encourage insightful discussions?

5. What things can a teacher do at the beginning of the year to create a climate that honors thinking and respect for everyone's thoughts and opinions?

Creating a Trusting, Intimate Environment for Literacy Learning

- Be respectful

- Be accountable for actions and words

- Look at those who are speaking

- Don't interrupt

- Listen attentively

- It is O.K. to disagree. Just do it respectfully

- Encourage talk and sharing of ideas

- Create authentic conversations. Avoid questions with known answers.

- Cherish quiet, thoughtful moments

- Encourage individuality and intellectual challenge

- Promote thoughtful discussion

- Encourage questions

Reflection Tool for Educators

As I look around my room, do I see children:

☐ sitting knee-to-knee and eye-to-eye, engaging in real conversation?

☐ working together in an atmosphere of trust?

☐ looking back into their books to justify their opinions?

☐ having the courage to say what they are thinking?

☐ feeling encouraged to develop their own opinions?

☐ agreeing or disagreeing with their peers, respectfully?

☐ who are deeply engaged in thinking about their reading?

☐ being kind to their peers?

☐ making connections to the text?

☐ using sensory images to deepen their understanding?

☐ questioning the text?

☐ using inferences to think more deeply?

☐ using talk as a tool for learning?

☐ engaged in authentic conversation for real purposes?

  Contributed by K. Francescani © 2005 by Linda Hoyt from *Spotlight on Comprehension*. Portsmouth, NH: Heinemann.

The Comprehension Classroom 9

JANE RAMBO

MEET THE AUTHOR

JANE RAMBO *is the Director of Reading for schools in Midland, Texas. She is an avid professional reader who is dedicated to lifelong literacy for all.*

FOCUS QUOTE

Does the classroom feature print on the wall that serves an instruction purpose? Are there models of summaries, persuasive pieces, or directions? Are there lists of comprehension and fix-up strategies? Does the featured text help students to become independent problem solvers and strategy users who understand how to comprehend?

The Comprehension Classroom: Primary

1. Is it a **print-rich environment** (text and print everywhere, poetry, children's writing displayed, books in all centers, labels, vocabulary banks, graphic organizers)?

Lots of Evidence   *Some Evidence*   *No Evidence*

2. Is there a **meeting area and evidence of explicit comprehension strategy instruction** in read alouds, science, social studies, and so on?

Lots of Evidence   *Some Evidence*   *No Evidence*

3. Are **read aloud selections displayed** for students to examine and reread?

Lots of Evidence   *Some Evidence*   *No Evidence*

4. Are there **charts on the walls listing the comprehension strategies?** Is there evidence that the students refer to and use the charts? Were these charts constructed with children, not laminated, so they can be revised?

Lots of Evidence   *Some Evidence*   *No Evidence*

5. Are **group discussions punctuated with learners turning knee-to-knee and eye-to-eye** to discuss their learning or does teacher call on one student at a time to share?

Lots of Evidence   *Some Evidence*   *No Evidence*

6. Is the **classroom library well stocked with fiction and informational texts?** Do students sort and re-sort it to match their studies of text features and genre? Are there at least eight books per child? Is there a range of difficulty levels represented? Are children invited to write book reviews and leave them with books for others to read?

Lots of Evidence   *Some Evidence*   *No Evidence*

7. Do students have **a special place for their personal collection of independent reading** books? (A ziplock bag, a covered cereal box or?) Is there a variety of genre included?

Lots of Evidence   *Some Evidence*   *No Evidence*

8. Are students taking home **nightly reading material thoughtfully chosen by the teacher** with a comprehension focus to consider while reading? (Bookmarks saying: Help me visualize as we read this; I Can Make Connections in This Book; Please ask me to retell this story after we read.)

Lots of Evidence   *Some Evidence*   *No Evidence*

The Comprehension Classroom: Primary *continued*

9. Is there evidence that **small group guided reading instruction** is happening daily—small group area, something for teacher to write on to make teaching points, leveled books, etc.?

Lots of Evidence   *Some Evidence*   *No Evidence*

10. Are there **small group focus areas** (writing, reading, word work, science, listening, poetry, math)?

Lots of Evidence   *Some Evidence*   *No Evidence*

11. Are there books in focus areas?—(Alphabet books in word work area, books in science area, books in math area, exemplary texts in writing area, etc.)

Lots of Evidence   *Some Evidence*   *No Evidence*

12. Are there **modeled/interactive writing/written retellings** that demonstrate author craft, text features, multiple genre (work displayed over time)?

Lots of Evidence   *Some Evidence*   *No Evidence*

13. Does **independent writing on self-selected topics** occur daily?

Lots of Evidence   *Some Evidence*   *No Evidence*

14. Is there an **interactive word wall** created by learners and teacher together? Does it change over time?

Yes _____ No_____

15. Is every available opportunity used to add text to student work? Art projects have written descriptions about how they were done, how they relate to a book or ? Math experiences are accompanied by written retells of the process, and so on.

Lots of Evidence   *Some Evidence*   *No Evidence*

16. Is **student performance data** collected as a natural part of each lesson and used to inform instruction (running records, informal and formal assessment)?

Lots of Evidence   *Some Evidence*   *No Evidence*

17. Is word work manipulative and interactive? **Learners are taught to cross-check meaning when sounding words out** to support comprehension and meaning.

Lots of Evidence   *Some Evidence*   *No Evidence*

18. Do readers use a variety of strategies for dealing with challenging words and blockages in comprehension?

Lots of Evidence   *Some Evidence*   *No Evidence*

The Comprehension Classroom: Intermediate

1. Is it a **print-rich environment?**—Class-created strategy charts, poetry, student writing samples, many books in various parts of the classroom, vocabulary banks, graphic organizers. Bulletin boards reflect learning from reading and discussion: Lists of powerful verbs, collections of sentence strips with terrific leads, a record of dialogue that serves different purposes, nonfiction text features and examples of their use. Units of study are obvious to an observer.

Lots of Evidence   *Some Evidence*   *No Evidence*

2. Are there **read alouds from fiction and nonfiction complete with think alouds** and comprehension strategy lessons? Is evidence of thinking is recorded on strategy charts?

Lots of Evidence   *Some Evidence*   *No Evidence*

3. Is there a **meeting area where students huddle close together on a carpet or with soft furniture** to create a community of learners? Discussions include a lot of eye-to-eye, knee-to-knee conversations between peers before individuals speak out.

Lots of Evidence   *Some Evidence*   *No Evidence*

4. Does **comprehension instruction carry across all curricular areas**—math, science, social studies? Student response journals, lists on the wall, reading strategies posted show evidence of inferencing, drawing conclusions, etc., in all curricular areas.

Lots of Evidence   *Some Evidence*   *No Evidence*

5. Is there **small group reading instruction to coach reading strategies?** Is there a small group area, something for teacher to write on to make teaching points, reading strategies posted, leveled texts, evidence of comprehension focus?

Lots of Evidence   *Some Evidence*   *No Evidence*

6. Does **independent reading time begin with a comprehension strategy focus lesson?** Readers understand that while they are reading, they will be consciously focusing on strategy use and will debrief content and strategy understandings at the end of the session.

Lots of Evidence   *Some Evidence*   *No Evidence*

7. Does **independent reading engage students with a wide variety of genre in fiction and informational texts?** The teacher confers with individuals during this time.

Lots of Evidence   *Some Evidence*   *No Evidence*

The Comprehension Classroom: Intermediate, *continued*

8. Is **nightly reading material based on student interest**—are reading logs, literacy bags, linked to whole class strategy focus to support synthesis of strategy use?

Lots of Evidence   *Some Evidence*   *No Evidence*

9. Is the **classroom library** organized well—with books grouped by author, themes, variety of genres? (Is there balance between fiction and informational texts? Are books attractively arranged? Do many have covers facing out? There are picture books and novels as well as magazines, newspapers, and other realistic texts. Reading material is easily available for readers of all achievement levels in the room. (Rule of thumb: 8 books per student)

Lots of Evidence   *Some Evidence*   *No Evidence*

10. **Word Walls/Vocabulary Banks** in the room?

Yes _____ No_____

(content area words, vocabulary for character description/feelings, words selected for structural analysis instruction, rich descriptors, simile, analogy, etc.)

11. Is **writing instruction** evident in that students' are writing in response to each curricular area? There is evidence that they are receiving daily independent writing time based on student selected topics. Modeled and interactive writing are used to demonstrate writers' craft. Writers Workshop teaches process and sustainable attention.

Lots of Evidence   *Some Evidence*   *No Evidence*

12. Is there **student performance data?** Is there evidence that each lesson is seen as an assessment opportunity rather than waiting to give an end of project grade? Running records, and informal assessments inform instruction and are collected regularly.

Lots of Evidence   *Some Evidence*   *No Evidence*

13. Is word work manipulative and interactive? **Learners are taught to cross-check meaning when sounding words out** to support comprehension and meaning.

Lots of Evidence   *Some Evidence*   *No Evidence*

14. Do readers use a variety of strategies for dealing with challenging words and blockages in comprehension?

Lots of Evidence   *Some Evidence*   *No Evidence*

Environments for Supporting Comprehension: Affirmations and Invitations

As you review the checklists on environments to support thoughtful literacy, consider your classroom carefully. In the columns below, first list affirmations that you noticed as you read the list. What is already in place in your classroom? In the second column, list things you would like to accomplish to further enrich the environmental supports for rich comprehension instruction.

Affirmations (already in place)   Invitations (things to add)

_____   _____

_____   _____

_____   _____

_____   _____

_____   _____

_____   _____

   Now, prioritize. What will you do first, second, and so on. . .
   Ask your students about the changes. Are these changes helping them as learners?
   Did your principal or your colleagues notice the changes? Can they tell by walking in your room what your instructional priorities may be? Which units of study you are now involved in? If students are focusing on comprehension all day long?

KEY QUESTIONS

1. How might checklists such as these be used by a single teacher, in a grade level group, or by a school?

2. What modifications might you make in the list to personalize it to your classroom goals, your school, your standards?

3. The checklist could be used by a principal to coach teachers. What might be the benefits of such coaching? How would this assist principals and teachers in crafting thoughtful environments?

4. The walls are clearly important. They send messages about what we are learning and the strategies we are utilizing to comprehend. What are core considerations in crafting walls that work as tools for learning rather than decorative add-ons to learning?

10 Check It Out

MARGE COLLINS,

MARION ODELL,

AND SUSANNE C. SCOTT

MEET THE AUTHORS

MARGE COLLINS *has led a very active professional life. She has worked as a classroom teacher, staff developer, and literacy specialist for the Palo Alto School District in California. She has most recently worked as a resource teacher. She and her husband love to travel.*

MARION ODELL, *Reading Recovery Teacher–Leader, is a member of the Literacy Training Team for new teachers in the Palo Alto Unified School District. She works as a Reading Specialist and has also taught regular classes and students with learning disabilities.*

SUSANNE C. SCOTT, *EdD, Reading/Language Arts Specialist, is a teacher on special assignment in the Palo Alto Unified School District. While working on curriculum and professional development initiatives, she also enjoys teaching and learning with her class of fifth grade students. She has presented at many conferences and leads K–5 staff development projects in the areas of reading, writing, and literacy.*

FOCUS QUOTE

The environment sets a tone, a stage for the learning, and that learning should show on the walls, in the book selections, and in the self-efficacy of the children.

A Comprehension Checklist

Learning Environment

- Safe, peaceful, comfortable, well-ordered classroom
- Students are thoughtful; "think time" is encouraged
- Partnerships are supported between and among students
- Talk is valued: partner conversations in each lesson
- Physical arrangement of classroom furniture provides for individual, small group, and whole class instruction
- A print-rich environment encourages children to read, write, and talk about text
- Areas are created around the room for small group work
- Flexible grouping practiced
- A rich display of student work
- A variety of fiction and nonfiction books, picture books, poetry, newspapers, magazines, and maps used for reading and writing, many face out
- Nonfiction as visible as fiction on walls
- Class-created "tools" for thinking are clearly visible
- Class-created lists—books that show emotion, books that show passing of time, etc.—are on walls.
- Music often played to create a thoughtful atmosphere
- Children have collections of books within reach during independent times, familiar favorites as well as new texts

What Are Teachers Doing?

- Modeling/thinking aloud to demonstrate strategies in fiction and informational texts
- Providing individual and small group instruction in strategic reading and writing behaviors
- Gathering assessment data as a natural part of lessons
- Providing daily time for read alouds and discussions
- Allowing children time to read and write independently, conferring one-on-one
- Supporting fluency with a focus on expression and meaning
- Charting children's thinking and:
  - activating prior knowledge
  - higher level questioning
  - verbal scaffolding
  - visualizing strategies
  - student-generated questions
  - encouraging comparisons
  - eliciting opinions/justifications
  - supporting inferential thinking
- Providing ongoing assessment and evaluation to improve and guide instruction; maintaining portfolios for all students
- Making careful text selections: some books to challenge thinking, others at just-right levels, many to match learner interest

What Are Students Doing?

- Engaging in authentic reading and writing tasks
- Engaging in deep vs. shallow thinking
- Participating in storytelling, drama, poetry, writing in response to reading experiences
- Actively listening/participating in partners, small group, whole class discussions
- Developing personal questions, making connections, visualizing
- Identifying important ideas and words
- Searching for evidence to support opinions
- Making comparisions
- Evaluating text
- Looking closely at author's craft
- Having opportunities to make choices about what to read and write
- Conferring with adults and other students
- Sharing individual work with other students
- Creating individual and group projects
- Working at an appropriate level of challenge to reach their full potential
- Using sketching, notetaking, conversation, and drama to interpret meaning
- Writing in response to reading
- Sharing innermost thoughts and connections to reading experiences

A Comprehension Checklist, *continued*

What to Look for in Kindergarten

- A print-rich environment
- Centers supplied with materials to encourage reading and writing
- Art work that is accompanied by print
- Students engaged in active listening
- Students engaged in various oral language activities; knee-to-knee responses to text
- Opportunities for children to learn early reading strategies in small group settings
- Daily modeled, shared, interactive and independent writing
- A well-stocked writing center which all students use regularly
- Illustrations enhanced by details and labeling or connected text
- Use of strategies in small and large group settings:
    - Guided reading picture walk
    - Making predictions
    - Guided retelling
    - Think alouds
    - Visualization
    - Charting children's thinking
    - Charting children's responses and ideas
    - Deep vs. surface conversations
    - Connections
    - Developing "I Wonder" questions
    - Making comparisons
    - Offering opinions
    - Thinking about meaning
    - Independent reading every day

What to Look for in Grades One and Two
Reading
- Daily read alouds: fiction and nonfiction think alouds and conversation about texts
- Shared reading
- Guided reading, just-right books
- Guided retelling, think alouds, summaries of texts, making predictions, visualization
- Independent reading of picture books, poetry, and nonfiction books. Strategies are applied personally
- Book Clubs/Literature Circles/Information Circles

Writing
- Designated time each day for teaching writing
- Use of literature as a model for student writing
- Evidence of children's writing in many genre of nonfiction

Vocabulary and Concept Development
- Students engaged in rich oral language and vocabulary activities; knee-to-knee response to text
- Charts of colors, shapes, number names, theme words, enlarged text, word walls
- Use of graphic organizers
    - Venn diagrams
    - Webs
    - Story maps
    - KWLQ
    - Sequence cards
    - Graphs
    - Labels
    - Diagrams
    - Timelines
    - Captions

What to Look for in Grades Three to Five
Reading
- Teaching of reading features: dialogue, literary devices, story maps, KWLQ, and other graphic organizers
- Students visualize, infer, make connections, summarize, determine importance, predict, compare, justify opinions, evaluate, read critically; knee-to-knee response to text
- Think alouds model comprehension strategies that are applied in content areas and independent reading
- Student-generated questions are used in every curricular area
- Worksheets/acrostics/time fillers minimized
- Directed Reading and Thinking (DRTA) or Directed Listening and Thinking (DLTA) focuses on predicting through narrative and informational text
- Book Clubs/Literature Circles/Information Circles
- Whole class novels are minimized
- Flexible grouping for varied instructional purposes: Small groups meet in each subject area
- Access to reference materials, both text and online

Writing
- Designated time each day for teaching writing
- Writing folders with self-selected topics
- Variety of genre explored

Vocabulary
- Theme words
- Dictionaries and thesaurus
- Test is taught as a genre

 Contributed by M. Collins, M. O'Dell, and S. Scott © 2005 by Linda Hoyt from *Spotlight on Comprehension*. Portsmouth, NH: Heinemann.

To create a literacy of thoughtfulness, the environment needs to support deep versus shallow thinking, extensive amounts of time with text, and offer rich immersion in high quality language. It must also emphasize the power of knee-to-knee converstions between learners and explicit teacher modeling of comprehension strategies. It is a place where high expectation, rigorous learning, and extensive scaffolds enable learners to reach new depths of understanding and develop a base of strategic, flexible strategies they can use across the curriculum. The environment sets a tone, a stage for the learning, and that learning should show on the walls, in the book selections, and in the self-efficacy of the children.

KEY QUESTIONS

1. What would you consider the non-negotiables in an environment that promotes comprehension and deep thinking?

2. What "tools" for learning should be on the walls? How could we recast wall space as a resource rather than simply a display?

3. Teacher space can take a lot of room for a desk, storage, etc. How can that space be minimized so that the learning needs of the classroom are taken into account first?

4. A central gathering area is a must as we create intimate classroom environments where learners can connect to demonstrations and communicate in an atmosphere of trust. What kind of gathering area have you created? How is it working?

5. A key feature in environments that stimulate comprehension is the way time is used. Learners need time to read, time to think, time to wonder, and to question. How are you addressing time issues to ensure that comprehension has time to develop?

Spotlight on Environment: Focus on Comprehension

☐ What are the strengths of the environment you have created in your classroom?

☐ In what way does your room arrangement facilitate/support comprehension?

☐ What do you wish you could improve?

☐ Do children have a voice in the room arrangement?

☐ Who owns and uses the walls? Are the walls covered with teacher made or commercial products?

☐ Are the walls filled with tools that students can use in their learning?

☐ How is your classroom library organized? Do the students organize it and participate in book selection? Is there a balance between fiction and informational texts?

☐ Do your students frequently resort the books to categorize them in groups that are useful to them or that match your current investigations of genre and text features?

☐ What would be an ideal addition to your environment?

☐ Does a colleague have a room arrangement that facilitates comprehension? What makes it work?

☐ If a visitor walked into your classroom, would that person be able to tell by looking at the walls which strategies you are currently investigating?

☐ Would the environment show a visitor what units of study are taking place?

☐ Are the students able to explain which strategies they are already using well and those which they are working on?

☐ Do students write about their strategy use?

☐ An intimate classroom should have a warm inviting feeling. The addition of a lamp, a bookcase with space dedicated to display, a cloth over a small table, a rug in the gathering area all add a sense of community. Would any of these additions work in your space?

☐ Is there space in your classroom to meet with a small group and confer 1–1 with learners?

☐ How do you store learning charts over time to ensure that students can return to them as needed?

☐ Do your walls show a record of your study of literary devices? Are there lists of books with similar themes, of those with foreshadowing, of those with fascinating dialogue or verb choice?

Helping Parents Help Us

Promoting Comprehension Through Parent Involvement

11

V. SUSAN
BENNETT-ARMISTEAD

I wonder how we could get parents to support what we are doing here?

Our comprehension instruction is so powerful, I wonder how we could share the information with parents?

MEET THE AUTHOR

V. Susan Bennett-Armistead *is currently a parent educator and early literacy specialist for Williamston Community Schools as well as an early childhood professional development consultant. Her doctorate from Michigan State University will be in teacher education with an emphasis on early literacy development. Prior to pursuing her PhD, Susan worked for fourteen years in the early childhood community as a teacher, director, and advocate for young children and their families. Presently a mother of three, Susan and her husband eagerly await adoption of two more children.*

FOCUS QUOTE

We want parents to see themselves as valuable contributors to their child's learning and to see that they are *already* modeling literacy uses.

Schools know that parent support is a critical component in student success. Unfortunately, teachers and administrators don't always know how to obtain that involvement and sometimes don't recognize the support. It all comes down to meaningfully connecting with families.

Others in this book will share with you a variety of ways to connect with children and support their literacy learning. In this chapter, I will share another piece of the puzzle: effective ways to reach out to, support, and welcome the involvement of families in their children's literacy lives. Just as other authors have told us that there is no one magic bullet for promoting children's comprehension, neither is there one best way to involve parents.

Joyce Epstein (1995) urges us to consider that involvement itself should not be viewed as one kind of practice. Often, when teachers talk about involving parents in their children's schooling they imagine the parent volunteer who comes in to work in the classroom. Epstein argues that there are in fact at least six different areas in which schools can support parent involvement: parenting, communicating, decisionmaking, volunteering, learning at home, and collaboration with the community. Within each area, a family might play out its involvement in different ways. For example, within volunteering, one family might be able to schedule a time to come in to school and listen to children read. Another, with small children, might prepare materials at home, like creating 32 blank books for use at school. Still another might come to school after work to facilitate a Family Literacy Night. Each family is involved, each on a schedule that fits their availability, and each with a task that they feel comfortable doing.

Williamston Literacy Project

Williamston Community Schools, a small suburban/rural district in Michigan, decided to try to reach all its families by designing a community-wide focus on literacy, supported through the role of a Parent Educator/Community Early Literacy Specialist, currently filled by me. The vision of this role is to reach all families with children from birth to second grade, *before* children are identified as at risk for literacy difficulties and, in the case of children already identified, to work with the family in improving the child's literacy skills. To do this, we had several basic assumptions:

- **All parents have much to contribute to their children's learning.** Using Luis Moll *et al.*'s (1992) work as a guide, we tried to keep in mind that every family has important information to share with their children, and with help from us, can be tapped to support their children's learning. Moll *et al.* refer to this as "Funds of Knowledge," and it might include knowing a great deal about agriculture, cultural traditions, music, folk medicine, etc. In our community, we found that parents are amazing resources on a wide variety of topics with a limitless store of skills.

- **Every parent is an expert on his/her own child.** While we know a lot about working with groups of children, no one knows an individual child better than his family. (Even in the rare cases where this wasn't true, our interactions with the family reflected our belief that it was.) This laid the foundation for a relationship based on mutual respect, or as Rasinski and Frederick (1989) describe it, a "co-empowerment."

• **Every child in the community could benefit from literacy support whether they are enrolled in our school or not.** To address this, we developed partnerships with family day-care homes, preschool programs, the local library, play groups, the bookstore, and parochial schools. The idea is to create a community-wide focus on literacy and serve as a resource to other groups.

• **Every parent wants to be involved in his child's learning, but there may first be barriers to overcome.** Some barriers include:

- Schedules
- Transportation
- Language
- Parents' previous unpleasant experiences with school
- Differing views of the roles of school (some parents perceive schooling as a task best left to the "experts" at school (Lareau 2000)
- Parents' perceptions that they have nothing to offer
- Parents' perception that they are unwelcome
- Teachers' perception that including parents means more work for them
- Teachers' previous unpleasant experiences with parents
- Teachers' inexperience/lack of training in working with parents

It is important to recognize that no *one* approach can overcome all of these challenges, but that a multifaceted approach might address many of them. To that end, we implemented:

• **Parent education nights:** A series of topics related to early literacy including creating a print-rich environment at home, oral language development, comprehension and literacy, and music and literacy. These were offered in a variety of settings throughout the community.

• **Home visits** to families that want them: Parents were invited to schedule a visit to gain more information on promoting literacy experiences at home. Visits are conducted at the family's convenience in the location of their choice (my office, their workplace, their home, the coffee shop in town . . . wherever they feel most comfortable meeting).

Literacy Eco Map
To facilitate this conversation, I use a Literacy Eco Map. This map illustrates for parents many of the elements of a comprehensive view of literacy

(reading, writing, listening, and speaking as well as viewing). Our conversation around this map allows me to address comprehension as the primary goal of literacy, and encourages parents to think beyond "sound it out" as a response to a reader. In addition to sharing information around the Eco Map, I leave a booklet of ideas for at-home activities and follow up by sending home a library book that is well suited to the child's passions and reading level.

- **Family Literacy Nights:** These themed events provide an opportunity for children and parents to engage in literacy-building games and comprehension activities that can be easily reproduced at home. In excess of two hundred people attended our first event. The key to success with this event was that children invited their parents and that parents viewed it as a worthwhile way to spend the evening with their children. Each participating family received a free book. Three such events were conducted this year.

- **Book Buddies Program:** An in-school parent volunteer reading program where parents read to and with pre-K to second graders needing extra literacy support. We provided training in comprehension strategies to help parents gain skills to use with their buddies and their own children as well.

- **Newsletter entries:** I regularly include literacy suggestions and activities in the school newsletters for families to do at home.

- **Book-lending program:** The infants, toddler, and preschool programs in our school-run childcare programs did not have access to the school library. Through donations, scavenging, and a small grant, a lending library was developed that allows every child to take home a book every week. These books include tips for parents about interacting with a child around the text and strategies for enhancing language and comprehension.

- **Ongoing consultation with teachers:** Information gained through home visits and other collaborations with families is shared with teachers to better help teachers meet the needs of children.

Goals for the Program

All of these connections provide opportunities for us to help families improve literacy skills in their children. The goals of these contacts are multilayered as well. We want parents to:

- see themselves as valuable contributors to their child's learning
- see that they are *already* modeling literacy uses and make them more evident to their children

Dear_____,

Our family is invited to the Family Literacy Night at Discovery Elementary
Media Center. It is on Monday, October 20 from 6:30–8:00. If we come, we
can do lots of activities and I get to choose a free book!

I hope we can go!

Love,

FIGURE 11–1 Students invite their parents to attend the literacy events.

- provide access to a variety of literacy materials including stories, informational text, magazines, coupons, writing materials, etc.
- gain a view of literacy that includes promoting comprehension through interactive reading
- see themselves as critical to providing primary experiences for children to draw upon when activating prior knowledge in literacy experiences
- see that virtually every activity can be connected to literacy with a little thought
- understand that their role as literacy models is more powerful than anything we can do at school

Your Community

Although our community is small and our program fairly new, there are
many elements of this project that can be used in communities different
from ours. The book-lending program for example, was based on the work
done in an urban setting in California (Madrigal *et al.* 1999). The home visits
are modeled after the work done by McIntyre and Kyle (2000) in Appalachian communities. The family literacy nights are designed to emulate the
work of Vopat's Parent Project in Chicago (1998). If you have a real desire to
reach your families and include them in the powerful role of building children's literacy, there are marvelous models all around us. We hope that you
can hear in your own district the music we heard in this parent's comment:

> I never knew that so much could be connected to literacy. I never
> knew it was that important. I can't wait to try this!

References

Epstein, J. L. 1995. "School/Family/Community Partnerships." *Phi Delta Kappan,* 76: 701–12.

Lareau, A. 2000. *Home Advantage: Social Class and Parental Intervention in Elementary Education.* Lanham, MD: Rowman & Littlefield.

Madrigal, P., C. Cubillas, D. Yaden, A. Tam, and D. Brassell. 1999. "Creating a Book Loan Program for Inner-city Latino Families." CIERA Technical Report #2–003. Ann Arbor, MI: CIERA.

McIntyre, E., and D. Kyle. 2000. "Family Visits Benefit Teachers and Families—and Students Most of All." *CREDE Practitioner Brief #1,* October.

Moll, L. C., C. Amanti, D. Neff, and N. Gonzalez. 1992. "Funds of Knowledge for Teaching: Using a Qualitative Approach to Connect Home and Classrooms." *Theory into Practice* 31: 131–41.

Rasinski, T. V., and A. D. Fredericks. 1989. "Dimensions of Parent Involvement." *The Reading Teacher* 43: 180–82.

Vopat, J. 1998. *More Than Bake Sales: The Resource Guide to Family Involvement in Education.* York, ME: Stenhouse.

KEY QUESTIONS

1. How might parent involvement efforts improve achievement in reading comprehension?

2. Which comprehension strategies might you specifically target for teaching to parents?

3. How can you ensure that all children have books in their homes?

4. What are barriers to parent involvement in your community?

5. What might you try that would involve parents who traditionally do not get involved at school?

Parental Involvement Questions

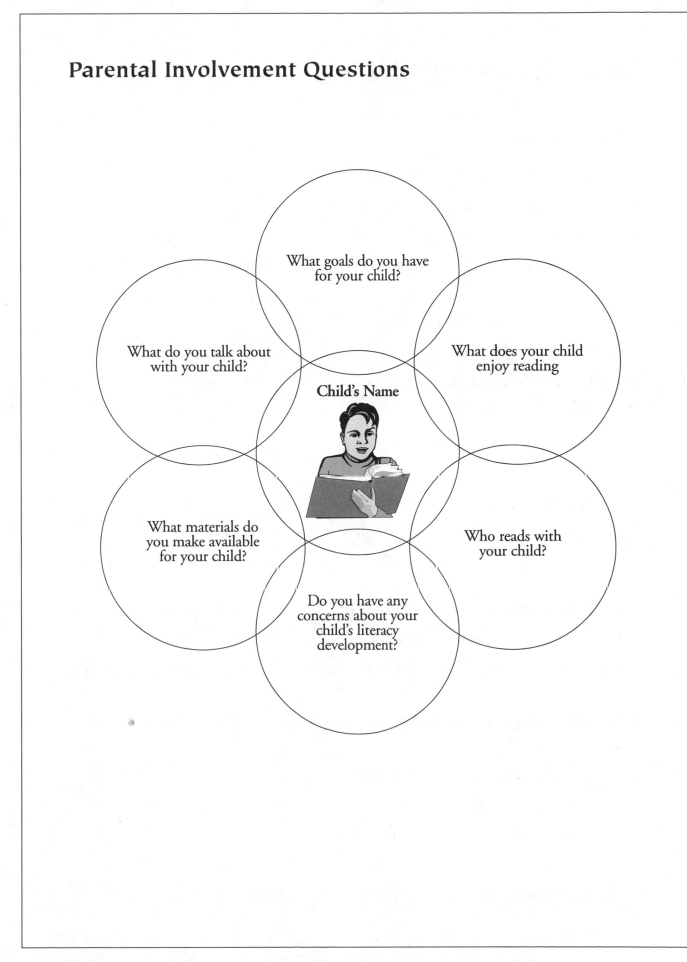

What goals do you have for your child?

What do you talk about with your child?

What does your child enjoy reading

Child's Name

What materials do you make available for your child?

Who reads with your child?

Do you have any concerns about your child's literacy development?

Parent Tips for Nurturing Readers

A Recipe for Comprehension

• Take your child to the library frequently

• Consider books as gifts for holidays and special occasions

• Let your children see you reading . . . don't wait until they go to bed

• Read aloud a LOT . . . from fiction and books about the real world

• When you read to your child, talk about the book. Share your opinions and encourage a conversation about what happened

   Try questions like:

   • What did you notice?

   • What did you like?

   • Did you learn anything new?

   • How did this make you feel?

   • I like the part when_____. What did you like?

   • Wasn't it funny when _____.

• Help your child think of connections to the book. "Remember the time we went on a picnic? It was a lot like the picnic in the story." Or "Remember that worm we found outside?"

• Try Pair Reading . . . read familiar books in unison

• Encourage independent quiet reading . . . while you read a magazine or newspaper, your child reads quietly too

• Practice summarizing the steps in everyday household activities like setting the table, making a taco, etc.

• Provide varied opportunities for writing:

   • write letters, notes, and emails

   • have your child write out your grocery list

   • make lists

   • be a note-writing family . . . write notes to each other

Recipe for Literacy

One relaxed child
Bathed, fed, and at peace with the world
One loving parent
Combine with one wonderful picture book
Simmer with read aloud and conversation
The result: A lifetime of comprehension

—Linda Hoyt

Part Three

Comprehending
Strategically

Questioning,
Inferring,
Summarizing

12 Guiding Comprehension Through Questioning and Coaching

ALISON MALONEY

MEET THE AUTHOR

ALISON MALONEY *is originally from Perth, Australia. She has many years of experience in classrooms and has done extensive professional development for teachers.*

She is currently serving as manager of Heinemann Seminars coordinating and teaching seminars all over the United States. For many years she was a consultant with Edith Cowan University in Perth and the First Steps Professional Resource for Learning.

FOCUS QUOTE

To help our students utilize their natural curiosities and use questions to extend and deepen comprehension, we need to assess the role of questioning in the classroom—who is asking the questions and why?

In 1991 at the Australian Reading Association conference, Dr. Peter Freebody suggested that teachers have been found to ask a question of students every eight seconds. With data like that, we have to ask, "Is that teaching or interrogation?" Historically, educators have asked students a barrage of questions under the guise of reading instruction, but there is little evidence to suggest that this practice has positive results.

I was recently working with a teacher who was teaching comprehension through guided reading for the first time. Mary-Ann, like many of us, felt that she needed extra support and so she decided to follow the teacher's guide from the series her school was currently using. She was partway through the lesson when several things occurred to her: (1) The teacher's manual was trying to cover too many concepts for the students to develop deep understanding, and (2) The questions suggested were not stimulating the students to think deeply about the text. It was at this point that she realized that she, and not the guide, knew the needs of the students and the questions that would best guide them through the text.

For many students and teachers, comprehension is defined by the questions supplied by the teacher's guide in the reading series. While these questions may represent a range from literal and inferential to evaluative, we must be cognizant of the fact that these questions are *assessing* comprehension, not teaching it. There is a place for assessment, but as the saying goes, "You don't fatten a pig by weighing it!" So, we can't improve students' comprehension by continually assessing without first teaching students how to think more deeply about the texts of their world.

To help learners develop a true definition for comprehension we need to reassess the role of questioning in the classroom—who's asking the questions and why? Are the questions being asked playing a critical role in learner development or are they just filling time? When a basal program suggests the points to stop within text for question and answer, we have to wonder if those stop points and questions are best for this group of learners at this moment in time? We have to wonder if these particular questions will really deepen understanding.

Questions Are Natural

I am reminded of my nephew when he was very young. He was constantly asking "why?" immediately followed by "why" and yet another "why." I wonder, when do we stop becoming curious? Is it because we somehow learned in school that there is one answer and then it is over? Is it because no one had the time (or interest) to answer the "why's"? But if we, like my young nephew, stay with a stream of questions it forces us to think more deeply about a topic. While no one wants to answer questions on "Why the sky is blue" in the middle of the parking lot with a cart full of groceries, we must acknowledge that the stream of questions represents true wonder and an innate need to know.

In classrooms we often ask a question of a student and if it is answered satisfactorily, we move on. Done, finished. If the answer we receive is unexpected we put it down to lack of comprehension. The constant flow of questions that drives a curious three year old cannot exist in an environment where teachers ask only ask questions that have predetermined answers.

FIGURE 12–1 Learners talk to each other about their books, asking genuine questions that stem from their interests.

To help our students utilize their natural curiosities and use questions to extend and deepen comprehension, we need to assess the role of questioning in the classroom—who is asking the questions and why? We need to explicitly teach students to question the text themselves. We need to assess the role of teacher as questioner.

Questions Help Us Engage with Text

Before we can decide how to teach questioning we need to consider the variety of ways in which we question texts. There are several kinds of questions that spring immediately to mind. One enjoyable question for me is, "What's going to happen?" This kind of question can keep me turning the pages in a novel a long time after I should have been asleep. There is also the "What about . . . ?" and the "Why?" that sparks the desire to learn and discover new things. As students develop critical literacy, their questions challenge the author, the text and the topic: Is it correct? What is the message? Is there bias in this writing? How does this other author discuss this topic? And of course, there is the "I Wonder" question that unleashes our sense of wonder about the world.

In Search of *Real* Questions

When I first attempted to teach my students to question text for themselves, I discovered that it is harder than it sounds. With the aim of teaching my students to generate questions, we started by listing questions on a flip chart. It looked all right at first, but then I realized that they were engaging in a

FIGURE 12–2 Real questions stimulate interest, add motivation, and deepen understanding.

well-known student strategy called "please the teacher." There was no passion in their questions. There was no genuine sense of wonder. Because these students believed comprehension was answering questions, when asked to generate their own, they believed any question would work. They had selected questions for which they already knew the answers!

To encourage my students to ask questions that stimulated and improved their reading, I needed to help them see which questions were real for them. My next step was to try the question-generating strategy with pictures instead of text. Using a picture helped students realize that they had no interest in and gained no support from questions at the literal level. The added benefit of a picture was that students wondered where or how we might find the answers. This took us to printed texts, to other photos, and also helped us learn an important lesson: sometimes there are no answers from anywhere but yourself.

Additional Modeling for Those Who Need It

The students who claimed to not have any questions when they were reading independently concerned me. These were often the students who generated their questions for my benefit. These students needed to see and hear me model the strategy more frequently and more explicitly. Even though I was continuing to model questioning for the whole class, I inserted modeling into the small group work I was doing with these students so they could observe again, in a more intimate setting, the way questions helped me as a reader.

Considering Purposes for Questions

As the students became increasingly interested in their own questions, they began to see how different questions performed different functions and that some questions were more helpful than others. We ended up with a rough table that defined best questions as:

- questions that move them through the text "what next . . . ?"
- questions that guided them to a particular book in the first place "why I picked it up/searched it out . . ."
- questions for the author
- questions about related texts and understandings
- questions about the world
- questions about the craft of the writing
- questions I still have after reading

Text Selection

Watch out for the text! One of the most important elements of teaching any comprehension strategy is carefully chosen text. This is especially true when teaching questioning. If the students have no interest in a topic, or if it is badly written, you will be lost.

Releasing Responsibility

In the early stages of teaching the questioning strategy, much of the work and responsibility was mine. Using the Gradual Release of Responsibility model, I was initially in control, explicitly demonstrating the language that would explain the questioning strategy and my thinking as I read. As I slowly released responsibility, with my end goal that the students be independent, much time was spent sharing, supporting, and guiding the students through the metacognitive process. Most of this occurred through guided reading and one-on-one conferences.

After feeling very confident that I was moving from the teacher-directed questions that we all know assess comprehension, to student-generated questions that support and develop *their* comprehension, I still felt the need to ask some probing questions of my students. In order to support their comprehension and their metacognitive process I need to know what's going on!

Teacher Questions: Questioning to Coach Readers

As I was struggling with my role as questioner in the classroom, I learned of the power of coaching. I was taking some courses in executive coaching in my personal time. During this training we talked often of the definition of a coach—it was different from both a teacher and/or mentor although contained qualities of both. Timothy Galway, famous for changing the nature of sports coaching from telling to leading, defines coaching as "unlocking a person's potential to maximize their own performance." It is helping others think about their own learning.

I am a great believer that students need explicit instruction to learn, and also that they need practice and guidance to become independent. As the students gained proficiency with questioning, I moved from teaching to

FIGURE 12–3 Verba and her students engage in a coaching conversation designed to deepen understanding through probing questions.

coaching. This meant that I, as coach, generate a continuing stream of questions that force the coachee to move deeper and be reflective about his or her own understanding. These open-ended probing questions lead to a dialogue based upon deep, reflective thinking and move students to a new level as a strategy user and a comprehender.

If we take a coaching stance in questioning, our goal is to:

- Compel the reader to consider the text and their response to the text
- Focus on a deeper level of thinking
- Guide the reader to consider his or her own questions and the role those questions played in comprehension
- Focus the reader on strategic behaviors that could be applied in other settings
- Encourage a descriptive and not judgmental response
- Provide a feedback loop for the teacher

Questions: Tools for Comprehension

Questions are natural. They flow as smooth extensions of thought when we are interested in a topic and are attempting to understand. They are tools for deepening understanding and making connections between the new and the known.

When readers consciously question texts, authors, and topics they engage in deeper levels of thought and are empowered to navigate the texts of their world.

When teachers offer explicit modeling and then shift to the role of coach, questions take on a new texture. They are honest, open, and supportive of long-term reading development.

Remember, the question that has one right answer is only good for that one moment in time. How might questions instead be recast as personal tools for learning?

KEY QUESTIONS

1. Who's asking the questions? Where do they come from?

2. Are the questions in the teacher guide worthy of learner time? Would students be better served by generating their own questions or having an open-ended questioning experience with their "coach"?

3. How might we ensure that learners focus on asking questions as well as thinking about how their questions affect their comprehension?

4. Will the relationship you have with students allow you to ask a stream of questions that forces their thinking to a deeper level without causing stress?

5. Are you modeling questioning as a comprehension strategy in all curricular areas?

Recording My Questions

Reader_____ Text_____

Readers ask questions continuously as they move through a text. They wonder, "Why?" "What about?" "How?" And so on. As you read today, think about your questions. You may have questions about a picture, a part of the text, or something the author did not say. Select a few questions to write down and be ready to talk with a partner about them.

While reading page   I wondered:

#_____   _____

#_____   _____

#_____   _____

#_____   _____

#_____   _____

At the end of the reading, I am wondering: _____

My questions helped me _____

_____

_____

_____

_____

_____

Teacher Observation

Teacher Observation

Student _____

This student asks questions that: Date _____

	Date observed								Notes
• Reflect connections (T-T, T-W, T-S)									
• Show interest in further study									
• Question the author's meaning									
• Question the author's craft									
• Show application of prior knowledge									
• Make inferences beyond the text									
• Give evidence of synthesis									
• Show critical thinking/evaluation									
• Indicate understanding of events, facts									

The Ease of Questioning 13

JOY SCURLOCK

MEET THE AUTHOR

Joy Scurlock *has been an educator for 17 years and is currently a literacy specialist for the Williamson County School District in Tennessee. She has had the opportunity to present on a national level as well as continue her work with students, teachers, parents, and community workers in her county.*

FOCUS QUOTE

Students who develop strategies for questioning gain ownership of the process, a process that will be used over and over not only in reading, but in problem solving and decisionmaking throughout school and life.

Questioning is a comprehension strategy that promotes engagement and keeps the learner involved in the topic. In *Strategies That Work,* Harvey and Goudvis (2000) state that "asking questions engages us and keeps us reading" (81–82). In life, our questions propel us through the newspaper, through a recipe, through the challenges of growing a garden, rearing children, and so on. Questions are natural to human development and are one of our strongest tools for understanding our world.

Questioning: Before, During, and After a Text

Questioning begins early in human development. We have all heard precocious three year olds asking, "Why?" over and over and over until we realize our patience is running thin. It is natural then to connect those questions to literacy. For preschoolers and early primary students, their questions flow as a natural extension of listening to the title or looking at the cover. The child's generation of questions continues throughout the actual reading of the story and at the conclusion as well. As older students progress in the application of the questioning strategy, questions can be recorded on think sheets or written on sticky notes and placed before, within, and after the text. The goal is to teach students to question to the point that questioning becomes a habit, and engagement occurs each time they read.

FIGURE 13–1 Students are genuinely interested in the questions and wonderings of their peers. Student-generated questions lead to deeper levels of motivation and understanding.

Questioning: Thin and Thick

Maureen McLaughlin and Mary Beth Allen in *Guided Comprehension: A Teaching Model* (2002) remind us of the terms, "thin and thick questions." **Thin** questions require specific answers based on specific information, while **thick** or open-ended questions initiate discussion and promote thought. Students should be taught the difference between these two types of questions and understand that each has its place. Thin and thick questions reinforce what students have read, but also cause students to think deeper about the text, and beyond the text searching for personal connections and life applications.

Thin questions are questions that can be answered from specific information in the text and usually have a one or two word response, i.e., "In the story *The Three Little Pigs*, what did the first little pig use to build his house?"

Thick questions are open-ended, requiring deeper thought and explanation, i.e., "In *The Stranger*, how did the farmer feel when he realized that the stranger did not sweat as he worked?" A student would take the information from the text, add previous knowledge, and provide an explainable answer.

Questioning: Queries to the Author

The authors of the book *Questioning the Author* (Beck *et al.* 1997) developed a questioning strategy that promotes engagement through actively searching for meaning while reading. Using queries or questions to the author during reading, this approach emphasizes an understanding of the author's purpose and meaning in the information presented. This approach can be utilized in all forms of text including narrative or expository texts.

Planning

The process of questioning the author begins with the planning of the text to be read and discussed. What are the students to read, and what information are they to know when finished? Planning allows the teacher to identify areas that students might have difficulty understanding, either due to a lack of prior knowledge or if the author did not develop the information thoroughly.

Segmenting

Segmenting the text follows the planning process in questioning the author. This involves reading the information and determining where in the text to stop and question for understanding. It must be noted that though text often lends itself to natural breaks at the end of paragraphs and chapters, the concept of segmenting in this case is to stop at points that need reinforcement or greater understanding. The process of segmenting works well with the before, during, and after questioning presented earlier in this chapter.

Developing Queries

This is the final step in the questioning the author process and is a natural lead-in to discussion of text. Each section of the text that was segmented is queried or questioned to guide students to a deeper understanding of the text. These queries are directed to the author and may or may not have a specific answer; however, the answers should be explainable or defendable though they are not answered at this time, but are noted or recorded. Initial querying is modeled by the teacher. The teacher may release this process to students when an understanding is in place and students can initiate questions appropriate to the text. This will be especially important in older age groups as students begin to feel ownership in the reading comprehension process.

Examples of some of the queries to the author as explained in the book *Questioning the Author* are:

INITIATING QUERIES

- Author, why did you write this?
- Author, what are you saying to me, to us?
- Author, when did you write this text?

FOLLOW-UP QUERIES

- Author, what did that word, sentence, paragraph mean?
- Author, why don't you tell me more?
- Author, does what you write now make sense with what you wrote before?
- Author, why did you use that particular word or phrase?

NARRATIVE QUERIES

- Author, why is the character like he is?
- Author, did you really solve this situation?
- Author, what is going to happen next, and why?

Discussion

Discussion is the final step in questioning the author. As the facilitator, the teacher poses queries as the text is read to promote thinking and discussion that would lead to a deeper understanding of the author's purpose. Also, the teacher sets ground rules for respectful and considerate discussion, rules such as: only one person speaks at a time; everyone shares before a person can speak a second time; students may disagree with one another, but do not say someone is wrong, just offer another perspective for consideration; etc. Again, the process of querying is eventually released to students, who then participate in student-directed discussion while the teacher monitors and directs.

Benefits to Explicit Instruction in Questioning

Empowerment

Since a goal of teaching is for students to learn how to learn, the effective application of questioning empowers students to do just that. Students who

FIGURE 13–2 When students write their own questions, they can experiment with many different formats of questioning.

develop strategies for questioning gain ownership of the process, a process that will be used over and over not only in reading, but in problem solving and decisionmaking throughout school and life.

Experience

Students should experience working with texts on an individual basis as well as in a group setting. A group setting is ideal as literature circles or guided reading groups. Each experience, whether small group or individual, actively engages students in the reading process and hones strategies needed to continue critical thinking while reading.

Enrichment

Students who are engaged in the questioning strategies will not only deepen their understanding but will also enjoy a feeling of success and accomplishment. The shared information and discovery that occurs during the discussion times provides greater comprehension for all reading levels as some students expose information based on prior knowledge while other students may submit more literal, often overlooked statements. Students' personal perspectives lead to questions and discussions with a greater sense of diversity. As comprehension is improved, the ability to communicate is enhanced. This enrichment cultivates a desire to learn. If we can instill in our students this desire, then we can make a difference. If we can equip our students with effective learning strategies such as questioning then we know that our students are well on the way to becoming lifelong readers and ongoing learners. They will but also be better communicators, problem solvers, and decisionmakers, characteristics that hold value in all aspects of their lives.

Excitement

The book was *A Single Shard* by Linda Sue Park. I had just finished teaching a questioning strategy. As students looked at the title and cover page, questions began to spring up, "Why did Crane-man live under a bridge? What happened to Min's parents? Why was Tree-ear so mean to Min?" As one student finished a question, another student quickly jumped in with a new question or thought. I smiled. I remembered my former frustration when I did not think I was equipped to teach reading comprehension effectively. As I looked around the room at the "engaged" students, I was excited. Now, I am beginning to feel like I have the knowledge and expertise to really make a difference, the type of difference I want to make in reading comprehension instruction.

References

Allsburg, Chris Van. 1986. *The Stranger.* New York, NY: Houghton Mifflin Co.

Beck, Isabel L., Margaret G. McKeown, Rebecca L. Hamilton, and Linda Kucan. 1997. *Questioning the Author: An Approach for Enhancing Student Engagement with Text.* Newark, DE: International Reading Association.

Bentley, Dawn. 1998. *The Three Little Pigs.* Kansas City, MO: Piggy Toes Press.

Harvey, Stephanie, and Anne Goudvis. 2000. *Strategies That Work: Teaching Comprehension to Enhance Understanding.* York, ME: Stenhouse.

Keene, Ellin Oliver, and Susan Zimmerman. 1997. *Mosaic of Thought: Teaching Comprehension in a Reader's Workshop.* Portsmouth, NH: Heinemann.

McLaughlin, Maureen, and Mary Beth Allen. 2002. *Guided Comprehension: A Teaching Model for Grades 3–8.* Newark, DE: International Reading Association.

Park, Linda Sue. 2001. *A Single Shard.* New York, NY: Scholastic.

KEY QUESTIONS

1. Student-generated questions are critical. How can we integrate them into every subject area?

2. "Thick and thin" questions provide labels for helping learners identify recall vs. deeper questions. What labels do you use to help learners see the difference in questioning quality?

3. How might student-generated questions replace the questions in basal teacher editions? In science/social studies textbooks?

4. How might student-generated questions change the way we read weekly newsmagazines?

5. Should learners expect that all of their questions have answers?

Developing Quality Questions

Question Developers _____   _____

Text/topic being reviewed _____

Good readers know that it is important to ask questions before, during, and after reading. Questions help us to stay interested in a topic, to make connections to what we already know, and to think more deeply.

Your job is to select three texts that have passages and questions. For each one, read the text with your partner then look closely at the questions. Your job isn't to answer them, it is to analyze them. What do you notice about the questions you find? Are they shallow, with right and wrong answers, or are they deep, causing the reader to really think about the topic and explain understandings?

Text #1: _____
# of shallow questions_____   # of deep questions_____

Text #2: _____
# of shallow questions_____   # of deep questions_____

Text #3: _____
# of shallow questions_____   # of deep questions_____

Select one of the passages and write your own questions. Make sure they are deep questions that will cause your reader to really think, to explain, or to make connections.

Meet with another team and share your passage and questions. Talk with them about your findings as you analyzed questions today.

Partner Think Alouds 14

LINDA HOYT

MEET THE AUTHOR

LINDA HOYT *continues to work on her ability to provide think alouds that are clear and concise. She believes strongly that think alouds need to be planned with key points clearly delineated before working with students.*

FOCUS QUOTE

Partners prepare a reading selection and a think aloud for each other. They understand that they are to read and think aloud to help their partner understand the strategy they are using for comprehension.

In a comprehension-centered classroom, we get used to integrating think alouds into our read alouds, science lessons, and guided reading sessions. As our students observe, they are gaining understanding of the strategies we emphasize but are also developing an understanding of the way a think aloud looks and sounds.

To extend strategy use, I frequently engage students in Partner Think Alouds. At these times, I ask learners to prepare a passage for sharing with a partner. They read the passage and plan the points where they will stop to open the window into their thinking. This level of preparation is just as important for the students as it is for teachers. When think alouds are planned in advance, the strategy comes into clear focus. Talking points are targeted and explicit.

Sometimes, I assign a strategy for the think aloud. This helps learners who are just beginning to apply a strategy to stay focused and helps them present the strategy clearly for their partner.

As learners gain control over multiple strategies, they choose the strategy they would like to share with their partner. Finally, students meet in partners to share their passages and think alouds. The listener focuses on active listening and asks questions about the selection that was read and about the strategy.

Students have told me how much they have learned through this process. They love the partner interaction and feel that they are synthesizing their understanding of the strategy as they plan and then execute their Partner Think Alouds.

As students gain confidence with peers in the classroom, Partner Think Alouds can be extended to cross-age buddy reading time. In this setting, an older reader plans a reading and think aloud for a younger student. After the sharing of the book and the think aloud, the younger student is invited to talk about what was learned as well as how the strategy might help them as a reader.

FIGURES 14–1 and 14–2 Partners prepare a reading selection and a think aloud for each other. They understand that they are to read and think aloud to help their partner understand the strategy they are using for comprehension.

FIGURE 14–3 Think alouds can be added to buddy reading times when cross-age partners meet to read and talk about books.

FIGURE 14–4 Bilingual partners can engage in read aloud/think aloud times in the language they find most comfortable.

KEY QUESTIONS

1. How might Partner Think Aloud work with your students?

2. Which strategies might you have them first use in a partner setting?

3. How might cross-age reading partners integrate think alouds into their times together? How might the younger partners gain from this?

4. What are the benefits of having students engage in think alouds for each other?

Planning a Think Aloud for a Partner

Reader _____ Date _____

You have probably noticed that your teacher uses "think alouds" as a way to help you understand the thinking inside of his/her head. Think alouds are an important way to share our thinking and our strategy use.

You are going to be doing a "think aloud" for a partner. You can select the strategy you would like to emphasize. Your job will be to help your partner understand what you are thinking and how you are using the strategy to go deeper in your comprehension of the text.

1. Select a strategy you would like to use in your think aloud. Write the strategy

    you have selected: _____

    _____

2. Think about your strategy. What is important to share about this strategy? What would your partner need to know to use it?

    I want my partner to understand that: _____

    _____

3. Look at the reading selection. Select a portion of it that you could use in a think aloud for your partner. Reread this section and think about the words you would use in a think aloud. List some important ideas/words you want to

    include in your think aloud: _____

    _____

4. Practice your think aloud. Try to use the words/ideas you listed above.

5. Meet with your partner and share the Think Aloud you have planned.

6. Did your partner understand the strategy? How do you know? How might you find out? Was your partner able to ask you questions about the strategy or about the passage?

Key Word Strategy

1. Read a short bit.

2. Stop!

 3. Think . . . . . . write one word
that seems especially
important.

4. Share your words with a partner.
Tell why you choose these words.

> The Key Word Strategy is powerful in
> helping students summarize and a
> perfect tool for partner think alouds.

15 Read It Again, Differently

FRANKI SIBBERSON

MEET THE AUTHOR

FRANKI SIBBERSON *has been teaching elementary children in the Dublin City Schools since 1987. She has taught kindergarten through fifth grade as well as reading intervention. She has co-authored two books,* Beyond Leveled Books *(Stenhouse, 2001) and* Still Learning to Read *(Stenhouse, 2003) as well as a video series entitled* Bringing Life to Reading *(Stenhouse, 2004).*

FOCUS QUOTE

We must teach our students that rereading is powerful and that when readers reread, they read *differently.* When readers reread, they choose to do so because they have a purpose.

Rereading Is Important

One day in early spring, I was taking my fourth grade students out for recess. Recess fell right after our read aloud time. We had stopped at an exciting part of *The Tiger Rising* and several of the kids continued their talk on the way out. I overheard Shea say to Casey, "That book doesn't have a theme!"

I was surprised, so I stopped to ask if they were talking about *The Tiger Rising.* Shea said, "Oh, no! I get the theme in that book, but the one we read a long time ago—*The Van Gogh Café* [which we had read in the fall]—that book doesn't have a theme. We still can't figure out what the point of it is." They looked at me with expectation.

I suggested that we pull a small group together and reread the book and try to figure out what we missed the first time that would help us understand Cynthia Rylant's work better. They both smiled and ran off to recess, yelling back over their shoulders, "Count me in for that group. I really want to read it again and find the theme!" And off they went.

As they ran off, I couldn't help but think about the messages I had previously given my students about rereading text. I wondered if my kids knew the value of rereading in understanding text deeply. I wondered if I supported their comprehension by offering opportunities for rereading in all aspects of the reading program.

Thinking About Our Own Reading Habits

I started to think about my own habits of rereading: How many times had I finished reading a book and wished it wasn't over? How many times had I ended the book with questions I still had about the story? How often had I reread a part of a story or maybe even the whole book to clarify my understanding? How often had I wondered about something in the story and found myself rereading until I was satisfied? Had I ever reread a book at a different time in my life to discover new things because of the changes in my life/age?

As I started to pay closer attention to my own rereading, it was clear that rereading was critical to who I was as a reader.

Valuing Rereading in Reading Workshop

Just like adults, when children read books that engage their thinking, they often want to reread. It comes as a natural result of thoughtful reading. For young children, rereading a favorite book over and over is important. Making rereading a valued part of our reading workshop with older students can encourage students to gain a deeper understanding and appreciation for many pieces of text.

Reading Again, Reading Differently

Rereading is a powerful strategy for readers. Rereading is more than reading a piece again. Often our intermediate readers are told to reread, but often they only read the piece again in the same way they read it the first time. We must teach our students that rereading is powerful and that when readers reread, they read *differently.* When readers reread, they choose to do so because they have a purpose. We hope to teach our students to consider the many possibilities for rereading and help them discover purposes for rereading.

I now teach my students that rereading is not simply reading again. Rereading is about reading something again, but differently. There are many books and pieces of texts worth reading more than once. In her book *When Kids Can't Read* (2003), Kylene Beers states "The first read of any sort of text

FIGURE 15–1 Rereading a text for a different purpose helps learners to look more deeply at the text.

yields the first draft of understanding. Readers revise the draft through every reading." (p. 18)

Reasons to Reread

There are many reasons to reread a text that include:

- to understand a line or phrase that is difficult
- to get ready to talk about the book
- to follow a thread throughout the book
- to support a theory or prediction
- to study the author's craft
- to think through an opinion about an issue in the text
- to think about how a work relates to others by the same author; in the same genre

Rereading Short Texts

Minilessons/strategy lessons   To help my students begin to understand the power of rereading, I try to use several short texts. I know if I use short texts, my intermediate readers can learn the power of rereading in a short time. With a short, yet thoughtful text, I can guide students through a rereading in a short amount of time and still teach a skill they will be able to use when they are reading longer texts independently. I try to find picture books, short stories, and poems that are talk-worthy and think-worthy. I search for pieces that have many layers of meaning—books that leave every reader with many questions. Some of my favorites are *The Stranger* by Chris Van Allsburg, *Emma's Rug* by Allen Say, *Stranger in the Mirror* by Allen Say, *Voices in the Park* by Anthony Browne, and *The Other Side* by Jacqueline

Woodson. When I share these texts with my students, I want to teach them to listen in ways that help them understand more layers of the text than they could possibly understand during a first read.

Rereading *The Other Side*

I decided one day to read *The Other Side* by Jacqueline Woodson. The depth of the story leads to many questions and thoughts after reading it for the first time. I read the book aloud to the class and when we were finished, I asked my students what questions or thoughts they had in response to the story. This is the list they generated:

> What is the significance of the fence?
> How does the fence connect to the theme?
> How did they become friends—the fence separated them?
> How did the other girls change?
> What is happening in the story when the fence is mentioned?
> What made the mom change so fast?
> How did the fence bring the two girls together?
> Why is color important?
> Why did the author choose to tell the story from the child's perspective? Why the black child?
> Why did she choose the title?
> What does this line mean? "This old fence is going to be torn down someday."
> Why do they love the fence?

The next day, I asked students to listen to a read aloud of the book again. I wanted them to think back to the questions they had from yesterday and really think about how they would listen differently. Each child chose a focus for his/her reading, setting purposes that would help them understand the text at new levels. To support this thinking, I provided them with the following form to track their thinking and to focus their thoughts.

It is easy to teach kids the power of rereading by using short books full of meaning. A picture book can be read aloud in a short period of time, so rereading it over a few days is not a problem. And, if they are learning to ask big questions like the ones above, they will be able to follow a thread throughout the story based on their questions and theories. For example, for the student wondering about the title, the reread could help them see lines that they hadn't noticed the first time through.

Rereading Unlocks Deeper Layers of Meaning

When you are reading a book for the second or third time, you don't have to wonder about how it's going to end or what happens to the characters. Rereading helps students see deeper layers of understanding and meaning in text.

Rereading—Reading Again, Reading Differently

Reader_____ Text_____

Date_____

This time, what will you read for?
What question do you have or what theory are you trying to prove?

Lines from the text	Why is it significant?

Contributed by F. Sibberson © 2005 by Linda Hoyt from *Spotlight on Comprehension*. Portsmouth, NH: Heinemann.

FIGURE 15–2 Purposeful rereading generates questions, clarifies theories, and unlocks layers of meaning.

Rereading Creates Communities of Readers

Rereading also binds us together as a community of readers, with individual quirks and a collective history. In her book *Reconsidering Read-Aloud* (2002), Mary Lee Hahn shares her class' celebration for each child's birthday. She says, "One of the privileges of your birthday celebration in my room is to pick the birthday read-aloud, an idea I borrowed from Lucy Calkins' *Art of Teaching Reading*. On the day we celebrate your birthday, you can pick any part from any previous read-aloud to revisit." (p. 41). I loved this idea so much that I used it to celebrate the end of the school year with my students. I assigned each student a day during the last month of school to choose our "Reread Aloud." Just like Mary Lee's students, my students had the opportunity to choose a part from a previously read book to revisit as a class. What a powerful experience it was for all of us! Not only did we get to revisit many of our favorite characters, but we were again reminded of the power of rereading.

References

Beers, Kylene. 2003. *When Kids Can't Read: What Teachers Can Do.* Portsmouth, NH: Heinemann.

Browne, Anthony. 1998. *Voices in the Park.* New York: DK Publishing.

Calkins, Lucy. 2000. *The Art of Teaching Reading.* New York: Longman.

DiCamillo, Kate. 2001. *The Tiger Rising.* Cambridge, MA: Candlewick Press.

Hahn, Mary Lee. 2002. *Reconsidering Read-Aloud.* Portland, ME: Stenhouse Publishers.

Rylant, Cynthia. 1995. *The Van Gogh Café.* New York: Harcourt.

- Say, Allen. 1998. *Stranger in the Mirror.* Boston: Houghton Mifflin.
- ———. 1996. *Emma's Rug.* Boston: Houghton Mifflin.
- Van Allsburg, Chris. 1986. *The Stranger.* Boston: Houghton Mifflin.
- Woodson, Jacqueline. 2001. *The Other Side.* New York: Penguin Putnam.

KEY QUESTIONS

1. What is the role of rereading in your classroom?

2. Think about your own rereading. Which books have been powerful to you during a second or third read? Which books would you like to reread in the future? What makes them worth rereading?

3. What are some books that would help your students understand the power of rereading? Which books have you shared with students that leave them with many things to talk and think about?

4. How can you support rereading in all aspects of your reading program—read aloud, strategy lessons, small groups, and independent reading?

End-of-the-Year Read Aloud

During the last month of school, we will be rereading favorite excerpts from books that we've already read as a class. Each of you will be able to choose a part of a book that you would like to have reread. Please see the attached schedule for your assigned date. Take some time over the next few weeks to think through the books and excerpts that you think would be worthy of rereading as a class. Once you have decided, fill out this form and return it to me. Choose a piece that can be read aloud in 10–30 minutes. It will be fun to relive some of our favorite moments in books!

Name _____

_____

Book that you'd like me to read from: _____

Which part would you like for me to read (include chapter number, pages, etc.)

_____

Why did you choose this book? _____

_____

Why did you choose this excerpt for the class to reread together?

_____

_____

What do you think you'll gain from hearing everyone else's choices being reread

aloud? _____

_____

_____

16 Inference
A Partnership with the Author

JUDY WALLIS

MEET THE AUTHOR

Judy Wallis *is the pre-K–12 administrator for language arts in Spring Branch School District in Houston, Texas. An educator for over 30 years, Judy has been an elementary teacher and a language arts specialist. She has authored chapters on reading comprehension, balanced literacy, working with English language learners, and school change. She consults with other districts across the United States.*

FOCUS QUOTE

Because inferencing requires active reading and a willingness to enter into partnership with an author, modeling the process many times through thinking aloud, guided practiced, and independent practice across the curriculum enables students to grow more skilled as readers.

The ability to make inferences is crucial for comprehension because inferencing facilitates a reader's ability to create personal and implied meanings from text. Inferences are constructed from two sources: prior knowledge and explicitly stated information. Inferences are reasoned assumptions about meaning not explicitly stated in the text or made clear by an illustration, photograph, or diagram. Keene and Zimmerman (1997) write: "To infer as we read is to go beyond literal interpretation and to open a world of meaning deeply connected to our lives" (149).

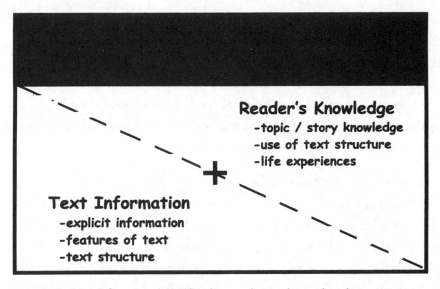

FIGURE 16–1 Inferences are made when readers go beyond explicit statements in a text and integrate knowledge of the world to make reasonable assumptions.

Under the umbrella of "inference" you might find: making predictions, interpreting meanings, using context clues, drawing conclusions, inferring cause and effect relationships, inferring character traits, and so on. While teachers may elect to teach each type in unique ways, it is important for learners to understand that all forms of inference require that personal knowledge be integrated with information from a text or situation to generate an inference.

An Equation for Inference

To help students understand the process of inferring, you might help readers think in terms of an Inference Equation. This equation provides a visual support system as readers strive to understand this essential comprehension strategy.

Information (clues) + reader knowledge = inference.

 +  =

Inference Minilessons

The notion of using think alouds and gradual release of responsibility to teach comprehension strategies is not new. An understanding that may offer new insights into the process, however, is that learners need a broad extent of experiences with each strategy in many different kinds of text. To fully integrate a strategy as complex as inferencing, learners must see the process modeled over and over and over again.

The following minilessons are kernels of possibility to demonstrate how multiple books and multiple exposures across read aloud, shared reading, guided reading, independent reading, and content-area study anchor deep understanding of a strategy. Once just isn't enough!

Minilesson 1: Understanding Inferring

Read *Seven Blind Mice* by Ed Young. As you share the book stop frequently to share your inferential thinking with the students. Model by selecting a stem such as: I can infer that _____. Or, based on what we have read so far, I can infer _____. Help students to realize that it is the mouse who uses *all* the information about the elephant to infer that they are dealing with an elephant. You might use the inference equation to illustrate how the clues from the text were added to the prior knowledge of that one mouse who then put the clues together, and created his ending inference: an elephant!

Minilesson 2: Looking for Inferences about a Character

Read *Old Henry* by Joan Blos (or another book with a strong character). Gather explicitly stated information from the text and ask the students to generate inferences about the character's traits. You might use the inference equation or a simple spider map to record their observations. It is important to have learners justify their thinking with evidence from the text as they generate inferences about character traits.

Minilesson 3: Inferring About Events

Remind students that there are many kinds of inferences. We infer by drawing conclusions, making predictions, etc. Explain that all of these require the reader-text partnership as in the inference equation. *The Keeping Quilt* by Patricia Polacco has several critical points where you might pause to engage in the process of predicting (generating possible outcomes), the need for drawing conclusions (to bring ideas to resolution), and to look for cause and effect relationships (to infer a link between two events). As you engage in your think aloud, help the learners to notice these various kinds of inferences.

As you demonstrate and model different kinds of inferences, you might consider making an archive chart that captures different types of inferences.

Sample archive chart:

INFERRING

> . . . a process that allows a reader to create personal and implied meanings from text.

Inferences are constructed from two sources:
- reader's prior knowledge or schema (about the world, genre, concepts, text structures)
- what actually appears in the text explicitly

Readers make inferences about . . .
- author's assumptions about the world
- characters' intentions and characteristics
- conclusions suggested by a text
- meanings of words or phrases
- connotations in text
- explanations for events
- pronoun referents
- other_____

Minilesson 4: Inferring in a Poem

Make an overhead of an age appropriate, narrative poem. Draw a line on the right side of the poem to make a blank column for jotting down inferences and notes as you read. Model how you make inferences within the text of the poem, using key words, images, etc., to support your thinking. Help learners to understand that it is especially important to infer in poetry because poets can't use as many words as authors of books. The reader must supply a good bit of the information. To build comprehension, the author gives clues and the reader puts them together to make inferences.

Minilesson 5: Inferring a Theme

Read *When I Was Young in the Mountains* by Cynthia Rylant, engaging in a think aloud as you wonder about the theme. Turn to the final page and read and talk about Rylant's words, "I never wanted to go anywhere else in the world, for I was in the mountains. And that was always enough." Share your thinking now, wondering, what might you infer about the theme? What clues helped you? Guide the students in discussing the gathering of clues that lead us to our inferences about theme.

Minilesson 6: Inferring in Informational Texts

It is essential to extend understanding of inference into science, social studies, and math. Learners need to understand that inferences are important tools in all of the texts we read. Using a nonfiction picture book or a transparency of a nonfiction text, do a think aloud using the "I can infer . . ." stem to show students how the same strategies will deepen their thinking in every text they read.

Extending Understanding

After experiencing several think alouds on inferencing, learners may be ready to consciously apply the strategy in their own reading. During shared or guided reading, a teacher can begin to back away from explicit instruction. This is a time when learners need to be prompted to make inferences. It might be very helpful to have an inference equation posted near the area where you conduct shared and guided reading.

When learners make inferences during independent reading, they are learning that they can make inferences independently and consciously. This intentionality of strategy use is important, as readers can now begin to see how the strategy can benefit them personally. Conferring with individuals during this time will provide assessment opportunities so you can determine if more think alouds and demonstrations are needed for the whole class or just for a small group.

To help readers "hold their thinking" through independent reading time, they might record inferences on sticky notes, record inferences and "justifications" in double-column journals, and so on. Giving students time to reflect on their ability to create inferences independently will also help to solidify their learning.

Inferring is complex. Because inferencing requires active reading and a willingness to enter into a partnership with an author, modeling the process many times through thinking aloud, guided practiced, and independent practice across the curriculum enables students to grow more skilled as readers.

Teaching Tips for Strategic Reading:

- Provide explicit strategy instruction, releasing responsibility to students gradually as they gain expertise.
- During strategy instruction that includes forms to record thoughts, point out the kinds of thinking embedded within the process.
- Make sure that students recognize that successful comprehension is the result of efficient and purposeful use of strategies.
- Make sure to use consistent language when discussing strategies. Use the language of strategies when "thinking aloud."

References

Keene, Ellin, and Susan Zimmerman. 1997. *Mosaic of Thought: Teaching Comprehension in a Reader's Workshop*. Portsmouth, NH: Heinemann.

Owocki, Gretchen. 2003. *Comprehension: Strategic Instruction for K–3 Students*. Portsmouth, NH: Heinemann.

KEY QUESTIONS

1. Independent reading is a great place to look for the "footprints" of previous instruction. How might you gather and record learner understanding about inferences during one-on-one conferences? How could the information help you in your planning?

2. Which picture books, poems, and informational texts are your favorites for think alouds with inferences? Why do you think these examples work so well for you?

3. Inferences happen everywhere in life. We infer the moods of family members by their posture, their expression, and their attitude. We make inferences in movies, about the weather, and about the kind of food likely to be served in a restaurant. How might we help students become more aware of daily inferences that are not related to reading?

Inferences

Inference Equation

Information (clues)   +   reader knowledge   =   inference.

Spend time really thinking about inferences. Try to notice times when you infer. If you smell something good coming from the kitchen, can you infer what it is? If you notice your teacher looking unhappy, can you infer what is wrong? Look all around in your life. Notice inferences in your reading. Record your inferences below.

Clues . . . (from real life or from a book)	What I know . . .	My inference:
Example: There are big, black clouds in the sky.	Dark clouds can mean rain.	I think it is going to rain.

Recording My Inferences

Reader_____ Text _____

Reading Response Sheet. Focus on inferences. Jot your thoughts as you read during independent reading today.

While reading, I was able to infer that:	Support for my inference is on page _____	Text + Me = Inference I was able to make this inference because:

Linking At-Home Reading to Class Strategy Lessons

Date_____ Book Title _____   Inference based
Inferences I made while reading at home.   on page _____.

1._____   _____

2._____   _____

3._____   _____

4._____   _____

Parent Signature _____

Date_____ Book Title _____   Inference based
Inferences I made while reading at home.   on page _____.

1._____   _____

2._____   _____

3._____   _____

4._____   _____

Parent Signature _____

Date_____ Book Title _____   Inference based
Inferences I made while reading at home.   on page _____.

1._____   _____

2._____   _____

3._____   _____

4._____   _____

Parent Signature _____

Making Inferences About Characters

Reader _____ Date _____

Character #1: _____

I think this character is: _____

_____ because

_____

Character #2: _____

I think this character is: _____

_____ because

_____

Character #3: _____

I think this character is: _____

_____ because

_____

When you compare these characters, what do you notice?

_____

_____

_____

_____

Part Four

Getting at Language
Words, Writing, and Reading Like a Writer

17 Comprehending at the Word Level

LINDA HOYT

MEET THE AUTHOR

Everyone loves a good laugh and Linda is no different. She and her husband have a lot of fun giving crazy white elephant gifts to friends and receiving some really outrageous gifts in return.

FOCUS QUOTE

If a reader sounds out a word but does not consciously think of how the word fits in the sentence or paragraph, that reader is not comprehending . . . he is simply decoding.

Proficient readers are focused on meaning. They monitor their comprehension and notice when they do or do not understand. They can identify confusing ideas and words, and then implement strategies to help themselves deal with the problem. Proficient readers have a rich collection of strategies that help them navigate challenges at the word level and within the text as a whole (Hoyt 2000).

Comprehension at the word level is crucial to a reader's ability to navigate a text and construct global understanding. At the word level, readers must simultaneously apply world knowledge, understandings about the structure of language, and visual cues (Goodman, Watson, and Burke 1996, Clay 1998). Comprehension at the word level is supported by skilled word recognition, decoding, and fluent reading (Duke and Reynolds 2005 in Chapter 2) *plus* constant consideration of the context in which the words occur. The process of considering word meaning within the context of a passage is critical. If a reader sounds out a word but does not consciously think of how the word fits in the sentence or paragraph, that reader is not comprehending . . . he is simply decoding.

Coaching for Word-Level Understanding

As I confer with individual readers or listen to partners reading together, I am constantly looking for evidence that students are comprehending as they read. When I notice a reader rereading and changing a word that had been read incorrectly on the first attempt, I celebrate. Self-correction suggests the child used meaning and realized that his first attempt at the word wasn't fitting well in the context of the sentence. I also celebrate when a reader looks around the page at pictures, headings, and so on to gain additional support for determining a word and its meaning.

The Schools That Beat the Odds studies (Pearson and Taylor 2004) report that the schools with the highest levels of achievement were engaged in more comprehension coaching than lower achieving schools. This coaching was occurring at the word level, at the story level, and in written responses to text. When teachers remind readers to think about meaning, especially after sounding out a word, they are coaching the reader to self-monitor understanding and empowering the child as a comprehender.

COACHING QUESTIONS TO CONSIDER:

- Does it make sense?
- Is there something in the picture that would help you?
- Does that sound right to you?
- Does it look right to you?
- What would make sense here?
- As you think about the story, what might the author be thinking here?
- Do you see a chunk in the word that will help you?
- What else can you do?
- Are you using the comprehension equation? (letters and sounds + meaning)

When I Get Stuck:

1. Look at the picture. 🌷

2. Go back and read the sentence again. ←go

3. Does it make sense? 💡

4. Use the first and last letters of the word. f__r = flower

5. Chunk it! Look for parts of the word you know. some thing

6. Skip it and go on. ⌢

7. Does it sound right? ♪

What do Good Readers do?

Good readers take a "book walk".

Good readers make good predictions.

Good readers form visual pictures.
*pictures in your head

Good readers ask questions as they read
I wonder? Why? What? H

Good readers make connections.

Good readers re-read when it doesn't make sen

FIGURE 17–1a, b Charts provide a visual support to readers as they strive to comprehend at the word level.

Word-Level Comprehension Equation

I teach students a simple equation to help them bring word-level comprehension to a conscious level. They learn that:

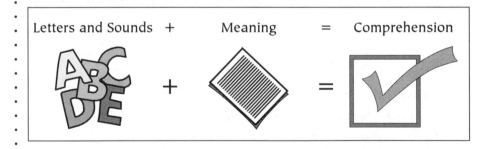

Letters and Sounds + Meaning = Comprehension

The following are strategies I have often used to support word-level comprehension for learners.

Oral Cloze

As you read aloud to your students, stop occasionally mid-sentence and ask: What word might come next? After they catch on, you won't need to cue them and you will find them quickly and joyously supplying words every time you stop. This teaches learners to trust their sense of meaning and

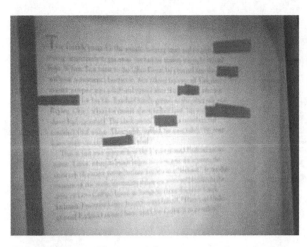

FIGURE 17–2 Placing sticky notes over key words in a passage teaches students to use context to cross-check word choices. Progressively uncovering the words gives strong phonic support as well.

language and to give them practice in using context to support comprehension.

Cloze at the Overhead

Make a transparency of a page from a literature selection or content-area text. (You may need to enlarge the text a bit to ensure that students can see the print clearly.) Place pieces of sticky notes over key words in the text. As the students read from the overhead, engage them in conversations about the covered words. What meaningful words might they put in those places? How do they know? Once they come to consensus about meaningful words, you can slip the sticky note material away one letter at a time, having them predict letters as you go. They love the sense of solving a puzzle and get wonderful phonics practice combined with comprehension of the passage.

Cloze in a Guided Reading Selection

Guided reading is a powerful context for focusing on comprehension at the word level. If you place strips of sticky notes over key words within the guided reading selection, students can engage in small group discussions about words that would make sense and then have the delight of personally peeling away the sticky strip to decode and cross-check the word. When I am first teaching this, I place the strips for the students. After they become more proficient, I have them do it for one another. I might give them a direction such as: "Reread this familiar title and place four sticky strips on nouns that you think are really important in this book." The students then reread, placing the strips in position and trade books with each other. This can be varied by having them cover verbs, words that have a short vowel, or whatever you

FIGURE 17–3 Cloze experiences can easily be provided in the context of guided reading to support word-level comprehension.

FIGURE 17–4 Readers of all levels benefit from this focus on word-level understanding. Photos reprinted with permission from National Geographic.

FIGURE 17–5 Phonics and comprehension work together in cloze experiences. Reprinted with permission from National Geographic.

like. The important idea, however, is that they select words that are important to the message of the book so they stay focused on comprehension.

To integrate context with first letter clues, place sticky notes in a book but leave the first letter of the word exposed. This gives a phonetic clue that will substantially narrow their choice of words and gives needed practice in integrating decoding with comprehension.

Word Substitution

Word substitution activities work well with materials from any subject area and will work on the overhead, on a chart, or in guided reading. This experience is designed to broaden understanding at the word level. This is also an excellent link to work with synonyms and to word choice in writing.

FIGURE 17–6 Word substitution broadens children's thinking about meaningful word choices, affecting reading comprehension and word choice in writing. Photograph used with permission from National Geographic.

For word substitution, I place a sentence on a chart and cover the verb. The sentence can come from a reading or content-area selection or be one that you create. Example: Maria _____ to the store. The students think of possible words to substitute for the blank while I jot down their ideas. Example:

Maria _____ to the store.

ran	skipped
dashed	raced
rode	flashed

Students can now talk about the meaning of the passage as a whole and discuss which words are better choices within the context of the whole piece.

To use this process in guided reading, I give students a sticky note and ask them to make a list of as many possible substitutions as they can. The sticky note fits nicely right on the page of the book and can support quality conversations among the group.

Word-level comprehension is the foundation for broader story understandings. When learners are carefully coached and supported, they can simultaneously develop strong skills as decoders, excellent fluency, AND comprehension.

References

Clay, Marie. 1998. *By Different Paths to Common Outcomes*. Portland, ME: Stenhouse Publishers.

Duke, Nell, and Julia Moorhouse Reynolds. 2005. "Learning from Comprehension Research: Critical Understandings to Guide Our Practice." In *Spotlight on Com-*

- *prehension: Building a Literacy of Thoughtfulness,* edited by Linda Hoyt. Portsmouth, NH: Heinemann.

- Goodman, Yetta, Dorothy Watson, and Caroyn Burke. 1996. *Reading Strategies: Focus on Comprehension.* Katonah, NY: Richard C. Owen.

- Hoyt, Linda. 2000. *Snapshots: Literacy Minilessons Up Close.* Portsmouth, NH: Heinemann.

- Pearson, P. David, and Barbara Taylor. 2004. "Schools That Beat the Odds." Presentation at the International Reading Association Convention, Reno, Nevada.

KEY QUESTIONS

1. How are your students doing with word-level comprehension? Do they remember to cross-check for meaning when they sound words out?

2. What visual supports to you have on your walls to encourage and remind them to think about meaning while they read?

3. How do you record your students' efforts to cross-check, self-correct, and so forth?

4. Do you have any students who are efficient word callers but have limited comprehension? What might you do for them?

Reader Self-Monitoring

Readers can engage in self-coaching if they listen to their own reading on tape while looking at a copy of the text. Their job is to listen carefully and stop the tape recorder when they notice that they have used a strategy. The reader then makes a tally mark to record the strategy and continues listening. Readers can then meet with partners or with their guided reading group to share their data and explain to others how they used the Comprehension Equation to comprehend.

Sample Monitoring Log I:

Name _____ Date _____ Book _____

Listen closely. Stop the recorder when you notice that you are using a strategy. Use tally marks to record each strategy used.

Self-correct	Backtrack/Read again	Pause to look at pictures	Sound out and think about meaning

What did you do well? _____

_____

_____

What might you improve? _____

_____

_____

What helped you to understand the passage?_____

_____

_____

Reader Self-Monitoring

Sample Monitoring Log II:

Name _____ Date _____

Book _____ Pages _____

As you listen to the recording of your reading, think about the ways
you were helping yourself to understand.

	Yes	No
My reading sounded like people talk.	☐	☐
When I came to a word I didn't know, I sounded it out **and** checked to see if it made sense.	☐	☐

When I got stuck on a word, I thought about what made sense and tried:

	Yes	No
the beginning of the word	☐	☐
the ending of the word	☐	☐
chunks in the word	☐	☐
the rest of the sentence	☐	☐
looking at the picture	☐	☐
When my reading didn't sound right, I stopped and reread the part that didn't make sense.	☐	☐
I paused occasionally to think about what I was reading.	☐	☐

The Comprehension Equation

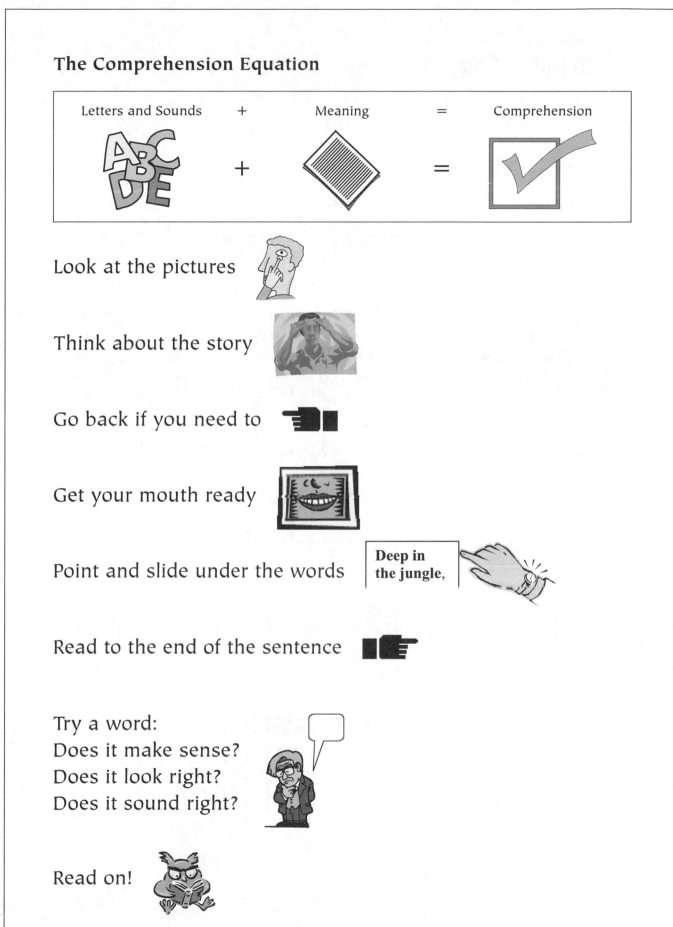

Letters and Sounds	+	Meaning	=	Comprehension

Look at the pictures

Think about the story

Go back if you need to

Get your mouth ready

Point and slide under the words

Read to the end of the sentence

Try a word:
Does it make sense?
Does it look right?
Does it sound right?

Read on!

Reading Log

Reader _____

			Strategies Used									Retell						
Date	Book	Page(s)	Picture clues	Prediction	Read on	Reread	Sound it out	Self-correction	Makes connections	Substitutes meaningful words	Reading rate appropriate to text	Characters	Setting	Problem/Solution	Theme	Events	Nonfiction/key ideas	Nonfiction connections

Key: + Strategy effectively used

• Strategy taught in conference

Building a Robust Vocabulary 18

LINDA HOYT

MEET THE AUTHOR

LINDA HOYT *loves to read and treats herself to personal reading whenever she can. Her favorite places to read include curled up by the fire, sitting sideways in a chair, on a blanket on the beach, on the deck with the dog by her side, or in a classroom full of learners who also find joy in books.*

FOCUS QUOTE

The best word-learning classrooms are filled with an intentional focus on vocabulary where students notice words and consider strategies for becoming word savvy.

Vocabulary and comprehension have a powerful relationship that is unparalleled in strength and importance (Duke and Reynolds 2005). While we know that overall vocabulary knowledge is an excellent predictor of comprehension ability, it is important to know how vocabulary is best developed.

Good vocabulary instruction is based on extensive and intensive reading experiences in which word-level awareness is nurtured and extended through discussion, modeling, and wide exposure to a diversity of richly written texts. In quality vocabulary instruction, the focus is on words that are interesting and/or have relationships to one another. Connections abound as students focus on relationships between words they already know and words they are learning. These words are then used multiple times in an array of meaningful contexts. Learners who are nourished by such an environment develop a strong sense of word consciousness (Graves and Watts-Taffe 2002) and a sense of wonder about words and how they can be used. The best word learning classrooms are filled with an intentional focus on vocabulary where students notice words and consider strategies for becoming word savvy.

How different this is from classrooms where well-meaning teachers pass out lists of unrelated words and ask students to write dictionary definitions, then use the words in sentences. Research suggests that this kind of rote

FIGURE 18–1 Word-learning classrooms bring words into focus. Words are savored in discussion, in conversation, in reading, and in writing.

response to vocabulary instruction simply does not work (Beck, McKeown, and Kucan 2002, Blachowicz and Fisher 2002, Stahl 1999.) and programs designed to teach vocabulary have often had surprisingly little affect on reading performance (Mazyinski 1983, Stahl and Fairbanks 1986).

Preteach Concepts Rather Than Words

Many experts suggest that we need to minimize preteaching of words before reading. If we preteach concepts instead of just words, the vocabulary that surrounds the concept will flow naturally and students enter a text with a conceptual knowledge to support comprehension. After the reading, individual words can be revisited using the context to assist in meaning making (Beck, McKeown, and Kucan 2002, Ohanian 2002).

Time and Exposure

Vocabulary knowledge has been compared to a light dimmer switch. At its lowest levels, you notice there is light; as the light increases, the illumination gives a clearer and clearer view of the surroundings (Blachowicz and Fisher 2002). When a learner is introduced to a word, there is rote recognition that is quickly lost if there is not meaningful, purposeful use of the word and interaction with the word in diverse contexts. It is the deep, flexible knowledge of a word that enables a reader to apply it in many contexts over time.

Beginning in Kindergarten

The best teachers of vocabulary then are those who intentionally focus on vocabulary from kindergarten on and make learning words and concepts a part of each element of the day. This intentionality of word awareness can be facilitated in a number of ways:

1. Ensure that students spend a lot of time reading from a wide range of texts with well-crafted language.
2. Read to learners from richly written fiction and nonfiction sources, discussing interesting words.
3. Create a word-rich environment, celebrate words on the walls of your classroom.
4. Use a rich vocabulary when conversing with learners.
5. Study the concepts that underlie words.
6. Identify relationships between words.
7. Connect new words to words already known.
8. Help students develop strategies for independent word learning.
9. Model good word learning behaviors and your own curiosity about words.
10. Invite students to be word detectives, collecting interesting words and words that are important.
11. Save words in a notebook.
12. Give students opportunities to use words in meaningful ways.
13. Engage with fewer words; don't try to cover so many that learning is superficial.
14. Link visualizations to word meanings.
15. Provide opportunities to make inferences about word meanings.
16. Have fun with language!

Max Brand (2004) writes that "word detectives are hidden in our classrooms, waiting for the opportunity to show their ability to uncover knowledge of words" (99). The following vocabulary support systems are designed

FIGURE 18–2 Vocabulary-focused interactions add rich support to language development and content learning at all grade levels.

to help your students find joy in word investigations and to develop the strategies they need to be independent vocabulary craftspeople.

Vocabulary Strategies

Vocabulary Teams

Divide the class into teams and ask each team member to find two words to bring to the attention of their group. They have a few days to select their words, mining them from their reading selections and from class read alouds. Each student explains what their words mean, tells why these particular words were selected, and explains why it is important for the group to know these words. Group members enter all words into their vocabulary logs with the goal of trying to use the words suggested by their teammates. They can use the words in conversation, in class discussions, and in writing. Team members support one another by trying to notice when a teammate uses one of the words.

After all words are presented, the team votes to select two of their words to submit to the class for whole class learning. The words nominated by the team for whole class learning must be accompanied by a rationale for why these words are important for everyone to know. Words selected for whole class learning are explored in depth through a variety of experiences throughout the week and will be posted on the wall to provide visual interest in the words. The following week, teams meet again and the cycle continues with a group of new words.

Personalizing Vocabulary

When personal connections can be made, vocabulary is more easily moved into long-term memory. To facilitate these connections, students can take vocabulary words and then consider ways to make connections.

Example: *Write about a personal connection.*

Thicket: This reminds me of the blackberry thickets that my mother used to make me navigate to help her pick blackberries.

Example: *Sketch a connection.*

Thicket:

Explain it in your own words.

A thicket is like _____.

Vocabulary Mapping

There are a wide array of ways to map vocabulary words. The important aspects of a map are the visual display and the opportunity to link words and ideas together.

Word Map Example

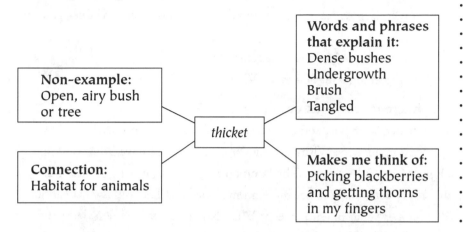

K.I.D. Vocabulary

K.I.D. Vocabulary is a strategy that integrates word recognition with important information related to the word and a visual reminder to make it memorable.

Vocabulary Word: *Murky*

Key Word	**I**mportant Information	**D**raw to remember
Muddy	Not clear	

 Where might you expect to see this word? How might it be used?

 Murky. I would expect to see this word in a description of a stagnant pond or in a poem about mud puddles.

 See Chapter 53 in this book by Amy Goodman for more examples of K.I.D vocabulary.

Word Theater

Similar to charades, teams of two review a reading passage and select words they think are interesting (Hoyt 1999). They then plan how to dramatize the words for another partner team. During the "word theater," the observing team cannot say the word out loud, but they have to find it in the text.

Word Wizards

Students focus on using target vocabulary words outside of the classroom and then report back on how the words were used.

Sketch a Word

Like the game *Pictionary,* students take turns sketching something that will bring a certain word to mind for their team. They continue drawing until someone in the team guesses the word. Words can be selected from content area studies, read alouds, or literature selections.

Word Replacement

Make a transparency of a page from a book, ensuring that the text is large enough for all students to read it easily. Underline a word or two and ask students to work in teams to suggest words that could replace the ones you underlined.

> Example: The tiger *bounded* into the jungle.
>
> Replacements for *bounded?* What would fit?

Use Inference to Focus on Vocabulary

Inferences can help extend and enrich vocabulary development.

> Example: Mrs. Wishy Washy. "Boys and girls, I have been thinking about Mrs. Wishy Washy. The book doesn't say this, but I can infer that she was really *determined* to get those animals clean. What could we say about *determined?* What might it mean? What happened in the book that would show she was very *determined?*"
>
> Example: Whales. "We have been reading about whales. As I think about the gray whale, the largest of them all, I think of the word *majestic.* Chat with your elbow partner for a moment about *majestic.* Why might I think that the gray whale is *majestic?* What do we know about whales that might make majestic a good word to describe them?"

Text Talk

Beck and McKeown (2001) introduced Text Talk as a research and development project designed to improve comprehension and vocabulary. They reviewed children's literature selections and chose three words from each to use for vocabulary focus. The books were read to children in an interactive style with stop points for open-ended questions during the read aloud. The three focus words were written in large bold letters and placed on a bulletin board next to the cover of the book. The teacher and students actively tried to use the words and placed a tally mark next to the focus word each time one was used in conversation or located in another book.

Exploring Prefixes and Suffixes

While prefixes and suffixes are not enough to fully determine word meaning, they can, at times, be helpful clues. Teaching students that the word *graph* can become *autograph, biography, geography, graphite, graphic,* and so on can give them assistance in difficult, technical reading. Similarly, having an awareness of common prefixes and suffixes can assist learners in determining word meaning when context is insufficient. The * indicates those that are most commonly occurring (Ohanian 2002) and make up half of the prefixed words in English.

Common Prefixes

ab-	away	Marlee is *absent* today.
bi-	two	My *bicycle* has a flat tire.
com-	with	In math we *combine* numbers to add them.
con-	together	Our teacher is at a *conference* today.
de-	not	I am going to *destroy* the weeds that are choking my garden.
*dis-	not	A *disadvantage* of living in Oregon is the rain.
*in-	not	That math problem is *inaccurate*.
*im-	not	The cast kept my ankle *immobile* for six weeks.
mis-	not	I made a *mistake* on that.
mono-	one	The speaker talked in a *monotone* and really put me to sleep.
pre-	before	Let's *preview* this chapter before we begin to read
re-	again	We will have to *repair* the roof.
super-	great	You were a *superstar* in science today.
tele-	over a distance	We just got a cordless *telephone*.
tri-	three	The *tricycle* is getting a little small for you.
*un-	not	You look *unhappy* today.

Common Suffixes

-able	able to	These shoes are really *comfortable*.
-al	referring to	She has a lot of *musical* talent.
-er	one who does	The *rancher* is rounding up his cattle.
-ful	full of	Those roses are *beautiful*.
-less	without	I have been *sleepless* for three nights.
-ly	like	My son is becoming very *manly*.
-ment	state of	The Nike *advertisement* had great new shoes.
-ness	state of being	This book is just filled with *foolishness*.
-ous	full of	The curves ahead look really *dangerous*.

Word Sorts

Word sorts (Hoyt 2003) can take many forms. This version emphasizes making connections between words and phrases to activate prior knowledge and ensure that students are seeing relationships between the terms. In this experience, learners will interact with the vocabulary words and phrases, before, during, and after reading.

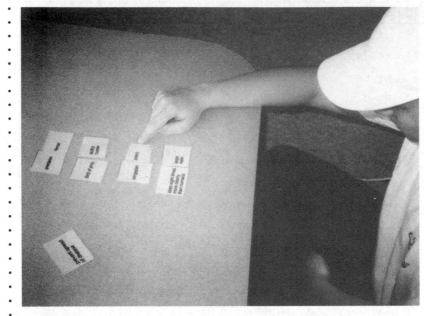

FIGURE 18–3 Students tear words and phrases apart then move them around to create categories, partner pairs, and triads. The emphasis is on relationships between words and ideas.

First, target key words and phrases from a passage (fiction or content area material), then have the students sort the words and phrases into categories that make sense to them. Have them tell why they have clustered the words and phrases as they did.

Next, have them group the words/phrases into partner pairs and make a statement that explains the connection.

Example: | Predator | | Fierce |

Connecting statement: *Predators* can be *fierce* hunters.

Then create triads, clusters of three words/phrases, and make a connecting statement to show how the words are connected.

Next, read the passage. When you find a word or phrase in the text that was in the sort, set it aside. If you finish reading and have words/phrases left, reread to try to find them in the passage.

Finally, use the words/phrases to support a summary of your reading.

Summary

Show learners your passion for words. Let them see that you have fun using new words and learning what they mean. Consider alternatives to dictionary exercises and writing traditional sentences to create a culture of word savvy thinkers. Your students will reap the benefits of better comprehension, better written language, and richer oral expression as well.

References

Allen, Janet. 1999. *Words, Words, Words: Teaching Vocabulary in Grades 4–12*. Portland, ME: Stenhouse.

Beck, Isabel, and Margaret McKeown. 2001. "Text Talk: Capturing the Benefits of Read Aloud Experiences for Young Children." *The Reading Teacher* 55 (1): 10–20.

Beck, Isabel, Margaret McKeown, and Linda Kucan. 2002. *Bringing Words to Life*. New York, NY: Guilford Press.

Blachowicz, Camille, and Peter J. Fisher. 2002. *Teaching Vocabulary in All Classrooms*. Upper Saddle River, NJ: Merrill/Prentice Hall.

Blachowicz, Camille, and Donna Ogle. 2001. *Reading Comprehension: Strategies for Independent Learners*. New York, NY: Guilford Press.

Brand, Max. 2004. *Word Savvy: Integrated Vocabulary, Spelling and Word Study, Grades 3–6*. Portland, ME: Stenhouse.

Duke, Nell, and Julia Moorhouse Reynolds. 2005. "Learning from Comprehension Research: Critical Understandings to Guide Our Practice." In *Spotlight on Comprehension: Building a Literacy of Thoughtfulness*, edited by Linda Hoyt. Portsmouth, NH: Heinemann.

Frasier, Debra. 2000. *Miss Alaineus: A Vocabulary Disaster*. San Diego, CA: Harcourt.

Greenwood, Scott. 2004. *Words Count: Effective Vocabulary Instruction in Action*. Portsmouth, NH: Heinemann.

Hoyt, Linda. 1999. *Revisit, Reflect, Retell: Strategies for Improving Reading Comprehension*. Portsmouth, NH: Heinemann.

Ohanian, Susan. 2002. *The Great Word Catalogue: Fundamental Activities for Building Vocabulary*. Portsmouth, NH: Heinemann.

Stahl, S. and M. Fairbanks. 1986. "The Effects of Vocabulary Instruction." *Review of Educational Research* 56: 72–110.

KEY QUESTIONS

1. Which of the vocabulary strategies in this article might you add to your collection of vocabulary support strategies?

2. How might you weave vocabulary connections into read alouds? What did you think of Text Talk?

3. How might you weave vocabulary connections into content-area studies? What modifications might you make?

4. How might you get kids excited about word learning?

A Checklist for Vocabulary Instruction

Does the physical environment show that vocabulary is important?
- ☐ Are there collaboratively made word lists on the wall?
- ☐ Is there a word wall?
- ☐ Is there a list of vocabulary strategies?
- ☐ Are content specific vocabulary words clearly evident?
- ☐ Do students keep a vocabulary journal?
- ☐ Is word play and word awareness a part of every day?

How does the teacher show that words are important?
- ☐ Are there two or more read alouds a day complete with discussion of interesting words?
- ☐ Is there a structure for students to collect words they find to be interesting?
- ☐ Is there a sense of excitement about word learning?
- ☐ Are interesting words explored in all dimensions of the curriculum?

Are strategies for exploring words modeled and practiced?
- ☐ Do learners engage in word sorts and word mapping?
- ☐ Are students encouraged to monitor their own attempts to use new words in daily conversation and in writing?
- ☐ Are strategies for understanding words modeled and demonstrated?
- ☐ Are word relationships and connections made evident?

Do the students have tools for word learning?
- ☐ Are they self-selecting vocabulary words to study?
- ☐ Are they comfortable with a dictionary and a thesaurus?
- ☐ Do they know how to use root words, prefixes, suffixes, and context to determine word meaning?
- ☐ Are they encouraged to use rich vocabulary in class discussions?
- ☐ Are students encouraged to create images or sketches to support word meaning?
- ☐ Are ELL's reminded to connect English words to native language counterparts?

Thinking About Words

Reader _____ Date _____

While you are reading, your job is to be looking for words that you think are interesting. Collect your words in column #1. Jot what you think the word means. Be sure to tell why you think that is the meaning.

Interesting word	Where I found it	I think it means... because
_____	_____	_____
_____	_____	_____
_____	_____	_____
_____	_____	_____
_____	_____	_____

Select the two words that you find most interesting. Look both of them up in the dictionary and the thesaurus. What did you notice?

Word 1	I noticed that:

Word 2	I noticed that:

Thinking About Words

Word Map

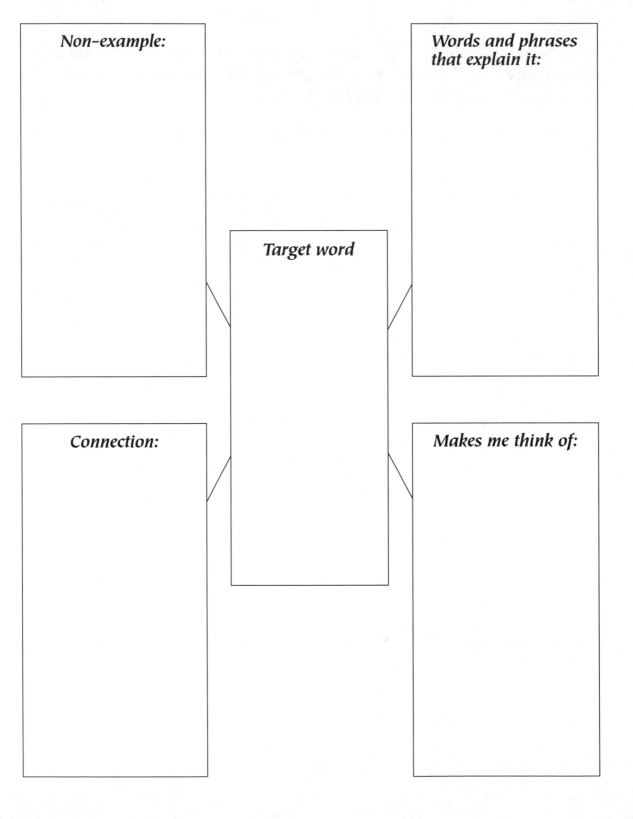

Non-example:

Words and phrases that explain it:

Target word

Connection:

Makes me think of:

Heads-Up on Vocabulary

Reader/Writer _____

When we study words and meaning, our writing and speaking get better. We understand what we are reading and pay better attention to interesting words. Your job is to collect and try to use interesting words. Pay attention to words while you are reading and select some really interesting words to place in this box.

[ ]

Select three words from those you collected. You are going to become good friends with these words, searching for them while you read and trying to use them in writing or in talking.

The word	I found it in: (books and page #)	I used it: in my writing or in conversation
1. _____	_____	_____
	_____	_____
	_____	_____
	_____	_____
	_____	_____
2. _____	_____	_____
	_____	_____
	_____	_____
	_____	_____
	_____	_____
3. _____	_____	_____
	_____	_____
	_____	_____
	_____	_____
	_____	_____

19

Alphaboxes and the Two-Word Strategy . . . Not Just for Little Kids

MOLLY HOUSE

MEET THE AUTHOR

MOLLY HOUSE *lives in Des Moines, Iowa. She was a classroom teacher for 29 years. She is presently a reading consultant for the Heartland AEA 11 Education Agency.*

FOCUS QUOTE

Active learning situations that allow students to engage with vocabulary in a nonthreatening way allow all of the student's energies to be focused on comprehending the text, not wondering what the words mean.

I teach middle school/high school. I'm not a reading teacher. In forty-two minutes, how can I possibly teach all this content and build comprehension with my students, too?

It's quite simple. Borrow Alphaboxes and the Two-Word Strategy (Hoyt 1999) from the elementary sector and watch the learning happen. Alphaboxes and Two-Word Strategies support vocabulary, promote content understanding, and are highly motivating to students. With these strategies in hand, everyone can be a reading teacher.

Knowing that Alphaboxes and the Two-Word Strategy were tools that elementary teachers use effectively to motivate struggling readers and English language learners, I just knew these strategies would work well with older students too.

Support for a Novel

Teacher Susan Anderson allowed me to work with her ninth grade students while they were reading *To Kill a Mockingbird*. This is a very diverse group of learners in an urban setting. From this rich and thought-provoking novel, I chose the words *discriminate* and *conflict* to initiate vocabulary work with the students and then utilized the following steps:

Step One: Think and Ink

Time: two minutes

Students were asked to write on a photocopy of an alphabox all the words they could think of for *discriminate*

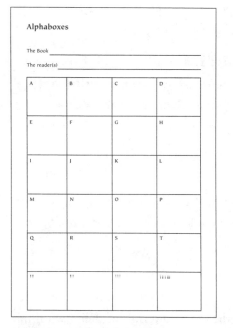

FIGURE 19–1 Alphaboxes

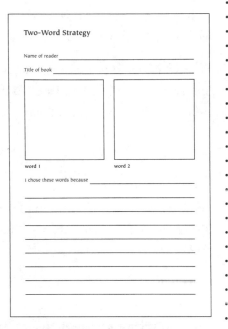

FIGURE 19–2 Two-Word Strategy

FIGURE 19–3 To access prior knowledge and stimulate connections, students use photocopies of an alphabox to record words related to the target vocabulary.

Step Two: Pair Share or Triad Share

Time: three minutes

Students work with assigned pairs or triads and share words they selected. They are invited to add words they hear from their partners that will extend their own understanding of the target vocabulary.

Step Three: Highlights

Time: one minute

Each student highlights two words that best represent discrimination.

Step Four: Whip Around (Everyone Shares!)

Students stand up, whip around the room, and share one word at a time. As each word is shared, it is written on a poster size alphabox. The whip continues until all words are written on the large alphabox poster.

Step Five: Setting the Stage for Active Learning

Students are then asked to listen to the story *Jemma's Journey* by Trevor Romain. While they listen, their task is to use their personal alphabox and add, in a different color ink, words or phrases that help their thinking about the meaning of *discriminate*.

Step Six: Add More Words

Students are once again invited to add words to the class alphabox. These additions will reflect their expanded understandings as a result of listening to *Jemma's Journey*.

Step Seven: Expanding with the Two-Word Strategy

Students now take photocopies of the Two-Word Strategy sheet and choose two words that they have found to be the most powerful for their own thinking. They record their two top words and write an explanation of why they selected these words.

FIGURE 19–4 Team sharing broadens thinking and builds deeper understanding.

FIGURE 19–5 Students share words that relate to *discriminate*. These words are added to a poster size alphabox.

Alphaboxes

The Book ___Jemma's Journey___

The Reader(s) ___Jihan Jackson___

A animosity anger	B blacks bullets bully bullying	C careless choosing categories crime cruelty	D dislike disrespect distinguish drama dumb difference
E election	F fights forgotten flag freedom	G genderism gays	H Hatred harassing harassment hater Hitler hyppocritical
I ignorant isolation	J jealousy Judging Jewish	K Klu Klux Klan	L loathe
M mean memories memorial	N nazi	O outspoken	P prejudice persecution preferred
Q	R racism racist	S Skinhead sexism seperation singled out sorry	T
U unfair unwanted	V violence voting	W whites	XYZ

FIGURE 19–6 Jihan's alphabox.

FIGURE 19–7 The alphabox words offer a rich resource from which students select their two top choices.

Two-Word Strategy

Name of reader   *Jessica White*

Title of book   *Gemma's Journey*

Segregation	Presecution
word 1	word 2

I chose these words because *they help me really define the word "discrimate". And both words have a lot of history behind them. Segregation and presecution were involved in WWI with Austria-Hungary and Serbia, in After the Slaves were freed until the Civil Right movement with the Coloureds and the whites, and in WWII with the Jewish, Gypsys and the Nazis*

FIGURE 19–8 The Two-Word Strategy allows readers to prioritize their thinking and to think more deeply about relationships between concepts.

Step Eight: Show My Thinking

These reflections show the depth and power of using these two very simple and quick strategies to "push" and deepen thinking. The following statements were generated during Show My Thinking:

"My thinking was different than normal and it was a lot easier to remember words that relate rather than memorizing the definition. I think I will use the strategy more often." Ben

"I thought it was very educational. I learned a lot of new tips for words. You made me think about the word." Alex

"It made me think a whole lot more than I usually would." Brittany

"What surprised me the most is *discriminate* can be used in a good way. I used to think it only had to do with race or religion but it's really a decision you choose in your life." Sarah

"I thought of stuff all related to *discriminate*. Then I thought of examples of new things . . . when we stopped I had so many ideas in my head not always on paper." Levi

"I was thrilled . . . their understanding." Mrs. Anderson, Teacher

And all this happened in less than forty minutes!

Step Nine: Reading *To Kill a Mockingbird*
The students will now enter the text with rich understandings of the concept of discrimination and can make stronger connections, ask more probing questions, and experience this novel with far greater comprehension because time was taken with Alphaboxes and the Two-Word Strategy *before* they began to read the book.

Applying the Process in Content-Area Studies
The eight steps provided for the lesson on *discriminate* will work across the curriculum. Alphaboxes and the Two-Word Strategy can be used effectively in science, social studies, health, science, music, and P.E. Select a concept that is central to the unit of study and you are ready to begin. When you get to the step that suggests reading to the students, you could either find a read aloud selection that is related to your content or provide a hands-on experience that will generate more thinking on the topic.

Extending the Strategies: Top Ten
Attention math and science teachers! Your content specific vocabulary can be overwhelming in number and usually not found in any student's background knowledge. Try Top Ten to really target the attention of your students (Hukee 2003).

Example:

Step 1: Choose the top ten words for a unit in algebra or geometry. Put them in a class alphabox using a blue pen.

Step 2: As students work their way through the content of the unit, encourage them to be searching for more words that are important to their understanding. When they locate words that they believe are important, have them add those words to the alphabox in a color other

FIGURE 19–9 As words are added to the master chart, students need to explain their rationale for the addition.

than blue. As new words are added, ask them to explain their thinking. "This word helped me understand more in geometry because . . ."

Step 3: Use the alphabox for review of the unit or add the Two-Word Strategy, asking students to find the two words that are most important and justify their thinking.

Students can use the Alphabox and Two-Word Strategy words in oral retells of the content, in their writing, and in their daily note-taking. Students will stay focused on essential content and vocabulary while solidifying their understanding of the concepts.

Here are the words I came up with for algebra and geometry. Limiting the list to 10 wasn't easy, but it made me think!

ALGEBRA: *difference, quotient, product, factor, multiple, function, equation, solve, graph*

GEOMETRY: *angle, line, segment, polygon, circle, plane, theorem, proof, area, perimeter*

Whether you select the Alphabox, the Two-Word Strategy, or a combination of both, the key is to remember:

1. Choose the most important words for the unit of study or lesson.
2. Incorporate the vocabulary into activities that build background knowledge and broaden connections.
3. Create active learning situations that allow students to engage with vocabulary in a nonthreatening way.

This allows all of the student's energies to be focused on comprehending the text, not wondering what the words mean.

References

Hoyt, Linda. 2002. *Make It Real: Strategies for Success with Informational Texts.* Portsmouth, NH: Heinemann.

———. 1999. *Revisit, Reflect, Retell: Strategies for Improving Reading Comprehension.* Portsmouth, NH: Heinemann.

Hukee, Julie. 2003. Math consultant; collegial sharing session.

KEY QUESTIONS

1. How might Alphaboxes work in my content area?

2. How might the Two-Word Strategy work in my setting?

3. How do I already teach vocabulary in my content area? Would any of the suggestions in this article work for me?

4. How might the Top Ten strategy assist my students in holding onto core understandings?

5. What vocabulary words do I want my students to be able to use in ten years?

6. What might be the benefits of having Alphaboxes filled with words hanging on your walls?

Recommended Books

There are many powerful children's books with thought-provoking content to stimulate vocabulary and concept development. Reading books that are rich in concepts and vocabulary stimulate students to think more deeply, think of the concepts which underlie the words, and to see the essential relationship between words and ideas.

A few suggestions:

Feathers and Fools. Mem Fox. 1989. New York: Harcourt, Inc.

Jemma's Journey. Trevor Romain. 2002. Honesdale, PA: Boyds Mills Press.

Just Like Josh Gibson. Angela Johnson. 2004. New York: Simon & Schuster.

Pink and Say. Patricia Polacco. (1994). New York: Putnam & Grosset Group.

The Story of Ruby Bridges. Robert Coles. 1995. New York: Scholastic.

White Socks Only. Evelyn Coleman. 1996. Morton Grove, IL: Whitman and Company.

What titles can you add?

_____

_____

_____

_____

_____

_____

_____

_____

Alphaboxes

The Book _____

The reader(s) _____

A	B	C	D
E	F	G	H
I	J	K	L
M	N	O	P
Q	R	S	T
U	V	W	XYZ

Two-Word Strategy

Name of reader _____

Title of book _____

word 1   word 2

I chose these words because _____

_____

_____

_____

_____

_____

_____

Language Banks, Imagery, and Poetry
Reading from a Writer's Point of View

20

MARY MONROE

MEET THE AUTHOR

MARY MONROE *is a teacher and an artist living in Redwood Valley, California. She is an active participant in the Redwood Writing Project and tries to incorporate best reading and writing strategies with her third grade students.*

FOCUS QUOTE

When students examine and use language from their reading in their writing, they internalize its meaning and enjoy it more.

There is so much pressure these days on improving the reading skills of our students that many teachers have become reluctant to take much time for the instruction of writing. However, it is my experience that when learners read from a writer's point of view, their understanding of and appreciation for the texts they are reading increases. When my students examine and use language from their reading in their writing, they internalize its meaning and enjoy it more. They begin to understand the concepts of audience and purpose.

When students read like a writer, they are more likely to notice the words a writer uses. They become sensitized to word choice and sentence fluency. They notice well-chosen nouns and powerful verbs (Greenwood 2004). This improves comprehension at the vocabulary level, especially for English language learners (ELL's).

The writing process itself helps learners to develop behaviors that serve them well in their reading. Students who write develop stamina; they reread and rewrite to make their word choices and intentions clear and strong. They learn how to focus for longer blocks of time as they develop their written messages. The revision process, which is inherent in writing, is based on meaning and purpose, ensuring that the reader can understand what the author is trying to say.

Writing and reading are reciprocal processes (Routman 2003). When readers have rich experiences with literacy that include both reading and writing, comprehension has fertile soil in which to flourish.

The following lessons are designed to emphasize reading-writing connections and to help learners understand that comprehension is enhanced through careful word selection and imagery.

Language Banks

For each language bank, we select a focus such as a part of speech or a literary device. I start things off with a read aloud and challenge the students to watch for great examples of adjective choice, simile, or whichever target I feel is appropriate. As examples are identified, we begin recording on a chart. The students continue the search by watching for outstanding examples in their reading over the next few days. The important part of these lessons is the *process* of searching through books, experiencing the excitement of the language and sharing our discoveries. These rich collections of adjectives, verbs, similes, idioms, etc., become an integral part of the reading/writing environment, hanging in our room all year.

If your students keep a writer's notebook they could create their own personal lists as well. Ready-made lists won't do the trick. Remember, it is the ownership of searching through books, brainstorming, and recording that excites the students and compels them to use the words and literary devices in their own writing.

Finding Powerful Verbs

Students need to understand that powerful verbs are crucial to us, both as readers and writers. They hold our attention and create strong images in our minds.

To set the stage for a focus on verbs, I ask the students to: "Close your eyes and imagine that Raquel *went* to the store." Now, tell a partner what you visualize . . ."

The verb *went* is so vague that they come up with a myriad of images. "She went with her mom in the car," and "She rode her bike," were a couple of responses. Then I asked, "What if she was supposed to meet a friend there in 5 minutes?" Students then responded with more precise verbs, such as *skipped* or *raced.* We began a word bank titled Powerful Verbs, which we added to for the next several days as we combed our books looking for precise and powerful verbs. They especially like jotting their words on sticky notes which they place directly on the chart to be transcribed more boldly later.

Similes

After reading Audrey Wood's, *Quick as a Cricket,* we brainstormed adjectives that could describe a person, then turned them into similes. When a student uses the adjective *tall* to describe someone, I ask, "*Tall* like what? A mountain? A tree?" When they say they are *fast,* I ask, "Like what?" One year someone wrote, "I'm as fast as a cheetah." The similes are recorded on a chart and hung on the wall. These can become the foundation for biographical collections about students in class, about parents, about the staff members of the school, or a way of extending thinking in science and social studies.

Figurative Language

When I read *Miz Berlin Walks* to my class I stop with amazement at the expression, "waiting cotton-quiet" and wonder out loud: "What would that be like, waiting like that?" We spend a period reading with the purpose of searching for expressions that make us stop and really visualize what we read. As with word banks, students spend time searching through books, heightening their own awareness as a reader as they try to find more examples of figurative language.

Foundations for Personal Narrative

Byrd Baylor's *I'm in Charge of Celebrations* is great for brainstorming personal experiences that are moments to celebrate. These are poignant topics for possible personal narratives and demonstrate beautifully the importance of self-expression as a purpose for writing. I had a student once who did not live with her parents and her moment to celebrate was when she got to see her mom. Another third grade boy with a learning disability was able to express his love for the outdoors, telling about fishing with a good friend and seeing an eagle.

Crafting Poems with Rich Imagery

I begin by reading picture books to model alliterative language and excite the students. We read several books with great verbs, adjectives, and alliteration and revel in the language. I particularly discuss *Some Smug Slug* by Pamela Duncan Edwards, *Toad* by Ruth Brown and *Timothy Tib* by

Liz Graham-Yooll. I tell the students that they will be choosing an animal as the topic of an alliterative poem, where many of the words begin with the same sound. First, though, they would be illustrating the poem with oil pastels and a watercolor wash.

I model the process of choosing an animal from a collection of *Zoo Books* and model drawing while looking at a photograph. Then I set the students loose, searching through books and magazines to make their selection. There is much excitement and sharing in this process.

The next step is to create two lists; one of verbs and the other of adjectives that describe their animal. I then model using the word lists to create a free form poem with alliteration. We underline words in one color that start with the same sound; like *stomp* and *stampede,* or perhaps *tremendous* and *trumpet.* Then while thinking aloud we put the words together in an order that we like. I think out loud about verb form, word order, figurative language, and so on. The students listen to me and wonder out loud: "Would the *-ing* form of these verbs work better? What order should we put them in? Does that sound right? Does that make sense? What images come to mind?" I also model line breaks and talk about what a poem looks like. By the end of the modeled writing, we come up with: "Stomping, stampeding elephants, thundering through thick forests. . . ."

Now it is time for the students to create their poems. I want my third grade students to write a free-verse poem that don't use a frame so each voice is unique.

We got so excited about phrases and images! We oohed and awed over "slink-slither snakes, happy, heroic horses and a golden stampede." Everyone loved Jay's "spicy red horses." Later he said, "I didn't think I could write poems."

We have used the same process with other student-driven topics. Several students wrote wonderful moon poems during our study of the phases of the moon. What a great way to integrate science and social studies into language arts!

When readers see text through the eyes of a writer, they notice the subtleties of language, of word choice, and of imagery. They are better able to savor the richness of a well-chosen verb or the beauty of a metaphor. When readers see text through the eyes of a writer, they savor the fine points, think about meaning, and comprehend more deeply.

Galloping horses Grazing On grass.
Spicy red horses Zapping through the
field.   short Soft horses flying
through breezy trees.
large living horses laying in the grass,
dancing jumping horses jumping in the air.

Jake

She attacks and playfully pounces On
her prey and pleased with her meat,
protective with her babies, she and
the pack are lazy in their den
she is wise beyond her years
        she
        the
        majestic
        wolf

gold as the moon.
glowy as the stars
Storms come by in White

BY Jessica Mendoza

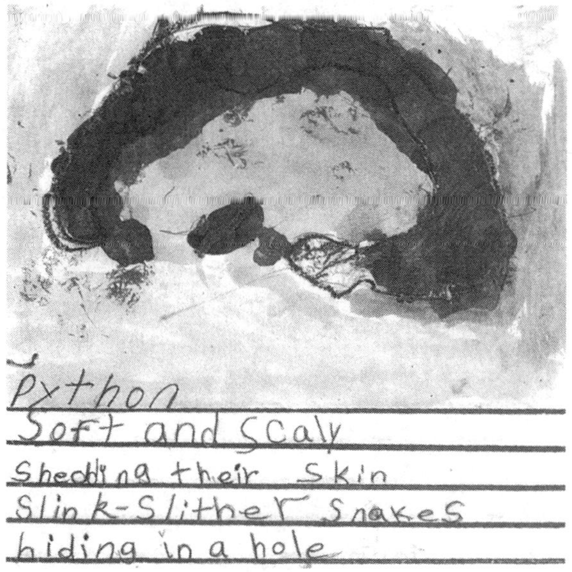

Python
Soft and Scaly
Shedding their skin
Slink-Slither snakes
hiding in a hole

FIGURE 20–1 Third graders use language banks to build rich imagery for their readers.

References

Fletcher, Ralph. 1998. *Craft Lessons: Teaching Writing K–8*. Portland, ME: Stenhouse.

Greenwood, Scott. 2004. *Words Count: Effective Vocabulary Instruction in Action*. Portsmouth, NH: Heinemann.

Lane, Barry. 1999. *The Reviser's Tool Box*. Shoreham, VT: Discovery Writing Press.

Routman, Regie. 2003. *Reading Essentials: The Specifics You Need to Teach Reading Well*. Portsmouth, NH: Heinemann.

Wood-Ray, Katie. 2002. *What You Know by Heart: How to Develop Curriculum for Your Writing Workshop*. Portsmouth, NH: Heinemann.

KEY QUESTIONS

1. What are some examples of writing that has inspired you? What stood out in the pieces?

2. How can you ensure that the language banks you create are used and refined over time?

3. What picture books are your favorite models for writing?

4. How can writing help your students' comprehension?

5. There are many ways to respond to reading through writing. What writing supports have you used that have enhanced reading comprehension?

6. How might we raise metacognitive awareness of the connections between reading and writing?

Books with Wonderful Language

Baylor, Byrd, *I'm in Charge of Celebrations* (Moments to celebrate!)

Brown, Ruth, *Toad* (great adjectives, gooey, yucky, sticky, odorous)

Chandra, Debra, *Rich Lizard and Other Poems* (free verse)

Crimi, Carolyn, *Tessa's Tip-Tapping Toes* (verbs)

Edwards, Pamela Duncan, *Some Smug Slug* (alliteration)

Esbensen, Barbara, *Words with Wrinkled Knees: Animal Poems*

Florian, Douglas, *Insectlopedia, Poems and Paintings*

Fox, Mem, *Possum Magic* (alliteration)

Graham-Yooll, Liz, *Timothy Tib* (descriptive language)

Kaur Khalsa, Dayal, *Tales of a Gambling Grandma* (hilarious)

Lesser, Carolyn, *What a Wonderful Day to Be a Cow* (great verbs)

MacLachlan, Patricia, *All the Places to Love* (all her books have great verbs)

Paulsen, Gary, *Dogteam* (figurative language, sentence fluency)

Steig, William, *Brave Irene* (strong verbs)

Wattenberg, Jane, *Henny Penny* (retold with great verbs)

Wood, Audrey, *Quick as a Cricket* (simile)

Yolen, Jane, *Miz Berlin Walks* (waiting cotton-quiet and more)

Zolotow, Charlotte, *When the Wind Stops* (great language)

Collecting Great Words and Phrases

Reader _____

As you read, keep your eyes open for words and phrases that are especially well chosen. Notice strong verbs, interesting nouns, places where you can visualize well. . . Read with the eyes of a writer, noticing the craft that makes a reading selection really special. Try to notice how the author used words to affect your understanding of the text.

Words/Phrases to Savor	Book/page #	I chose this because

Select one or two that you would like to add to your writers notebook or to a class language bank. Share your selections with a partner and tell why you chose these particular examples.

Reading Like a Writer

Writers do many things to help readers comprehend. While you are reading, think closely about the author. Try to think about what the author is doing with words. How is the author helping you to understand? Example:

The book	This author helped me comprehend by	I have used this practice in my own writing. (quote yourself)
Blueberries for Sal	Creating visual images. Using descriptive words. Matching illustrations to words. Using carefully chosen verbs.	Visual images: The seagull stretched its wings in the sun.

The book	This author helped me comprehend by	I have used this practice in my own writing. (quote yourself)
_____	_____	_____
_____	_____	_____
_____	_____	_____
_____	_____	_____
_____	_____	_____
_____	_____	_____
_____	_____	_____

21

Strategies Authors Use to Aid Comprehension

PAT ADKISSON

AND JOYCE PRICE

MEET THE AUTHORS

PAT ADKISSON *has been in education for 29 years with 21 years teaching kindergarten through the sixth grade. For the last six years she has worked in the Central Office and her various responsibilities include training, coaching, and modeling for new and developing teachers in all areas of the curriculum. Pat also serves as a system writing trainer for the state of North Carolina.*
JOYCE PRICE *has worked in the Union County Public Schools in North Carolina for over 30 years. She has taught grades 2 through 6. After 25 years of classroom work, she is now a curriculum coordinator whose responsibilities include training new teachers, doing model lessons, and conducting staff development. She is a state and local trainer in the area of writing.*

FOCUS QUOTE

As students increase their awareness of writer's craft, they also improve their reading comprehension.

Students who reside in classrooms where books are loved, where books and reading materials are within easy reach, and where authors are valued as mentors, grow as readers, as writers, and as comprehenders. Creating a classroom atmosphere where reading and writing are deeply intertwined with explicit instruction in how readers make sense of text is a challenging, yet rewarding gift for the learners we serve.

In a classroom where quality literature is treasured, analyzed, and seen as a mentor to writers, students begin to notice the conscious decisions writers make. They are better able to understand what they read. Teachers can help students by providing examples of strategies that effective authors use and show those strategies in action with beautifully crafted texts. The list of strategies can be short. We suggest using a framework of eight strategies that appear in texts that teachers and students love to read and talk about. These eight strategies are manageable both for the teacher to teach and the students to learn. The strategies are recognizable, teachable, and enable students to better understand the text. After discussing the strategy and the text in which it was demonstrated, open-ended questions are posed to students. These higher-level questions get students thinking about the author's use of the strategies and how these strategies help them to comprehend and to write.

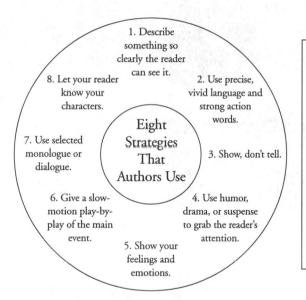

1. Describe something so clearly the reader can see it.
2. Use precise, vivid language and strong action words.
3. Show your readers what is happening, bring them into the action.
4. Use humor, drama, or suspense to grab the reader's attention.
5. Show your feelings and emotions.
6. Give a slow-motion, play-by-play of a main event.
7. Use selected monologue or dialogue.
8. Let your reader know your characters.

FIGURE 21–1 Eight Strategies (shown two ways)

Setting the Stage

We believe it helps to organize literature in tubs to represent each of the eight strategies. Read the books aloud, invite students to read them repeatedly and talk about how these books inform us. Repeated reading and conversation will show readers how the writer uses the target strategies to bring us into the world of the text.

Craft a Reading/Writing Environment

Treat your students as readers, as writers, and as comprehenders. As they continue to read and reread the target books, cast them as researchers with questions such as: What do you notice about the way these authors help us get to know their characters? What do you notice about the way these authors bring us into the heartbeat of the action? How can we accomplish this in

FIGURE 21–2 Books can be organized according to the writing/comprehending strategy you are teaching.

FIGURE 21–3 When books are grouped according to writing attributes, readers become sensitized to the craft of the writer and the nuances of meaning. (Photos taken in Karen Hodges' third grade classroom, Union County, North Carolina)

our own writing? How might we use our writers notebooks to explore this strategy?

Comprehenders and Writers

When readers read like writers and writers think about their audiences, the result is deep, reflective thinking about how understanding is achieved. Our goal with these eight strategies is to help accomplish both deep comprehension and improved writing proficiency. A powerful combination!

Mentor Books

The mentor texts provide rich examples of the strategies at their best. Students read and reread these mentors, comparing the way the authors applied the target strategy.

The best books to use are those you have at your disposal. Use the books you love and those that are of interest to your students. Incorporated in this chapter are a list of the books that we use to help teach the eight strat-

FIGURE 21–4, 21–5 When readers read like writers, they see more deeply into the content. They think about what is happening and how the writer brings action to life for readers.

egies. We sometimes put paper clips on the pages that we want students to notice or place a sticker on the front of the book with page numbers for examples of the strategies in use they won't want to miss!

The Process

We teach the strategies one at a time so learners can think deeply about the strategy from the view of a reader as well as a writer. As students analyze the mentor texts, they write about the author's craft. We then engage the students as apprentices to the mentor books, having them attempt to apply the strategy in their own writing.

With each of the strategies, we have provided our focus questions, the list of the mentor texts we used, and a sample of a student analysis of one mentor text. Notice how comprehension and composition are so intricately tied together.

Strategy 1   Describe something so clearly the reader can see it.

• How does the author describe _____ so clearly that the reader can see him/her/it? What were the key words that helped paint a picture in the reader's mind? How does this help the reader better understand the text?

• Example: **As I strolled along the sandy beach, I spotted a shimmering pink starfish resting at the edge of a shallow pool of foamy water.**

Mentor Books: Describe something so clearly the reader can see it

See the Ocean by Estelle Condra

The Seashore Book by Charlotte Zolotow

Rain Talk by Mary Serfozo

A New Improved Santa by Patricia Rae Wolff

The Velveteen Rabbit by Margery Williams

The Rainbow Fish by Marcus Pfister

The Rainbow Fish
Marcus Pfister

How does the author describe the cave so clearly that the reader can see it? What were the key words that helped paint a picture in the reader's mind? How does this help the reader better understand the text?

The auther described the cave as dark and the key words that helped paint a picture in my mind are darkness, glare and emerged. It helps me understand that the rainbow fish is scared of the wise octopus who hides in the cave.

FIGURE 21–6

Strategy 2   Use precise, vivid language and strong action words.

• Which words or phrases did the author use to make this writing lively? Can you give some examples? How does this help the reader better understand the text?

• Example: **Holly straddled the horse, slapped his sides with the reins, and shouted "Yahoo!" as the horse shot down the dusty path.**

Mentor Books: Use precise, vivid language and strong action words

The Relatives Came by Cynthia Rylant

When I Was Young in the Mountains by Cynthia Rylant

Night Noises by Mem Fox

Owl Moon by Jane Yolen

In November by Cynthia Rylant

Dream Weaver by Jonathan London

Water Dance by Thomas Locker

Mississippi Mud by Ann Turner

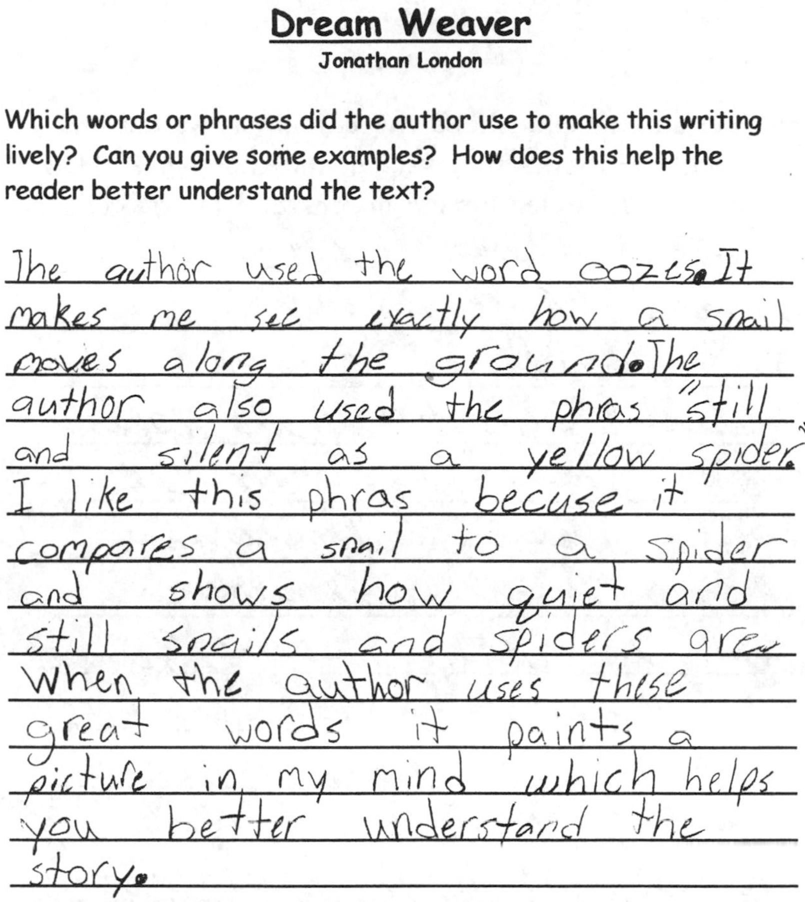

Dream Weaver

Jonathan London

Which words or phrases did the author use to make this writing lively? Can you give some examples? How does this help the reader better understand the text?

The author used the word oozes. It makes me see exactly how a snail moves along the ground. The author also used the phras "still and silent as a yellow spider." I like this phras becuse it compares a snail to a spider and shows how quiet and still snails and spiders are. When the author uses these great words it paints a picture in my mind which helps you better understand the story.

FIGURE 21–7

Strategy 3   Show, don't tell.

• Can you find an example where the author shows actions or feelings rather than simply telling what happens? How does this strategy help the reader better understand the text?

• Example: I walked into the kitchen. My dog, Jigs, had my new shoe in his mouth. Threads were dangling from the sides. I stomped my foot, my face turned red, and my eyes bulged. I pointed my finger and shouted, "Bad dog!"

Mentor Books: Show, don't tell

Ramona Forever by Beverly Cleary
Ramona the Brave by Beverly Cleary
The One in the Middle Is a Green Kangaroo by Judy Blume
Shiloh by Phyllis Reynolds Naylor
Alvin Ailey by Andrea Davis Pinkney
The Ghost-Eye Tree by Bill Martin, Jr.

Shiloh
Phyllis Reynolds Naylor

Can you find an example where the author shows actions or feelings rather than simply telling what happens? How does this help the reader better understand the text?

The author shows Shiloh's feelings by saying, "his tail was going like a windshield wiper, fast speed." Shiloh was happy to see him. He leaps up almost as high as Marty's shoulder. Shiloh is very happy. Because if he leaps as high as his waist or his shoulder he is very happy. Instead of saying, "Shiloh is happy." It makes you feel the action.

FIGURE 21–8

Strategy 4   Use humor, drama, or suspense to grab the reader's attention.

• How did the author use humor, drama, or suspense in this text? What mood does this story create? How does this keep the reader's attention?

• Example: Tyler came home from school on Friday. He grabbed a snack and flopped down on the sofa to read his new book, *Frindle,* while he waited for his mom and dad to get home from work. He thought he heard a noise coming from upstairs. "No," he said to himself, "I'm just hearing things." He went back to his reading. Suddenly, "Boom!" came a sound from right above his head. Tyler thought there must be a burglar up there! He started to tremble and ran for the phone. Just as he started to dial 911, he heard footsteps on the stairs. He looked up as Grandma Ruth said, "My, my, Tyler, I didn't know you were home from school so early. I just got in from Florida. Come up and help me unpack this huge suitcase."

Mentor Books: Use humor, drama, or suspense to grab the reader's attention

The Magic School Bus by Joanna Cole
Skinnybones by Barbara Park
McBroom Tells the Truth by Sid Fleischman
McBroom's Ear by Sid Fleischman
McBroom and the Big Wind by Sid Fleischman
Cinder-elly by Frances Minters
Little Red Cowboy Hat by Susan Lowell

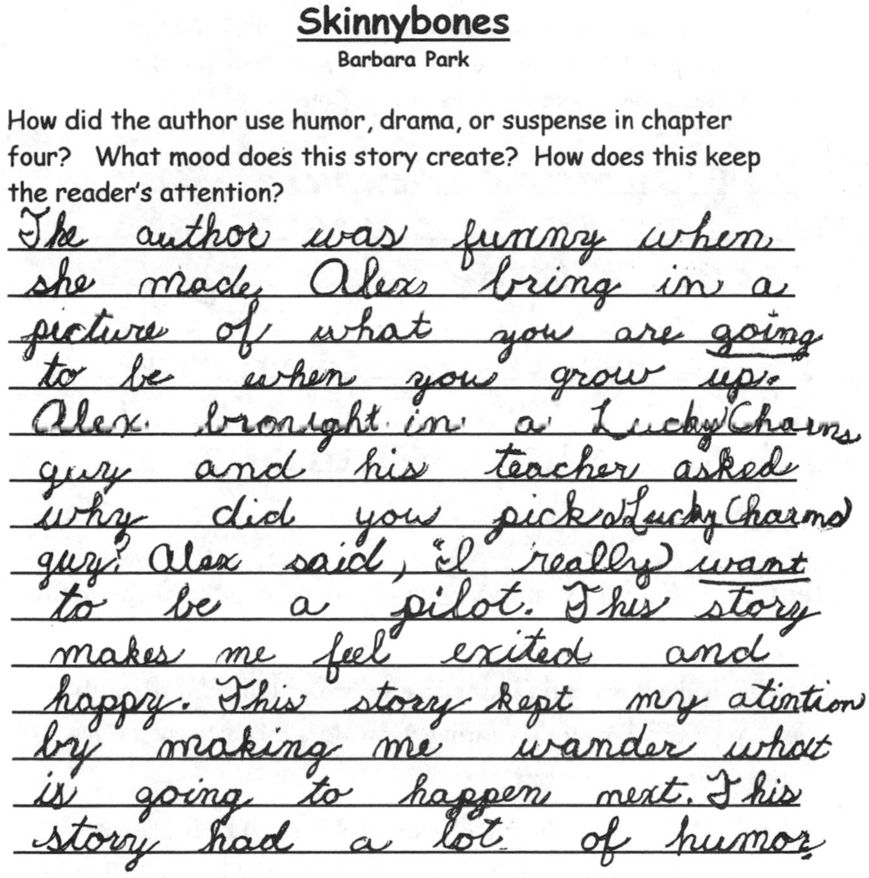

Skinnybones
Barbara Park

How did the author use humor, drama, or suspense in chapter four? What mood does this story create? How does this keep the reader's attention?

The author was funny when she made Alex bring in a picture of what you are going to be when you grow up. Alex brought in a Lucky Charms guy and his teacher asked why did you pick a Lucky Charms guy? Alex said, "I really want to be a pilot. This story makes me feel exited and happy. This story kept my atintion by making me wander what is going to happen next. This story had a lot of humor

FIGURE 21–9

Strategy 5 Show your feelings and emotions.

- What feelings or emotions are expressed in this text? Why do you think it is important for the author to let us know these feelings or emotions?
- Example: **Jose's cheeks turned beet red as he stood in front of the class to give his first science presentation.**

Mentor Books: Show your feelings and emotions

Alexander and the Terrible, Horrible, No Good, Very Bad Day by Judith Viorst

- *The Tenth Good Thing About Barney* by Judith Viorst
- *Today was a Terrible Day* by Patricia Reilly Giff
- *Wilfrid Gordon McDonald Partridge* by Mem Fox
- *Ira Sleeps Over* by Bernard Waber
- *Ira Says Goodbye* by Bernard Waber
- *Stevie* by John Steptoe
- *I Love My Hair* by Natasha Anastasia Tarpley

<u>Stevie</u>
John Steptoe

What feelings or emotions are expressed in the story? Can you give some examples? Why do you think it is important for the author to let us know these feelings or emotions?

> Robert was feeling mad because Stevie broke his toys. He also stepped on Roberts bedspred. I think it is important for a book to have feelings so we know how the characters feel and so it will be more interesting.

FIGURE 21–10

Strategy 6   Give a slow-motion, play-by-play recount of the main event.

- What is the main event in the chapter/story? How did the author slow down this part of the writing? How does this help the reader better understand the text?

- Example: **Pat sat in the big black swivel chair. The hairdresser picked up the scissors and with a funny little grin asked, "What kind of cut would you like today, Miss Pat?" Before Pat could answer, he grabbed a lock of her shoulder length hair, and snipped six inches off right the back. He continued to snip another and another, until he got to the front. To Pat's surprise, her hair was only a few inches long from her scalp to the ends. She looked down at the floor. She looked back in the mirror. She glared at the hairdresser. Tears filled her eyes. The hairdresser asked, "How do you like it?" Pat was speechless!**

Mentor Books: Give a slow-motion, play-by-play recount of the main event

- *Charlie Anderson* by Barbara Abercrombie
- *Grandpa's Garden* by Shea Darian

Erandi's Braids by Tomie diPaola

Shaggy by Marcus Pfister

Storm in the Night by Mary Stolz

Where the Big Fish Are by Jonathan London

Erandi's Braids

Antonio Hernandez Madrigal

What is the main event in this story? How did the author slow down this part of the writing? How does this help the reader better understand the text?

> The main event is when Erandi got her braids cut off. The author explained exactly what the barbor and Erandi did. The barbor measured Erandi's braids, the picked up the scissors and started to snip. Erandi felt tears on her eyes. She asked the barbor if he hair would grow back and he said they would. The author slows the story down and this helps me understand the story better. It helps me because I can paint a better picture in my mind.

FIGURE 21-11

Strategy 7 Use selected monologue or dialogue

• Where did the author use monologue or dialogue in the story? What is the reason for the monologue or dialogue? How does this help to move the story along?

• Example: It was Saturday afternoon at Lake Brannon. Joyce and Pat were baiting their fishing hooks with wiggly worms. They were hoping to catch a few fish to cook for dinner. Joyce yelled to Pat, "Hey, let's have a contest to see who can catch the biggest fish!" They decided that would be a great idea.

MENTOR BOOKS: USE SELECTED MONOLOGUE OR DIALOGUE

Martha Speaks by Susan Meddaugh

Martha Calling by Susan Meddaugh

Koi and the Kola Nuts by Verna Aardema

Painted Words/Spoken Memories by Aliki

Fables by Arnold Lobel

Shrek by William Steig

The Table Where Rich People Sit by Byrd Baylor

Martha Speaks

Susan Meddaugh

Where did the author use monologue or dialogue in the story?
What is the reason for the monologue or dialogue? How does this
help to move the story along?

> The author used dialogue
> when they say "How did you
> know he was robbing our house?" asked
> Helen. "We got a call at the station,"
> said the officer. "Some lady named
> Martha." Helen was curious and
> it answers Helen's question. It
> changed their feeling from worried
> to happy.

FIGURE 21-12

Strategy 8   Let your reader know your characters.

> • Use one word that best describes (character). Give several examples
> from the text that support your answer. Can you give a quote in the au-
> thor's own words that proves your choice?

> • Example: A word that best describes the character India Opal in the
> book *Because of Winn-Dixie* is "smart." She shows this in the grocery
> store when the dog is running around destroying the place. When the
> manager is yelling, "Call the pound," Opal says "No! That's my dog,"
> even though he wasn't. She did this to save his life. Then, when she
> got home with the dog, she told her dad that she had found a dog.
> He said, "You don't need a dog." She said, "I know, but he needs
> me." That was quick thinking on her part. When Opal was three, her
> Mother left her. She always wanted to know about her mother, but
> her father didn't want to talk about her. The author, Kate DiCamillo,
> writes, (Opal to dad) "I've been talking to Winn-Dixie and he agreed
> with me that, since I'm ten years old, you should tell me ten things
> about my mama. Just ten things, that's all." . . . The preacher (her
> dad) said to Winn-Dixie, "I should have guessed you were going to
> be trouble."

MENTOR BOOKS: LET YOUR READER KNOW YOUR CHARACTERS

> *Amber on the Mountain* by Tony Johnston
> *Wombat Divine* by Mem Fox
> *Brave Irene* by William Steig

Doctor DeSoto by William Steig
Miss Rumphius by Barbara Cooney
The Wednesday Surprise by Eve Bunting
My Great-Aunt Arizona by Gloria Houston

Brave Irene

William Steig

Use one word that best describes Irene. Give several examples from the story that support your answer. Can you give a quote in the author's own words that prove your choice?

I think the word to best describe Irene is full of courage since she didn't let the wind get the best of her. She sprand her ankle and kept going. When the wind tells Irene to go home she says, "I will do no such thing".

FIGURE 21-13

Summary

As students increase their awareness of writers' craft, they also increase their reading comprehension. With an atmosphere of investigation, the eight basic strategies empower students to think more deeply, write with greater clarity, and have a better sense of how comprehension is built for the reader and the writer. The open-ended questions that are part of each investigation focus learners on the strategy and invite comparisons across the mentor texts.

Once the students understand the strategies and see the patterns across multiple works, literary analysis can be woven throughout the literacy block. These questions should recur throughout the reading program in shared reading, guided reading, read alouds, and independent reading. The questions should be recurring in high quality literature as well as in leveled texts and program materials. Students will quickly learn to evaluate the texts they read for quality and often reach new depths of understanding when they realize that comprehension challenges sometimes occur because of poorly crafted text.

The rewards for students will be an increased love of literature and new depth of understanding as readers and as writers.

· References

· Allington, Richard. 1999. *Teaching Struggling Readers: Articles from the Reading Teacher.* Newark, DE: International Reading Association.

· Boyles, Nancy. 2001. *Teaching Written Response to Text: Constructing Quality Answers to Open-Ended Comprehension Questions.* Gainesville, FL: Maupin House.

· Lane, Barry. 1999. *Reviser's Toolbox.* Shoreham, VT: Discovery Writing Press.

KEY QUESTIONS

1. What are the benefits to learners as they engage in this kind of comparative study of reading and writing?

2. How might you extend this into analyzing novels?

3. What would the study look like if you were to do a comparative study of quality informational texts by authors such as Seymour Simon and Russell Freeman?

4. How might a strategy focus impact your guided reading lessons?

Comparing Texts on My Own

Reader _____

The eight strategies you have been learning are everywhere! Your job is to continue searching for examples as you read. When you notice a strategy in a book, list the title in one of the boxes at the top of this page and then check off the strategies you noticed. Be prepared to share with others as you compare and contrast books you are reading.

Date	Strategy	Title of Book								
	1. Describe something so clearly the reader can see it.									
	2. Use precise, vivid language.									
	3. Show action rather than tell about it.									
	4. Use humor, drama, or suspense to grab the reader's attention.									
	5. Show your feelings and emotions.									
	6. Give a slow-motion, play-by-play of a main event.									
	7. Use selected monologue or dialogue.									
	8. Let your reader know your characters.									

Planning My Writing

Your job is to review your writing folder. Go back through pieces you have already written and analyze them. Can you find any of these strategies in your own writing? Can you find places where you could do some revision and use one of these strategies to improve your piece?

1. Describe something so clearly the reader can see it.
2. Use precise, vivid language.
3. Show action rather than tell about it.
4. Use humor, drama, or suspense to grab the reader's attention.
5. Show your feelings and emotions.
6. Give a slow-motion, play-by-play recount of a main event.
7. Use selected monologue or dialogue.
8. Let your reader know your characters.

While reviewing my writing folder, I noticed: _____

_____

_____

The strategy I am using the most is _____

_____

_____

A strategy I am going to work at using more is_____

_____

_____

Meet with a partner and share your thinking about your own writing.

Interactive Paragraphs 22

LINDA HOYT

MEET THE AUTHOR

LINDA HOYT *has worked in kindergarten through eighth grades and feels very fortunate to have had experience with students at so many levels of development. One of the greatest surprises in her career was learning that middle schoolers often enjoy the very same learning experiences that delight primary age students. These older learners still love to be actively engaged and, like their younger counterparts, place special value on social interaction.*

FOCUS QUOTE

Interactive paragraphs focus students on comprehension and word knowledge but also teach the invaluable skills of revision and editing.

We know the power of interactive writing. When learners share thinking about a topic and then share a pen to craft letters, words, and sentences they are using what they know about content, word order, and phonics in one synergistic experience. Comprehension is built in tandem with print knowledge.

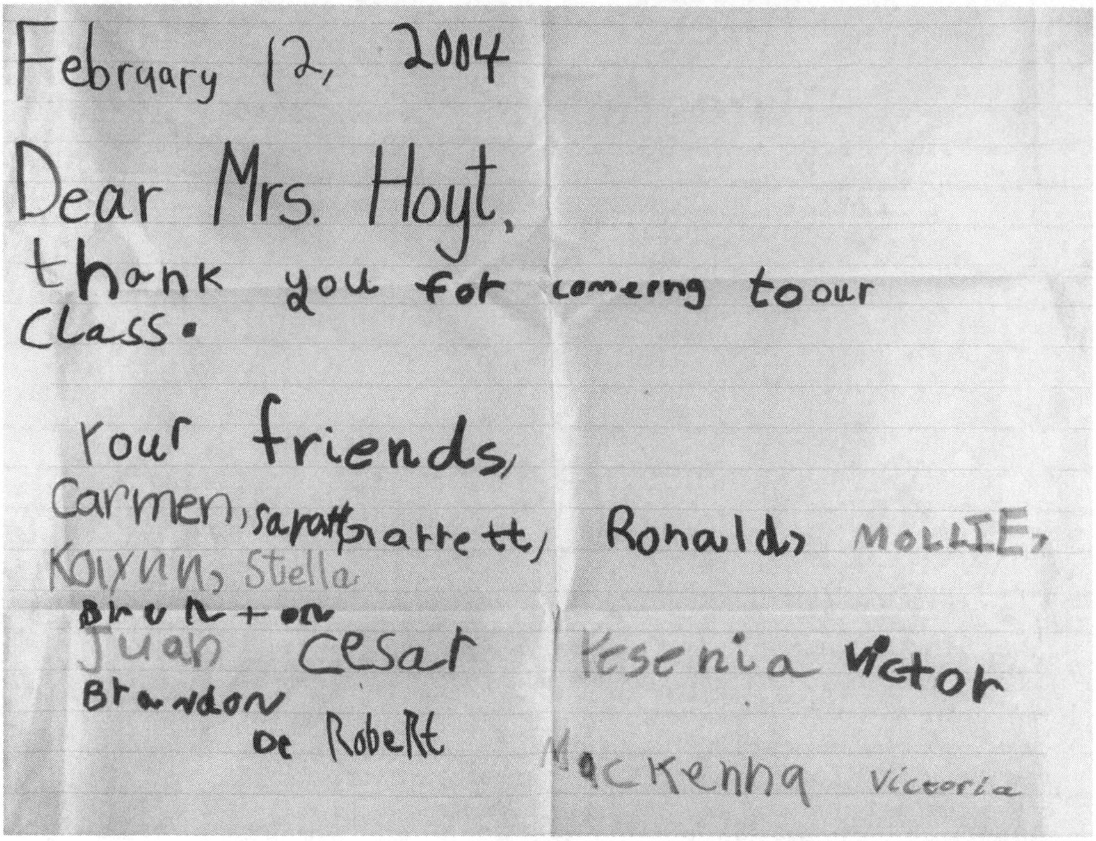

February 12, 2004

Dear Mrs. Hoyt,

thank you for comering toour Class.

Your friends,

Carmen, Sarah, Garrett, Ronald, MOLLIE, Kaixun, Stella, Brunton, Juan Cesar, Yesenia Victor, Brandon, De Robert, Mackenna, Victoria

FIGURE 22–1 First graders in Ms. Freeman's class wrote this interactive letter.

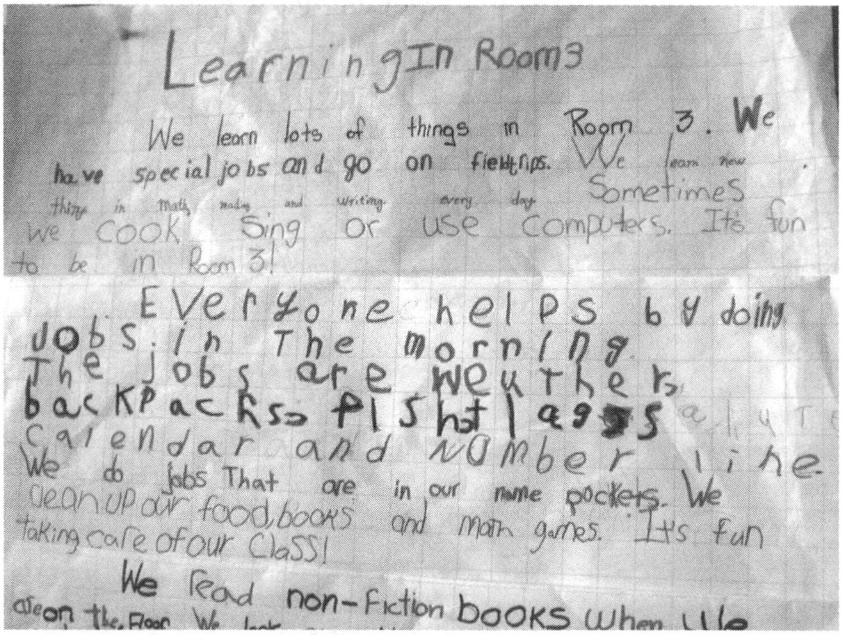

Learning In Room 3

We learn lots of things in Room 3. We have special jobs and go on fieldtrips. We learn new things in math, reading and writing every day. Sometimes we cook, sing or use computers. It's fun to be in Room 3!

Everyone helps by doing jobs in the morning. The jobs are weather, backpacks, flshtlag salute, calendar and number line. We do jobs That are in our name pockets. We clean up our food, books and math games. It's fun taking care of our class!

We read non-fiction books when we are on the floor. We look

FIGURE 22–2 Students in Room 3 used interactive writing to focus on their classroom as a community of learners.

Extending Fluent Readers and Writers

As learners become more fluent users of print, interactive paragraphs are a logical step. They focus students on comprehension and word knowledge but also teach invaluable skills of revision and editing. Interactive paragraphs provide more independence for learners as they work in partner pairs, crafting individual sentences before a paragraph is constructed.

The Process

To build an interactive paragraph, learners reflect on an experience, a book, or a topic of study, recalling important ideas and content points. Then, the teacher presents a topic sentence in a pocket chart. The topic sentence keeps the writers focused so that a cohesive paragraph can be shaped. The students are then told that they are going to use the topic sentence as the opening of a paragraph that they will create together.

FIGURE 22 3 The teacher writes a topic sentence and students understand that their sentences need to fit the topic sentence.

Next, partners are given strips of paper torn from a roll of adding machine tape or sentence strips and a colored felt pen. It is helpful if each partner-team has a pen of a different color so their sentences can be easily identified in the chart.

The partner-pairs discuss the topic and think of a sentence that would fit well with the topic sentence. They understand that both partners must agree on the sentence. It cannot be just one partner's idea. They also understand that they will pass the pen as they write the sentence, trading off after each word. To ensure that partners really understand collaboration, a lot of modeling is done to show how to come to agreement about the sentence, how to share the pen, and how to check with each other on spelling before each word is written.

If partners think that their sentence is too long for the strip of paper that they have, do not let them add a second line on the same sentence strip.

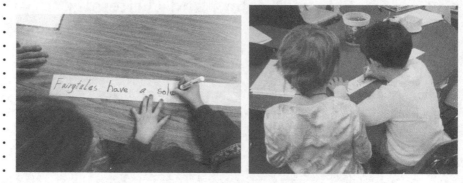

FIGURE 22–4a, b Partners come to agreement about the sentence they are writing and then pass the pen back and forth on every word.

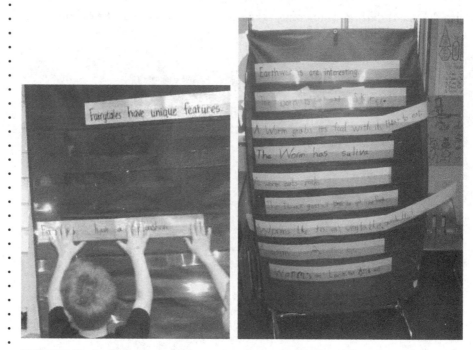

FIGURE 22–5a, b Students add sentences in random order. When this is done as a whole class experience, the chart can be very full.

They need to get another strip to continue their sentence. This is important as sentences will be torn up during the revision process.

Partners proofread their sentences to check for content and spelling, then they are ready to add their sentences to the chart. Students place their sentences in the chart in random order. They do not try to sequence for content or rearrange for sentence fluency at this time.

Revising the Paragraph: Deepening Thinking

Now, the thinking really deepens . . . Assemble the students around the chart and read the sentences in the order they appear. Ask questions such as: "How does this sound?" "Does it make sense?" "Is this telling the most important things we learned about _____?" Questions such as these initiate the process of revising for meaning. Encourage students to talk about sentences they think should come first and sentences that might make a good ending for the paragraph. As suggestions are made, move the sentence strips around so the students can read with the changes in place and decide if they like them.

A question students especially like is: "Do any of these sentences say the same thing?" Invariably, there will be several sentences that say the same thing or are even identical. If the sentences are identical, place one behind the other in the chart, telling the students that both great ideas are right there together.

The situation is also likely to arise where two sentences have the same meaning but are written a bit differently. Then, you can ask: "Is there a way we could put these two sentences together?" As the students generate ideas, they may select the beginning of one sentence and the end of the other. The teacher **tears** the parts of each team's sentence that are being kept and sets the rest aside. The first time you tear up a strip, they will gasp. After that, they look forward to the merging of ideas and rearranging of sentences. Occasionally, the group will decide to add a word or two, so have some extra strips and a pen handy.

It is important to respect the authors' work. When a suggestion for change is made, refer by pen color to the authors . . . "Red team, are you O.K. with this change? Or, "Blue team, the group has suggested we add a word to your sentence, is that O.K. with you?"

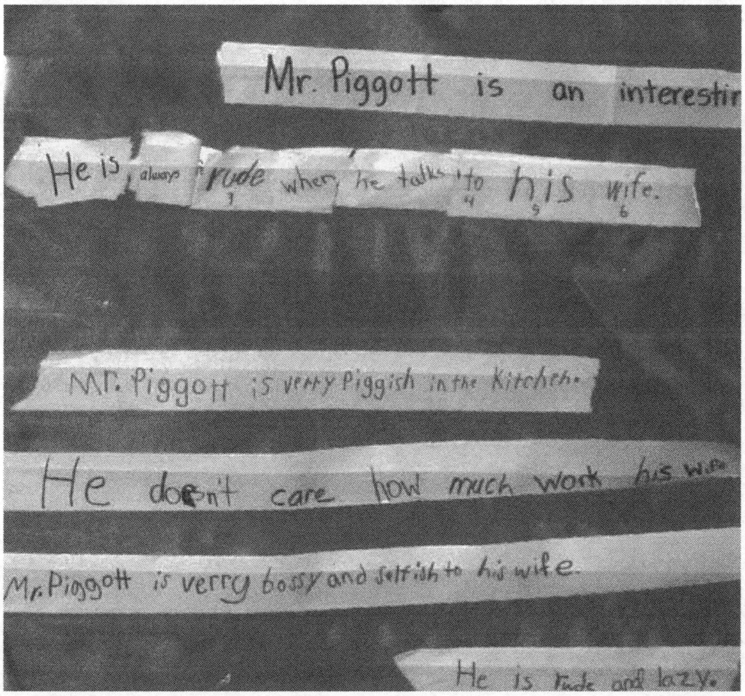

FIGURE 22–6 Notice how line two is torn into words. This sentence was crafted from four contributions, each of which were very similar.

Discussion of the content, sentence order, word choice, editing, and punctuation follow the same order as writing process. Work on the content first, then come back and focus on editing, spelling, and punctuation.

Continuing the Process

Interactive paragraphs support almost any dimension of writing, from word choice to voice to conventions. Comprehension is continuously developed as the group reads and rereads the passage. Revisions could continue over several days.

As you close the discussion for the day, ask the students to consider: "If you were to write a paragraph of your own on this topic, what would you want to include? What did you learn about writing today that you can use in writers workshop?" Be sure to leave the chart out and invite students to think about it. Many times, individuals or partners will ask if they can work on combining more sentences or rearranging the order of the paragraph during their free time.

Multiple Paragraph Pieces

Mutiple paragraph essays can be developed by hanging two or three pocket charts with a topic sentence in each. Partner-pairs are assigned one of the topic sentences to address with their sentence, and teams can meet around the pocket charts to work collaboratively to organize and revise their paragraphs. Multiple paragraphs offer significant levels of independence for teams and create a climate for intense involvement.

Supporting Writing Development

Interactive paragraphs help readers think about getting their messages across in clear and concise ways. They support organization, deeper thinking, and help determine importance. They also teach writing in deliberate and meaningful ways that can easily be applied across the curriculum and in writers workshop.

References

Brecktel, Marcia. 2001. *Bringing It All Together: Language and Literacy in the Multilingual Classroom.* Carlsbad, CA: Dominie Press.

McCall, Jan. 2003. *Interactive Paragraphs.* In "Navigating Informational Texts: Easy and Explicit Strategies K–5," video program by Linda Hoyt. Portsmouth, NH: Heinemann.

Swartz, Stanley, Adria Klein, and Rebecca Shook. 2002. *Interactive Writing and Interactive Editing: Making Connections Between Writing and Reading.* Carlsbad, CA: Dominie Press.

KEY QUESTIONS

1. How might interactive paragraphs be used in math, science, and social studies?

2. How would they be adapted for English language learners?

3. What ideas do you have about uses for interactive paragraphs with your students?

4. How might you use interactive paragraphs to teach proofreading and spelling?

Designing Interactive Paragraphs: The Steps

1. Refresh students' thinking about a book or unit of study, focusing them on the main ideas.

2. Place a topic sentence into a pocket chart. Explain that they will be writing sentences that will fit with that topic sentence.

3. Pass out adding machine tape or sentence strips and felt pens in a variety of colors.

4. Partners generate sentences, coming to agreement on the wording and the spelling of each word. Partners pass the pen after each word.

5. Sentences are placed in the chart and the group comes to agreement about sentence order, word choice, and conclusion. Sentences with the same or similar meanings are combined, respecting the thinking of all teams.

6. The paragraph is edited for spelling, punctuation, and capitalizaion.

7. Multiple paragraph pieces can be generated after students undertand the process and are ready to work in collaborative teams to complete revisions.

Text to Tunes

Extending Understanding by Writing Songs

23

MARISSA OCHOA

MEET THE AUTHOR

Marissa Ochoa *is a second year teacher at Valley Elementary in San Diego, California. She is currently teaching third grade. Ms. Ochoa received her BS from UCLA and her teaching credential from Cal State San Marcos. In her free time she plays tennis and racquetball and enjoys taking her dog to the beach.*

FOCUS QUOTE

The songs provided students with a creative medium to present their information to the class. Through the songs written by the students, the class learned about a variety of sea animals.

My students were studying oceans so I decided to use their love of music as a support system as they moved toward synthesizing their learning. To begin, I shared examples of songs written about the ocean that I found on the Internet. We sang the songs, talked about the information presented in each, and then wondered about songs we might create to share our own learning about the ocean.

We next wrote a class song collaboratively about our field trip and set up criteria for a good "learning" song. We wanted to be sure that the song made sense, reflected our learning, and utilized what we knew about rhyming words.

The Field Trip
(Tune: "Row, Row, Row Your Boat")
By Team 16

There goes Team 16
In Pt. Loma Bay
Lookin' for fish and more
On this great Tuesday

We found a lionfish
Acting strong and brave
It warned the others to stay back
In the rolling waves

We spotted octopi
And they had 8 legs
They're showing off their tentacles
While they're laying eggs

The next step was to write songs individually, each one based on a different ocean animal. Even though the students were doing individual research, I asked them to work with a learning partner. I knew the partnerships would increase conversation and collaboration and bring a stronger content review and richer language use. Each student selected an ocean animal to research. They listed words and phrases that were important to understanding this topic and used summarizing strategies. Partners actively reviewed the research together, making suggestions, asking questions, and reviewing our ocean books for additional ideas.

FIGURE 23–1 Students worked with learning partners as they drafted their songs.

Once their content was solidified, the students chose a popular children's song such as *Twinkle, Twinkle, Little Star, I've Been Working on the Railroad, Row, Row, Row Your Boat, This Land is Your Land,* etc., and began to draft lyrics.

Our earlier work on the collaborative class song had made it clear that it wasn't enough for a song to be cute and rhyming. They understood that their song needed to teach and to share important content. I continually stressed that content was the focus of this experience. Learning partners worked together often as they shared tentative lines, asked confirming questions, and sought "just-right" vocabulary to fit their lyrics.

As part of the review process, students presented their songs to the class for suggestions and comments, often returning to draft new lines or search for better word choices. The class learned each song and table groups came up with different body movements and actions to accompany each set of lyrics.

Our final step was to record the songs on a class *Oceans Songs* CD. Knowing that a CD would be created from their finished products inspired

FIGURE 23–2a, b Performing the songs was grand fun and a wonderful time to extend our understanding about ocean animals.

the students to be more creative and develop pride in their work. Each student received a copy of the CD as a celebration of our learning about the ocean.

Writing songs provided students with expressive choices as they shared their learning about an ocean animal. It gave them a format they were more comfortable with (other than a written report) and enabled them to use a creative medium to present their information to the class. Through the songs written by the students, the class learned about a variety of sea animals in a format much more entertaining than a textbook or lecture. Students of all ability levels were able to learn the information and had an enjoyable time throughout the process.

This process was a lot of hard work, but it was worth it! Students used every dimension of the writing process as they made draft after draft of their songs. They read and reread their resources to confirm their facts and worked on word choices. The partner-teams, even though working on independent projects, supported one another through discussion, shared research, and collaboration on vocabulary. The experience was powerful and could easily be applied to a variety of subjects such as history, math, and other science units.

References

Hoyt, Linda. 1999. *Revisit, Reflect, Retell: Strategies for Improving Reading Comprehension.* Portsmouth, NH: Heinemann.

KEY QUESTIONS

1. How might music be used to extend thinking in your students?

2. Would writing lyrics based upon research fit a standard in your state or district?

3. What benefits would this experience provide for English Language Learners? What might you do for ELL students who are not familiar with popular children's songs in English?

4. The recording of the CD at the end gave learners an authentic purpose for elevating quality and bringing pride to their work. How else might CD and video technology be used in a comprehension-centered experience?

Samples from *Ocean Songs* CD

From Marissa Ochoa's students:

I'VE BEEN LOOKING FOR A SEA OTTER
(Tune: *"I've Been Working on the Railroad"*)
By Christine

I've been looking for a sea otter
In the Atlantic Ocean
Sea otters move with flippers
Throughout the water's motion
They swim over water and rocks
And play all day with their toys
Otters are gentle and playful
So stay quiet and don't make noise

THE STINGRAY
(Tune: *"I've Been Working on the Railroad"*)
By Brianna

I've been lookin' for a stingray
In the coral reef
I've been lookin' for a stingray
One that's really neat
It has its mouth on the bottom
Its eyes are to the side
A stingray hunts its prey all day long
Here comes food along . . . MUNCH!

Samples from *Ocean Songs* CD, *continued*

THIS OCEAN IS YOUR OCEAN
(Tune: "This Land Is Your Land")
By Branden

As I was swimming
In that big ocean
I saw upon me
Some seaweed floatin'
I saw below me
Thousands of fishes
This ocean was made for you and me

THE OCEAN
(Tune: "Twinkle, Twinkle Little Star")
By Xavier

Stingray, stingray, glide to me
So you can shock the crab at my feet
When you eat the little crab
He looks like a little dab
Stingray, stingray, glide to me
So you can shock the crab at my feet

Writing Songs to Share Our Learning

Names of researcher/songwriters: _____

The topic you have been learning about _____

To craft a song about your topic, you will need to think about helping someone else to understand what you have learned about your topic. Create a song that will teach others what you know.

1. Important information to include in our song:

   _____

   _____

   _____

   _____

   _____

2. Selecting a song. What tune will you use for your song? (A few ideas: "The Farmer in the Dell," "Mary Had a Little Lamb," "Home on the Range," "Yankee Doodle," "Somewhere over the Rainbow," "Down in the Meadow").

   Select a tune: _____

3. Write your draft making sure to remember that you job is to teach someone something, not just to create rhymes.

4. Perform your song!

Part Five

Comprehension Instruction

Read Alouds,
Guided Reading, and
Independent Reading

24

Building Comprehension Through Read Alouds with Picture Books

TERESA THERRIAULT

MEET THE AUTHOR

TERESA THERRIAULT *has been involved in education for over thirty years working as a classroom teacher, with talented and gifted programs, Title 1, and special needs. She has worked as a district-level literacy facilitator and as a district Language Arts Specialist. Teresa and her husband live in San Diego where she works as an independent literacy consultant.*

FOCUS QUOTE

Finding a text that becomes our teaching partner is a key ingredient as we nurture readers to think, strategize, and actively comprehend.

A good book draws children in, makes them wonder, and allows them to connect to a world beyond their classroom walls. Finding a text that becomes our teaching partner is a key ingredient as we nurture readers to think, strategize, and actively comprehend.

Picture books can provide the tools we need to introduce content and to model strategies for visualizing, making connections, and inferring. They can form a foundation from which we learn how to determine important words and ideas, summarize, or study an author's craft.

There are countless reasons to read aloud to students of all ages and it is essential to ensure that picture books aren't just reserved for the youngest children. Learners of all ages benefit from the fine illustrations and carefully crafted texts that characterize quality picture books. With thoughtful selection, picture books can support almost any learning target while exposing students to well-crafted language and thought-provoking content.

I used to worry that students had heard a book before, but now I celebrate rereading. I realize that a first reading is like a first introduction to a person. This is a time to get acquainted. The first reading of a picture book gives surface understanding, but continued interactions, over time, free the learner to notice details, look for fine points, notice the craft of the author, and to think deeply about the theme.

Repeated readings are also wonderful times to show learners how we can implement a variety of strategies to take ourselves into high levels of thinking. We might model how we use questioning to get acquainted with a book on the first reading. Then, on a second reading, emphasize how visualizations help us notice details and to create the sensory images that the author is trying to portray. A third reading could revisit one of these strategies or link up with a third strategy such as making connections. As we get to know favorite books, just like when we become better acquainted with our

FIGURE 24–1 Well-crafted picture books can be revisted again and again to deepen comprehension.

friends, we have richer understandings and can reach higher as comprehenders.

Jim Trelease reminds us that students whose teachers frequently read to them are better readers and have higher achievement. Shortcut your search for a great picture book for your next read aloud by checking out some of my favorites in the following list. As you consider these beautiful possibilities, please also consider which comprehension strategies you might be able to model with each selection. Carefully modeled comprehension strategies and engaging books are a winning combination.

Title	Author & ISBN	Year	Library of Congress Summary	Grades	Comments
Amelia and Eleanor Go for a Ride	Ryan, Pam Munoz 0–590–9075–X	1999	A fictionalized account of the night Amelia Earhart flew Eleanor Roosevelt over Washington, D.C. in an airplane.	2nd & up	Social studies: This is a book to return to year after year! Author's note is packed with information.
When Marian Sang	Ryan, Pam Munoz 0–439–26967–9	2002	An introduction to the life of Marian Anderson, extraordinary singer and first African American to perform with the Metropolitan Opera, whose life and career encouraged social change.	3rd & up	Social studies: This remarkable story of one American's life is worth sharing. Eleanor Roosevelt plays a part in Marian's life, too.
Wilma Unlimited: How Wilma Rudolph Became the World's Fastest Woman.	Krull, Kathleen 0–15–202098–5	1996	A biography of the African American woman who overcame crippling polio as a child to become the first woman to win three gold medals in track in a single Olympics.	2nd & up	Social studies: *Wilma Unlimited* was my first Kathleen Krull book. It certainly wasn't my last! She's an amazing author who has many popular books for young readers. <www.kathleenkrull.com>.
M Is for Music	Krull, Kathleen 0–15–201438–1	2003	Alphabet book introducing musical terms from *allegro* to *zarzuda*.	3rd & up	Social studies & music: Compelling illustrations & vocabulary. Author's note is packed with information. A unique alphabet book that could be a model for informational writing.
Lives of the Musicians Good Times, Bad Times (and What the Neighbors Thought)	Krull, Kathleen 0–15–248010–2	1993	The lives of twenty composers and musicians, ranging from Vivaldi, Mozart, and Bach to Gershwin, Gilbert and Sullivan, and Woodie Guthrie, are profiled in this eclectic, humorous, and informative collection.	3rd & up	Social studies & music: Includes bibliographical references, index of composers, musical terms, and further ideas for reading and listening. Even if you are not a music history enthusiast, this title is a gem!

Title	Author & ISBN	Year	Library of Congress Summary	Grades	Comments
The Boy on Fairfield Street: How Ted Geisel Grew Up to Become Dr. Seuss	Krull, Kathleen 0–375–82298–4	2004	Introduces the life of renowned children's book author and illustrator Ted Geisel, popularly known as Dr. Seuss, focusing on his childhood and youth in Springfield, Massachusetts.	3rd & up	Social studies: There's hardly a reader out there who hasn't been impacted by Ted Geisel. This book speaks to the aspirations in all of us to become what we were meant to be.
Martin's BIG WORDS: The Life of Dr. Martin Luther King, Jr.	Rappaport, Doreen 0–7868–2591-X	2001	"Dr. M.L. King, Jr.'s life is chronicled through the "big words" he was determined to use as a child. They are simple and direct, yet profound and poetic."	2nd & up	Social studies: A familiar title to many, but it's just too good to leave off this list! Unbelievable illustrations; author and illustrator notes; important dates; additional books and websites.
Aunt Harriet's Underground Railroad in the Sky	Ringgold, Faith 0–517–88543–3	1992	With Harriet Tubman as her guide, Cassie retraces the steps escaping slaves took on the Underground Railroad in order to reunite with her younger brother.	2nd & up	Social studies: Similes & symbolism. If you liked Ringgold's *Tar Beach* (0–517–88544–1), which earned the 1992 Coretta Scott King Award and was named a Caldecott Honor Book, you'll be impressed with this title.
My Dream of Martin Luther King	Ringgold, Faith 0–517–88577–8	1995	The author recounts the life of Martin Luther King, Jr. in the form of her own dream.	3rd & up	Social studies: Caldecott Honor artist brings her unique voice and art to the life of M. L. King, Jr. and the Civil Rights Movement. Another picture book that brings life to our history for both students and adults.
Talking to Faith Ringgold	Ringgold, Faith; Freeman, Linda & Roucher, Nancy 0–517–885465–8	1996	An interactive biography of the African American artist and children's author, detailing her experiences, perspectives, and inspiration for her art. At intervals in the text, the reader is asked related questions.	3rd & up	Social studies: What a remarkable book! This is not your ordinary memoir! Also included are: list of Ringgold's books, videos about Ringgold, and lists of museums where her works are housed. This book is a marvelous model for memoir writing.
Frederick Douglass: The Last Days of Slavery	Miller, William 1–880000–42–3	1995	An introduction to Frederick Douglass and the tragedy of slavery	3rd & up	Social studies: You may be familiar with Miller's *Zoar Hurston and the Chinaberry Tree*. For more books by Miller visit <www.leeandlow.com/booktalk>.

Title	Author & ISBN	Year	Library of Congress Summary	Grades	Comments
Follow the Drinking Gourd	Winter, Jeanette 0–679–81997–5	1988	"It sounded like a simple folk song sung by slaves, but it was really a map to freedom, for hidden in the lyrics were directions to the escape route known as the Underground Railroad. Winter tells the story of a brave family who followed the drinking gourd, the Big Dipper, north to liberation."	3rd & up	Social studies: This lovely picture book opens up a portion of American history to the younger readers, yet speaks to all of us about a unique part of African American history. Includes author's notes, a song, and additional factual information regarding the North Star.
The Story of Ruby Bridges	Coles, Robert 0–590–57281–4	1995	For months, six-year-old Ruby Bridges must confront the hostility of segregationists when she becomes the first African American girl to integrate Frantz Elementary School in New Orleans in 1960.	3rd & up	Social Studies: Ruby Bridges Hall is my contemporary and she is my hero. Her book and her life have inspired me and I have inspired children by sharing her story, our country's story. Don't miss this one.
Across AMERICA I Love You	Loomis, Christine 0–7868–2314–3	2000	Describes various landscapes of America, from the Rocky Mountains and Alaska's wild lands to the giant sequoias of California, relating the parent-child relationship to the natural settings.	3rd & up	Social studies: The breathtaking paintings share the grandeur of America while the ". . . lyrical ode to this great country is mirrored in a mother's loving serenade to her child."
America the Beautiful	Bates, Katherine Lee 0–689–85245–2	1993	An illustrated edition of the nineteenth-century poem, later set to music, celebrating the beauty of America.	K–5th	Social studies: How many times have we smiled or grimaced when we've heard our students substitute words and distort the meaning to our national songs? Neil Waldman has added stunning paintings to each phrase of "America the Beautiful" so that students can see the meaning of Bates' 1893 poem.
RED LEGS: A Drummer Boy of the Civil War	Lewin, Ted 0–688–16024–7	2001	A young boy participates in a Civil War reenactment with his father.	3rd & up	Social studies: "Lewin dramatically captures one of the many battles waged in the bloodiest war fought on American soil. He pays a moving tribute to the brave Civil War soldiers and to the dedicated reenactors who preserve their memory."

Title	Author & ISBN	Year	Library of Congress Summary	Grades	Comments
The Yellow House: Vincent van Gogh & Paul Gauguin Side by Side	Rubin, Susan Goldman 0–8109–4588–6	2001	"A wonderful introduction to the world of artists for young readers, this thought-provoking story about how artists generate and share ideas and how they work."	4th & up	Social studies & art: Includes reproductions of actual paintings, bios of Vincent van Gogh and Paul Gauguin, notes from the author and artist.
The Yellow Star: the Legend of King Christian X of Denmark	Deedy, Carmen Agra 1–56145–208–4	2000	Retells the story of King Christian X and the Danish resistance to the Nazis during WWII.	3rd & up	Social studies: Presents a story that was unfamiliar to me and demonstrates how important a true leader is and how collectively, we can make a difference.
Luba the Angel of Bergen-Belsen	McCann, Michelle 1–58246–098–1	2003	Biography of the Jewish heroine Luba Tryszynska, who saved the lives of more than fifty Jewish children in the Bergen-Belsen concentration camp during the winter of 1944/1945.	3rd & up	Social studies: This story is a must read! Epilogue includes current photo of the grown-up "children" that Luba saved. Included are: bibliography of books, articles, videos, letters, personal interviews and websites.
Earth from Above	Arthus-Bertrand, Yann 0–8109–3486–8	2002	Presents aerial photographs of various scenes from around the world including fishermen in Morocco, a farm on the island of Crete and a mangrove forest in New Caledonia. Beautifully crafted text supports photos.	4th & up	Science & geography: This is a coffee table book, a gift for young and old. "Robert Burleigh's text enriches the experience, revealing the fascinating story that each photograph tells. This magnificent full-color book offers more than forty globe-trotting images. Now every child can travel around the world!"
Red-Eyed Tree Frogs	Cowley, Joy 0–590–87175–7	1999	This frog found in the rainforest of Central America spends the night searching for food while also being careful not to become dinner for some other animal.	K–5th	Science: Many of us know Joy Cowley from her big books and guided reading books. Little did I know that she is also particularly fond of frogs. This beautifully photographed book will speak to the naturalist in all of us.
Animal Lives: The Frog	Tagholm, Sally 0–7534–5215–4	2000	Describes the life cycle of frogs, discussing how they are born, develop, feed, play, and breed.	3rd & up	Science: Rich language drew me to this book and meaty content held my interest. Exquisitely written, particularly for informational text. Voice, word choice, sentence fluency, strong organization shout from these pages.

Title	Author & ISBN	Year	Library of Congress Summary	Grades	Comments
Watch Me Grow: Frog	Magloff, Lisa 0–7894–9629–1	2003	"Colorful photographs and lively text make learning about the life cycle fun! Includes fantastic facts about frog species from all around the world."	K–5th	Science: I love this book. Kids love this book. See more in the same series by accessing <www.dk.com>.
Bullfrog at Magnolia Circle	Dennard, Deborah 1–931465–39–8	2002	A young male bullfrog avoids a hungry heron and searches for a calling site in his bayou home.	2nd & up	Science: Smithsonian's Backyard series has "entertaining stories with an educational message that answers the many questions about the habits and habitat of the animals in their own backyard." Included are: audiobooks and stuffed animals developed by the Museum of Natural History.
Once Upon a Starry Night	Mitton, Jacqueline Balit, Christina 0–7922–6332–4	2003	Beautifully narrated and illustrated, this book artfully combines mythology and astronomy.	2nd & up	Science: This National Geographic book is a companion book to *Zoo in the Sky* 0–7922–7069–X. Another Mitton book is *Kingdom of the Sun* 0–7922–7220–X .
Park Beat	London, Jonathan 0–688–13994–9	2001	Rhyming text describes activities and sights during the four seasons.	K–5th	Science: "Pumpkins grinnin', Snowballs flyin', Birds chirpin', Hot dogs roastin' give you a taste of this rappin', tappin', finger snappin' celebration of the seasons."
Sky Tree	Locker, Thomas 0–06–443750–7	1995	Sky tree; seeing science through art.	1st & up	Science & art: Whoa! What a beautiful book. It captures the magic of a tree through poetry and paintings. "Questions at the bottom of each page lead to a unique discussion in the back of the book, where art and science are intertwined, and further depth is added to the wonder of *Sky Tree*."

Title	Author & ISBN	Year	Library of Congress Summary	Grades	Comments
Water Dance	Locker, Thomas 0–15–201284–2	1997	Water speaks of its existence in such forms as storm clouds, mist, rainbows, and rivers. Notes include factual information on the water cycle.	2nd & up	Science: Personification and lyrical language. Locker's books are models for presenting factual information through poetry. Detailed scientific information on the water cycle is included at the end of the book. Read all of Locker's books about nature including *Mountain Dance* and *Cloud Dance*.
Animals Nobody Loves	Simon, Seymour 1–58717–155–4	2001	"Seymour Simon unveils the fascinating truths about twenty of nature's most misunderstood animals, from the downright savage to the surprisingly timid."	3rd & up	Science: If Seymour Simon's name appears on a book, pick it up and check it out. He is the author of over 200 science books for children. For more information, visit his website at <www.seymoursimon.com>.
What Do You Do with a Tail Like This?	Jenkins, Steve & Page, Robin 0–618–25628-8	2003	"Explore the many things animals can do with their ears, eyes, mouths, noses, feet, and tails in this beautifully illustrated interactive guessing book."	K–4th	Science: This book is a Caldecott Honor Book. Other books by Jenkins include *Hottest, Coldest, Highest, Deepest,* and *What Do you Do When Something Wants to Eat You?*
Pumpkin Circle: The Story of a Garden	Levenson, George 1–58246–078–7	1999	Rhyming text and photographs follow a pumpkin patch as it grows and changes, from seeds to plants to pumpkins ready to harvest, to jack-o-lanterns and then to seed again.	2nd & up	Science: This is an unusually crafted book that is more than just a children's story about a pumpkin patch. Levenson's lyrical language " . . . Twisting tendrils grasp like hands stretching out to cling . . ." is supported by amazing photographs. For more information visit <www.pumpkincircle.com>.
Human Body Revealed	Davidson, Dr. Sue & Morgan, Ben 0–7894–8882–5	2002	Cutting-edge graphics and compelling facts and figures fill the pages of this remarkable informational text.	4th & up	Science & health: "Amazing transparent pages are unique, created with hundreds of medical images and the latest computer imaging techniques." You, along with your students, will be amazed with this stunning resource. An unusual, but worthwhile read aloud by DK Publishing.

· Reference

Trelease, Jim. 1995. *The Read-Aloud Handbook.* New York: Penguin Books.

KEY QUESTIONS

1. Which picture books have you found to stimulate deeper thinking in your students?

2. As you model comprehension strategies during read aloud times, which strategies are you becoming most comfortable with? Which ones are you working on?

3. Which informational picture books have you found that invite children in as comprehenders?

4. Are you returning to the same books again and again to see them with new eyes and think more deeply about their messages?

Rereading Picture Books

It is important to revisit high quality picture books, to see them again through new eyes. Each time a book is reread, new details emerge and deeper comprehension can be supported. Possible comprehension strategies in read alouds include: Visualizing, Questioning, Giving Opinions/Evaluating, Determining Importance, Inferring, Skimming/Scanning, Previewing/Predicting, Noticing author's craft, Comparing, Connecting, Summarizing, Determining Theme, and so on.

Title	Rereading the Same Book with New Eyes. . . . Record the strategies and insights gained with each reading.		
	Strategy emphasized, date and reflections	Strategy emphasized, date and reflections	Strategy emphasized, date and reflections

25 Listening Is Comprehension Too!

MICHAEL F. OPITZ
AND MATTHEW D. ZBARACKI

MEET THE AUTHORS

MICHAEL F. OPITZ *is a Professor of Reading at the University of Northern Colorado, where he teaches graduate and undergraduate literacy courses. He is a consultant in several areas of language literacy and is the author or co-author of several articles and books from Heinemann on the subject, including* Reaching Readers *(2001),* Rhymes and Reasons *(2000), and* Good-bye Round Robin *(1998).*

MATTHEW D. ZBARACKI *is an Assistant Professor of Reading at the University of Northern Colorado, where he teaches graduate and undergraduate courses in children's literature and literacy. Zbaracki's love for children's literature began when he taught grades four through six and culminated in his PhD in children's literature from Ohio State University.*

FOCUS QUOTE

Listening has not occurred unless comprehension has occurred.

How often have you heard teachers say to their students, "Are you listening to me?" We ask children to listen every day in schools. And outside of the classroom, they listen for 45 percent of the time (Hunsaker 1990). Expecting children to listen as much as they do in and out of school points to the need to help students by providing them with strategies for *how to listen*. This article is designed to introduce you to some ideas of how to do just that.

So What Is Listening?

Ask children this question and you're likely to get answers that range from those that focus on behaviors (e.g., not interrupting the speaker) to those that focus on comprehending what has been heard (e.g., learn from what you hear) (McDevitt 1990, Donahue 1997).

Listening is a complex process that is far different from hearing. Hearing is merely being able to discriminate among the spoken sounds with little or no comprehension. Listening, on the other hand, is an active process that includes attention to the meaning of the spoken message. Most importantly, listening has not occurred unless comprehension has occurred.

There are several good reasons to teach listening (Opitz and Zbaracki 2004). One reason is to show children how to listen for specific details. Merely expecting children to listen for details is quite different from showing them how.

Guided Listening Experiences

Doug wanted his fifth grade students to become better at listening for details while simultaneously learning how to construct a historical timeline. He decided to use *Carl Sandburg: Adventures of a Poet* (Niven 2003) because of the many details it provides about Sandburg's life as well as some of his poetry. What's more, when reviewing the book, Doug noticed that it included a timeline that showed the major events in Sandburg's life juxtaposed with historical events. The timeline was connected with train tracks marked with the years in which the events occurred. He saw this as a perfect listening guide.

On a blank piece of paper, he drew the train tracks down the middle of the page. On each railroad tie, he wrote the appropriate year(s) leaving spaces on either side for students to write associated details (see Figure 25-2). Once prepared, Doug then told students how to use the guide: "Listening for details and big ideas are very important skills in life. That is going to be the focus of today's lesson." He then went on to explain how to use the listening guide, saying something like, "While I am reading the book, you need to listen for at least one detail that tells about Sandburg's life and one that tells about a historical event for each of the years shown on your train track. You then need to write these on the listening guide." Finally, he began reading the book, stopping occasionally to give students time to write what they heard about the given years shown on the train track. Once the reading was finished, he showed students the timeline in the book. Students compared their guides with the one in the book. Doug closed the lesson by reminding students how they could use this focused type of listening in their everyday lives. "So the next time you are wanting to get specific information from someone who is talking to you, think first about what it is you want to know, pay really careful attention, and then make notes so that you can remember what you heard."

FIGURE 25–1 Listening is comprehension and a skill
that is vital throughout life.

Another strategy for teaching precise listening and highlighting a different kind of listening guide are found in the Give Me Five Strategy. This is one of several strategies that appear in *Listen Hear!* (Opitz and Zbaracki 2004).

Give Me Five

Grade Levels: 1–5

Description:

Precise listening invites listening for specific information such as the main point a speaker is trying to make or the details associated with it. What is most important is that the listener understands the purpose for listening at the outset. Providing students with some sort of listening guide is one way to establish a purpose for listening and provide concrete evidence that the listener did indeed accomplish the purpose. Using Give Me Five, you tell students what to listen for and provide a structured guide on which students can make note of their discoveries.

Teaching Suggestions:

1. Choose a children's literature selection that highlights the specific skill you are trying to help students learn. For example, if you want students to listen for details, a selection with several details is needed.

2. Construct a listening guide that can be used by children to make notes.

3. Show the book and the listening guide to the students.

4. Explain to children the purpose for listening to the read aloud and how they are to complete the listening guide. Make sure students understand that they are to listen for at least five details and write each in

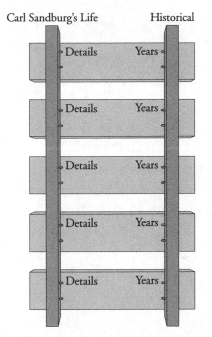

Carl Sandburg's Life   Historical

Details   Years

Details   Years

Details   Years

Details   Years

Details   Years

FIGURE 25–2 Doug's Listening Guide

the appropriate space on the guide. Once they have five details, they can write additional details in the space provided.

5. Distribute the listening guide and read the book.

6. Have children fill in their listening guides, as you read the book.

7. After reading the book, review the listening guide with the children and provide them with some time to give you and their classmates five details they were able to glean from the listening experience.

Students can also be invited to listen to the details their classmates share and note likenesses and differences among them.

SUGGESTED TITLES:

Cerullo, Mary M. 2003. *Sea Turtles: Ocean Nomads.* New York: Dutton.

Cherry, Lynne. 2003. *How Groundhog's Garden Grew.* New York: Scholastic.

Curlee, Lynn. 2003. *Capital.* New York: Atheneum.

Davies, Nicola. 2003. *Surprising Sharks.* Cambridge, MA: Candlewick.

Drummond, Allan. 2003. *The Flyers.* New York: Farrar, Straus & Giroux.

Fleming, Denise. 2003. *Buster.* New York: Henry Holt.

Harness, Cheryl. 2003. *Rabble Rousers: 20 Women Who Made a Difference.* New York: Dutton.

Hiscock, Bruce. 2003. *The Big Caribou Herd.* Hoesdale, PA: Boyds Mills.

Lasky, Kathryn. 2003. *The Man Who Made Time Travel.* New York: Farrar, Straus & Giroux.

Mastro, Jim. 2003. *Antarctic Ice.* New York: Henry Holt.

Niven, Penelope. 2003. *Carl Sandburg: Adventures of a Poet.* San Diego, CA: Harcourt.

Schwartz, Amy. 2003. *What James Likes Best.* New York: Atheneum.

Sobol, Richard. 2003. *Adelina's Whales.* New York: Dutton.

Swinburne, Stephen R. 2003. *Black Bear: North America's Bear.* Honesdale, PA: Boyds Mills.

Symes, Ruth. 2003. *The Sheep Fairy: When Wishes Have Dreams.* New York: Scholastic.

Van Leeuwen, Jean. 2003. *The Amazing Air Balloon.* New York: Penguin.

References

Donahue, M. 1997. "Beliefs About Listening in Students with Learning Disabilities: Is the Speaker Always Right?" *Topics in Language Disorders* 17(3): 41–61.

Hunsaker, R. A. 1990. *Understanding and Developing Skills of Oral Communication.* Englewood, CO: Morton.

Jalongo, M. R. 2003. *Early Childhood Language Arts.* 3rd ed. New York: Allyn & Bacon.

Opitz, M., and M. Zbaracki. 2004. *Listen Hear! 25 Effective Listening Comprehension Strategies.* Portsmouth, NH: Heinemann.

McDevitt, T. 1990. "Encouraging Young Children's Listening." *Academic Therapy* 25(5): 569–77.

KEY QUESTIONS

1. Do your students need explicit instruction in listening comprehension skills?

2. How might you get them to take an active stance as a listener?

3. How do you show your students that you have listened carefully to them?

4. Classroom arrangements do affect speaking and listening behaviors. How might you arrange a room to stimulate precise listening?

5. What are the parallels between listening and comprehension?

Give Me Five

Name _____

Title of Book _____

Five Details I Heard:

1. _____

2. _____

3. _____

4. _____

5. _____

Other Details:

_____

_____

_____

_____

_____

_____

Contributed by M. Opitz and M. Zbaracki © 2005 by Linda Hoyt from *Spotlight on Comprehension*. Portsmouth, NH: Heinemann.

Taking an Active Stance as a Listener

Listener/Researcher _____ Date _____

Your job is to become highly aware of listening behaviors . . . Look closely at others when they talk to each other. Notice their listening behaviors. Look around the room when your teacher is talking; what do you notice about the listening behaviors of your classmates?

As a researcher, record your observations:

I noticed that when someone is listening carefully, that person _____

_____

_____

When someone is just hearing sounds and not really listening, it shows. I noticed

that _____

_____

_____

If you were to give advice about being an active listener who understands and uses what is being said, what would it be? _____

_____

_____

Think about yourself as a listener. What do you do well? What might you set as a goal for improving your active listening skills? _____

_____

_____

Making Connections

Building Companion Collections for Guided Reading

26

LINDA HOYT

MEET THE AUTHOR

LINDA HOYT'S *greatest pleasure in her work as an educator comes at moments when a child has a breakthrough in understanding text. Learners who have become strategic and see links in their learning remind her that there is no better profession in the world.*

FOCUS QUOTE

Knowing that comprehension is deepened when I link companion sets together for guided reading, I also have to consider the impact of times when I can link a read aloud or a shared reading to guided reading experience.

During my early years of teaching, I remember how important it was that we taught in thematic units. We struggled to build connections across the curriculum so we could be engaged in a unit on farm animals and have activities for farm math, farm science, farm spelling, and so on. As the years went by, it became quickly evident that these units were often fun, but they lacked so much. The activities we created to cross the curriculum were often inauthentic and stilted. While involved in units I often had a nice collection of related read aloud books but had few resources in multiple copy sets that the students could engage with for reading instruction. Considering this was all occurring in the name of reading instruction, we did very little reading!

Today we are certainly wiser in the ways of matching readers to texts and teaching comprehension instead of just assessing it. But I do have a concern. The instruction I see in guided reading is often focused on providing materials "at the child's level." The focus on getting the child through the leveled material then creates a pattern of hopping from topic to topic to topic and from author to author with little sense of connection. All too seldom do guided reading lessons explore multiple works by the same author or multiple books on the same topic. Those connected explorations are often saved for read alouds or literature circles.

When I first started guided reading, level was all I looked at as I carefully took my running records and charted learner progress. When I really looked at my own practice, I realized that it was entirely possible for a guided group to read about hot air balloons one day, snakes the next, and Sammy the Seal the day after. While learners seemed to be happy, I wondered if they were playing the age old "keep the teacher happy" game. I had to wonder if this was, in fact, the best I could be offering my students.

Further light was shed on my wonderings as I was working with a second grader who one day read with wonderful fluency and comprehension in a level 17 book. The next day I offered him another level 17 book and he fell completely to pieces, having no clue what he had read. I puzzled over the problem until I reminded myself that all level 17 books are not equal. Their challenges are really quite different IF we consider background, knowledge, and experience. In thinking about this particular child, I realized that the book he read successfully was about vehicles and things that move, a personal passion for this young man. The level 17 that was way over his head was about a sailor on the ocean who was talking to his bird. Not only had this young boy never seen the ocean, he had never experienced a talking bird and had little interest in the book.

What a good reminder of a basic understanding! The more we know on a topic, the easier it is to read materials on that topic. The more interested we are in a topic, the more likely we are to read with success. Having spent 30 years focusing on reading instruction means that *The Reading Teacher* and my other professional journals are comfortable reading for me. My husband is very knowledgeable about the electrical industry and reads journals for pleasure that I can barely decode, much less comprehend. Our differing backgrounds govern our comprehension in deep and powerful ways. This is happening to our young readers as well. Background knowledge and/or the lack of it are pivotal in comprehension. To keep background knowledge in mind as I am creating matches between learners and texts, I want to take into account the child's:

- approximate reading level
- interests
- first-hand experience related to a topic
- related reading: other books on the same topic or by the same author or in the same genre

With a focus on comprehension and this broader view of text-to-child matching, I stand a better chance of helping the child to be successful. But, I have discovered that it can get even better!

If I make a conscious effort to cluster books together by topic or author or genre, I have created a link between the guided reading experiences that make the reading easier. A child who has read two or three Joy Cowley books quickly realizes that she is going to have fun with the reader and that there will be a very clear problem/resolution structure to her work. A child who has read three poetry collections is building up background in poetic language so that each successive poem is getting easier to interpret.

Building Content Knowledge and Vocabulary

When learners have repeated experiences with the same vocabulary and content, the vocabulary is more easily assimilated into long-term memory. The repeated exposure, especially when it occurs in different texts, deepens the connections readers are making between words and concepts. So, when a guided reading group reads three books on frogs, they are building up content knowledge and vocabulary about frogs. As successive books are encountered, these children can now read *frog* books at a higher level of difficulty. The background knowledge they have gained about frogs and the repeated exposure to the concepts and terms have made technical vocabulary like *amphibian* and *lungs* a piece of cake.

Linking Books by Topic

Companion books such as those in Figure 26-1 are examples of how linking guided reading selections by topic can support reader development while broadening world knowledge. As content knowledge grows, you can begin to move to books of increasing difficulty on the same topic. The previous content knowledge scaffolds the reader to be successful with the more difficult material.

FIGURE 26–1 Companion collections broaden world knowledge and enable readers to successively handle more difficult texts.

When companion collections are of similar levels, guided reading groups can often move to higher levels of difficulty with the support of the familiar vocabulary and content knowledge they are gaining.

English language learners, especially, benefit from linking books together as the long-term interaction with the content helps to sustain their vocabulary development in English and to ensure that comprehension is developing side by side with language.

Considering Companion Collections

Title	Level	Series	Publisher
Things That Grow			
In the Garden	A	PM Plus	Rigby
My Garden	A	Real Readers	Rosen
What Plant Is This?	B	Windows on Literacy	National Geographic
How Flowers Grow	C	Real Readers	Rosen
How to Grow a Plant	C	Vision Series	Wright Group
Wheels			
Wheels	B	Windows on Literacy	National Geographic
Things on Wheels	C	Little Red Readers	Sundance
Wheels	C	Discovery Links	Newbridge
Wheels	E	Explorations	Eleanor Curtain
Transportation			
All Kinds of Trucks	B	Little Blue Readers	Sundance
What's on the Road?	B	Windows on Literacy	National Geographic
Wheels	B	Windows on Literacy	National Geographic
Buses, Cars, and Trains	C	Safari	Mondo
Machines That Travel	C	Little Blue Readers	Sundance
Making a Road	C	Little Blue Readers	Sundance
The Bus	C	Twig Books	The Wright Group
The Transportation Museum	C	Little Red Readers	Sundance
Wheels	C	Discovery Links	Newbridge
Frogs			
Fascinating Frogs & Toads	F	Factivity Series	Dominie
Introducing Frogs & Toads	F	Factivity Series	Dominie
How Do Frogs Grow?	G	Discovery Links	Newbridge
Ribbit Ribbit	G	Safari	Mondo

FIGURE 26–2 Read alouds on the same topic as guided reading sessions build background knowledge and activate vocabulary, which can enable guided reading sessions to push readers to deeper levels of understanding in more complex texts.

Broadening the Connection to Read Aloud

Knowing that comprehension is deepened when I link companion sets together for guided reading, I also have to consider the impact of linking a read aloud or a shared reading to guided reading. Now I can wonder, if I am going to create links by topic, by author, or by element of writers' craft, is there a link I can make between a current read aloud or strategy lesson I am using with the whole class? Would there be a benefit to doing a read aloud just for the guided reading group of a book on the same topic they are about to read, of another book by the same author, or perhaps a book that demonstrates a writing element that I want to be sure they notice in their guided reading selection? While guided reading isn't designed for read aloud, could there be benefits if I frontload language and content with a small group read aloud? Would the learners comprehend better if I make thoughtful choices about my whole class read alouds that will connect to their guided reading selection?

When learners are shown that there are connections between books and asked to look for them, they become more strategic and focused on understanding. They begin to realize how consciously they can apply their prior knowledge when reading new material.

Extending to Independent Reading

Knowing that independent reading is a time when some students struggle to find books at comfortable reading levels and on topics they enjoy, I often build mini–companion collections for independent reading. If you are reading a book on frogs in guided reading, why not give the child a small companion collection of books on frogs to enjoy during independent reading? I place these little companion collections in a ziplock bag so they are easily car-

FIGURE 26–3 Small companion collections can be provided for independent reading to extend interaction with the topic and the related vocabulary.

ried around. Many learners really benefit from extending their exploration of the topic and working with the familiar vocabulary in independent reading time.

Creating Multilevel Companion Collections

Multilevel companion collections are a way to bring just-right reading material to learners in every subject area. In a multilevel companion collection, I want to reach a broad range of achievement levels so that all learners in the classroom can be reading at their just-right level AND be focused on a unit of study. For these broader class collections, I gather sets of six guided reading books each, on a wide range of levels, all linked to a content standard I need to teach. With this support, it is easy to bring core science, health, or social studies concepts into the language arts block. Guided reading groups can focus on the core unit of study within guided reading, helping control curricular overload. Similarly, I could conduct literature circles during content-area time using these companion collections to ensure that readers have access to content books at a comfortable reading level.

Some possibilities for linking guided reading selections and deeping understanding:

- Link guided reading selections together by creating companion collections of guided reading titles based on:
  - topic
  - author
  - writing trait
  - theme or _____
- Do a read aloud before guided reading to build content knowledge and vocabulary on the topic.
- Link guided reading to a unit of study in science or social studies.

FIGURE 26–4 Multilevel companion sets give the entire class access to books at their just-right level while engaging in core content-area studies. Multiple copies of each title make guided reading and literature circles a natural part of content study.

Have guided reading groups read the social studies text and a resource book on the same topic and discuss similarities and differences in the way the information was presented, compare the content, examine author style, etc.

- Create mini–companion collections so students can extend their learning in guided reading into independent time.
- Build multilevel companion sets based on your standards and/or core curriculum. Focus on multiple copy sets of books that reach the full range of developmental levels in your class. Many schools build these sets collaboratively and put them in a central place where they can be shared.

KEY QUESTIONS

1. What are your reactions to the notion of linking guided reading selections by topic, by author, by genre, or by writing craft rather than simply by level of difficulty?

2. What benefits would there be in creating companion collections for guided reading?

3. How might multilevel companion collections work for you? Would your colleagues be willing to work with you to build collections that could be shared?

4. How might you create more links between read aloud and shared reading with guided reading? Links by reading strategy, topic and so on . . .

Companion Collections to Consider

Titles	Level	Series	Publisher
Magnets			
Fun with Magnets	B	Real Readers	Rosen
My Magnet	B	Literacy Tree	Rigby
Magnets	E	Discovery Links	Newbridge
Magnets	G	Factivity Series	Dominie
Fun with Magnets	K	Rigby Focus	Rigby
Magnetic and Nonmagnetic	L	My World of Science	Heinemann Classroom
Magnets	L	My World of Science	Heinemann Classroom
Magnets	L	Windows on Literacy	National Geographic
Magnets	N	Science All Around Me	Heinemann Classroom
Wheels			
Wheels	B	Windows on Literacy	National Geographic
Things on Wheels	C	Little Red Readers	Sundance
Wheels	C	Discovery Links	Newbridge
Wheels	E	Explorations	Eleanor Curtain
Using Wheels	F	Little Red Readers	Sundance
Wheels Go Round	G	Safari	Mondo
Wheels at Work	H	Little Blue Readers	Sundance
Solar System			
The Sun	B	Rigby Focus	Rigby
Our Earth	C	Real Readers	Rosen
The Moon	C	Rigby Focus	Rigby
Pictures in the Stars	D	Cambridge Reading	Dominie
The Moons of Jupiter	E	Cambridge Reading	Dominie
A Trip to Space	F	Story Steps	Rigby
Look at the Stars	G	Rigby Focus	Rigby
Our Sun	G	Real Readers	Rosen
A Trip into Space	H	Little Red Readers	Sundance
The Earth	H	Windows on Literacy	National Geographic
The Moon	H	Factivity Series	Dominie
The Stars	H	Factivity Series	Dominie
Mars	I	Rigby Focus	Rigby
Mars: The Red Planet	I	Real Readers	Rosen

Companion Collections to Consider, *continued*

Titles	Level	Series	Publisher
Solar System, *continued*			
On the Moon	I	Windows on Literacy	National Geographic
Planet Earth	I	Rigby Focus	Rigby
The Moon	I	Twig Books	The Wright Group
Planets Around the Sun	J	Seymour Simon	SeeMore Readers
Our Solar System	K	Safari	Mondo
A Trip Through Our Solar System	L	Real Readers	Rosen
Super Space Station	L	Real Readers	Rosen
Planets of Our Solar System	M	Rigby Focus	Rigby
Rocks from Space	M	Rigby Focus	Rigby
Space Quest	O	Discovery World	Rigby
Space Rocks: A Look at Asteroids and Comets	O	Real Readers	Rosen
All About the Moon	P	Real Readers	Rosen
Inside the Sun	P	Real Readers	Rosen
Moving and Shaking	P	Book Web	Rigby
Our Changing Planet	P	InfoQuest	Rigby
Our Place in Space	P	Info Quest	Rigby
Solar Storms	P	Real Readers	Rosen
There's No Place Like Home	P	Chapter Books	Orbit
Across the Solar System	Q		Heinemann Classroom
Space Junk	Q	Sails	Rigby
Sky Watch	Q	Explorers	The Wright Group
Exploring Space	S/T	Reading Expeditions	National Geographic
The Mystery of Life on Other Planets	V/W		Heinemann Classroom
Asteroids, Comets, and Meteors	X		Heinemann Classroom
Stars and Constellations	X	InfoSearch	Heinemann Classroom
Venus	X		Heinemann Classroom
Riddles of the Universe	Z	Chapter Books	Orbit
Animals Hiding			
Animals Hide	B	On Our Way to English	Rigby

Companion Collections to Consider, *continued*

Titles	Level	Series	Publisher
Animals Hiding, *continued*			
Animals at Night	C	Windows on Literacy	National Geographic
Hiding	C	Literacy Tree	Rigby
Animals Hide	D	Discovery Links	Newbridge
Chameleons	F	Factivity Series	Dominie
Looking Like Plants	G	AlphaKids	Sundance
Chameleons	I	Twig Books	The Wright Group
Can You See an Insect?	J	Windows on Literacy	National Geographic
Camouflage	K	Rigby Focus	Rigby
Camouflage	L	Cambridge Reading	Dominie
Hide to Survive	L	RHCC	Rigby
In Hiding: Animals Under Cover	L	Pair-It Books	Steck-Vaughn
The Hiders	M/N	Sails	Rigby
Surviving in the Wild	N	Rigby Literacy	Rigby
Birds			
Birds	B	Rigby Focus	Rigby
A Bird Flies By	D	Windows on Literacy	National Geographic
Baby Birds	D	Windows on Literacy	National Geographic
Birds	E	Windows on Literacy	National Geographic
Every Bird Has Feathers	F	Factivity Series	Dominie
Every Bird Has a Beak	F	Factivity Series	Dominie
Super Seabirds	I	AlphaKids	Sundance
Bird Families	K	AlphaKids	Sundance
Rainforest Birds	K	AlphaKids	Sundance
Using a Beak	L	Sails	Rigby
Bird Watchers	M	Chapter Books	Storyteller
Birds of Prey	M	Chapter Books	Storyteller
What Makes a Bird a Bird?	N	Book Shop	Mondo
Birds of Prey	O	Book Shop	Mondo
My Life with Birds	O	Sails	Rigby
Waterbirds	O	InfoQuest	Rigby
Birds: Modern-Day Dinosaurs	P	Real Readers	Rosen

Companion Collections to Consider, *continued*

Titles	Level	Series	Publisher
Birds, *continued*			
Feathery Fables	P	A Collection of Traditional Tales	Rigby
Flight Path	T	InfoQuest	Rigby
Classifying Birds	U		Heinemann Classroom
The Life Cycle of Birds	U		Heinemann Classroom
Frogs			
Tadpoles and Frogs	D	AlphaKids	Sundance
Where's the Frog?	D	Discovery Links	Newbridge
Fascinating Frogs & Toads	F	Factivity Series	Dominie
Introducing Frogs & Toads	F	Factivity Series	Dominie
How Do Frogs Grow?	G	Discovery Links	Newbridge
Ribbit Ribbit	G	Safari	Mondo
Fantastic Frog Facts	H	AlphaKids	Sundance
The Frog Report	I	Rigby Focus	Rigby
How a Frog Gets Its Legs	J	Real Readers	Rosen
Frogs	K	Windows on Literacy	National Geographic
Tadpole Diary	K	Informazing!	Rigby
Frog	M		Heinemann Classroom
Frogs	N	Book Shop	Mondo
Water			
Water Changes	D	Discovery Links	Newbridge
Rain Is Water	E	PM Plus	Rigby
Water	E	On Our Way to English	Rigby
Water, Ice, and Steam	E	Real Readers	Rosen
Water	I	Windows on Literacy	National Geographic
Water Liquid, Solid, Gas	J	Twig Books	The Wright Group
Where Does the Water Go?	J	Windows on Literacy	National Geographic
The Wonderful Water Cycle	L	On Our Way to English	Rigby
Water	L	My World of Science	Heinemann Classroom
Water	M	Materials, Materials, Materials	Heinemann Classroom
Watching Every Drop	M	RHCC	Rigby
Water for the World	M	RHCC	Rigby
The Shapes of Water	O	Chapter Books	Orbit

Companion Collections to Consider, *continued*

Titles	Level	Series	Publisher
Insects and Bugs			
Ants	B	Discovery Links	Newbridge
Ants Love Picnics Too	B	Literacy 2000	Rigby
Butterfly	C	AlphaKids	Sundance
Is It an Insect?	C	First Stories	Pacific Learning
Bumble Bee	D	Pacific Literacy	Pacific Learning
The Praying Mantis	D	Pacific Literacy	Pacific Learning
All About Ants	E	Real Readers	Rosen
Spiders	E	Discovery Links	Newbridge
Caterpillar Diary	E	Informazing!	Rigby
Busy Bees	F	Real Readers	Rosen
How Spiders Live	F	Sunshine Books	The Wright Group
Insects	F	Rigby Focus	Rigby
Spiders	F	AlphaKids	Sundance
Spiders!	F	Real Readers	Rosen
Tarantulas Are Spiders	F	Book Shop	Mondo
A Butterfly Is Born	G	Life Cycles	Newbridge
Tarantula	G	AlphaKids	Sundance
Insects	H	AlphaKids	Sundance
Amazing Ants	I	AlphaKids	Sundance
Ants	I	Factivity Series	Dominie
Beetles	I	Factivity Series	Dominie
Flies	I	Factivity Series	Dominie
Insect-Eaters!	I	Rigby Focus	Rigby
Introducing Anthropods	I	Factivity Series	Dominie
Spinners and Weavers	I	Factivity Series	Dominie
Wasps and Bees	I	Factivity Series	Dominie
Don't Stomp on That Bug	J	Rigby Literacy	Rigby
Fireflies!	J	Twig Books	The Wright Group
The Secret of Silk	J	Rigby Focus	Rigby
Cockroach	L		Heinemann Classroom
Dragonfly	L		Heinemann Classroom
Earwig	L		Heinemann Classroom
Looking at Insects	L	Discovery World	Rigby
Mosquito	L		Heinemann Classroom

Companion Collections to Consider, *continued*

Titles	Level	Series	Publisher
Insects and Bugs, *continued*			
Thinking About Ants	L	Book Shop	Mondo
Caterpillars	M	Book Shop	Mondo
Spiders	M	Book Shop	Mondo
The World of Ants	M	Life Cycles	Rigby
Social Insects	K	AlphaKids	Sundance
Busy as a Bee	M	Plants	Rigby
Bugs on the Menu	M/N	Sails	Rigby
Billions of Bugs	N	On Our Way to English	Rigby
The Insect Army	O	InfoQuest	Rigby
A Colony of Ants	P		Heinemann Classroom
Insects	S	Book Shop	Mondo
Classifying Insects	U		Heinemann Classroom
The Life Cycle of Insects	U		Heinemann Classroom
Weather			
Learning About Clouds	A	Real Readers	Rosen
Learning About Rain	A	Real Readers	Rosen
In the Sky	B	Little Red Readers	Sundance
Rain	B	Little Reader Twin Texts	Sundance
Rainbows	C	Safari	Mondo
Watch the Sky	C	Windows on Literacy	National Geographic
Wind and Rain	D	Factivity Series	Dominie
A Storm Is Coming	F	Explorations	Eleanor Curtain
Map the Weather	G	Safari	Mondo
What Is Rain?	G	Factivity Series	Dominie
What Is Wind?	H	Factivity Series	Dominie
Weather Watching	I	AlphaKids	Sundance
Wild Weather	I	Rigby Focus	Rigby
It's a Blizzard!	J	Real Readers	Rosen
Rain, Snow, and Hail	J	Discovery World	Rigby
Super Storms	J	Seymour Simon	SeeMore Readers
When a Storm Comes	J	Windows on Literacy	National Geographic
Big Freeze	L		Heinemann Classroom
Drought	L		Heinemann Classroom

Companion Collections to Consider, *continued*

Titles	Level	Series	Publisher
Weather, *continued*			
Heat Wave	L		Heinemann Classroom
Looking at Clouds	L	Discovery Links	Newbridge
The Wonderful Water Cycle	L	On Our Way to English	Rigby
Clouds	M	Literacy Tree	Rigby
Snow	M		Heinemann Classroom
Watching the Weather	M		Heinemann Classroom
Weather Watching	M	Rigby Focus	Rigby
Chasing Tornadoes!	O	Rigby Literacy	Rigby
Measuring the Weather	P	Chapter Books	Orbit
Precipitation	V		Heinemann Classroom
Wind and Air Pressure	V		Heinemann Classroom
Weather and Climate	V/W	Reading Expeditions	National Geographic
Turbulence Ahead	W	InfoQuest	Rigby
Global Warming	X/Y	Reading Expeditions	National Geographic
Rainforest			
A Rain Forest	A	Rigby Focus	Rigby
Animals of the Rainforest	B	Sails	Rigby
Rainforest Plants	F	AlphaKids	Sundance
Rainforests	G	Little Green Readers	Sundance
Life in the Rain Forest	I	Real Readers	Rosen
Saving the Rainforest	I	AlphaKids	Sundance
Rainforest Birds	K	AlphaKids	Sundance
Animals of the Tropical Rainforest	L	Real Readers	Rosen
The Rain Forest	L	Windows on Literacy	National Geographic
Tropical Rainforests	L	Factivity Series	Dominie
Rainforest	P	Cambridge Reading	Dominie
Up a Rainforest Tree	P		Heinemann Classroom
The Living Rain Forest	Q	Chapter Books	Orbit
The Rain Forest	Q	Action Packs	Rigby
A Rain Forest Adventure	R	Discovery Links	Newbridge

Companion Collections to Consider, *continued*

Titles	Level	Series	Publisher
Night Creatures			
Bats, Bats, Bats	A	Real Readers	Rosen
What Comes Out at Night?	B	Little Red Readers	Sundance
Coyotes	H		Heinemann Classroom
Opossums	H		Heinemann Classroom
Raccoons	H		Heinemann Classroom
Dark Dwellers	I	Factivity Series	Dominie
Hunting in the Dark	I	AlphaKids	Sundance
Creatures of the Night	L	Rigby Focus	Rigby
Bats	M	Literacy Tree	Rigby
Creatures of the Dark	M	Literacy Tree	Rigby
Owls	M	Discovery Links	Newbridge
Flowers and Plants			
In the Garden	Step Up	Windows on Literacy	National Geographic
Plants in the Park	Step Up	Windows on Literacy	National Geographic
Flowers	A	Explorations	Eleanor Curtain
In the Garden	A	PM Plus	Rigby
My Garden	A	Real Readers	Rosen
What Plant Is This?	B	Windows on Literacy	National Geographic
How Flowers Grow	C	Real Readers	Rosen
How to Grow a Plant	C	Vision Series	Wright Group
Leaves, Fruits, Seeds, and Roots	C	Reading Science	Pacific Learning
Grow Seed Grow	D	Discovery Links	Newbridge
Growing a Plant	D	Discovery World	Rigby
Plants	D	AlphaKids	Sundance
Planting and Growing	D	On Our Way to English	Rigby
Dangerous Plants	D	Explorations	Eleanor Curtain
Amazing Plants	F	Explorations	Eleanor Curtain
How Does My Garden Grow?	F	Windows on Literacy	National Geographic
Growing a Plant	G	Discovery World	Rigby
Growing in My Garden	G	Factivity Series	Dominie
Seeds and Plants	G	Factivity Series	Dominie

Companion Collections to Consider, *continued*

Titles	Level	Series	Publisher
Flowers and Plants, *continued*			
Plants and Seeds	I	Sunshine Books	The Wright Group
Seashore Plants	I	AlphaKids	Sundance
Seeds	I	Read and Learn	Heinemann Classroom
The Busy Harvest	I	Discovery Links	Newbridge
Flowers	J	Read and Learn	Heinemann Classroom
From Field to Florist	J	Windows on Literacy	National Geographic
How Do Plants Grow?	J	Real Readers	Rosen
Plant ABC	J	Read and Learn	Heinemann Classroom
Grandma's Garden	K	Rigby Focus	Rigby
Flowers, Fruits, and Seeds	M		Heinemann Classroom
Strange Plants	M		Heinemann Classroom
Wetland Plants	M		Heinemann Classroom
How Plants Survive	N	Discovery Links	Newbridge
Power-Packed Plants	O	InfoQuest	Rigby
Strange Plants	O	Windows on Literacy	National Geographic
Plant Power	S/T	Reading Expeditions	National Geographic
Classifying Nonflowering Plants	U		Heinemann Classroom
Plant Parts	V		Heinemann Classroom
Plant Reproduction	V		Heinemann Classroom
How Food Grows			
Watermelons	Step Up	Windows on Literacy	National Geographic
All About Apples	A	Real Readers	Rosen
Food from Plants	D	Rigby Literacy	Rigby
Vegetables and How They Grow	D	Real Readers	Rosen
Sunflower Seeds	D	The Story Box	The Wright Group
Growing Tomatoes	E	AlphaKids	Sundance
Food Comes from Farms	F	Windows on Literacy	National Geographic
Growing Beans	F	Little Blue Readers	Sundance
Seeds Grow into Plants	G	Windows on Literacy	National Geographic
Plants on My Plate	G	Windows on Literacy	National Geographic
An Apple a Day	H	Early Science	Newbridge

Companion Collections to Consider, *continued*

Titles	Level	Series	Publisher
How Food Grows, *continued*			
Growing Strawberries	H	AlphaKids	Sundance
Big Red Tomatoes	I	Windows on Literacy	National Geographic
Growing Radishes and Carrots	I	Book Shop	Mondo
Potatoes	I	Windows on Literacy	National Geographic
Where Does Food Come From?	I	PM Plus	Rigby
Corn	J	Windows on Literacy	National Geographic
Plants We Use	J	On Our Way to English	Rigby
Rice	N	Windows on Literacy	National Geographic
Worms			
How to Make an Earthworm Farm	C	Little Green Readers	Sundance
Worms	D	Literacy 2000	Rigby
Worm Rap	F	AlphaKids	Sundance
Earthworms	J	Rigby Focus	Rigby
My Worm Farm	K	AlphaKids	Sundance
Worm	L		Heinemann Classroom
Silkworm	M		Heinemann Classroom
The Amazing Silkworm	M/N	Windows on Literacy	National Geographic
Worm Work	P	Sails	Rigby
Transportation			
All Kinds of Trucks	B	Little Blue Readers	Sundance
What's on the Road?	B	Windows on Literacy	National Geographic
Wheels	B	Windows on Literacy	National Geographic
Buses, Cars, and Trains	C	Safari	Mondo
Machines That Travel	C	Little Blue Readers	Sundance
Making a Road	C	Little Blue Readers	Sundance
The Bus	C	Twig Books	The Wright Group
The Transportation Museum	C	Little Red Readers	Sundance
Wheels	C	Discovery Links	Newbridge

Companion Collections to Consider, *continued*

Titles	Level	Series	Publisher
Transportation, *continued*			
Transportation over the Years	D	Discovery Links	Newbridge
What Did They Drive?	D	Windows on Literacy	National Geographic
The Train Race	E	AlphaKids	Sundance
The Plane Ride	F	Little Red Readers	Sundance
Trains	F	Little Blue Readers	Sundance
Building a Strong Bridge	J	Twig Books	The Wright Group
Bullet Trains	J	On Deck	Rigby
Cruise Ships	J	On Deck	Rigby
Supersonic Jets	J	On Deck	Rigby
The Bridge Builders Gruff	J	Safari	Mondo
Wheels, Wings, and Other Things	J	Rigby Literacy	Rigby
Emergency Vehicles	K	PM Plus	Rigby
Trains	K	AlphaKids	Sundance
Work Vehicles	K	Windows on Literacy	National Geographic
Bridges	L	Discovery Links	Newbridge
Tunnels	L	Windows on Literacy	National Geographic
Emergency Vehicles	M		Heinemann Classroom
Boats and Ships	M		Heinemann Classroom
Riding the Steam Train	M	Pacific Literacy	Pacific Learning
How Do Airplanes Fly?	O	Real Readers	Rosen
Trains	P	Literacy Tree	Rigby
Building the Transcontinental Railroad	W	Reading Expeditions	National Geographic
The Ocean			
Big Animals of the Sea	A	Sails	Rigby
Tell Me About Turtles	A	Real Readers	Rosen
In the Sea	B	Little Red Readers	Sundance
Ocean Facts	B	Real Readers	Rosen
On the Seashore	B	Sails	Rigby
See the Boats Go!	B	Windows on Literacy	National Geographic
Whales in the Ocean	B	Real Readers	Rosen
What Can a Diver See?	B	Windows on Literacy	National Geographic

Companion Collections to Consider, *continued*

Titles	Level	Series	Publisher
The Ocean, *continued*			
Who Lives in the Sea?	B	Book Shop	Mondo
The Baby Shark	C	Windows on Literacy	National Geographic
Hiding in the Sea	E	AlphaKids	Sundance
Whales	F	AlphaKids	Sundance
Sea Turtles	G	Little Green Readers	Sundance
Tidal Pools	G	Little Green Readers	Sundance
Diving Down	H	Safari	Mondo
Living in the Ocean	H	Factivity Series	Dominie
Sea Horses	H	AlphaKids	Sundance
Sea Turtles	H	Little Reader Twin Texts	Sundance
Butterflies of the Sea	I	Factivity Series	Dominie
Kelp Forests	I	Factivity Series	Dominie
Sea Animals	I	Little Red Readers	Sundance
Sharks	I	AlphaKids	Sundance
What Do You Know About Dolphins?	I	Windows on Literacy	National Geographic
Incredible Sharks	J	Seymour Simon	SeeMore Readers
Jellyfish	J	AlphaKids	Sundance
Killer Whales	J	Seymour Simon	SeeMore Readers
Sea Giants	J	AlphaKids	Sundance
Starfish & Urchins	J	Factivity Series	Dominie
Under the Sea	J	AlphaKids	Sundance
Whales on the World Wide Web	J	AlphaKids	Sundance
Fish That Hide	K	Factivity Series	Dominie
Monsters of the Deep	K	Factivity Series	Dominie
Ocean Tides	K	Real Readers	Rosen
Sea Snakes	K	Factivity Series	Dominie
Sea Turtles	K	Factivity Series	Dominie
Sharks	K		Heinemann Classroom
Turtles in Trouble	K	AlphaKids	Sundance
Blue Whale	L		Heinemann Classroom
Eels	L	Factivity Series	Dominie

Companion Collections to Consider, *continued*

Titles	Level	Series	Publisher
The Ocean, *continued*			
Encyclopedia of Fantastic Fish	L	Rigby Literacy	Rigby
Dolphins	L		Heinemann Classroom
Life in the Ocean	L	Windows on Literacy	National Geographic
Octopuses, Squid, and Cuttlefish	L	Factivity Series	Dominie
Rainbows of the Sea	N	Book Shop	Mondo
Sea Animals	N		Heinemann Classroom
Whales	N	Book Shop	Mondo
Exploring Tide Pools	N/O	Windows on Literacy	National Geographic
In the Deep	O	Discovery Links	Newbridge
What's in the Sea?	O	Real Readers	Rosen
Oil on Water	P	Sails	Rigby
Searching for Sea Lions	P	Chapter Books	Orbit
Amazing Sharks	Q	Science Spectacular	Newbridge
Sharks and Rays	Q	Explorers	Shortland Publications
Divers of the Deep Sea	Q/R	Windows on Literacy	National Geographic
Oceans and Seas	R/S		Heinemann Classroom
Beneath the Waves	T	InfoQuest	Rigby
Octopuses	T		Heinemann Classroom
Sea Horses	T		Heinemann Classroom
Whale Tales	T	Chapter Books	Orbit
The Oceans Around Us	U/V	Reading Expeditions	National Geographic
Oceans of the World	W	InfoQuest	Rigby
Protecting the Seas	X/Y	Reading Expeditions	National Geographic
Energy			
Making Electricity	I	Little Blue Readers	Sundance
Power from the Sun	I	Little Green Readers	Sundance
Water Power	I	Little Green Readers	Sundance
Sun Power	J	Windows on Literacy	National Geographic
At the Coal Mine	K	Rigby Focus	Rigby
The Power of Wind	K	On Our Way to English	Rigby
Wind Power	K	Windows on Literacy	National Geographic
The Power of Water	L	RHCC	Rigby
Fossil Fuels	M	Rigby Focus	Rigby

Companion Collections to Consider, *continued*

Titles	Level	Series	Publisher
Energy, *continued*			
Using Energy Wisely	M	Discovery Links	Newbridge
Steam Power	N	Rigby Focus	Rigby
Energy	R	Sails	Rigby
Using Energy	V/W	Reading Expeditions	National Geographic
Natural Disasters			
Rumble, Bumble, Boom!	D	Reading Science	Pacific Learning
Hurricanes	H	Little Reader Twin Texts	Sundance
Facts About Forest Fires	I	Real Readers	Rosen
Forest Fire!	I	On Our Way to English	Rigby
Hurricanes and Tropical Storms	I	Real Readers	Rosen
Avalanche!	J	Real Readers	Rosen
Facts About Tornadoes	J	Real Readers	Rosen
Natural Disasters	J	AlphaKids	Sundance
Facts About Earthquakes	K	Real Readers	Rosen
Volcanoes	K	AlphaKids	Sundance
Earthquake!	N	Discovery Links	Newbridge
Geysers	N		Heinemann Classroom
Warning: Volcano! The Story of Mount St. Helens	N	Real Readers	Rosen
Volcanoes	N		Heinemann Classroom
Flood!	O	Rigby Literacy	Rigby
Shake, Rattle, and Roll	Q	Rigby Literacy	Rigby
Volcanoes	Q	Explorers	The Wright Group
Volcanoes	Q/R	Windows on Literacy	National Geographic
Eathquakes	R	Explorers	The Wright Group
Forest Fires: Run for Your Life!	R	Book Shop	Mondo
Disaster Plan	V	Book Web	Rigby
Hurricanes	V		Heinemann Classroom
Our Changing Earth	V	Chapter Books	Orbit
Shake, Rattle, and Rumble	V	InfoQuest	Rigby
Tornadoes	V		Heinemann Classroom
Volcanoes and Earthquakes	V/W	Reading Expeditions	National Geographic
Twisting Up a Storm	Z	Chapter Books	Orbit

Comprehending Nonfiction

27 Using Guided Reading to Deepen Understandings

TONY STEAD

MEET THE AUTHOR

TONY STEAD *has taught in elementary schools, lectured at the University of Melbourne, and is the past president of the Melbourne Chapter of the Australian Reading Association. He is the author of many publications, including* Is It A Fact? *(Stenhouse, 2002). His latest is a video series "Time For Nonfiction," which highlights his recent work with several teachers at the Manhattan New School.*

Tony currently works extensively in literacy education with school districts across the United States, Canada, and Australia. His greatest love is learning from children.

FOCUS QUOTE

The results of this practice have been phenomenal. Not only are our learners now successfully navigating science and social studies texts presented in content studies, they are also actively selecting nonfiction as part of their independent reading.

As an educator I always ensure that guided reading is an integral component of instruction in a comprehensive language program. The powers of guided reading in facilitating comprehension are evident. Mooney (1990), Clay (1993), Fountas and Pinnell, (1996) and Taberski (2000), to name a few, have highlighted that when a teacher is able to meet with a small group of children at their instructional reading level, they are able to build on each child's independent reading level. It enables the teacher to monitor children's reading development, assess what they need, and guide them along the literacy continuum to deepen and strengthen their understandings as readers.

But what about nonfiction? What is its place in the guided reading forum? It is not surprising that when I ask teachers the percentage of nonfiction material utilized in guided reading, their answer is around 3 percent. The implication of this limited practice is that many of our learners are unable to access, process, and communicate nonfiction information. They are in essence only partially literate.

Partial Literacy?

This notion of partial literacy became evident to me when assessing children's capacity to deal with informational texts during pre-assessments. Mandy, a third grader, typified what many of our children do when faced with informational texts. With her fictional reading she was able to read complex texts and discuss setting, plot, character development, and reactions. However, this was not the case with nonfiction. While certainly able to read the words, she lacked comprehension and was barely able to explain any of the information presented by the author. This told me that her level for instruction with nonfiction was different than that of narrative texts. Mandy was not the only learner who struggled with nonfiction. In a class of 29 children, almost half had instructional levels substantially lower with nonfiction than that of their fictional reading. Many colleagues have informed me that these results typify their findings when comparing children's instructional nonfiction levels with that of fiction.

Is Nonfiction Harder to Comprehend?

Do these findings therefore imply that nonfiction reading is harder for children than fiction? I think not. I believe the answer lies in our lack of immersion, teacher demonstration, and use of informational texts in daily instruction. Duke and Pearson's (2002) research would appear to support this notion. Duke and Pearson found that less than 4 percent of instruction in classrooms centered on nonfiction. I am sure that this percentage is even less when we consider the instruction taking place with informational texts during guided reading instruction.

Balancing Fiction/Nonfiction

In the classrooms where I work, we now aim for at least 50 percent of all guided reading engagements to be with nonfiction texts. This instruction begins in kindergarten so that children are exposed to the language, structures, and features of nonfiction from the onset of their schooling. In many of our third-to-fifth grade classrooms, we are aiming for nearly 70 percent of guided reading encounters to be centered on informational texts. The results of this practice have been phenomenal. Not only are our learners now successfully navigating science and social studies texts presented in content studies, they are also actively selecting nonfiction as part of their independent reading.

When working with nonfiction as part of guided reading instruction, there are a number of considerations and guidelines that I utilize to help facilitate teaching and learning. See the following Table 27–1.

It is important to select nonfiction material at the children's instructional level. This should be material that the children can almost read and comprehend independently. (Slightly higher than their independent level of decodability with comprehension.) Many times children are able to decode informational texts higher than their comprehension level. If this is the case, I select texts where the children begin to lose comprehension, which will be lower than their ability to simply decode. Guided reading is about comprehension—making meaning and understanding, not simply decoding.

Considerations for Assessment and Instruction

The following table lists some of the considerations I take into account when assessing children's comprehension of nonfiction texts. These considerations are also important in planning comprehension instruction. It needs to be noted that depending on the piece being read, not all the considerations presented in the table are processed within each reading. These are an overall roadmap for assessing and teaching comprehension with informational texts. (Refer to the end of this piece for a rubric that may be useful for tracking children's understanding when working with informational texts.)

FIGURE 27–1 It is important that the resources used for guided reading be at the learners' instructional level.

TABLE 27-1
Considerations When Assessing and Teaching Comprehension with Informational Texts

Is the student able to:

• Recognize the purpose of the piece? E.g., Was it written to describe, instruct, explain, present an argument, retell a series of events, etc.?

• Make predictions as to the content of the piece being read?

• Understand the information presented by the author in the piece?

• Synthesize the information presented?

• Understand information presented in visual forms such graphs, diagrams, photographs, and tables?

• Infer from the information presented?

• Raise questions?

• Make connections?

• Understand the difference between fact and opinion?

• Use text features such as table of contents, index, and glossary?

• Evaluate the validity of the piece?

Prepare for the Lesson

When selecting material for the guided reading session, I familiarize myself with the material so that I am aware of the challenges it may bring to the readers. If I need to point out more than a handful of challenges to the group, then the book is probably going to be too hard and will not be suitable at this time. If children struggle with too many challenges, comprehension and enjoyment become compromised. We need to keep in mind that a guided reading session is about setting the group up for success.

Use a Variety of Different Forms of Nonfiction

Nonfiction is far more than just books about animals and space. Some of the purposes for reading nonfiction and the various forms associated with these major purposes are listed in Table 27-2. Exposing children to a variety of forms and purposes for reading nonfiction ensures that our learners gain valuable insights into how to read for a multitude of purposes.

Select a Comprehension Focus

I find it imperative to be clear on what I am attempting to achieve when working with a group during guided reading. In selecting a focus, I often look to the content areas such as science and social studies and the specific reading strategies I am working on in whole class strategy instruction. I then highlight these same strategies in small group instruction only at each group's instructional level. In this way I am able to further assist my learners as they synthesize strategies demonstrated during whole class discussions. Table 27-3 highlights some of the strategies I concentrate on over the course of a year in

TABLE 27–2
Key Purposes and Forms of Nonfiction Texts

Some of the Key Purposes for Nonfiction	Common Forms or Examples Relevant to Elementary School Children That Can Be Used for Guided Reading Instruction
To describe (Descriptive reports)	personal descriptions such as wanted posters, missing posters, etc. poetry scientific reports about animals, plants, and machines reports about countries definitions, labels, captions, illustrations
To explain	scientific explanations on how and why a phenomenon occurs personal narratives that explain how and why something happens elaborations, reports illustrations, captions, labels
To instruct	recipes, rules, directions experiments, games lists, maps, letters, email illustrations, captions, labels
To persuade	debates, reviews advertisements, evaluations book reports letters, email poetry posters, cartoons, illustrations
To retell information about a person or past event:	reports autobiographies/biographies
Nonfiction narrative	letters poetry journals, scripts historical retellings
To explore and maintain relationships with others	cards, letters, email questionnaires, interviews poetry

Adapted from Stead, Tony. 2002. *Is That a Fact: Teaching Nonfiction Writing.* Portland, ME: Stenhouse Publishers.

small group settings. What is important is that I focus on only a limited number of strategies at one time so that I don't overload children with too much to process during the guided reading session.

Don't Try to Achieve Too Much

My golden rule is: Less is best. Often during guided reading sessions we attempt to get through a large body of text in one sitting. I have found it far more effective to take just one section, and in some cases, one page, for my point of instruction. This allows the discussions and reflections to go deep and helps facilitate comprehension. If children can successfully navigate a small portion of the text then they are able to transfer these understandings to the remainder of the text.

TABLE 27–3
Comprehension Focuses with Informational Texts

Strategies in Making Meaning
Predict/confirm/change predictions
Locate specific information (skim/scan)
Understand the difference between fact and opinion
Find new facts
Cause and effect
Problem/Solution
Main Idea/s
Compare and contrast
Identify bias of author
Text-to-text connections
Text-to-self connections
Text-to-world connections
Sequencing (events, instructions)
Retelling in own words
Find supportive details
Infer
Raise questions from the texts read

Strategies in Working with Text Features
How to use a:
table of contents
index
bibliography
glossary
Interpreting Visual Information
maps, diagrams, labels, photographs,
pictures, graphs, charts, timelines

Utilize Ongoing Monitoring Procedures to Plan for Future Learning

I find it crucial to keep ongoing records of how children are interacting with texts in order to plan their future needs for subsequent guided reading sessions. I record how successfully the children understood the focuses set during the guided reading session. This in turn allows for better future instruction and flexibility in groupings.

Use Follow-Up Activities Cautiously

Any follow-up activity must support the teaching and should only be used if beneficial. Sometimes the best follow-up is to have the children reread the text independently or with a partner, listen to the book on tape for fluency and phrasing, read another book on the same topic, and so on.

Broadening Reading Strategies

When guided reading with informational texts becomes a core of daily practices the results become evident. Children begin to think and process information differently. No longer are they simply looking for plots, character developments, and elements of story. They begin to understand how to process information about the real world. This in turn has a profound impact on their independent reading. They begin to naturally select nonfiction material as part of their independent reading because they see these texts as intriguing and exciting. As Linda Hoyt (2002) so beautifully puts it in her publication

FIGURE 27–2 Ongoing assessment informs instruction and helps teachers to craft meaningful instruction.

Make It Real, "I saw that students' natural curiosities were aroused. They were reading because of their own personal interests."

References

Clay, M. 1993. *An Observation Survey of Early Literacy Achievement.* Portsmouth, NH: Heinemann.

Derewianka, B. 1990. *Exploring How Texts Work.* Rozelle, New South Wales, Australia: Primary English Teaching Association.

Duke, N. K., and V. S. Bennett. 2003. *Reading and Writing Informational Text in the Primary Grades.* New York: Scholastic.

Duke, N. K., and P. D. Pearson. 2002. "Effective Practices for Developing Reading Comprehension." In A. E. Farstup and S. J. Samuels (eds.) *What Research Has to Say About Reading Instruction.* Newark, DE: IRA.

Fountas, I., and G. S. Pinnell. 1996. *Guided Reading: Good First Teaching for all Children.* Portsmouth, NH: Heinemann.

Harvey, S. 1998. *Nonfiction Matters: Reading, Writing, and Research in Grades 3–8.* Portland, ME: Stenhouse Publishers.

Hoyt, L. 2002. *Make It Real: Strategies for Success with Informational Texts.* Portsmouth, NH: Heinemann.

Mooney, M. 1990. *Reading To, With, and By Children.* New York: Richard C. Owen Publishing.

Stead, T. 2002. *Is That a Fact? Teaching Nonfiction Writing K–3.* Portland, ME: Stenhouse Publishers.

Taberski, S. 2000. *On Solid Ground: Strategies for Teaching Reading K–3.* Portsmouth, NH. Heinemann.

KEY QUESTIONS

1. If you examine the balance between fiction and informational texts in your guided reading lessons, how would the percentages look for each?

2. How might a school ensure that assessment procedures include children's abilities to work with nonfiction texts?

3. Apart from those listed in this article, what are some other considerations that need to be taken into account when planning for guided reading with informational texts?

4. How might content studies such as social studies and science be incorporated into guided reading?

5. What considerations should a school take into account when purchasing materials for guided reading?

Observation Rubric for Tracking Children's Comprehension When Working with Nonfiction

Child's name _____

Independent Nonfiction Reading Level _____

Key :
1: Not evident
2: Early understandings
3: Strengthening understandings
4: Strong understandings

Date				
Recognizes the purpose of the piece				
Makes predictions as to the content of the piece being read				
Understands the information presented by the author in the piece				
Synthesizes the information presented				
Understands information presented in visual forms such graphs, diagrams, photographs, and tables				
Infers from the information presented				
Raises questions from information read				
Makes connections				
Understands the difference between fact and opinion				
Uses text features such as table of contents, index, and glossary				
Able to evaluate the validity of the piece				

Contributed by T. Stead © 2005 by Linda Hoyt from *Spotlight on Comprehension*. Portsmouth, NH: Heinemann.

Planning for Nonfiction Guided Reading Lessons

Week of _____ Guided Reading Group Members include:

_____

_____

The approximate guided reading level for this group is _____

The text(s) I will use _____

Challenges in these texts include _____
(look at topic specific vocabulary, text features, etc.)

My teaching points will be _____
(nonfiction text features, nonfiction forms, the comprehension strategy from our
whole class comprehension discussions, and so on)

Observations: Suggestions for Further Instruction:

_____   _____

_____   _____

_____   _____

_____   _____

_____   _____

_____   _____

_____   _____

_____   _____

Nonfiction Guided Reading Record

Student: _____

Year: _____

Date	Title of Nonfiction Selection and Level	Running Record Observations for this text	Running Record Accuracy Score ____ %	Strategies Observed	Use of text features (table of contents, glossary, maps, etc.) (1–5)	Description	Explanation	Instruction	Persuasion	Retell/Nonfiction Narrative	Comprehension Strategy Addressed Record strategy and score understanding (1–5)

Form/genre of nonfiction in this selection

Contributed by T. Stead © 2005 by Linda Hoyt from *Spotlight on Comprehension*. Portsmouth, NH: Heinemann.

Guided Reading

More Than Just Decoding and Retelling

28

JANE RAMBO

MEET THE AUTHOR

JANE RAMBO *is the Director of Reading for schools in Midland, Texas. She is an avid professional reader who is dedicated to lifelong literacy for all.*

FOCUS QUOTE

Remembering/recalling the content of guided reading books or stories in student anthologies should not be the purpose for guided reading lessons. The guided reading text is a vehicle for teaching students reading comprehension strategies that are applicable for future reading.

Before I shift into the independent reading portion of a guided reading lesson, I always ask the following: "What can you do if you get stuck or have a problem with your reading?" Most of the time students will tell me they can sound out a word or look for chunks in words. It is rare for students to tell me they reread a sentence, make inferences, stop and think about the author's message, or use the sentence context to figure out unknown words, etc.

These student responses, or lack of them, show their reading strategies are at the word knowledge level and not at the author's message level (Routman 2002). These responses remind me that I have a lot of work to do if these readers are to become strategic comprehenders! These responses also remind me of the importance of seeing small group instruction, including guided reading, as a time when we can lift up our instruction and elevate the quality of support we offer our students.

FIGURE 28–1 The think aloud gains intensity in a small group format.

FIGURE 28–2 With a strategy focus, the content is learned and foundations are laid for generalizing to other texts.

Therefore, in planning my guided reading lessons, I ask myself: What comprehension strategy can I integrate into this guided reading lesson that will support these learners in many texts? Should I select one that links to our whole class strategy lesson? Have I observed a specific comprehension need in these particular readers that I can address in this small group environment? Which text might I select that will be at their instructional level and give us a solid vehicle for practicing the strategy?

This kind of thinking is what separates guided reading from the reading groups of thirty years ago (Opitz and Ford 2002). Guided reading isn't about getting through a particular selection. It is about teaching a strong, well-crafted strategy lesson and using the book as a vehicle for practicing and applying the strategy. Guided reading is about building a strategic base that will support readers in the wide variety of texts they encounter in the world.

Accurate decoding or simply remembering/recalling the content should not be the purpose for guided reading lessons. Interactions built around recall are only effective when married to conversations about *how* to create a summary and a discussion about how to generate summaries in many different kinds of texts.

As a result of this kind of thinking, my guided reading lessons often look like a small group version of the strategy lessons I teach to the whole class (Hoyt 2002). It is not unusual to see me or a student in the small group doing a think aloud as we work together to bring our strategy use into focus. You would also be likely to see students reading silently and independently during guided reading while I circulate to listen to individuals and to assess their ability to apply the strategy while reading independently.

You may ask: Is that guided reading? You bet! This is guided reading that doesn't just chalk up the number of books covered. It is focused, strategic, and never loses sight of the purpose: To empower these learners for the books they will pick up for the rest of their lives, not just the book they are looking at today.

Guided Reading with a Strategy Focus

THE STEPS:

1. Select a comprehension strategy.

2. Select a book at their instructional level that will be the vehicle for practicing the strategy.

3. Provide a prereading conversation to activate prior knowledge/vocabulary and so on if needed.

4. Present a minilesson with a think aloud or a review of the strategy

5. Have the students read independently while you circulate and assess individuals. Sticky notes are used during this time to mark points where the strategy is applied.

6. Wrap up. The group discusses the selection they read, sharing their insights into the content as well as sharing points where they were able to use the strategy. The group then talks about other texts in which they could use the strategy. Would it work in math, science, the newspaper, another book by this same author, and so on?

Prove It—A Guided Reading Lesson on Inferencing

Inferencing: Using the author's hints (words, ideas, or thoughts) in combination with what you know about the world. This allows us to imply things that may not be directly stated by the author.

1. Select a photograph or illustration from which inferences can be drawn. For example: the picture might be of a child's birthday party where the dog has knocked the birthday cake over while the candles are still burning. Guide inferences about the pictures asking the students to use the stem, "I can infer that _____." Model pointing out the part of the picture that supports your inference.

2. Show the students a chart with a text such as the following:

> Tommy's Mother met him at the front door. His new shirt was covered in mud. He knew from the frown on her face that he would have to stay in his room for the rest of the day. His mom had told him to change his shirt before going to play baseball.

Do a think aloud about this text using the stem ("I can infer . . ."). Explain to the students that you will need to justify your thinking and place a sticky note under the part of the text that supports your inference.

Example: "I can infer that Tommy's mother is upset. I am going to put my sticky note under the word *frown* in the third sentence because that helped me to make my inference."

3. Have the students begin reading silently from their guided reading books with the understanding that they are going to be marking with sticky notes the places where they are able to pause and make an inference. Some students may benefit from jotting their inference right on the sticky note and leaving it in the text next to the support they found for the inference.

FIGURE 28–3 Students use sticky notes to mark the places in the text where they were able to use the strategy.

4. The group may benefit from having the teacher ask one or two inference questions from the portion of text read silently then having the students search for the evidence/support in their books. (Students who miss inferencing questions often don't understand the relationship to the evidence the author gives in the text. Many times students can answer a general question, but going back in the text to find evidence can be a challenge.)

5. Guide the group in discussing inferences. How do we make them? Why is it important to find justification? What other contexts might provide practice?

References

Hoyt, L. 2002. *Make It Real: Strategies for Success with Informational Texts.* Portsmouth, NH: Heinemann.

———. 2000. *Snapshots: Literacy Minilessons Up Close.* Portsmouth, NH: Heinemann.

Opitz, M. F., and M. P. Ford. 2002. *Reaching Readers: Flexible and Innovative Strategies for Guided Reading.* Portsmouth, NH: Heinemann.

Routman, R. 2002. *Reading Essentials: The Specifics You Need to Teach Reading Well.* Portsmouth, NH: Heinemann.

KEY QUESTIONS

1. What are the advantages to elevating guided reading to a strategy lesson?

2. What benefits would students find if every guided lesson closed with a conversation about applying the strategy in other contexts?

3. If you were to select core comprehension strategies that should be integrated into guided reading, which ones would be first on your list?

4. How might we ensure that every comprehension strategy is practiced and supported in fiction as well as nonfiction selections?

Guided Reading with a Strategy Focus:
A Template for Success

1. Comprehension Strategy Focus: _____

   _____

   _____

2. Focus Text(s) at instructional level for this group_____

   _____

   _____

3. Prereading conversation needs to include: (concepts/core vocabulary)_____

   _____

   _____

4. The strategy minilesson (focus and resources needed) _____

   _____

   Key point for think aloud: _____

   _____

5. Independent reading/use of strategy: _____

   _____

6. Wrap-Up/discussion/debriefing of strategy use _____

   _____

Guided Reading Strategy Log

Reader _____

Notice as your teacher presents strategies in your guided reading lessons. Some of these will link up to the work you do with the whole class. Sometimes you will learn a new strategy in your guided reading lesson. This log will give you a way to save your thinking.

Date	Strategy Focus	What did you learn?	How did the strategy work for you today?	Where else can you use it?

Reading Response Sheet

Focus on inferences. Jot your thoughts as you read during independent reading.

Date _____ Book Title _____

Inferences I made while reading.   My inference was based on page _____, paragraph #_____, life experience, other text, or ?

1._____   _____

2._____   _____

3._____   _____

4._____   _____

Date _____ Book Title _____

Inferences I made while reading.   My inference was based on page _____, paragraph #_____, life experience, other text, or ?

1._____   _____

2._____   _____

3._____   _____

4._____   _____

Date _____ Book Title _____

Inferences I made while reading.   My inference was based on page _____, paragraph #_____, life experience, other text, or ?

1._____   _____

2._____   _____

3._____   _____

4._____   _____

From Doubt to Celebration

Strategy Instruction in Independent Reading

29

CAROL UPDEGRAFF

MEET THE AUTHOR

CAROL UPDEGRAFF *has been in education for 31 years. She has taught for 29 of those years at Hopland Elementary in the northern California wine country. Carol has taught the full range of primary grades and is currently teaching in a multiage/multigrade first, second, and third classroom.*

FOCUS QUOTE

In the process the students have become interested in books other students have read, styles of authors and illustrators, and have improved their ability to express themselves to others.

Everyone provides time for independent reading. I did provide some reading but then I heard a presentation about changing the structure of my independent reading so that it opened with a comprehension-based minilesson and closed with a sharing circle focused on the same strategy (Hoyt 2000; Taberski 2000). I thought, "Ya. Sure." I could hardly get my students to sit still for the quiet reading time; how was I going to add all of that?

Getting Past the Doubt

When I began to implement this change, I did so with much doubt and skepticism. I had heard how effective the sharing circle could be for the development of reading strategies, but I wasn't sure that it could still work with my highly diverse group of first, second, and third graders. But, I plunged on knowing that this might sound great in theory, but wasn't likely to be so in reality. Boy was I wrong! My students loved it and it worked beautifully.

First Steps

I started by first chatting with Linda Hoyt, who was doing a residency in our school. I felt strongly that I had to focus first on keeping my young readers on track during independent reading time. Linda suggested that I start really simply by modeling how to use sticky notes to mark my favorite parts of a book during read aloud time. Then I told the students that during independent reading, they would have a chance to do the same thing in their independent reading books. Linda then suggested that I briefly model the strategy again in a minilesson just before we started independent reading time.

With my doubts in hand, I followed her suggestions and modeled the strategy twice. As I passed out the stickies, my fingers were crossed in hopes that the adhesive strips didn't turn into missiles rather than a support to deeper thinking. Armed with a sense of purpose and a clear understanding of the task, my students went to work. They read, marked favorite places in their books, and read some more. They were attentive, on task, and really focused.

At the end of the independent reading time, I called them together in a circle and invited them to go "knee-to-knee" with a partner to share their favorite points in their books. It was magical. They really cared about each other's ideas. They got excited about the books they saw their partners reading. They loved the chance to talk one-on-one about their reading. They really looked at each other and at their books.

The last step is to close with a class discussion about the strategy. The question was: *How did marking your favorite points help you as a reader? How did this strategy work for you today?*

FIGURE 29–1 At first they just marked favorite parts with sticky note strips. As time went on, they began determining importance and selecting their #1 favorite part and writing a full sticky note about why it was their favorite.

FIGURE 29–2 Students take their partner sharing very seriously. They are active listeners as they discuss the books they read and the strategies they used.

There's No Stopping Now

I have been using this format for independent reading for about six months now and I am so impressed with my students. If I forget to provide a comprehension minilesson or neglect to remind them about the strategy focus for the day, they remind me! Common questions from my students are now: "Are we meeting today? What are we to look for? Do you want us to use stickies?"

Higher Levels of Achievement

The information that my students now give about their books and schemas is amazing. They have covered plot development, character development, character traits, summaries, favorite parts, and genre characteristics to name just a few. In the process, the students have become interested in books other students have read, styles of authors and illustrators, and have improved their ability to express themselves to others.

Stretching Myself and My Students

This process has kept me on my toes with planning and learning how to stretch my students and encourage good reading practices. Modeling for my students, guided practice, independent practice, and time to reflect are all part of our class routine for independent reading. This is a format I will be continually improving upon as the students and I become more adept at it.

Armed with Tools for Comprehension

My students now enter independent reading armed with tools for comprehension. They have a clear understanding that they will get to talk to a part-

FIGURE 29–3 We close each circle with a discussion of the strategy and give a few students the opportunity to stand up and share with the class.

ner at the end of the reading time to share their observations and wonderings about their books. They also know that we will share as a class and talk about the strategy of the day and how it helped us to grow as readers.

Modifications I Have Tried

• At the end of the independent time, the students fill out their reading log for one of their books, and then move to the circle area on the rug, bringing their book with them. A further modification might include having them make a note about the strategy they used and how it worked for them.

• To heighten their sense of responsibility for the final class sharing, I have a cup with everyone's name written on a popsicle stick. Each time I draw a stick, the student stands up, illustrates the strategy we have been learning, and tells a bit about their book. I draw at least four students, and sometimes six. My class has gone from having fingers crossed hoping to not being chosen, to begging for me to call on more so they can talk about the strategy in front of the class.

Making the Learning Visible

We have added a strategy chart to our classroom. Now as we add strategies to our repertoire, we list them on the chart and make a conscious effort to continuously review our good reader strategies. The chart is a reference for us as we enter reading challenges in science, social studies, guided reading, and so on. We use it as our guide and a reminder of the many tools we have to create meaning while we read.

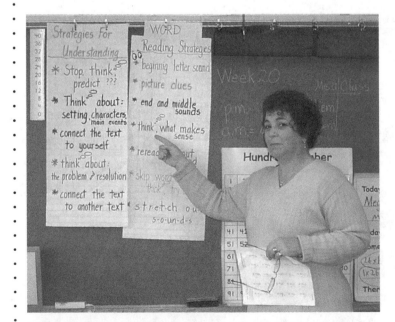

FIGURE 29–4 A strategy chart is a strong visual reminder that keeps Carol and her students focused on the important comprehension strategies they are applying in all the texts they read.

Comprehension Strategy Instruction in Independent Reading: The Steps:

1. Introduce a strategy during read aloud or shared reading.

2. Briefly reteach/remind students of the strategy in a minilesson just before independent reading.

3. Be sure they understand that they are expected to apply the strategy while reading independently, then talk about it at the end of the session.

4. Read.

5. Bring the class together so they are knee-to-knee and eye-to-eye with a partner with the goal of sharing their observations about the strategy and what they gained from the book.

6. Reflect as a class about the strategy and consider other contexts and ways in which it might be used.

Adapted from Hoyt, Linda. 2000. *Snapshots: Literacy Minilessons Up Close.* Portsmouth, NH: Heinemann.

References

Hoyt, L. 2000. *Snapshots: Literacy Minilessons Up Close.* Portsmouth, NH: Heinemann.

Taberski, S. 2000. *On Solid Ground: Strategies for Teaching Reading K–3.* Portsmouth, NH: Heinemann.

KEY QUESTIONS

1. What comprehension strategies do you believe are most important for children to apply independently with books of their own choosing?

2. Are you using a Strategy Chart to keep the strategy learning visible? If so, what strategies do you have on it?

3. Carol's students really gained from the knee-to-knee conversations with a partner. How might this kind of interaction be woven across the day? Would it fit into read aloud, shared reading, science, math, etc.? How can you ensure that the conversations include a focus on the strategy?

4. Are there other ways in which comprehension can be solidified in independent reading?

Personal Reading Strategy Log

Reader_____

Strategy I Used: Date   Reflection: How well did it work? Have you used it in more than one book? Does it seem to work best with one kind of text?

_____   _____   _____

_____   _____   _____

_____   _____   _____

_____   _____   _____

_____   _____   _____

_____   _____   _____

_____   _____   _____

_____   _____   _____

_____   _____   _____

_____   _____   _____

_____   _____   _____

Reading Log for Conferencing During Independent Reading

Reader_____ Teacher/Listener_____

Look for evidence of strategy use during one-to-one conferences. List the date when you observe the strategy in use and note if it is observed in a fiction or informational text.

	Date Observed			Fiction/Info	
Uses picture clues					
Predicts					
Reads on past unknown words					
Rereads to cross-check					
Self-corrects					
Makes meaningful substitutions					
Breaks words into chunks					
Adjusts reading rate to match text					
Can skim/scan					
Identifies favorite/important parts of text					
Finds key words/ideas					
Questions the text					
Makes inferences					
Makes connections					
Determines importance					
Creates visual images					
Identifies story elements:					
Setting					
Characters					
Events					
Main Idea					
Problem/Solution					
Theme					

Reading Partnerships
Grasping Deeper Layers of Meaning

30

STACI MONREAL AND
JENNIFER WHITE

The only way we could have done this work was to live alongside the children and teachers. It was from watching them in action that our path became clear.

MEET THE AUTHORS

STACI MONREAL *has spent her career teaching and learning about reading and writing, as a teacher, as Director of Literacy, and currently as principal at Central Elementary. She works with teachers in an inner-city school and together they are striving to create a school where all students achieve at high levels.*

JENNIFER WHITE *has many years of teaching experience in elementary classrooms. She has worked as the Assistant Director of Literacy for San Diego City Schools and is currently the principal of Webster Elementary in San Diego City Schools.*

FOCUS QUOTE

The partnerships have supported students' development of academic language, and most importantly, their identities as readers. One of the greatest benefits has been watching our children's love of reading emerge and spill over into their everyday life.

W̶e eavesdropped on Melissa and Ablo while they were analyzing and discussing a "Junie B. Jones" book. Listen to what they said:

Ablo: Lucille is acting like she is all "that." This part right here where she said, "Have you ever noticed my satiny-smooth skin?"

Melissa: Yah, she is so about herself.

FIGURE 30–1 Melissa and Ablo deep in discussion.

Can you hear how annoyed Melissa and Ablo are at Lucille? By talking to each other about this character, these two children better understand her.

In our classroom, reading partnerships emerged as a result of our noticing minimal engagement while children were reading independently. At first glance, it was exciting to see what appeared to be a class full of readers. But as we lingered longer and studied each of the readers, a disturbing reality surfaced. We had lots of questions about what we were seeing. But the big question that lingered was: Why are our children having such great conversations and reacting with such wild enthusiasm to text read aloud to them, but silently and robotically plowing through the books they were reading on their own? So, we gathered together a team of teachers to figure out why this was happening so we could take action. It didn't take long to realize that all of our readers (K–6) were new readers and needed greater levels of support to be able to independently have rich conversations between themselves about the text they were reading on their own. Our first step was to build from the rich conversations we were hearing in read aloud and shared reading. We asked ourselves, what if children had a partner to keep them company and help them think as they made meaning in the text they were reading on their own?

A Closer Look At What Our Children Were Doing

During independent reading children were passive, they lacked any emotional response to the books they were reading. Many were reading books that were much too difficult for them and didn't even know it. Children just picked books because they were at their level not because the book was engaging. When children talked about books it was limited to retells that sounded robotic.

We noticed that children appeared to be doing one of the following during independent reading:

1. Pretending to read
2. Decoding the words without thinking about the meaning
3. Reading at the surface level
4. Flipping through the pages
5. "Plowing" through one book after another, stacking them in piles (primary grades)
6. Abandoning books (a new chapter book each day)

Getting Started—Awakening the Thinking Reader

We launched our study of reading partnerships as one vehicle to support children to become independent readers who choose to read, read with purpose, and think critically. To do this well would require very focused deliberate modeling, demonstration, and coaching. Teachers were enthusiastic to begin this work and were full of questions:

Forming Reading Partnerships

How do we put partners together (reading level, interest, etc.)?
What if I don't have an even number of children?

Gathering and Selecting Books

Don't we need two of each book?
Do the children select their own books?

Teaching the Reader and the Partnership

What do I teach them?
What do they talk about?
Do I give them a list of questions?
How many pages do they read before they talk?

FIGURE 30–2 Mark and Judith in Patricia Craig's sixth grade class.

What if they don't talk?

Do they read out loud or silently?

ASSESSING THE READER AND THE PARTNERSHIP

How do we confer in partnerships?

Forming Reading Partnerships

We discovered that there is a lot to consider when forming reading partnerships. Through trial and error, teachers have learned that they have greater success when they carefully match up the readers. Jesse Wills, a third grade teacher, says when she forms partnerships she generally thinks about reading level, interests, and conversational skills. Sometimes she will partner children who are at different levels. Jessie encourages the stronger reader to serve as a coach. The stronger reader plays this role for a short period of time and then moves back to a partnership that will push their own reading. She has also noticed that placing children in triads has been highly successful for children who need additional language support.

Gathering and Selecting Books

Selecting books   When we first started partnership reading, teachers found that the partnership got off to a better start when they were supported with book selection. Over time teachers modeled book selection conversations and coached partnerships toward independently selecting their own books.

How many books?   Initially, teachers thought readers would each need to have their own book. In upper grades if children are reading longer novels, this is generally true. However, we quickly discovered that children settle in closer to each other and often share the reading, coaching each other along the way, when they shared the same book. We also noticed children in primary classrooms snuggled in next to each other, pointing to pictures and text, and having rich conversations. We have observed upper-grade children having the same kind of success when sharing poetry and short stories.

Teaching the Reader and the Partnership

Explicit teaching is key to developing partnerships that cultivate readers who think and talk with understanding and passion around what they have read. The table below shows how teachers organize for partnership reading to ensure this time is used to teach, practice, assess, and revise.

The Teaching of Partnership Reading

Teaching Lessons on How to Expand Understanding:	Teacher models reading strategies and/or how partnerships work together (Read aloud/shared reading).
Practice with Support:	Partnerships have the opportunity to practice thinking and talking about the reading the whole class has done with the teacher.
On Their Own:	Partners set goals for reading and discussing their book, and begin reading together.
Observing Assessing, Coaching, and Teaching:	Teacher observes, confers, and coaches with partners and may gather the class for a moment during reading partnership time to reinforce or teach what children need.
Self-Evaluation:	Partners use partnership rubric to self-evaluate the strength of their reading partnership.
Feedback and Teaching:	Class gathers back together for feedback and teaching based on teachers observations.

Lessons to Expand Understanding

Initially teachers asked us, "What are the lessons we need to teach to develop children who can think and converse at deep levels?" The answer was, "We don't know. But we believe if you watch your children closely, they will tell you." And they did. We went into classrooms with teams of teachers and studied this question while watching and listening closely to children as they were reading in partnerships. We constructed a list of lessons children needed based on what they already did as readers and partners.

The following lists include lessons to support deeper thinking around reading and how to make partnerships more effective. Each list begins with a sample lesson followed by a list of possible lessons your children may need:

Lessons to Support Deeper Thinking

Sample Lesson: (Lili Sadeghian, Grade 4)

Lili had noticed that her children were making judgments about characters that weren't grounded and supported by evidence in the text. This lesson brings children back to focusing on character analysis and using evidence from the text to draw conclusions about the characters. During the lessons Lili asks children to identify ways to analyze characters that will assist them in better understanding the characters. She then reminds them that their analysis needs to be supported with evidence from the text.

Teacher: As readers we need to take a deeper look into a character in order to better understand the story and draw conclusions about the characters. Let's discuss ways we can look closely at our characters and what we can pay attention to when we are reading. Take a minute and talk to your partner and get ready to discuss this.

(Children talk. The teacher listens in to gauge the level of understanding.)

Teacher: Let's talk about ways we can look closely at our characters and what we can pay attention to when we are reading.

CLASS RESPONSES:

> We can look at the character's actions
>
> We can look at how the characters treat others
>
> We can look at what the characters say
>
> We can look at how characters react to things
>
> We can look at how characters interact with the world
>
> We can pay attention to how the author describes the character

Teacher: Today, when you read in your partnerships, find time to look closely at the characters in your book and analyze the characters. Use some of your classmates' suggestions as a way of looking closely at the characters. Use evidence from the text to support your analysis. Partners, make sure that you are holding each other accountable to provide evidence. Ask, "What makes you think that? Where in the text did you find that? How did you draw that conclusion?"

O.K. readers, let's get going.

Possible Lessons

Deepening the Reading and the Conversation

- Studying a character (If you were in his/her shoes; character's attitude and behavior toward others; personality)
- Forming opinions about what we read
- How reading several books around a topic or interest leads to greater understanding
- Rereading when the conversation isn't going so well
- Questions to help you get the conversation going
- Coaching your partner when they are stuck
- Keeping track of thoughts over time
- Evaluating the quality of our conversations (see Talk Rubric, Figure 30–4)

Ways of Engaging with a Reading Partner

- What it looks and feels like to really be into your reading
- Things that happened in your book that surprised and amazed you that you hadn't counted on happening
- What to say when your partner begins retelling what you both just read
- How to use evidence in the text to support what is being said

Lessons to Support More Effective Partnerships

These lessons are often live within the lessons listed above or are taught during the wrap-up of partnership reading.

Sample Lesson: (Alicia Crockett, Grade 2)

During a lesson that focused on asking each other how and why questions in nonfiction text, she inserted the following teaching because her kids needed this support:

Teacher: I have been noticing that we need to work on getting right to our reading because we don't have a moment to waste. Justin and I are going to start our partner reading. Watch what we do and give us some ideas on how to solve our problems.

(Teacher and student modeling)

Teacher: I want to read first.

Student: No. I'm going to read first.

Teacher: You read first last time.

Student: Did not.

Teacher: (Groans and pouts)

Alicia: (Asks the class) What is the problem? What can we do about this? Give us some ideas to solve our problem:

Class Responses:

> You can take turns. Justin can read first today and you can read first
>   tomorrow
> Do rock paper scissors
> Who cares who goes first, you'll get a turn to read
> Whoever picked the book goes second
> Offer for them to go first. Just say you can go first

Now you are going off to do your thinking work, but if you're having trouble getting started, try out one of these suggestions.

Possible Lessons

- How do we select a book?
- How to sit when we read (knee-to-knee, side by side, etc.)
- How to negotiate and set reading goals?
- How do we negotiate and select a reading focus?
- How we read the book together (aloud, in our head)?
- How often will we stop and talk?
- What we do when our partner isn't talking?
- Using stickies and jotting quick notes to prepare us for our talk.
- What do we do when the book we are reading isn't working for us?
- What we do when our partner is not here

Charting Along the Way—Co-constructing Charts to Support Independence

To support the reading work when children are on their own, teachers often engage children in problem solving to promote ownership and independence. During lessons, teachers and children chart specific information for partners to access while working together.

Observing, Assessing, Coaching, and Teaching

In the beginning, teachers were very concerned about how they would be able to confer with each of their readers if they reduced independent reading time to allow for partnership reading time. They quickly discovered that eavesdropping on partnership conversations gave them a window into the reading work without having to interrupt the readers. Teachers take notes

FIGURE 30–3a, b A class-created chart is an easy reference for independent reading.

on reading behaviors and make the following decisions about what they want to do:

- Leave them alone.
- Coach the readers.
- Coach the partnership.
- Reread with the partners and participate in the conversation.
- Pull an individual aside for a one-to-one conference.

Eavesdropping and conferring help teachers construct the lessons to come. Lili eavesdrops and listens to the children's conversation. At times she will casually enter into the conversation and coach in order to lift the children's thinking by asking a question, making a suggestion, or providing explicit feedback about what she is noticing in their work.

Alicia Crockett, a grade 2 teacher, will sometimes gather kids around a partnership to study what the partnership does well or use the other children to help coach the partnership. This is only done when she knows a large number of children will benefit from this quick meeting.

Self-Evaluation

The children work with the teacher to build a tool such as a rubric to measure the quality of the children's reading and thinking. The rubric evolves

Talk Rubric

pretty bad

1 — not saying very much
— not listening to your partner
— no real talk
— talking off topic - not much talk about the book

so-so okay

2 — just talking about a favorite part or 1 thing only in the book
— talking a little more
— on topic
— retells

pretty good

3 — talk about what the book reminds you of
— more of a conversation (talking back and forth to each other)
— tell what you think about the book
— add on to what your partner says
— have reactions to the book - how the book makes you feel

great

4 — real conversations - lots of talk
— tell your opinions - agree/disagree
— Questioning - Wondering why
— Practicing the strategy we are working on
— thinking about characters action - telling what you would do and how the characters are feeling
— Showing Evidence in the book

Rubric for Partner Reading/Talking

Great Day for Partner Reading/Talking ☺
— Focus on our reading & staying focused
— Having a deep "juicy" Conversation
— Helping my partner ✦ Support answers with evidence from book
— Talking/Discussing only the book

So-So Day for Partner Reading/Talking ☹
— Read & stay focused most of the time
— Discussed the book only about ½ the time
— Conversation wasn't very juicy

Oops! We had a bad Day for Partner Talk/Read ☹
— Playing around, not focused, "pretending" to read
— Talking/disrupting others, wasted "precious" reading time
— Not helping partner

FIGURE 30–4a, b Class-generated rubrics for evaluating partner talk.

and is used throughout the school year to shape the reading and thinking work.

Feedback and Teaching Following Partnership Reading

Following the partnership reading, children gather back together to learn about their learning. It is a time when the children's thinking is lifted through explicit examples of observed reading and thinking work.

Organizing Instruction to Get to Deeper Understanding

Our initial theory about why children were not thinking deeply and critically about text was that instruction was not scaffolded enough for children to feel what it was like to think off their own reading. Going from great conversations in read aloud and shared reading appeared to be too big a step to independent reading. Jill Bryson, a grade 2 teacher, came up with the following schedule. It takes children from the most supportive reading and talk experiences and gradually releases the levels of support to independence. Although we agree there will always be a place for reading in socially organized ways, our goal is to coach for independence. Jill's schedule is titled, "For the Moment" because she will gradually adjust her schedule based on what her children need for their learning.

Jill Bryson's Schedule "for the Moment"

READ ALOUD

- Teacher models thinking (reading strategy)
- Partnerships think and talk off the teacher's reading

SHARED READING

- Model reading strategies and/or how partnerships work together
- Partnerships think and talk off the reading done with the teacher
- Partnerships practice and evaluate the quality of their talk

PARTNERSHIP READING

- Partners set goals for reading and begin reading
- Teacher observes and coaches the reading
- Partners use partnership rubric to self-evaluate the strength of their partnership
- Class gathers back together for feedback and teaching

INDEPENDENT READING/SMALL GROUP

- Minilesson—model/Try-on/Practice reading strategies for independent reading (thinking while reading—keeping the conversation going while reading on their own)

Simultaneously children engage in one of the following:

- Children read independently
- Teacher meets in small groups (read aloud, guided reading, shared reading, etc.)
- Children work independently on literacy related work based on their need

Stages of Development: Developing Active Readers

By watching children in our rooms, we began to see patterns emerge. Looking closely at how well and to what degree children were developing as active readers and critical thinkers, we noticed differences in the level of emotional connection to what they read, critical thinking, interaction between reading partners, and level of responsibility and ownership in shaping reading plans. The stages below describe what we discovered. Our teachers use these stages to guide their work and coach their children in their reading partnership work.

Developing Active Readers

Stages	Emotional Engagement	Reading Work	Talk Behaviors	Reading Plans
4	• React: Giggle, gasp, argue, criticize, defend, change their mind	• Children do not rely on a set of questions to guide their discussions—Children have internalized how to converse about what they read • Children think critically • Speculate • Theorize • Arrive at big ideas, themes • Understanding is shaped and challenged over the course of the conversation	• Thinking is challenged and researched in text • Children listen to one another and share their thinking • Ideas are considered, challenged, and grown	• Read and talk across authors, topics, genres • Children read widely and deeply • Children organize their reading plans with intentions beyond that of the teacher
3	• Responsive: Notice and respond to humor, tragedy, changes to what they read	• Talk beyond text and confirm ideas using text • Children discuss beyond the text and confirm ideas using text	• Responses are connected • Readers look at each other and listen to each other	• Children keep track of ideas for next day and across texts • Partners stop to talk when needed
2	• Developing: Moments of interest	• Children retell only (e.g., "and then, and then, and then . . .")	• Partners take turns talking and listen to each other	• Children set goals based on text
1	• Passive: Little reaction, going through the motions	• Children respond to a set of pre-identified questions that are posted/charted • When questions have been asked and answered, reading work flounders	• Partners follow a turn taking pattern and • Children listen to self only	• Teacher sets plans for the children

Considerations for English Learners

We are beginning to see significant language progress for English language learners (ELL's). The partnership structure requires ELL's to produce more language. When ELL's are shaky on understanding the reading, they can lean on their partner to untangle and enhance the meaning. Many teachers are experimenting with having children write on their own about questions, ideas, and themes in their reading to prepare for partnership talk. This allows for the ELL to prepare and rehearse their language before they use it.

The Benefits We Have Discovered

As our study continues to unfold we are learning how the teaching of conversations in reading partnerships leads children to fully engage in rich reading lives. We have noticed that our readers now use conversations to gain a deeper understanding of the texts they read and how they now coach one another to analyze, evaluate, and synthesize what they read.

The partnerships have supported students' development of academic language, and most importantly, their identities as readers. One of the greatest benefits has been watching our children's love of reading emerge and spill over into their everyday life. We now see children:

- Finding deeper layers of meaning
- Coaching each other as readers
- Using and practicing academic language
- Maintaining a reading identity
- Joyfully reading

Here are two readers who are fully engaged in a conversation about what they are reading. They are thinking critically about the characters and show us that they are developing a discerning stance through their relationship with each other and the book.

Sample Lesson: (Michael Knauf, Grade 6)
Two girls discussing *Maniac Magee*.

Shatiya: She is stereotyping him because she does not know anything about him.

Britany: Yeah, she doesn't even know him.

Shatiya: I can look at you all day long without stereotyping you.

Britany: Yeah, but Amanda is used to that.

Shatiya: Yeah, but the only reason why she is used to that is she's in the east end and she is used to the attitude and all that because they are split-up. There are no white people there.

Britany: They have to stay on their side and she has to stay on her side and they have a big street between them. I think Maniac Magee will teach her to not judge a book by its cover. Don't judge him by his cover. To judge him because what you see on the outside.

Shatiya: You have to put yourself in the character's shoes and understand what they are going through.

Britany: Yeah, if you were brought up like that you would have an attitude.

Shatiya: Okay let's read from here to . . .

If the children are not learning to read, think, and talk deeply, it is because we have not taught them how!

References

Angelillo, Janet. 2003. *Writing About Reading: From Book Talk to Literary Essays, Grades 3–8*. Portsmouth, NH: Heinemann.

Calkins, Lucy McCormick. 2001. *The Art of Teaching Reading*. New York: Addison Wesley.

Cole, Ardith Davis. 2003. *Knee To Knee, Eye To Eye: Circling In On Comprehension*. Portsmouth, NH: Heinemann.

KEY QUESTIONS

1. What are your readers doing when they read on their own? Are they really reading? Do they react while reading (smile, laugh, frown)?

2. How do your readers authentically communicate about what they have read? Do they typically retell what they have read or do they talk about the big ideas, what it means, and how it makes them think and feel?

3. How are you currently teaching children to critically think about what they read? Are you satisfied with the results?

4. What changes might you make in your teaching to explicitly teach children to critically think and authentically communicate about what they read?

5. How much language are your children producing each day? Study one English learner and keep track of total minutes of language production. Is it enough time?

Partnership Observations

Partners: _____

Date	Book Being Read and Discussed	Partners are actively listening	Both partners take responsibility for talk	Partners support/assist each other	Conversations include:								
					Looking closely at characcters	Forming opinions	Asking questions	Use of evidence from text	Connections(T-T,T-W,T-S)				

Part Six

....

Tackling Texts (and Tests) Across the Curriculum

The Power of Rereading Informational Texts

31

LINDA HOYT

MEET THE AUTHOR

LINDA HOYT *has spent most of her teaching career working with students in Title 1 schools. She believes that these learners need more, not less, of what makes learning exciting. She believes that these learners benefit greatly from a comprehension-rich environment in which they can learn about the world while they learn to read.*

FOCUS QUOTE

I believe that rereading informational text is a survival skill. Informational texts challenge us with specialized vocabulary, densely packed concepts, and sentences that often lack elaboration and imagery. We have to work harder in informational texts to wrestle with the information load. Rereading can allow us to uncover layers of meaning gradually and with increasing sensitivity to the content.

M y husband and I purchased a dresser recently. We had been impressed by the very reasonable price and quickly told the salesperson we were ready to buy. After completing our transaction, we pulled around to the back of the building where we found the loading dock supervisor waiting for us with a cardboard box, a nice *flat* cardboard box. We had just purchased an "unassembled" product.

Rereading to Understand

Needless to say, that afternoon we read, we reread, and we reread again. The directions became a lifeline as we looked at what appeared to be five thousand screws and small metal parts plus a phenomenal array of wooden pieces. There were directions with pictures and labels and nicely numbered steps. The manufacturer provided us with everything we needed except a screwdriver. It should have been easy. The dresser took five hours to transition from a dizzying array of pieces to a functional piece of furniture with drawers. Rereading saved the day.

Rereading to Wonder, to Question, and to Think

Last night, we went out to dinner. The menu was delivered and . . . here I go . . . I read it, reread it, and was still rereading when the waitress arrived to take our order. I asked for "a minute more" and, guess what, I read it again! As I continued to reread, I was noticing ingredients that hadn't caught my eye on the first or even the second pass. My rereadings helped me notice side dishes and stimulated internal questions about fat, calories, carbs, substitutions I might request, and so on. I didn't count the times I reread the menu . . . but I know it was a lot. Did I have to reread? No. Did I reread because I didn't understand? No. I reread because I wanted to and because it was part of the fun of making a selection.

Good Readers Reread for Many Purposes

Good readers reread all the time. They reread when something strikes them as humorous, when they are puzzled, and when they want to think more deeply. They reread when they are composing a piece of text, when they want to learn, and when they are trying to understand. Regie Routman reminds us in *Reading Essentials* (2002) that rereading may be one of the most powerful strategies we can teach our students.

Rereading in Informational Sources

I believe that rereading informational text is a survival skill. Informational texts challenge us with specialized vocabulary, densely packed concepts, and sentences that often lack elaboration and imagery. We have to work harder in informational texts to wrestle with the information load and to hold onto the most important points (Hoyt 2003).

Rereading: Not Just When Meaning Breaks Down

I used to tell readers that they need to reread when they realize that a passage doesn't make sense. I coached them to use rereading as a repair or a fix-up strategy. I realize now that while this is an important support to readers, my coaching about rereading gave learners the idea that you only reread when things didn't make sense!

I have learned to see rereading with new eyes, to pay better attention to my own behavior as a reader, and to coach learners to use rereading in a plethora of ways. I want the readers I work with to understand that rereading is a tool which can be used with all the texts in our lives and used for a wide range of purposes.

Researching Rereading

To help learners see rereading with new eyes, I ask them to focus on the strategy consciously for a day or so. They are challenged to really notice when they read something, especially an informational text, a second or a third time and to be aware of the benefits that they find in rereading. We talk about our observations and create a chart listing reasons to reread and the kinds of texts that we might expect to reread.

Teaching Strategies to Support Rereading

My focus on rereading has caused me to rethink instructional routines that I have taught over the years and to wonder what affect rereading might have on students' comprehension if we added rereading to those familiar routines.

Read, Cover, Remember, Retell

I have been teaching this strategy for years, encouraging students to read short sections of a text, cover it with their hand, and consciously think about the content before sharing a retell of the segment with their partner.

FIGURE 31–1 Second graders use Read, Cover, Remember, Retell to enhance understanding and support summarizing.

Now, I also teach students to Read, Cover, Remember, *Reread!* As partners engage with this process, they follow the steps listed above with this variation: After pausing to think and remember, I challenge learners to, "Reread to see what else you notice."

I encourage them to wonder:

- Did you notice an important fact that hadn't caught your attention on the first read?
- Did you notice something about the craft of the author?
- Did rereading cause you to think of a question you would like to ask?
- Was one rereading enough or would you like to do it again to help yourself think more deeply?

The students then tell about changes in their thinking that occurred as a result of rereading. This conscious reflection on rereading as a tool for deepening meaning empowers readers to think more deeply, and they do seem to remember more.

References

Hoyt, L. 2002. *Make It Real: Strategies for Success with Informational Texts.* Portsmouth, NH: Heinemann.

———. 1999. *Revisit, Reflect, Retell: Strategies for Improving Reading Comprehension.* Portsmouth, NH: Heinemann.

Routman, R. 2002. *Reading Essentials: The Specifics You Need to Teach Reading Well.* Portsmouth, NH: Heinemann.

KEY QUESTIONS

1. Can you think of something you reread recently or a movie you watched a second time? What did you notice on the second time through? What were your purposes in watching or reading again?

2. How might we help learners to broaden their understanding of rereading so they don't think rereading only happens when they realize that they have lost comprehension?

3. How might rereading fit into read alouds, guided reading, content reading, and so on?

Rereading for Information

Reader_____ Date _____

Your job is to notice times when you reread and to think about why you are re-reading a passage. Did you like it so much you wanted to enjoy it again? Were you trying to think about the writing style of the author? Were you thinking about the meaning or trying to remember the content? Keep a record of your thinking.

● I reread _____ because _____.

While I was rereading, I noticed _____

_____

● I reread _____ because _____.

While I was rereading, I noticed _____

_____

● I reread _____ because _____.

While I was rereading, I noticed _____

_____

● I reread _____ because _____.

While I was rereading, I noticed _____

_____

Meet with a partner and share what you learned about rereading. Be sure to tell how you think rereading helped you as a reader.

Bookmarks

Cut these out and use with your books.

Read

Cover

Remember

Retell

Read

Cover

Remember

REREAD!

(Think about *why* you are rereading)

A Recipe for Success

32

Comprehension Strategies Across the Curriculum

JODI SNYDER

MEET THE AUTHOR

JODI SNYDER *has a substantial background in teaching primary grades as well as a special love of supporting children with special needs in the inner city. She is currently facilitating professional development as a literacy coach through Cornerstone, a Nationwide Literacy Initiative that provides embedded staff development for teachers of kindergarten through grade 3.*

FOCUS QUOTE

Assessment needs to be built into every lesson, not just based on a final exam or project.

Comprehension needs to be taught all day long, not just during reading and writing time. While students read in any of the content areas they apply comprehension strategies. They activate and build schema, determine importance, question, and synthesize information. To ensure this happens, it is important to build a classroom climate of inquiry and rigor where students readily apply these critical comprehension strategies across the curriculum.

Ingredient 1: Establish a Classroom Climate of Inquiry

When inquiry is encouraged, students will rigorously seek out answers to their questions. Students are more apt to investigate and challenge their thinking when they feel they can freely take risks. In a classroom of inquiry, questions are valued, recorded, and extended. The questions of the learners become the focus of discourse and of learning.

Ingredient 2: Fill the Classroom with Books, Books, and More Books

Informational books, not just fiction. Nonfiction literature needs to be at a wide range of levels so that students can read at their independent reading level and actively apply comprehension strategies. These selections must have high quality photos and illustrations, represent the full range of informational text structures, and cover topics that will pique learner interest. They must be organized in a way that makes them accessible to the learners.

Ingredient 3: Read Aloud from Nonfiction

Quality nonfiction texts should be read aloud, with the teacher explicitly modeling comprehension strategies as in fiction selections. Read alouds of nonfiction texts can also emphasize nonfiction text structures and features such as the table of contents, bold print, headings, and captions.

Ingredient 4: Time

Students need ample time to make meaning of the informational texts they are reading. Providing adequate time to read informational texts allows students to apply comprehension strategies outside of the literacy block and helps solidify their content learning. Students may work independently, with a partner, or as part of a small group in order to facilitate their learning.

Ingredient 5: Conversation

We value our conversations about text during fiction reading. We must also value literate conversations during informational reading. When learners take time to consciously analyze a text for author's craft, development of the topic, relationships to other topics and texts, and so on, they deepen content knowledge while building a richer understanding of how informational text works.

Conversations surrounding informational texts can also be directed to the comprehension strategies learners employ. With conscious focus on strategy use, learners gain critical insights into their own behaviors and the strategies that best help them understand their reading. Rich conversations extend thinking, explore diverse understandings, and increase strategic comprehension.

Ingredient 5: Assessment

Assessment needs to be built into every lesson, not just based on a final exam or project. To support comprehension strategy development, each lesson needs to be designed to scaffold students' learning while analyzing how

FIGURE 32–1 Personal conferences provide important insights into learner understanding. One-to-one conferences are important with nonfiction reading as well as with fiction reading.

JAGUARS

JAGUARS ARE IN THE CAT FAMILY

JAGUARS HAVE A SPOTTED BLACK COAT

JAGUARS' WHISKERS HELP THEM GO THROUGH THICK GRASSES

JAGUARS TAKE NAPS IN TREES

JAGUARS' SHARP CLAWS HELP THEM CLIMB UP TREES

JAGUARS EAT MEAT

JAGUARS' BIG JAWS HELP THEM EAT OTHER ANIMALS

JAGUARS ARE THE MOST POWERFUL ANIMALS IN THE RAINFOREST

EDWARD TYRONE KELLY

FIGURE 32–2 After reading about jaguars, this student synthesized the information and created a poem to demonstrate his knowledge.

strategy development is progressing. Through teacher/student conferences, a teacher is easily able to identify the strengths and weaknesses of a student and provide appropriate interventions in order to increase strategy use and content-area learning.

By observing conversations in which learners discuss their strategy uses in informational texts, teachers can assess the strategies students perceive they are applying, as well as the depth of their content knowledge.

In addition, work samples and writing offer insights into students' synthesis.

As the teacher gains insight into the student's learning and needs, small groups of students might be gathered to provide additional small group strategy instruction. These small groups might gather because of a need for strategy support, understanding of text features, or a broadening of content understanding.

Ingredient 6: Provide Visible Supports for Learning

Learning can also be scaffolded by creating and displaying anchor charts (Harvey and Goudvis 2000). Anchor charts are created with the students and contain their thinking and ideas. Information on anchor charts may include

FIGURE 32–3 This science project illustrates the student's knowledge of sharks as well as his competence in determining what was important as he read multiple books on sharks.

definitions and examples of comprehension strategies such as schema, determining importance, questioning or synthesis, and how they apply to the content areas.

The key is to use the charts. Creating them and hanging them on a wall isn't enough. As learners continue to add their thinking to the charts, they use them as tools for thinking and learning. Students become more responsible for their learning by accessing these charts when necessary and using them as tools for accessing meaning.

Jodi's Recipe

Climate of inquiry

Fill the classroom with quality informational books

Read aloud from nonfiction and model strategies or text features

Provide lots of time for nonfiction reading

Engage learners in literate conversations around nonfiction topics and nonfiction strategy uses

Build assessment into every lesson, not just the final product

Provide visible supports for learning: charts and lists

Trusted Authors for Science Inquiries

- Jim Arnosky
- Melvin Berger
- Gail Gibbons

- Theresa Greenaway
- Graham Meadows and Clair Vial
- Seymour Simon

References

Harvey, S., and A. Goudvis. 2000. *Strategies That Work: Teaching Comprehension to Enhance Understanding.* Portland, ME: Stenhouse.

Hoyt, L. 2002. *Make It Real: Strategies for Success with Informational Texts.* Portsmouth, NH: Heinemann.

Keene, E., and S. Zimmerman. 1999. *Mosaic of Thought.* Portsmouth, NH: Heinemann.

KEY QUESTIONS

1. How often do my students read authentic texts during content-area time?

2. In what ways can I incorporate the reading of quality literature into lessons other than reading?

3. How can I model comprehension strategies across the curriculum?

4. In what ways can students apply comprehension strategies to content-area learning?

A Lesson Plan: Focus on Whales

Text Focus: Nonfiction Text Features
Strategy Focus: Determining Importance

As students learn about animals during science class, they read a variety of nonfiction texts building their schema, determining what is important, questioning, and synthesizing the information.

• I begin by gathering the students on the carpet for a whole group lesson. I read aloud *Whales* by Melvin Berger. As I read, I direct the students' attention to how the author uses the features of nonfiction to help me recognize what is important. For example, Berger uses captions under photographs and bold print to draw the readers' attention to important details. Next, I create an anchor chart with the class listing the important facts about whales. This chart will be displayed prevalently in the classroom in order to provide a resource for the students.

• Students then have an opportunity to independently read books at a level that is just right for them. They will determine what is important by using the features of nonfiction, which they have just learned about in the whole group lesson. Students use sticky notes to mark the place where they discovered new facts in the books they are reading. The facts they gather are recorded and saved.

• The whole class reconvenes to discuss their learning. The discussion will center on not only the new knowledge they have gained through reading nonfiction texts, but also how they acquired this knowledge. The students will share and consequently teach each other how they applied comprehension strategies to elicit their new learning.

Assessment of Lesson

• Every lesson needs an assessment so I observe closely and take notes as learners discuss their learning. I watch for demonstrations of content knowledge and indications of which students understand determining importance. These observational notes from the discussion can be combined with information gained during individual conferences so I can determine who needs more support with this strategy and who is using it independently.

• Subsequent lessons will focus on synthesizing information from nonfiction texts. During synthesis, students may incorporate facts gained from reading into formats such as free verse poetry to integrate thinking.

33

A Teachable Moment for a Teacher
Nonfiction for Emergent Readers

MARLEE WRIGHT

MEET THE AUTHOR

MARLEE WRIGHT *is a primary teacher who loops with students between first and second grades. She teachers in a Title 1 school in Thomasville, North Carolina, and is looking forward to working with an ESL clustered group next year.*

FOCUS QUOTE

My students were starved for information about the real world. As we used the texts that supported their interests, their reading skills began to grow and develop. My students were more excited about reading than they had ever been before . . . and in truth, so was I.

I was involved in a special teachable moment . . . but instead of being the teacher, I was the learner! I was a first grade teacher at Thomasville Primary School in Thomasville, North Carolina, a Title 1 school with a fairly large ELL population. I attended a workshop that I was looking forward to but had no anticipation that it would initiate a significant change in my practices and in the classroom culture that I had so carefully crafted.

The day of my "teachable moment," I heard:

We need to rethink the kinds of literature we use in our classrooms, and . . . we need to use expository literature to a much greater extent than most of us are currently using it. Informational texts need to be at the heartbeat of our classroom lives, woven into read alouds and every other component of the day.
(Linda Hoyt)

As I left the workshop that day, I began mulling over the content of the session. Over the next few weeks I began to examine the books that I had been using in my classroom and, to my dismay, I realized that my selections had been leaning, to a great extent, toward fiction. I had actually been shying away from using expository texts. I had to admit that my read alouds, small group experiences, and comprehension strategy lessons were almost exclusively built around fiction.

Through the spring I spent a lot of time reflecting on the texts I had been using in my teaching, and I came to believe that I needed to make some changes! I began to read books about teaching reading and found that they all supported the need to use more expository texts in our work with learners of all ages. It seemed that everything I read that spring pointed me in that direction. At that point I decided that I would like to explore the infusion of informational texts across my day but the year was almost over! I asked my principal about the possibility of looping with this group to the second grade and was happily given the opportunity to start the following year with a running start.

As I continued to read, to attend more workshops, and to work with my students in new ways, I realized how many kinds of expository texts are available all around us—and how crucial it is that we teach our students how to use them appropriately! I began to consciously focus on using these texts for read aloud time, as well as for guided reading. We wove informational sources into independent reading and we reorganized our classroom library to create a better balance between fiction and nonfiction. As we added informational texts to our classroom library, they quickly became the most-read books on our shelves!

The students and I explored many different features of informational texts, such as glossaries, indexes, charts, maps, and tables of contents. Each student authored an informational book about polar bears or penguins, highlighting an informational text feature on each page. We did reports about animals, using graphic organizers to guide our research.

My students were even fascinated with our dictionaries! They pored over our classroom dictionaries, looking up words from our research, exploring the maps and charts, and simply looking at the illustrations. Another teacher donated a set of encyclopedias to our class, and those also became favorite free-time reading selections. During our book exchange time in the media center, my students began making the majority of their selections from the nonfiction shelves. The students were even interested in the texts I received from my workshops, and the way I had taken notes and highlighted special passages in the book!

My students were starved for information about the real world. As we used the texts that supported their interests, their reading skills began to grow and develop. My students were more excited about reading than they had ever been before . . . and in truth, so was I. I have come to believe that this excitement about learning is one of the most important gifts we can give our students as we help to prepare them for their futures.

My teachable moment has changed my life as an educator and better empowered me to lead children to new heights in literacy. That teachable moment helped me look with clear eyes at my own practices and the environment that I had created for learning. The reflections, the changes, and the letting go of old practices were all difficult. I am on a new path now. My students and I are ready for more teachable moments as we now surge with confidence into all of the texts of our world.

References

Hoyt, L. 2002. *Make It Real: Strategies for Success with Informational Texts.* Portsmouth, NH: Heinemann.

———. 1999. *Revisit, Reflect, Retell: Strategies for Improving Reading Comprehension.* Portsmouth, NH: Heinemann.

Keene, E. O., and S. Zimmerman. 1998. *Mosaic of Thought: Teaching Comprehension in a Reader's Workshop.* Portsmouth, NH: Heinemann.

KEY QUESTIONS

1. How is the balance between fiction and nonfiction in your classroom?

2. When you look at your classroom library, guided reading selections, and read aloud options, do you have a wide and diverse range of informational texts available?

3. If you have a central book room in your school, are the collections at each level balanced between fiction and nonfiction?

4. If you are using a program, check out the informational selections. Do they represent the wide range of informational texts we see in the world or do they focus mostly on descriptions?

5. How might you build enthusiasm for nonfiction to get your students excited about a rich diet of informational reading and writing?

How to Help Emergent Readers

Questions for Readers

After looking at the cover and the title:

Do you think this text will be for information or will it be for entertainment?

What text features do you see when you browse through the book?

As you browse through the book, what are some of the things that you wonder about?

What are some words you think you will encounter as you read?

Questions for Teachers

What new and different kinds of informational texts can I find that are appropriate for my class? (recipes, the minipage from the newspaper, the Internet, maps, globes, etc.)

What new books can I add to my classroom library, and do I have enough books on different reading levels but the same topics?

How can I manage my time better so that I am able to monitor each student's understanding of the texts?

Am I remembering to take running records in fiction and nonfiction selections?

How can I best arrange my classroom to achieve a balance of structure/nonstructure in which the students and I can explore nonfiction questions?

How can I help the students learn to coach each other and be supportive of each other as they work together in nonfiction texts and diverse topics?

What kinds of writing can the students do that reflect their learning and that will enhance their writing skills?

Searching for Balance

A Challenge for Teachers

• Look at the walls of your classroom. What is the balance between fiction and nonfiction sources on the wall?

• Check out your classroom library. How is the balance there? How are the books organized? Who organized them? Could the students sort nonfiction titles, cluster them, and label them in ways that are meaningful to them?

• Examine your think alouds carefully. Are you balancing comprehension strategy instruction with demonstrations in fiction and nonfiction selections, with demonstrations in newspapers, textbooks, and magazines?

• Be conscious in your selection of read alouds. Can you balance fiction and nonfiction or shift to two read alouds each day, one fiction, one informational?

• Look at your reading instruction. Could you teach a phonics or grammar lesson in a nonfiction text? Could you work on fluency with nonfiction passages?

• Are your students having information circles as well as literature circles?

• Look closely at the writing experiences your students are provided. Are they writing in informational formats every day and incorporating informational text features such as boldface type, captions, headings, labels, and so on into these writing experiences? Are they writing in a wide range of nonfiction genre: descriptive, procedural, and persuasive?

Informational Text Forms

Type	Examples	Traits
Description:	Report	Impersonal, objective language
	Summary	Timeless present tense
Explanation	To explain phenomena	Impersonal language
	Scientific explanation	Timeless present tense
	(How digestion works)	Cause/Effect
Procedure	Directions/Instructions	Detailed
	Recipes	Directive language
		Numbered steps or linking words related to time (*next, then, when, after*)
Recount	Diary	Simple past tense language
	Time-ordered summary	Linking words to do with time
	Retell	Specific to who or what
Persuasive	Advertisements	Presents a point of view
	Letters to the editor	Linking words associated with reasoning (*therefore,* and *so*)
Narrative	Biography	Clearly defined characters
		Descriptive language
		Past tense

Look for opportunities to include these forms in reading and writing experiences for your students. Check out your classroom library and media center for examples of each form. Analyze instructional resources to determine which forms are present and which ones need to be added.

Adapted by Linda Hoyt from First Steps Professional Development and the work of Tony Stead.

Science Notebooks

34 Developing Understanding and Strategies

RACHEL JORDAN

MEET THE AUTHOR

RACHEL JORDAN *has been a classroom teacher at the elementary and middle school levels. Currently, she is a Science Resource Teacher, providing professional development to K–8 teachers for the Palo Alto Unified School District in California.*

FOCUS QUOTE

This is a fabulous opportunity to teach students about graphic organizers such as tables, charts, diagrams, and graphs as well as honing their skills of observation.

S cience notebooks are a powerful tool for expanding content understanding while modeling essential strategies for reading and writing expository texts. When I introduce this tool to students, I explain that scientists use notebooks regularly to document the observations, questions, and conclusions that they form as a result of their work. In industry, science notebooks are extremely important. In fact, they are often kept in a locked, secure room and used to document proof of work eligible for U.S. patents. In the classroom, they are an invaluable source of developing expository reading and writing skills in addition to solidifying science content knowledge. They become a long-term record of our investigations and a place where learners can explore a variety of reading strategies and text features that are particularly important in informational texts.

Modeling the Strategies

Recording in science notebooks, like any other teaching tool or strategy, needs to be modeled. An invaluable tool in this process is a large-sized (24″ × 36″) spiral-bound blank notebook. With this enlarged space for recording, I use metacognitive teaching strategies by explaining aloud to my students why I am making each entry as I record it. This class notebook serves as a model for students to use as they begin to work in their own science notebooks. When students are learning a new skill in expository reading or writing, I may simply model the technique as a think aloud. I model strategies for recording and labeling, summarizing, jotting notes, using elements of expository text such as tables of content, titles, headings, and clear graphical organization of data.

As students become more proficient, I engage the class in pre-experiment discussions regarding how we might organize data or how to record questions to help them internalize the strategies for recording in their own science notebooks. My goal is to empower students to independently decide how best to organize their questions, observations, and conclusions so that their thinking is clearly understood by any reader and to ensure that they are using a wide range of tools in their writing and reading during science class.

STRATEGIES TO MODEL AND APPLY IN SCIENCE NOTEBOOKS

data entry	developing a table of contents
selecting a title	locating information
summarizing	headings
developing questions	graphic organizers (tables, charts, diagrams, graphs)
underlining or bolding key words	identifying main idea in reading and in your own writing
drawing conclusions	writing in a way that makes sense to a reader
applying skills and observations	writing hypotheses
underlining	using larger font for headings and important words
drawing/sketching to collect data	

Determining What Data to Record

An important step for students is to determine what data they will need to record, and how they can organize it to make sense to the reader. This is a fabulous opportunity to teach students about graphic organizers such as tables, charts, diagrams, and graphs as well as honing their skills of observation. For example, if students are conducting an experiment to determine the effect of the number of coils on an electromagnet, they need to figure out how to organize their data so that they, or any reader, can quickly make sense of it. I will either elicit or suggest (based on the age and skills of the students) a graphic organizer that students can use to organize their data as they collect it.

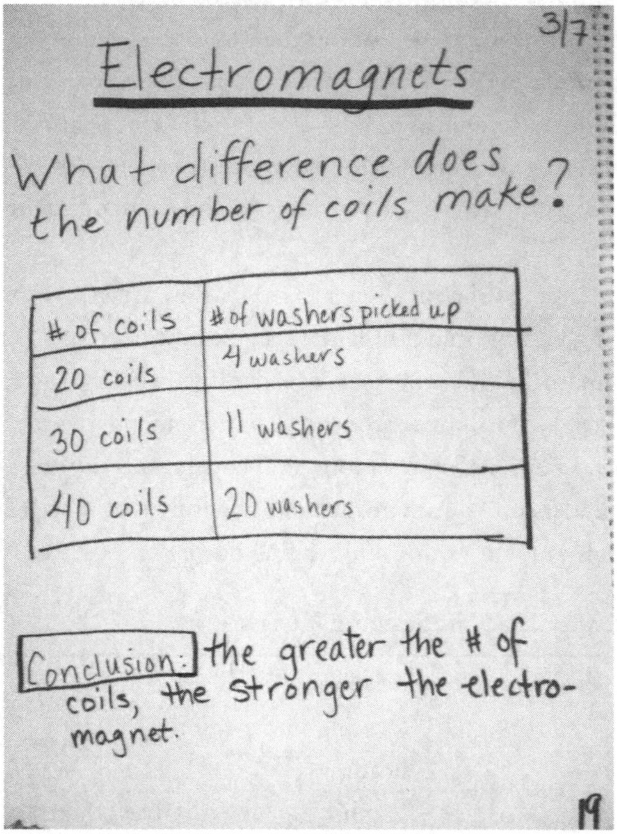

FIGURE 34–1 This data chart was modeled in the demonstration-size science notebook before students began the experiment. They then created charts in their own science notebooks.

Titles

We use our science notebooks in every science lesson so the pages quickly fill with records of our learning. Early in the year, I spend time modeling how to choose a title for each science experience. When we begin each lesson in science, I usually give students a quick description of the activity and demonstrate how to select a title that is easily identifiable when we want to reread later in the year. I then record a title in our class notebook. This is a good time to point out and expect the use of underlining or a larger font to indicate titles and headings.

As my students build their skills, I diminish my modeling of titles and explain that I will be looking at their notebooks to see how well their titles reflect the main idea of the science experiment as well as the data and the conclusions they are recording. The title students select is actually a powerful assessment, as it tells me a great deal about how well they understand the content and how they are developing as an expository writer.

Table of Contents

It is important to explain and demonstrate how a table of contents helps a reader find information quickly and easily. Once a few titles and experiments have been recorded in my demonstration notebook, I can show students how to create a Table of Contents at the front of the science notebook.

Like any professional Table of Contents, it should list the given title and the page number. I have found that periodically returning to the table of contents page and reviewing the title for each piece of work in the notebook not only teaches the purpose of a table of contents, but also helps us remember what we have been learning in science. We use the table of contents to quickly locate information in our own science notebooks when we have forgotten information, want to answer a question, or even to search for connections between the findings of our investigations.

Table of Contents	
Magnetic Materials	p. 1
Which magnet is Stronger?	p. 3
Magnet, Magnetic + Non-Magnetic	p. 4
Light the bulb!	p. 5
A Complete Circuit	p 9
Conductors/Insulators	p. 10
Circuit Diagram Key	p. 13
Parallel + Series Circuit	p. 15
Electromagnets	p. 21
Telegraphs	p. 22

FIGURE 34–2 Table of contents from the demonstration-size science notebook.

Forming Conclusions

I have found that it is very difficult for students to form conclusions. Typically, they tend to simply restate the data instead of forming a statement that will generalize the data to multiple situations. Therefore, I model making conclusions in a class science notebook extensively before I ask students to form their own conclusions. For example, with the data in Figure 34–1, many students will state that their conclusion is that "for 20 winds it picked

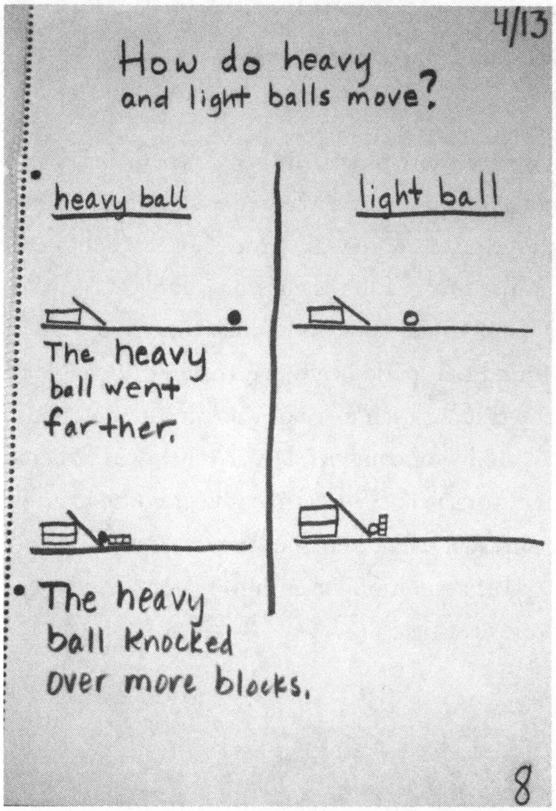

FIGURE 34–3 This chart demonstrates drawing to collect data and support conclusions.

up 4 washers, and for 30 winds it picked up 11 washers." In this case I rely on sentence frames to move students from observations to general inferences or conclusions. For example, "The greater the _____ the _____ the electromagnet."

With younger students, I often record conclusions with drawings based on their class discussion of observations from a given experiment. For example, when working with first graders in an experiment where they determined how balls of different masses (weights) move, I used pictures to represent their data. After looking at the drawings and discussing them, we were able to form sentences that explain the drawings. "The heavy ball went farther. The heavy ball knocked over more blocks."

Science notebooks help me to teach and model explicit forms of expository writing while also meeting my responsibilities to teach content. They are powerful logs of learning that provide a record of learning over time, serve as a vehicle for ongoing assessment, and when combined with explicit metacognitive demonstrations, teach my students critical strategies for reading and writing.

KEY QUESTIONS

1. How might notebooks guide learners in inquiry for math, social studies, health, physical education, or music? What writing and reading skills could be taught to support the content understandings?

2. Modeling is a key factor in helping students to internalize the strategies. Which strategies might you model first if you were to initiate learning notebooks with your students?

3. What are the benefits to students when they have a year-long record of their learning in a content area?

4. How might learning notebooks be linked to state standards?

Assessment of Learning Notebook

Subject area _____

Name of Learner_____ Grade___

The learning notebook shows evidence of the following:	Date observed:	Quality of work (1–5) 1 does not understand 3 beginning to get it 5 top notch . . . really has it	Suggestions for instruction
Titles that reflect main idea			
Data clearly presented			
The most important ideas are recorded			
Use of drawings as a data gathering tool			
Shows skill in observation			
Ability to clearly summarize learning			
Records questions about the learning			
Identification of important words (boldface or underlined)			
Titles and headings are bolded or in a larger font			
Opinions are supported by evidence			
Table of Contents correctly formatted			
Can locate information in the learning notebook			
Can locate information in resources			
Draws conclusions that reflect a generalization			
Uses charts			
Uses graphs			
Uses diagrams			

I See What
You Mean

Using iMovie In the
Reading Workshop

35

MARY LEE HAHN

MEET THE AUTHOR

Mary Lee Hahn *has been teaching fourth and fifth grades for 20 years, currently in the Dublin, Ohio, school district. She is the author of* Reconsidering Read Aloud *(Stenhouse 2002).*

FOCUS QUOTE

When I watched with a critical eye, I saw not just technology, and not just composing, but a concrete use of reading comprehension strategies that would inform our conversations about comprehension all year long.

The first time I turned my students loose to play around with the iMovie tutorial, I wrote it in my lesson plans as a technology experience. If pressed to go to my content standards to justify the activity, I might have gone to the Language Arts Standards and referenced the composing standards in Writing.

However, the more I watch students work with iMovie, the more I am amazed by all the ways iMovie brings abstract reading comprehension strategies to life for students in interactive, hands-on ways.

What is iMovie? Quite simply, it is a piece of computer software that allows a novice to make a movie. It's so easy to use that a not particularly techno-savvy adult can quickly and easily learn enough of the basics to get students started. (And then the adult can learn from the students!) It is not the *only* movie making software on the market, but it's the software that comes as a part of the standard built-in software package in the newer Macintosh computers I have in my classroom.

For this practical reason, it's the only movie making software with which I'm familiar. So my purpose here is not to sell iMovie in particular, and I'm not going to attempt to teach you much about how to use it. The most important thing I want you to know about iMovie is that you do not have to own or have access to a digital video camera to film the clips of video that will become your movie. iMovie comes with a built-in tutorial to help you learn to use the iMovie tools. The tutorial includes a set of video clips of two children in various stages of washing their dog. See Figure 35–1, screen shot 1.

Early in this school year, my fourth graders explored iMovie for the first time ever through this tutorial. When I watched with a critical eye, I saw not just technology, and not just composing, but a concrete use of reading comprehension strategies that would inform our conversations about comprehension all year long.

FIGURE 35–1 Screen Shot 1. Reprinted by permission from Apple Computer, Inc.

Visualization

One of the cognitive strategies proficient readers use to comprehend text is visualization (Keene and Zimmerman 1997). The first thing I had my students do when we began working with the iMovie tutorial was simply to watch all of the clips to determine what kind of a story the clips might tell.

So often we talk to our students about visualization as "making a movie in their mind" while they read or while they listen to a read aloud. For a proficient reader, that abstract analogy makes sense. For *all* readers, and especially for the less proficient readers, that abstract analogy becomes concrete while viewing the video clips in the tutorial. There is no accompanying text with the clips and no other way to comprehend what the story might be *except* by visualizing!

This experience early in the school year of visualizing the story in the iMovie tutorial has been followed throughout the year by many conversations about visualizing what we read, whether it is a poem on the overhead, an article in TFK, our own reading, or the class read aloud.

I even have an informal assessment record of the growth of each child's ability to visualize a story because I invite my students to draw a picture of their favorite part of the book after we finish every read aloud. I can assess how strong a student is in the strategy of visualization by looking at the details from the story included in the pictures he/she draws. Jennifer's meticulous picture of the climactic scene at the end of *Love, Ruby Lavender* (Wiles 2001) captures perfectly the moment when Ruby comes to the rescue of her arch-enemy Melba Jane on stage during the town operetta.

FIGURE 35–2 Jennifer's picture shows her visualizing skills.

Jennifer included the auditorium full of all the townspeople of Hallelujah, Mississippi, the heavy red velvet curtains on stage, and Mrs. Varnado playing the piano, waiting for Melba Jane to start her soliloquy. Melba Jane's wig has been snagged off her head by the chicken wire holding the prop apple tree together, revealing her cropped blue hair (leftover from an accident earlier in the book involving one of Ruby's chickens, a ladder, and a can of blue paint). Melba's expression registers shock, while Ruby, with her head full of unruly, curly red hair, is giving Melba a "say-something! look" (178).

In the same way that visualizing the story in the clips of the iMovie tutorial is the foundation for creating an iMovie, visualizing the story or information contained in the words of a text is an essential component for comprehension. Without visualization, my students wouldn't have been able to move on to sequencing the clips in the tutorial.

Sequencing

After the students have had the chance to play each clip in the iMovie tutorial, and they have an idea of what story the clips might tell, they are ready to put the clips in order. Proficient readers are able to determine the important information or events in a text, and they can sequence the information or events to retell or synthesize what they've read (Keene and Zimmerman 1997), so this sequencing of the clips is another example of an abstract reading strategy made concrete with iMovie.

FIGURE 35–3 Sequencing movie clips. Screen shots reprinted by permission from Apple Computer, Inc.

Initially, most students just drag whole clips from the clips pane to the clips viewer. Their stories are linear, predictable, and quite simple: The dog is in the mud. The kids catch the dog and prepare its bath. The kids bathe the dog.

The work of sequencing is built on the foundation of visualization. The iMovie brings both visualization and sequencing to life on the screen. Similarly, the pictures my students make at the end of every read aloud of their favorite parts of the book give us another concrete example of the link between visualization and sequencing. After all of the students have completed their pictures (visualization), we share them, putting each picture into order with the others as we go, asking ourselves, "Did this happen before or after that?" over and over again, giving every reader a refresher course in the valuable strategies of determining importance and then sequencing to retell or synthesize.

Chunks: Clips, Scenes, Paragraphs, Chapters

As the students learn the editing tools in iMovie that make it possible to select portions of the clips by cutting sections off, or by cropping to select a middle portion of a clip, their stories become more sophisticated. Some of the clips actually contain bits of video footage that are out of order so that the tutorial user has a reason to practice cutting and cropping clips, or so that the student has a reason to practice more refined sequencing skills. We now began to talk about scenes, as well as talking about clips. Organizing and sequencing all the clips of the dog in the mud became "the mud scene." Similarly, finding, grouping, and ordering all the clips of the kids preparing the bath became "the bath scene."

Those early discussions about the visual bits of the story in the iMovie—the clips and scenes—began our year-long conversations about the ways that authors organize text to give the readers clues to help with comprehension. A paragraph is like a clip, and an author gives the reader a series of paragraphs that create a scene, or a chapter.

Sometimes in the middle of a chapter, the author gives us a wide break in the text as a clue that there is a scene change within the chapter. My students have learned to interpret those wide breaks in the text and mentally prepare for the big change of time or place that the break often indicates. In their iMovies, they indicate these "wide breaks" by using the transition tools that allow them to fade in and out between clips.

Point of View and Flashback

When the students were able to see that sequencing the story in the tutorial could be more than just the simplistic, linear stories with which they began, they were ready to start thinking about some of the more sophisticated ways that authors choose to tell their stories.

The tutorial gave us a common "text" for exploring point of view. How would we order the clips if the dog is telling the story? The kids? The person holding the camera (code for a third person narrator)? And we played around with the idea of showing the dog in the mud in the middle of the bath scene, and discussed when and how authors use flashback.

Final Thoughts

Because these conversations around the iMovie tutorial came early in the year, they set the tone for the way we have talked about reading and writing all year long. This early experience with comprehending text as a concrete, hands-on process that is parallel to the manipulative, creative process of composing text, gave my students a more flexible way of approaching and understanding what they have read. All of the movie metaphors for comprehending and creating stories are easy to understand and relevant to their media-saturated lives.

Resources

Keene, Ellin Oliver, and Susan Zimmerman. 1997. *Mosaic of Thought: Teaching Comprehension in a Reader's Workshop*. Portsmouth, NH: Heinemann.

Wiles, Deborah. 2001. *Love, Ruby Lavender*. San Diego, CA: Gulliver Books, Harcourt, Inc.

KEY QUESTIONS

1. In what other ways might media or technology be used to support reading comprehension?

2. Which comprehension strategies might be good matches to technology?

3. If we believe that composing is comprehending, how might iMovie experiences affect the craft of our students' writing?

Reflecting on My Comprehension Strategies

We use our ability to comprehend in many ways through our lives. We might make an *inference* that a friend is feeling sad when we see that person sitting alone and looking down. We might *visualize* on the way to the pizza parlor just how that pizza is going to look and taste. When we use technology, we are often using comprehension strategies as well. When you watch TV, you might make a *connection* to another program. When you respond to a friend's email, you might *question* what that person meant before you write an answer.

Think about the technologies you use: the television, radio, CD player, the computer, or movies on the DVD and VCR. Be a good observer of your own thinking. Notice when you are using comprehension strategies . . .

Be watching for: predicting, inferring, questioning, visualizing, making connections, deciding what is important, evaluating, summarizing, or _____.

The technologies in my life: **Comprehension strategies I use with each**

- _____   _____

- _____   _____

- _____   _____

- _____   _____

- _____   _____

- _____   _____

- _____   _____

- _____   _____

- _____   _____

- _____   _____

Paint Pots of Poetry

36

Deepening Comprehension Through Cooperative Poetry Discussion

BARBARA COLEMAN

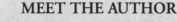

MEET THE AUTHOR

BARBARA COLEMAN *has many years' experience in elementary schools as a classroom teacher, assistant principal, and principal. She is currently a curriculum specialist in a Title 1 school. Her love for children's books is evident not only in staff developments that she conducts but in her home library as well.*

FOCUS QUOTE

When learners think about the meaning of a poem in cooperative groups, they are exposed to multiple views and usually understand with greater depth.

P oetry is a genre that requires a variety of consciously applied comprehension strategies. A reader of poetic language must be prepared to visualize, to search for main ideas, and to understand that there is often more than one interpretation of the meaning.

Poetry can extend our imagination and confirm our understandings of ourselves and our world. It can help us find unity with one another and see the metaphors in daily living.

To maximize language learning and comprehension, I like to engage students in cooperative teams as they work with poetry. This increases student-to-student conversation, teaches teamwork, and tends to expand comprehension as diverse ideas are shared. When learners think about the meaning of a poem in cooperative groups, they are exposed to multiple views and usually understand with greater depth.

Poetry is a wonderful context in which to explore word meanings. Because of the creative uses of language and metaphor often found in poetry, words are often used in new and unique ways, which, when consciously addressed, expand student vocabulary.

Paint Pots of Poetry: The Process

Students will work in teams of four-to-six students to collaboratively read poems using the questions provided on paint sticks to guide their reflections on the poem. The purpose is to give students an opportunity to enjoy a variety of poems and to be able to think about the "big idea" in cooperative groups. The "paint pots" are a metaphor to help students make the connection to the visual imagery that poetry creates. You might want to consider setting up stations with a different poem at each station. Groups could then rotate from station to station and experience a variety of poems.

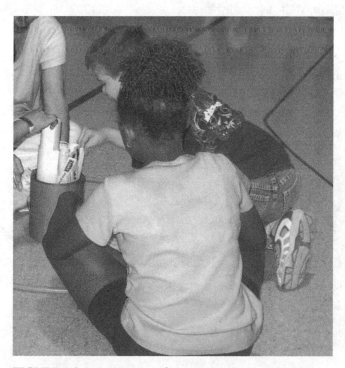

FIGURE 36–1 Learners work in cooperative teams to explore the deeper meanings of poems. Vocabulary can be enriched when learners think about the variety of ways words and phrases support meaning in a poem.

Materials

- Each station will need a Paint Pot (empty paint can or bucket) and paint sticks with questions written on them
- Poetry selections (chart size or a photocopy for each reader)

Procedures

Each cooperative group is given a different poem poster or set of photocopies for a poem and a "Paint Pot" with questions

Steps:

1. Each student reads the poem silently at least twice.
2. The group then reads the poem chorally.
3. Each student in the group selects a paint stick from the paint can.
4. Each student rereads the poem silently for the answer to *their* question.
5. Each student reads their question out loud and shares their thinking about the answer.
6. The group discusses the question and thinks about possible answers. They are encouraged to come up with more than one answer for each question.
7. The process continues until each group member has shared a question and guided the discussion around possible answers.

Possible Questions for Paint Sticks

What is the "big idea" of this poem?

What is the theme of the poem?

How does the speaker feel about the subject of the poem?

What is the tone or mood of the poem?

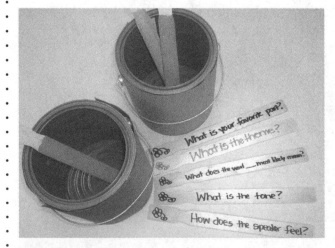

FIGURE 36–2 Paint sticks (free from a paint store) carry questions that students can use to guide them in thinking more deeply about poetry.

Select an interesting word or phrase. In this poem, it probably means _____.

If you could ask the author one question, what would it be?

What do you visualize as you read this poem?

Does the author have a message for the reader?

Variations

Each cooperative group becomes an expert group on one question. (Example: Group 1 might have, "What is the theme of the poem?" Group 2 might have, "What do you visualize?") As each group rotates to all the poems in the room, they search for the answer to that single question. As a result, the theme group would have explored the theme for several poems and might then discuss what they noticed about the way authors express theme in poetry. The visualizing group could share how different authors supported visualization for the reader.

Expert groups could leave their thinking on sticky notes at each poem station. This would allow other students to read and see what other groups are noticing about each poem.

At the end of the lesson, the poems and sticky notes could be displayed for a "gallery walk" so learners could view the variety of responses.

KEY QUESTIONS

1. How might Paint Pots of Poetry support the learners you serve? Would you make any modifications of the process?

2. Poems appear frequently on standardized tests. What questions might you place on stir sticks that would help prepare students for the standardized tests they will encounter?

3. How might you extend this deeper kind of reading to passages you lift from favorite picture books or novels?

4. Could you extend this kind of experience to reading passages from a unit of study in science, social studies, health, and so on? What kind of questions would best support this approach to content-area reading?

Analyzing Poetry

Reader _____ Date _____

While reading and discussing poetry today, I thought:

The most interesting theme was _____.

My favorite poem was _____

_____ because _____.

_____

I was able to get the best visualization when I read _____

_____. The author helped my visualization by

_____

_____

_____

The big ideas were easier to identify when I remembered to _____

_____

_____

If I were to write a poem, I would want to be sure to _____

_____

_____

_____

Sharing Our Visualizations

Poetry Reader_____ Date _____

Read at least five poems. List their titles and authors below. As you read focus on creating sensory images/visualizations.

_____   _____

_____   _____

_____   _____

_____   _____

Put a star by the one that you found helped you elicit the clearest images.

Why do think this poem brought stronger images for you? _____

_____

_____

Meet with a partner to share the poem you starred. Read your poems aloud to each other then share the visual images that you created. Talk together about the poet's style of writing and what was done to support visualization for the reader.

_____

_____

_____

_____

Understanding Passage of Time

Poetry Readers _____ _____ _____

Date_____

Your job is to read an array of poems and watch for those which show passing of time. Record the title, tell a bit about the setting, determine how much time passes, and record the clues that describe the passing of time.

Title	Setting	How much time passes?	Lines/words that signal passing of time
_____	_____	_____	_____
_____	_____	_____	_____
_____	_____	_____	_____
_____	_____	_____	_____
_____	_____	_____	_____
_____	_____	_____	_____
_____	_____	_____	_____
_____	_____	_____	_____
_____	_____	_____	_____
_____	_____	_____	_____
_____	_____	_____	_____
_____	_____	_____	_____
_____	_____	_____	_____
_____	_____	_____	_____

Math + Literature = Comprehension and Concepts!

37

CATHY BERNHARD

MEET THE AUTHOR

Cathy Bernhard *is an editor of* The Oregon Mathematics Teacher *magazine and is past president of the Oregon Council of Teachers of Mathematics. After many years of teaching in the classroom and working as a District math specialist and TAG facilitator, Cathy has retired and is working as a math consultant to numerous Oregon school districts.*

FOCUS QUOTE

The learning of a difficult subject becomes fun when the students are engaged in an engrossing book with follow-up activities to enhance the comprehension.

Comprehending math can be difficult. "Math texts present challenges for even the most seasoned reader." (Miller 2003, 100). They are laden with specialized vocabulary, complex concepts, and language patterns that are vastly different from those of oral speech. The understanding of math concepts at the elementary level, however, can definitely be enhanced through the use of appropriate children's literature.

Both fiction and nonfiction literature offer a variety of opportunities to explore comprehension of mathematical concepts. Fiction introduces the math concepts in a story format and makes these concepts more meaningful through real-life applications. Nonfiction materials are usually very colorful and model a variety of informational text features, such as diagrams, tables, and photographs. Combining a piece of literature with a follow-up experience increases the learning and adds an element of fun to a subject some consider confusing or tedious.

Broader Standards

The study of mathematics is no longer confined to basic number facts and operations, but, according to the new standards set by the National Council of Teachers of Mathematics (NCTM) in 2000, now also should include the strands of algebra, geometry, measurement, data analysis, and probability at all levels. The following lessons and accompanying comprehension follow-ups demonstrate how powerful it can be when math standards are linked to literature and the focus is on comprehension of the concepts and language.

Numbers and Operations

Counting books offer a unique way to integrate numbers with literature at any grade level. Usually these number books are written around a theme that ties to another content area, such as social studies or science. Once the children have read a counting book, the book's format can also serve as a prototype for individual or classroom books that students create. This type of follow-up activity integrates writing, reading, and mathematics in any chosen content area.

The reading *Counting Is for the Birds* provides an excellent example of a counting book that gives detailed science information. The art work includes very accurate drawings of ten common birds that come to a backyard bird feeder. Labeled diagrams explain scientific facts. Beginning with zero and ending with twenty, the accompanying text is written in rhyme and tells the tale of a conniving cat who lurks beneath the feeder waiting for a chance to make a meal of the visiting birds. The surprise ending is devoid of the anticipated violence and gore because a squirrel frightens away all of the birds on the feeder just as the cat prepares to pounce. The squirrel gets the food remaining on the feeder, the birds fly safely down the street, and the cat goes away hungry. A guide to the birds featured in the book appears at the end and gives further information about each species of bird.

Comprehension follow-up As a meaningful follow-up, you might facilitate comprehension by having the students create a counting book. Following the pattern of the bird book, their counting book could have one page for each number with illustrations and text provided by the children.

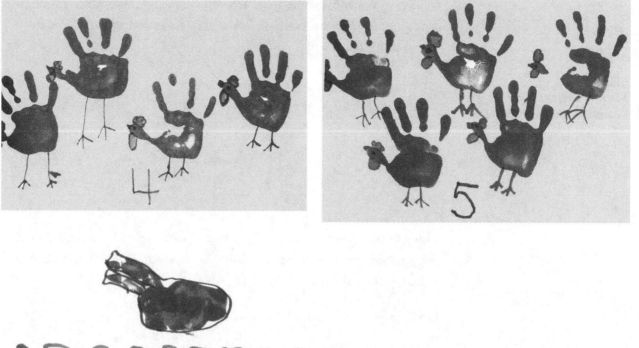

FIGURE 37–1a, b, c Even emergent learners can create books with mathematical concepts.

Algebra

The reading *Two of Everything* is a delightful retelling of a Chinese folktale about a poor farmer who discovers an antique brass pot buried in his garden. He has no idea how to use it, but as he struggles to haul it home, he drops his coin purse with five coins into it. As his wife examines the mysterious pot, she drops her only hairpin into it. When she reaches inside to recover the lost hairpin, she discovers that there are now two hairpins and two coin purses with ten coins. The old couple eagerly tries doubling other items, until the old woman accidentally falls into the pot. When the farmer pulls her out, he discovers that she also has been duplicated. Students have fun predicting how the farmer can solve his problem of two wives.

Comprehension follow-up The idea of a magic brass pot that duplicates everything makes a nice introduction to a common math activity called the "In/Out Game." This game is used to introduce the algebraic idea of a function to young students. A mathematical function has numbers that remain in a constant relationship with each other and follow a set rule. Using the example of the brass pot, it is easy to explain to students that the rule the pot follows is doubling everything ($2n$). When one hairpin goes in, two hairpins come out. When five coins go in, ten coins come out. As a different number is put in, the same rule is always followed to get the output. This can be shown using a T-Chart:

IN Rule: n	OUT $2n$
1	2
5	10
3	6
4	?

This game has many variations. The students are eager to predict what output accompanies a given input and then to determine the rule from looking at examples on the chart.

Geometry

The reading   The study of geometry at the elementary school level is based heavily on an understanding of vocabulary. *G is for Googol* is a math alphabet book that cleverly illustrates and defines many geometric terms. Every letter of the alphabet is tied to a math word with whimsical illustrations, accurate mathematical definitions, and humorous stories and activities. Sometimes a word is defined in the negative, as in the case of "diamond," which the author makes very clear is not a proper mathematical term.

Comprehension follow-up   "Alphabet Time" is a simple activity that can be used either to pre-assess the background knowledge of students in any content area or can be used as a culminating activity to ascertain what the students have learned during a unit of study. The teacher lists all of the letters of the alphabet on a chart or overhead transparency. The challenge is for the students to fill in at least one word related to the topic that begins with each letter. For example, if the topic is geometry, the word *quadrilateral* could follow the letter "q." In a geometry "Alphabet Time," it is often difficult to find words for the letters "j" and "k," however, creative students will find a solution. (*Juxtapose* and *kite* will work.)

Measurement

The reading   Measurement is a content strand that encompasses many topics, including linear measurement, weight, volume, time, money, and temperature. *Measuring Penny* is an unusual book that actually includes all of these topics in one story. Given a homework assignment to measure something in a variety of ways at home, Lisa chooses to measure her dog, Penny. Using both standard (inches and centimeters) and nonstandard measurement (dog biscuits), Lisa measures Penny's height and tail length. She weighs

Penny and measures the volume of water she drinks. Time, money, and temperature are also included in Penny's story. The book has diagrams and charts and stresses the importance of always including the correct unit in a measurement.

Comprehension follow-up   "Just My Size" is an activity that allows students to practice measurement by using objects that are familiar. The teacher should select a small moveable object in the classroom. Working in teams, the students estimate the object's height in inches and centimeters and its weight in grams and ounces. After the estimates are written down, students are given instruction on how to weigh and measure the object accurately. Then, the object is weighed and measured. Honor the students who are the closest in estimating the actual size and weight. As an extension, find other objects in the room that are approximately the same size and weight and measure and weigh them.

Data Analysis

The reading   Reading charts and graphs is a vital part of data analysis. *Tiger Math* provides an opportunity for students to interpret information that is displayed in a variety of different ways. This nonfiction book features a unique format, which is explained by the authors on the opening page:

> Graphs are math pictures that make it easy to see and understand information about numbers. This book will introduce four different kinds of graphs: picture graphs, circle graphs, bar graphs, and line graphs. If you want to read the story of T.J. the tiger without the math, you can read only the right-hand pages of this book. Then to learn more and see exactly how T.J. grew, you can look at the graphs on the left-hand pages. (Nagda and Rickel 2000)

T. J. is a tiger cub who was born at the Denver Zoo and the students can follow his activities and growth as they read the book and interpret the graphs.

Comprehension follow-up   Teachers who provide a daily graph encourage students to interpret data on a regular basis. Personalizing the information on graphs increases student interest. To create individual data markers, glue a magnetic strip (available at craft stores) to the back of a small digital photo or student picture of each child. Post the daily graph on a magnetic board or metal cookie sheet and let each student put his/her personal marker in the appropriate location on a bar graph.

Probability

The reading   *Probably Pistachio* is an extremely humorous book about a boy named Jack who is having a very bad day. Because his father has made him a tuna fish sandwich (which he hates) for lunch, he spends his math class calculating the probability of getting a pastrami sandwich (which is his favorite) in a trade with Emma, who actually had pastrami sandwiches for four days last week. The trade fails because Emma's father has made her a liverwurst sandwich. As he goes through the rest of the day, Jack calculates the probability of getting his favorite ice cream at home, his favorite snack after soccer practice, and a chance to play on a team with his friend. All of these choices are graphically displayed in illustrations so that students can easily calculate the probability of each event.

Comprehension follow-up   Using spinners or dice to make some decisions in the daily class routine, such as which group lines up first or which person does a job, provides an engaging way to focus student attention on probability. The teacher should make several spinners, some of which are "fair" (half red and half blue with an equal chance of being selected) and some of which are "unfair" ($\frac{3}{4}$ red and $\frac{1}{4}$ blue). After discussing the probability that an event will occur, the teacher spins the spinner to determine which person or group wins. For example, if half of the class is labeled red and half is blue, over a period of time, each group should get the opportunity to line up first an equal number of times if a "fair" spinner is used. Keeping a tally of who lines up first for several weeks will show this equality. Switching to an "unfair" spinner produces different results. The practice provided by this spinner activity makes probability a part of each student's daily life, and makes spinner questions on a test much easier to understand and answer.

Literature and Mathematics Enhance Comprehension

Linking literature with the teaching of math concepts provides a high interest level and diminishes some of the fear some students may have of math. The learning of a difficult subject becomes fun when the students are engaged in an engrossing book with follow-up activities to enhance comprehension.

References

Hong, Lily Toy. 1993. *Two of Everything*. Morton Grove, IL: Albert Whitman & Company.

Leedy, Loreen. 1997. *Measuring Penny*. New York: Henry Holt and Company.

Mazzola, Frank, Jr. 1997. *Counting is for the Birds*. Watertown, MA: Charlesbridge.

Miller, J. 2003. "Guided Reading In Mathematics," In *Exploring Informational Texts: From Theory to Practice*. edited by L. Hoyt, M. Mooney, and P. Parkes. Portsmouth, NH: Heinemann.

Murphy, Stuart. 2001. *Probably Pistachio*. New York: HarperCollins Publishers.

Nagda, Ann, and Cindy Rickel. 2000. *Tiger Math*. New York: Henry Holt and Company.

Schwartz, David. 1998. *G is for Googol*. Berkeley, CA: Tricycle Press.

KEY QUESTIONS

1. How might combining literature, math concepts, and a hands-on experience deepen comprehension?

2. What are your favorite books that include mathematical concepts? What hands-on learning might you offer with each one to solidify comprehension?

3. How might writing be added to the combination of literature, math concepts, and hands-on experience? What benefits would there be for comprehension instruction?

4. Have you talked with your students about the reading strategies we use in mathematics texts? What strategies would you hope they would consciously employ during mathematics?

Selecting Books to Match Math Standards

	Children's Literature Selection/Author	Comprehension Follow-Up	Writing Extension
Number	Counting is for the Birds By Mazzola	Count classroom objects	Create class book
Operations			
Algebra			
Geometry			
Measurement			
Data Analysis			
Probability			

Building Comprehension of Mathematics

A Reader of Mathematics Text Needs to:

• Preview the text before reading, notice visuals and diagrams.

• Think about what you know on the topic.

• Visualize the mathematics function you are reading about.

• Make connections to things in the real world.

• Reread often.

• Notice the structure of the writing in the math selection:

> *Narrative:* Tells a story. This could be a piece of literature with mathematics concepts or a story problem.

> *Expository:* Explains and defines concepts and vocabulary.

> *Procedural:* Explains the steps in doing something.

• Think about the author's purpose. What does the author want you to learn?

• Look for key words in the text. Jot them down and use them to summarize.

• Other: What can you add?

Is Pluto a Planet?

38 How Inquiry Curriculum Supports Comprehension

CATHY TOWER

MEET THE AUTHOR

CATHY TOWER *recently completed her PhD in educational psychology at Michigan State University. Her research and teaching experience is in the area of literacy, especially nonfiction writing. Prior to graduate school, she was a fourth grade teacher who delighted in engaging in inquiry with her students. Dr. Tower is currently an assistant professor of curriculum at the University of Toledo.*

FOCUS QUOTE

An inquiry curriculum takes children's questions as the central concern of classroom life.

Inquiry curriculum also requires a shift in the way texts are typically used. Instead of sole reliance on a single text (such as a science textbook), inquiry curriculum includes investigation of many different texts and engages communication systems such as art, drama, language, dance, music, or math.

I am a great believer in the power of inquiry to support student (and teacher!) learning in varied ways (Tower 2000). To begin, let's consider an example from my fourth grade classroom. My students engaged in a whole-class inquiry related to space and the solar system. We began by sharing our prior knowledge about the topic with each other and by collecting and sharing a wide variety of sources on the topic. One of the texts that my students and I came upon during our space inquiry was a short newspaper article that said that the IAU (International Astronomical Union) was considering whether or not to demote Pluto from a planet to something they called a "Trans-Neptunian Object." My students were stunned that something they had long regarded as a fact was being challenged: Pluto is the ninth planet! They could not believe that a "fact" could be changed, just like that, by a bunch of people in a room somewhere.

A Flood of Questions

This new idea resulted in a flood of new questions: What are the defining characteristics of a planet? Why have we decided to call some things planets, but other things asteroids or meteors or stars or moons? Who gets to decide? What would it mean if there were suddenly only eight planets?

These new questions led to new purposes for reading and to the selection of new sources (and a return to old ones with a new purpose). This new idea also helped students to better understand how it is that scientific sources can become out of date. If Pluto's status were changed, then all of a sudden every book on planets in our classroom library would be inaccurate. The new idea also helped students to understand the constructed nature of knowledge.

Interests Drive Inquiry Processes

In our classroom inquiry, this concern over the status of Pluto, and the new questions it raised, was but one of many space-related topics that we discussed, read about, researched, and wrote about. When it came time for small groups to choose subtopics for their inquiry, one group chose Pluto and wrote an informational book titled "Pluto: The Smallest Planet?" Other projects focused on the universe, Mars and the Pathfinder, satellites, the Milky Way, and John Glenn. My students and I closely followed the IAU story, and we were greatly relieved when the astronomers decided to leave Pluto alone.

Extending to Writing

My students' new, more sophisticated stance toward the nature of knowledge was revealed in the writing that they produced. For example, one group wrote:

> Some scientists believe that Pluto was once Neptune's moon, but escaped from its orbit around Neptune. Most people now consider it one of the nine planets, but around September or October of 1998, scientists started debating about whether Pluto really was a planet, or just some Trans-Neptunian object. But in February 1999, they made their final decision that Pluto was still a planet. One of the reasons they questioned Pluto being a planet is because it switches places with Neptune. Right now, Pluto is the farthest planet from the sun.

In this excerpt, it seems pretty clear that these students have come to understand the world (indeed, the universe) in a more sophisticated way. Their use of language such as "some scientists believe," "most people now consider," and "scientists started debating" suggests that they understand that knowledge is constructed and negotiated. This understanding is critical in supporting the kind of reading behavior that fosters deep comprehension of a wide variety of texts from many different sources.

What is Inquiry Process?

My understanding and use of the term "inquiry process" or "inquiry curriculum" is based on the writings of such scholars as Harste (1994) and Short and Burke (1996). An inquiry curriculum takes children's questions as the central concerns of classroom life. It requires a major shift from the more traditional practices of schooling. For example, in an inquiry curriculum, students are expected to be problem posers, not just problem solvers. They are involved in every aspect of the curriculum, from posing questions and finding sources to assessment.

FIGURE 38–1 Inquiry brings natural motivation into the learning environment as children explore their own questions and take a part in planning their study.

FIGURE 38–2 Students learn to pose questions and actively engage with the topic.

FIGURE 38–3 Art, writing, and visual expression can be a part of the inquiry process.

Inquiry curriculum also requires a shift in the way texts are typically used. Instead of sole reliance on a single text (such as a science textbook), inquiry curriculum includes investigation of many different texts and engages communication systems such as art, drama, language, dance, music, or math. This opens the dialogue wide and allows a variety of perspectives (sometimes competing perspectives) to be discussed and considered. By opening the door to many systems of communication, art, music, and drama can become essential elements of building understanding.

Inquiry Process and Comprehension

Critical Steps
1. Identify purposes for reading/inquiry
2. Build background knowledge
3. Engage in critical questioning
4. Express learning through multiple communication systems

The nature of an inquiry curriculum and the shift in the way texts are used provide unique opportunities to support reading comprehension. First, *purposes* for reading are critical. As purposes develop, they will dictate what gets read, when, and how. In an inquiry curriculum, students set the purposes for reading by asking compelling questions and exploring a topic of interest. Second, activating *existing prior knowledge* and *building new background knowledge* are important processes that support both inquiry and comprehension. In inquiry, students start by sharing what they know, and then they build on this knowledge as they become expert on a topic of interest. Third, *critical questioning* of the author, the texts, and students' own assumptions encourage the kinds of strategic reading behavior that supports comprehension. In inquiry, students often encounter conflicting sources, and they must then use critical reasoning to decide what information is most credible.

Merging New Learning with Prior Understandings

As the Pluto example illustrates, inquiry curriculum can open the door to multiple points of view, sometimes disrupting the knowledge that students take for granted and spurring them to pursue new, more sophisticated understandings of the world.

Support to comprehension   Teachers who implement an inquiry curriculum in their classrooms are creating multiple opportunities to support the comprehension of their students. Comprehension is enhanced when readers

- activate and connect to their prior knowledge
- read selectively
- have clear purposes for reading
- set goals and monitor their progress toward those goals
- consider the context surrounding a text (including the author, the time period in which it was written, the source of the text, etc.)
- read critically and question the texts as they go along (Duke and Pearson 2002)

The goals and purposes that drive an inquiry curriculum match well with our goals for supporting students' reading comprehension. In inquiry curriculum, students engage in the kinds of discussions and reading activities that encourage critical questioning and reflection, and that result in powerful learning experiences. Perhaps such engagement will motivate a student to join the IAU and continue the fight to defend Pluto's honor. Certainly, such engagement encourages students to be active meaning-makers who seek new understandings of the world around them.

References

Duke, N. K., and P. D. Pearson. 2002. "Effective practices for developing reading comprehension." In *What Research Has to Say about Reading Instruction* (3rd ed.), edited by A. E. Farstrup and S. J. Samuels, 205–42. Newark, DE: International Reading Association.

Harste, J. C. 1994. "Visions of literacy." *Indiana Media Journal* 17 (1): 27–32.

Short, K. G., and C. Burke. 1996. "Examining our beliefs and practices through inquiry." *Language Arts* 73 (2): 97–104.

Tower, C. 2000. "Questions that matter: Preparing elementary students for the inquiry process." *The Reading Teacher* 53 (7): 550–57.

KEY QUESTIONS

1. Think back to a powerful learning experience of your own, preferably a time when you sought answers to a personally meaningful question. This may not have happened within a school context! What were the elements that made it powerful and memorable? What role did texts play in this experience? How can we engage children in such memorable experiences in a classroom?

2. In what ways can you envision an inquiry curriculum supporting the comprehension development of your students?

3. What are some strategies for engaging students in asking personally meaningful questions?

4. How might a teacher model the inquiry process for her students?

5. What role do texts play in the inquiry process? How might your use of texts change when adopting an inquiry-based curriculum?

Inquiry Planning Sheet

Researcher_____ Date _____

Our classroom inquiry is _____

My personal questions are_____

_____

_____

This topic is important to me because _____

The resources I am going to use in my inquiry include _____

_____

_____

As I read and gather information, the good reader strategies I am going to con-sciously apply include _____

_____

_____

I am going to present what I have learned through (choose as many as you like)

☐Drawing ☐Writing ☐Doing an oral presentation ☐Creating Power Point slides

☐Dramatizing ☐Other _____

_____

_____

Comprehending Standardized Tests **39**

LINDA HOYT

MEET THE AUTHOR

LINDA HOYT'S *family is the heartbeat of her life. She and Steve have been married for 33 years and have three children. Brenden was born in 1978. Megan and Kyle, the twins her husband has lovingly dubbed their "variety pack," were born in 1980.*

FOCUS QUOTE

There is a huge difference between test practice and test preparation. Test *practice* happens when teachers pass out reams of practice passages and questions that students dutifully complete. Test *preparation* occurs when passages and their corresponding questions are carefully analyzed by a team of students while they talk about HOW they might navigate the passage and HOW they might address the questions.

Tests have become a hallmark of this era in education. Like newspapers, magazines, poetry, and fiction narrative, tests are part of our current world. The best advice that can be offered is to teach the attributes of "test" as a genre (Calkins, Montgomery, and Santman 1998). When children pay attention to the attributes that make a test a test and notice the way this particular genre works, they develop an understanding of the structure of a test, and of the inherent game that is played by the test designers.

When learners explore testing as a genre, they begin to see that there are strategies that will help them negotiate this particular kind of writing. They are better able to focus on the content of the selections when the big day arrives. Testing can be fraught with stress and trauma for many children. How wonderful it would be if children could understand the genre so well that they would have an arsenal of comprehension-seeking strategies ready for navigating a test. How wonderful it would be if they could move quickly and efficiently past the hurdle of *test day* so teachers could get back to the business of raising deep thinkers and explicit writers for the challenges of the future.

Test Practice or Test Preparation?

There is a huge difference between test practice and test preparation. Test *practice* happens when teachers pass out reams of practice passages and questions that students dutifully complete. Test *preparation* occurs when passages and their corresponding questions are carefully analyzed by a team of students while they talk about HOW they might navigate the passage and HOW they might address the questions. Correct answers are important, of course, but the talk focuses on the structure of the test, understanding what the questions are really asking, and so on. The critical difference falls in the category of strategy use and comprehension. When students learn to apply strategies to test taking, and have a deep knowledge of the genre of "test," the content of individual passages becomes much less of a hurdle.

Study the Genre of Test

We study the genre of poetry, of biography, and of persuasive writing. Why not study the genre of testing? What makes a test a test? How is it different from a textbook and its questions? What is the goal of the test writers? How do the writers' goals affect their writing and the way we should read a test? What do we notice about the questions? Is there a pattern to the way questions are worded, to the order in which questions appear? Can we discern what the test developers are thinking when they write? Is there a pattern to the kind of passages they include? What is the balance between fiction and nonfiction in the passages? Are the nonfiction passages all narratives (descriptions), or are there menus, invitations, poems, or directions?

Test Taking Strategies
focus "game face"
predicting
★read instructions/directions
memory
context clues
"codes" help you
wear your glasses if you have them
post-it notes on answer sheet
Never skip a question—just guess
Read the questions BEFORE the story

FIGURE 39–1 Students discuss test-taking strategies and create their own lists of strategies to remember for test taking. This list was created on the first day of studying the genre of test. As the study continued, the list became richer and more well developed.

Consider Stamina for Testing

Lucy Calkins, *et al.* (1998) remind us of the importance of stamina for testing. They report that the average test of reading comprehension at grade 3 takes 60–70 minutes to complete, yet third graders average less than 15 minutes of sustained independent reading each day. How can we possibly expect children to have the new experience of sustaining attention for such a long time AND do their best thinking about the content of the passages and follow the game of testing all at the same time? We can't. We must take stamina seriously. Children need to be engaged in independent, sustained reading for at least 30 minutes a day and have one day a week where they stretch to 60 minutes. If they do this every week all year, they will build stamina for independence and for sustaining attention just as a runner builds stamina before a big race. The development of stamina will allow the learner to focus on content when testing day arrives.

Read Tests with a Different Purpose

When we read a novel, we expect characters to unfold, for events to hold us spellbound, and for the sense of intimacy between author and reader to carry us into higher levels of thinking. Not so with a test! In a test, we need to read like the writer of the test. We need to figure out the tricks they are playing with us and the clues they have left behind. We need to beat them at their own game.

If you read a test with the idea that you are outguessing the writer, that is a completely different mindset than we use in normal reading. That is a strategy for comprehending that we don't use with any other kind of print. Figuring out the test writers' thinking, their tricks and their distracting questions, enables a reader to comprehend the test in a way that transcends the passage and leads to higher levels of success.

Model the Thinking of a Good Test Taker

We all understand the power of thinking aloud and opening a window into our thought processes for students. Why not do think alouds using test passages and questions? During think alouds you can model all of the good test-taking strategies you want the students to employ. You can model reading the questions first or show the way you go back and forth continuously between the passage and the questions searching for answers. A think aloud allows you to demonstrate the way you paraphrase a question in your own words and try to figure out what the test writer is really after. You could model the process of elimination that you use as you consider the various answers to questions and think out loud about how you select one answer.

Have you ever watched "Who Wants to Be a Millionaire?" on television? The contestants do a lot of thinking out loud as they choose answers. They will explicitly say things like: "I was drawn to C but I am not going to choose it because_____, or A and D both make sense to me, I am going to choose A because _____." While our students can't poll an audience or place a phone call to a friend as they do on the program, they can benefit from the same kind of verbalization.

Model the Language of Tests

Test questions and directions are often written in a formal register that is very different from that of oral speech, and certainly different from most of the literature we read to our students. Embedding test-style language into your daily interactions with students and weaving this formal register into your conversations about books will help learners to become familiar with these often unfamiliar structures. I place a chart near my read-aloud area with these stems as a helpful reminder to include them in my conversations with students.

Study Lots of Questions

Engage the students in analyzing test questions. Encourage them to wonder: What is this question really asking? Could I paraphrase this question in my own words? Could I sort these questions into categories such as questions that are answered right in the text, questions that require an inference, and so on? Help them notice that in the genre of test, we cannot rely heavily on our world knowledge. This is a genre that requires reliance on the text more than on our ability to make connections.

Test Question Stems:
The main idea of the story...
passage
selection
• A detail that supports the main idea...
Identify the inference.
• This story is mainly about...
• _____ are also known as _____
• Which of these happened first?
• Which sentence from the story ... an opinion?

FIGURE 39–2 Students analyze the formats of questions and collect question stems that appear to be common formats.

The Language of Tests

How was the central problem resolved?

What unexpected event happened?

The mood/tone of this writing could best be described as _____.

What conclusion can you draw?

Which statement is not true?

This story is mostly about _____.

A good title for this story would be _____.

Why did _____ happen?

What did _____ probably mean?

The best answer is _____.

There is enough information to suggest that _____.

This selection was written to_____ (inform, explain, describe . . .)

If another paragraph were added it would probably tell that ____.

What would happen if ____.

The purpose of this is to_____.

Which of the following is not true?

Which sentence best tells _____.

All of these are true except _____.

All of the above. None of the above.

Use this selection to consider   .

When the author writes _____, it probably means that _____

The main purpose of this is _____.

The main idea of this is _____.

Which of the following does not belong in the paragraph?

Why was _____?

According to this selection, _____.

This story is told from the perspective of _____.

How do you know that _____?

The most important ideas in this selection are _____.

There is enough evidence to say that (name of character) is probably____.

What would be most likely to happen after the end of the story?

What was the first thing she did?

This was written mainly to: (explain, show, describe, celebrate)

This would be most likely to be found in a book entitled, _____.

The word _____ in paragraph 2 means _____.

In which sentence does the word _____ mean the same as in the sentence above?

Select an answer in which the underlined word has the same meaning.

To _____ is to _____. (Example: To *cut* is to *slice*.)

A _____ is someone who_____.

I was *gratified* when _____. *Gratified* means: _____

In the selection _____ means _____.

A synonym for _____ would be _____.

As students look at categories of questions, it can also be helpful to notice patterns in the way the questions are worded. Are there typical formats to watch for? What are the signal words in the question, such as: "Which of the following is *not* true?" "There is enough information in this passage to *suggest* that___." "The *main purpose* of this article is to_____." Familiarity with these signal words can help readers to comprehend the purpose of the question more clearly, leading them to find the answer more easily.

Have Students Write Test-Style Questions

I model writing test-style questions about a book we have shared, a math experience, or a unit in science. I show the class how I think of the question and then design four possible answers. Students really get a charge out of watching me first position the correct answer and then come up with three almost correct distractors that are designed to "trick" the reader. When students watch the process several times, they begin to understand the relationship between questions and answers and see more clearly the game-like pattern that they must unravel.

Once the students understand the process, they are ready to design their own test-style questions. I like to have them work in pairs, sharing the pen and thinking together as they design the question, the correct answer, and the distractors. Over time, I ensure that they have practice writing questions with several formats, including vocabulary analysis such as: "In paragraph two, the word _____ probably means_____."

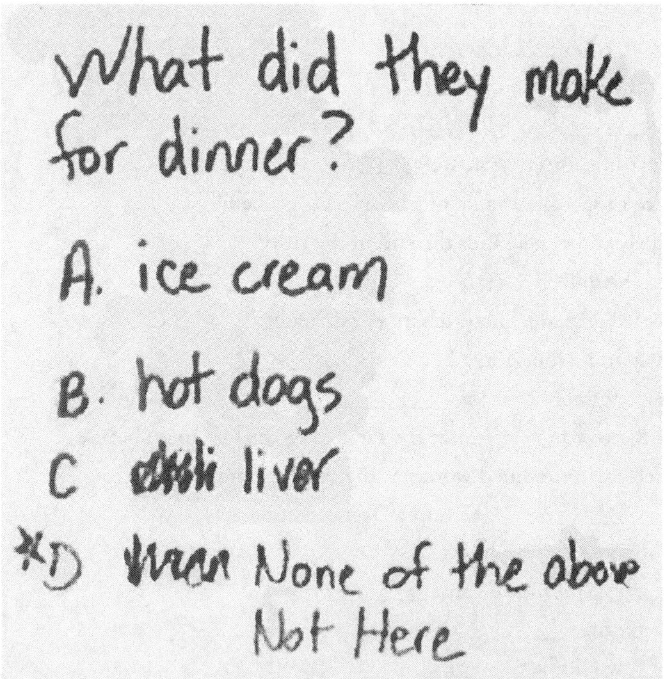

> What did they make for dinner?
>
> A. ice cream
>
> B. hot dogs
>
> C ~~chili~~ liver
>
> *D ~~None~~ None of the above
>   Not Here

FIGURE 39–3 A variety of question/answer formats, including "none of the above" can be modeled to build familiarity for students.

Children love to quiz each other with their questions. As soon as the questions are drafted the students circulate, quizzing each other and thinking aloud about how they could solve the question. Since we are designing the questions around our literature studies, science, social studies, and math curriculum this is a wonderful content review that keeps us focused on core content while we are learning about tests.

Beat the Teacher

Another twist that students really enjoy is "Beat the Teacher." After designing questions, I place myself on the hot seat and they get to ask me their questions. They work really hard to review their passages and pick challenging questions that they sincerely hope I cannot answer. After a few rounds of "Beat the Teacher," I often have the students number off from one through four. Then, as the student-generated questions are brought to the front of the room, I can say: "O.K., number threes. On your feet, you are the teacher!" Now the students who are number threes come forward, put their heads together to discuss the question, and then think out loud for the class about their answer.

Student-generated test questions offer a huge advantage when compared to packaged test materials. The test materials are rarely related to core curriculum and take a great deal of time away from teaching time in science,

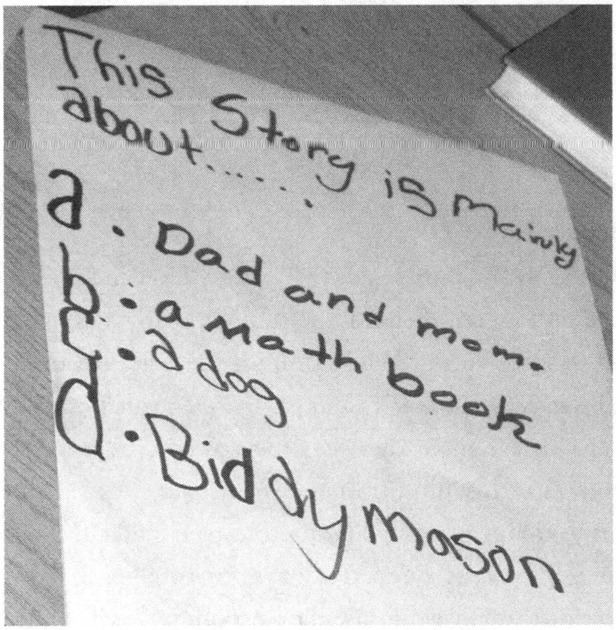

FIGURE 39–4 Students work in pairs to generate questions and answers about the a literature selection, science, social studies, or math content.

math, etc. When students generate their own questions about curriculum we are already studying, they have the advantage of deepening their content knowledge while they are learning about testing.

Fact or Fib: Creating True/False Statements

If the test in your state includes a true/false portion, you might find it helpful to work with *Fact or Fib* (Wilson 1999). In this format, students review literature or content-area studies. Then they create statements, some of which are true and some of which are deliberately false. In the following second grade examples, students used their study of bats as a source of information for Fact/Fib statements. As in "Beat the Teacher," students love to exchange their Fact/Fib sheets and try to trick each other.

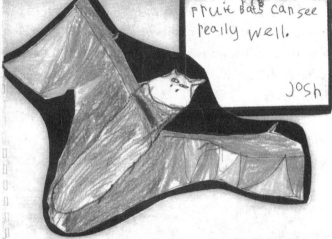

FIGURE 39–5a, b As you can see in Josh's example, he made the statement: Bats are blind. Under the flap, he clarifies: Fib! Fruit bats can see really well.

Not a Matter of Choice

When learners prepare for testing by thinking at the strategy level and trying to understand the genre of testing, they better understand how to navigate tests with confidence and success. When teachers support those investigations with explicit modeling of test-taking strategies and student-generated questions built around existing curriculum, learners stay focused on core curriculum while exploring a genre that they must come to understand.

Students must learn to comprehend standardized tests. If students do not score high enough on reading tests, no matter what other evidence we may have of their growth in reading, we can lose the freedom to teach in the ways we know are best for children. When test scores are high, there is trust in the school and in the practices of our profession.

Testing is not teaching (Graves 2002), but we can teach how to comprehend the standardized tests that are a reality in the lives of our children.

References

Calkins, Lucy, Kate Montgomery, and Donna Santman. 1998. *A Teacher's Guide to Standardized Reading Tests: Knowledge Is Power.* Portsmouth, NH: Heinemann.

Graves, Donald. 2002. *Testing is Not Teaching: What Should Count in Education.* Portsmouth, NH: Heinemann.

Scruggs, Thomas, and Margo Mastropieri. 1992. *Teaching Test-Taking Skills: Helping Students Show What They Know.* Newton Upper Falls, MA: Brookline Books.

Wilson, Jodi. 1999. "Fact or Fib." In *Revisit, Reflect, Retell: Strategies for Improving Reading Comprehension* by Linda Hoyt. Portsmouth, NH: Heinemann.

KEY QUESTIONS

1. How do you assist students in developing a strategic stance toward tests?

2. What do you know about the genre of the test in your state? Do you know the balance between fiction and nonfiction? Common question formats and signal words? How might you help students better understand these formats?

3. How might student-generated questions, Beat the Teacher, or Fact or Fib fit into your work with students?

4. What are some test preparation strategies that have worked well for you and your students?

Observation Guide: Focus on Test-Taking Strategies

Researcher(s)_____ Date _____

You and your fellow researchers will need to gather some test practice passages and questions. Your job is to really look closely at the way they are formatted. What do you notice about the way the pages look? What do you observe about the questions and so on. Jot your observations below:

Now, you are going to work with one passage and set of questions as a team. Read it together. Then look at the questions. Don't just answer the questions, you want to think about the strategies you use to find the answers. Think out loud. Tell each other how you are finding the answers. Jot your strategies here.

Look closely at the questions and their answers. Talk with each other about how to eliminate some possible answers very quickly. What helps you know what can't be right? What strategies can you use when you don't know the answer to a question? Talk to each other about strategies that might help. Jot your thinking below.

Good test takers think of this like a game. Talk to your team. How is this like a game? What strategies will help you focus on outsmarting the test developers? Your job is to "get" the answers. Write your strategies below.

Now, try your strategies with another passage. Think out loud about what you are doing. Talk to each other about what is working. Have you added any strategies to your list or taken any away?

What advice would you offer to someone who is about to take a test?

Helpful Test-Taking Strategies

- Read the questions first. Then read the passage to find the answers.

- Move continuously back and forth between the passage and the questions.

- Remember this is like a game. Your job is to think like the test writer and "get" the answer.

- Use the passage to confirm your answers. Don't just rely on memory.

- Consider what the questions are really asking.

- Look for key words in the question.

- Use a process of elimination to select answers. Cross out answers you know are wrong so you have less to think about.

- Use a sticky note to mark your place on the answer sheet.

- If the question asks for main idea, remember that all answers are probably from the story. You need to think about the big key idea that reflects the whole passage.

- When a question tells you to choose the "best" answer, that means it is just better than the others. All may be correct and it is possible that none of them are perfect.

- Be careful of answers with words like *always* or *never*. Unless it is specifically stated in the passage, absolute answers are rarely correct. (Calkins, Montgomery, and Santman 1998).

- Always answer every question, even if you have to guess.

- Don't get stuck on any one question. If you have time, you can come back to the tricky ones.

- Notice boxes before a selection. Their content is very important.

40

Puzzled About Comprehension and Standardized Testing?

BARBARA COLEMAN

MEET THE AUTHOR

Barbara Coleman *is a curriculum specialist at Wingate Elementary, a Title 1 school in Monroe, North Carolina. High standards and rigorous instruction have led learners to significant levels of achievement while nurturing a deep love of learning.*

FOCUS QUOTE

How do you achieve an authentic fit between reading comprehension and standardized testing? How do you remain true to your strongly held beliefs about how children become literate individuals and still meet the demands of high-stakes testing?

How do you achieve an authentic fit between reading comprehension and standardized testing? How do you remain true to your strongly held beliefs about how children become literate individuals and still meet the demands of high-stakes testing? It saddens me to walk into classrooms where teachers have resorted to teaching to the test, emphasizing "correct" answers at the cost of reading for deep meaning, authentic purpose, and relying on instruction in the strategies that empower learners.

In reading Lucy Calkins' (Calkins, Montgomery, and Santman 1998) book *A Teacher's Guide to Standardized Reading Tests,* I realized that she was feeling the same frustration in her work with her colleagues. She quotes Kathleen Tolan "Test practice is not test preparation" (p. 70).

Teach "Test" As a Genre

Tests are a unique genre. They have attributes not seen anywhere else in print. We need to teach children about how this genre works so that they understand how to navigate its challenges. Just as we teach the fine points of poetry, biography, and nonfiction we need to teach the structures and comprehension strategies to enable our children to do their best on standardized reading tests. As we explore the workings of "test," it is imperative that children do not expect to have deep connecting thoughts and discussions, but rather to outguess the test makers (Calkins, Montgomery, and Santman 1998) and solve the puzzle that each test passage presents.

Teach Tests as a Puzzle

Have you ever thought that you would find the answer to this troublesome question in a jigsaw puzzle? The following lesson series is built on the belief that reading comprehension needs to be taught with a variety of authentic texts in a nurturing and strategic way. The intent of these lessons is to describe and demonstrate to children that good reader strategies can be applied to the genre of testing.

A Metaphor for Standardized Tests

Think about a jigsaw puzzle as a metaphor for standardized reading tests. I believe most people keep the box lid with a picture of the completed puzzle in front of them while they are putting a puzzle together. Sometimes they focus on the picture as whole, and at other times, they look closely at one particular section. They move back and forth conceptually and physically between the picture and the puzzle pieces. Doesn't that sound like the good test takers we've watched as they navigate their way through standardized reading tests? The good test takers move back and forth between the questions and the passage, looking sometimes at the big ideas and sometimes more closely at a fine point. These good test takers use strategies to solve the puzzle of the test. It is this metaphor of putting together a puzzle that I used to help students successfully put the pieces of reading comprehension and testing together as a genre.

The Lessons

I have very purposefully designed the lessons to be taught over a period of days. I did this in order to give students an opportunity to process their own thinking and strategy use. Learners come up with many compelling questions about tests and how they work, so it is important to give them time. This isn't just about filling out practice pages; it is about understanding "testing as a genre" and the strategies that will best help them succeed. The ultimate goal of these lessons is to gradually release responsibility to the students in putting all the pieces of the puzzle together.

DAY 1/PART ONE:

- Give each student a handful of puzzle pieces from a 100–200 piece puzzle.
- Do not show them the picture on the puzzle box.
- Give the instructions that they are not allowed to ask questions, to talk to one another, or to help one another.
- Give them about a minute to work their pieces.
- Stop them. Tell them to turn to a partner and talk about this experience. They should then be ready to share with the group after two minutes.
- Record on chart paper the feelings/thoughts of the students. (Keep this chart for future reference and label it Chart #1.)

In part one of the lesson, the students had no idea what the puzzle was supposed to look like or even if they had all the pieces. Many times students just dive right into reading a testing selection much the same way—not previewing the title, not thinking about their prior knowledge, or not asking questions before they read.

DAY 1/PART TWO:

- Now, give the students (cooperative groups) an entire puzzle to work (around 50 pieces or less) along with the box cover of the puzzle.
- The instructions are different this time: they work as a group and talk with one another. They should be "thinking aloud" with their group as they decide where to place the puzzle pieces.
- It is important that the students are very specific in their conversation with each other about this experience compared to the first experience.
- One member of each group should be the recorder of the thoughts and comments.
- Record on chart paper the thoughts of the class from this experience. (Keep this chart for future reverence and label it Chart #2.)

The purpose of part one is to get students be realize the significance of "before" reading strategies such as:

- **Preview the text** ~ looking at the picture of the puzzle (part two)
- **Activate prior knowledge** ~ knowing how to put a puzzle together
- **Making predictions** ~ trying to see if a puzzle piece fits
- **Asking questions** ~ deciding where to start, such as with forming the border first or working directly with a particular section of the puzzle

DAY 2:

- Put the two chart papers side by side (Chart 1 and Chart 2).
- Discuss with the students the differences and likenesses.

- Talk about which puzzle was easier to work with and why.
- Which strategy was most helpful and why?
- Lead the students in conversation/responses by "implanting" good reader strategies such as:
  - Landmarks or key words = colors, objects, etc., on the puzzle
  - Citing/referencing the text = looking at the picture of the puzzle
  - Prediction = trying a piece to see if it fits
  - Confirming = placing a piece down

The purpose of this lesson is for students to begin making the connection that working a puzzle is very similar to the Before, During, and After strategies that good readers use. It would be good to create a T-chart comparing "puzzle" strategies with good reader strategies.

Sample T-Chart

Good Reader Strategies	"Puzzle" Strategies
Previewing the text	Looking at the picture of puzzle
Activating prior knowledge	Knowing how to put a puzzle together
Asking questions	Deciding where to start
Making predictions	Trying a piece to see if it fits
Confirming or changing predictions	Placing a piece down
Identifying key ideas or concepts	Matching colors, objects, etc., on the puzzle
Using context and clues to get meaning	Looking at the picture of the puzzle and pieces of unknown words that are not yet worked in the puzzle

The following chart from *Revisit, Reflect, Retell* (Hoyt 1999) can be very helpful as the students discuss helpful strategies. They might review this and then create their own version labeled, "Good Test-Taker Strategies."

BEFORE I READ

- I take time to think about what I already know on this topic.
- I look through the pages to think about charts, boldfaced headings, and pictures.
- I ask myself "I Wonder" questions before reading.

WHILE I READ

- I stop often to think about what I understand.
- I continue to consider my questions about the topic.

- I use context and all possible clues to get to the meaning of unknown words.
- I try to identify key ideas and concepts.

After I read

- I turn back through the pages and reflect on what I have learned.
- I think about my "I Wonder" questions.
- I use what I have learned by writing or talking about it.

Day 3: (Before-Reading Test Strategies)

Many students are not clear as to what a test question is actually asking them. This lesson focuses on understanding questions through a question sort. (Students are not going to work with the passage yet.) First, students cut the questions apart so they can be handled and easily moved around. Next, they identify key words in each question and then place the question in a category such as those listed in the box below. Have them save the questions in an envelope, as they will be used again in a later lesson.

Main Idea/Supporting Details	Author's Purpose
Text Features	Vocabulary in Context

Example of questions students created:

- What is the purpose of the first subheading in the selection?
- What is the main idea of the selection?
- Based on the context of paragraph 3, what does _____ mean?
- With which statement would the author most likely agree?
- Based on the selection, what will most likely happen next?
- Which of the following best describes Joe?
- What is the significance of Joe's decision to buy the bicycle?

The purpose of this lesson is to analyze the questions by looking at key words and deciding what each question might be asking. It is important that students paraphrase each question, putting it in their own words, so they understand that the strategies they use in all their reading is done with the genre of testing as well.

Day 4: (During-Reading Test Strategies)

- This will be the first time the students actually see the test selection.
- It is helpful to enlarge the passage so the text is very large.
- First, tell the students to cover up the selection and read the title only.
- To activate their prior knowledge, have them predict words or phrases they think may appear in the passage.
- Next, have them read the purpose or summary statement and underline the main idea or key words
- Last, tell the students to read the selection. As they read, they should write key words in the margin (Hoyt 1999) or draw a quick sketch. If your testing rules do not allow writing on the passage, you can have the students write their key words on sticky notes to the side of the passage.
- Guide a discussion about strategies they used to navigate the passage.

The purpose of this lesson is to look carefully at the passage, marking key words and main ideas.

Day 5: (After-Reading Test Strategies)

- Return the enlarged selection and the envelopes of questions to the students.

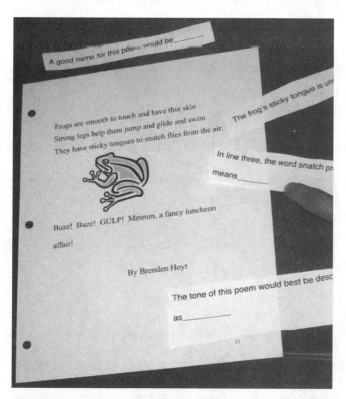

FIGURE 40–1 Learners tape questions next to the passage where the source of their thinking is listed.

- Tell the students to skim/scan the selection and "tape" their questions where they think the answer is found.
- Have them underline in the selection their answer choice.
- Then ask students to share with their groups what they "notice," such as the questions are not necessarily answered in the selection in numerical order, the variety of questions asked, etc.
- Put Charts 1 and 2 back up. Record students' observations and compelling questions and add to the T-chart if that was done on Day 2.

The purpose of this lesson is putting all the pieces of test comprehension together.

Day 6: (Putting it all together)

- Now give each student the actual test selection with the questions and answers and have them "complete the puzzle."
- Show them how a test designer creates one correct answer and three distractors, or uses negative wording like: "Which of the following is not true?" causing a shift in their puzzle-solving pattern.

References

Calkins, L., K. Montgomery, and D. Santman. 1998. *A Teacher's Guide to Standardized Reading Tests: Knowledge Is Power.* Portsmouth, NH: Heinemann.

Hoyt, L. 1999. *Revisit, Reflect, Retell: Strategies for Improving Reading Comprehension.* Portsmouth, NH: Heinemann.

KEY QUESTIONS

1. What strategies do you think learners should develop as good test takers?

2. How might these lessons support your students in better understanding the genre of test?

3. What other lessons might focus your students on the attributes of test as a genre?

4. If you were to repeat this series of lessons for poetry, informational text, and other genres likely to appear in a standardized test, what categories would you select for the question sort?

5. Could test practice booklets have a place in this analysis of test as a genre?

Sample Questions for Puzzle Lessons

A good name for this poem would be _____

_____

✂ -

In line three, the word *snatch* probably means

_____

✂ -

The tone of this poem would best be described

as _____

✂ -

The frog's sticky tongue is used for _____

_____

✂ -

Sample Passage for Puzzle Lessons

Frogs are smooth to touch and have thin skin

Strong legs help them jump and glide and swim

They have sticky tongues to snatch flies from

the air.

Buzz! Buzz! GULP! Mmmm, a fancy luncheon

affair!

By Brenden Hoyt

Sample Questions

A good name for this poem would be _____

   A. A Frog Has a Sticky Tongue
   B. All About Frogs
   C. Amphibians
   D. Lunch

In line three, the word *snatch* probably means _____

   A. squash
   B. catch quickly
   C. step on
   D. send away

The tone of this poem would best be described as _____

   A. imaginary
   B. serious
   C. a little silly
   D. sad

The frog's sticky tongue is used for _____

   A. holding onto lollipops
   B. sticking to trees
   C. diving in the water
   D. catching food

Part Seven

Understanding Comprehension and the Emergent Reader

41 Comprehension for Emergent Readers

LINDA HOYT

MEET THE AUTHOR

LINDA HOYT *is fascinated by the role of expectations in the learning of children. She believes that teachers who have high expectations, who talk to learners using rich, adult language, foster self-esteem and help learners to reach greater heights in literacy.*

FOCUS QUOTE

Emergent readers can and should be exposed to a wide range of meaning-seeking strategies so they understand from the beginning that reading is about comprehension. Anything less is not reading.

The old adage: "First you learn to read and then you read to learn" was often used to support a phonics first approach to literacy. But current thinking, including "No Child Left Behind" and "Reading First," suggests that we must simultaneously address phonemic awareness, phonics, fluency, vocabulary, AND comprehension from the earliest grades. Environments that overemphasize word study without concurrently supporting the development of comprehension are operating without the support of research (Stahl 2004).

. . . research does not suggest that these things [phonics, phonemic awareness and fluency] should be in place before comprehension instruction occurs. On the contrary, comprehension instruction and instruction in word recognition and decoding can occur side-by-side, and even work synergistically. (Pearson and Duke 2002; Pressley and Wharton-McDonald 2002; and Stahl 2004; from Duke/Reynolds, 2005, see Chapter 2).

If we accept that comprehension instruction needs to occur from the beginning, we then might wonder, what kind of comprehension instruction? Should this beginning instruction start with rote level recall or broaden to deeper levels and comprehension-seeking strategies?

Children Naturally Seek Meaning

Children naturally engage in higher-order thinking as they navigate their world. Toddlers learn very quickly to infer that when a parent frowns and looks stern, the parent is not happy. Prior knowledge tells the toddler that the refrigerator and cabinet are the places to look for food. Preschoolers ask questions incessantly in their zeal to understand their world. Babies learning to talk determine importance in words with their very first speech efforts. These first single word babblings include words of core importance such as "wawa . . . mama . . . dada . . . baba," long before full sentences can be generated.

Use the Language of Deep Thinking

Read alouds are a magical time in the primary grades when we can stretch learner thinking in literature that they cannot yet read on their own. During this time, our think alouds give significant insights into how readers think about meaning, how we make connections, ask questions, and so on.

An important dimension of the think aloud is the language we are modeling for primary students. As we attempt to make our thinking transparent for children, the words we use to talk about our thinking shape their understanding. The words we use to talk about thinking will spill over into the children's language and evolve in their partner talk. When we use rich language to talk about texts, we are modeling the language of comprehension and empowering learners with phrases they can use to support their own thinking.

STEMS TO BROADEN THINKING AND IMPLANT LANGUAGE:

I can picture this in my mind. . . .
I can infer that . . .
I am trying to think more deeply about this and I wonder . . .
I'd really like to ask the author about . . .

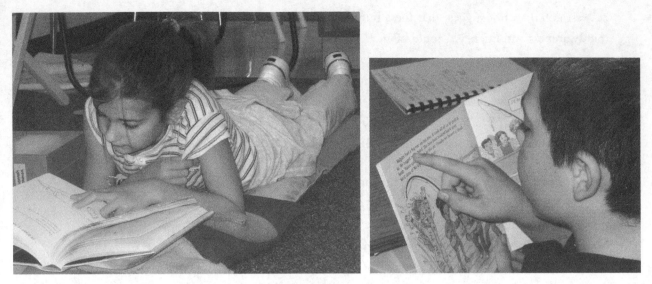

FIGURE 41–1a, b Emergent readers can and should be exposed to a wide range of meaning-seeking strategies so they understand from the beginning that reading is about comprehension. Anything less is not reading.

When I think about all of these bits of information, I know that

_____ must be really important because_____.

This makes me think about the time when I . . .

I can make a connection between this story and *When The Relatives Came!*

When I compare *Mrs. Wishy Washy* to *Mr. Dishy Washy,* I notice . . .

If I tell what happened, I am using surface thinking. If I think about *why* it happened, I am using deep thinking. Let's try to do some deep thinking together.

Research-Based Practices

There is a base of research focused on comprehension for our youngest learners. This research suggests that certain instructional approaches have been proven to deepen comprehension in primary grade students (Stahl 2004). Some of those research-based practices include:

- *Guided Retelling:* Students retell a story in their own words, taking care to include story elements such as problem, solution, characters, and setting.

- *Story Maps:* Students map story elements using drawings or written text to create a visual representation of the story elements.

- *Teacher-Generated Questions* to probe and deepen thinking: Open-ended teacher questions push learners to make comparisons, offer opinions, generate predictions, and extend their thinking.

- *Question Answer Relationships (QAR):* Right There, Think and

Search, Author and You, On My Own (Raphael 1986) are question categories that help readers understand how to locate answers to questions. Studies show positive affects of experiences in primary readers who learn to identify question types.

• **Reciprocal Teaching** (Palincsar, Yolara, and Brown 1992) is a during-reading process that engages readers in predicting, questioning, clarifying, and summarizing segments of text. In the primary grades, teachers integrate the four processes into read aloud and small group strategy lessons. (For more information on how to explicitly use reciprocal teaching, see *Make It Real* [Hoyt 2002]).

• **Targeted Discussion** of Background Knowledge (schema): Studies suggest targeting discussions of background knowledge to fit tightly around the topic of the text and then looking for justification in the text. This is important as young children sometimes rely on inaccurate or irrelevant knowledge and then quickly drift off topic. Inaccurate assumptions based on prior knowledge have even been found to override contradicting information stated explicitly in a text (Stahl 2004).

• **Directed Listening and Thinking Activity (DLTA):** In the late 1960s, Russell Stauffer designed DLTA to encourage prediction throughout a read aloud. Frequent pauses in reading encouraged predictions and encouraged justification of the prediction with evidence from the text.

• **DRTA (Directed Reading and Thinking Activity)** transfers the process to small group settings where learners have their own copy of a text. In this setting, sticky notes are placed at strategic points to cue the reader to stop, predict, and discuss before reading on.

• **Literature Webbing**/Event and Picture Sort: The teacher writes text events on cards or presents pictures from the text in a mixed-up order. Students place the cards and pictures in an order that makes sense to them before the book is read. The teacher reads the book and then students return to the cards and pictures to arrange them in the order in which they actually appeared in the selection. At this point, text-to-text connections, personal responses, and extensions to further reading and writing are included.

• **Visual Imagery:** Deliberate and conscious training in visual imaging has been found to make a positive difference in comprehension for primary students, even those identified as lowest achieving. You can begin by showing them a real object such as a stuffed animal or an apple. Cover the object with an upside down paper bag and ask the students to visualize the item. Encourage them to talk about what they see in their visualization, then uncover the item so they can look again. From

FIGURE 41–2 Students sort photographs before reading.

basic lessons like this, you can quickly branch out: "Boys and girls, can
you visualize yourself in bed this morning, when you were just beginning to wake up? What were you wearing? What was around you?
What woke you up? Chat with your elbow partner and tell about wak-
ing up." You will soon be engaging in visualizing during read alouds,
guided reading, and even mathematics.

• *Text Talk:* Beck and McKeown introduced Text Talk in 2001 as a research and development project designed to improve comprehension
and vocabulary. They reviewed children's literature selections and chose
three words from each to use for vocabulary focus. The books were read
to children in an interactive style with stop points for open-ended questions during the read aloud. The three focus words were written in
large bold letters and placed on a bulletin board next to the cover of the
book. The teacher and students actively tried to use the words and
placed a tally mark next to the word each time one was used in conversation or located in another book.

• *Video:* Documentary video can build bridges between the world of
experience and schooling. Videos of stories bring complex story lines to
very young students in a highly familiar format. When video, read
alouds, and guided reading are partnered with higher-order thinking,
research suggests that young children benefit.

• *Transactional Strategy Instruction (TSI):* This is a multistep approach to strategic interaction with text. The steps include: 1. setting
purposes, 2. activating and using prior knowledge, 3. getting the gist
during reading, 4. using text structure, 5. making predictions, 6. gener-

ating questions, 7. creating mental images and graphic representations, 8. summarizing, 9. using think aloud, and 10. using a variety of fix-up strategies. TSI can be modeled in read-aloud then used in guided and other small group formats to ensure learners are applying a rich range of strategies to make meaning as they read.

Finding Our Way

The important issue is to support comprehension from the beginning. Explicitly teach and support internalization of the strategies you want children to employ for the rest of their lives. Model comprehension strategies using language that the youngest children can synthesize into their own language banks as they learn to engage in literate conversations. Select teaching strategies that are proven to work with primary-age students. There is no evidence that comprehension should wait under after decoding is in place. There *is* evidence to suggest that as many as 20–25 percent of struggling students in fourth grade have strong word recognition and decoding skills (see Chapter 2) but have had inadequate support and preparation to comprehend the texts of their world.

References

Beck, I., and M. McKeown. 2001. "Text Talk: Capturing the Benefits of Read Aloud Experiences for Young Children." *The Reading Teacher* 55: 10–35.

Cole, Ardith Davis. 2004. *When Reading Begins: The Teacher's Role in Decoding, Comprehension, and Fluency.* Portsmouth, NH: Heinemann.

———. 2003. *Knee to Knee, Eye to Eye: Circling in on Comprehension.* Portsmouth, NH: Heinemann.

Duke, Nell, and Julia Moorhead Reynolds. 2005. "Learning from Comprehension Research: Critical Understandings to Guide Our Practice." In *Spotlight on Comprehension* edited by Linda Hoyt. Portsmouth, NH: Heinemann.

Hoyt, Linda. 2002. *Make It Real: Strategies for Success with Informational Texts.* Portsmouth, NH: Heinemann.

Owocki, Gretchen. 2003. *Comprehension: Strategic Instruction for K–3 Students.* Portsmouth, NH: Heinemann.

Palincsar, Ann Marie, David Yolara, and Ann Brown. 1992. *Using Reciprocal Teaching in the Classroom: A Guide for Teachers.* Ann Arbor, MI: University of Michigan.

Raphael, Taffy. 1986. "Teaching Question Answer Relationships, Revisited." *The Reading Teacher* 39: 516–22.

Stahl, Katherine Dougherty. 2004. "Proof, Practice, and Promise: Comprehension Strategy Instruction in the Primary Grades." *The Reading Teacher* 57 (7): 598–609.

Stauffer, Russell. 1969. *Directing Reading Maturity As a Cognitive Process.* New York: Harper and Row.

KEY QUESTIONS

1. Which comprehension strategies do you first teach to emergent readers?

2. To engage young children in deep thinking, we must offer them texts with something to think about. What are your favorite literature selections that help young children to think deeply and well?

3. How many times do you model a strategy before you begin to notice the children using the language of your think aloud when they talk about books?

4. How might you apply the research in this article about video for children with limited world experience?

My Reading Strategies

Reader_____ Book_____

Today when I read:

1. I made predictions

2. I made a movie in my head

3. I made a connection

4. I also _____

Draw a picture of your favorite part of the story and tell why you liked this part.

Retell Reflections

Reader_____ Story_____ Date _____

When I do a retell, I remember to:

	Yes	I will try to remember next time
Look at my audience	☐	☐
Think about the story	☐	☐
Speak clearly	☐	☐
Tell my favorite part and why I like it.	☐	☐

Include:

	Yes	I will try to remember next time
The beginning of the story	☐	☐
The middle of the story	☐	☐
The ending	☐	☐
Characters	☐	☐
Setting	☐	☐
The Problem	☐	☐

My rating of this story: It deserves _____ stars because _____

_____

_____

I am getting better at _____

I am going to work a little harder on _____

_____

_____

Strategy Log for Primary Readers

Reader _____

Date	Book Read	Decoding Fix-Up Strategies Used	Running Record Notes	Retell Score (1–5)	Comprehension Strategies Used

Observation of Comprehension Strategies

Reader_____

Look for evidence of a learner applying comprehension strategies The strategy was observed in:

a. read aloud
b. shared reading
c. guided reading
d. partner talk

e. class discussion
f. science
g. social studies
h. math

Note the date the strategy was observed and the setting in which it was used. Look for strategies to be used multiple times in many settings.

List date(s) strategy is observed and *context:*

Predicting								
Setting a Purpose								
Monitoring Understanding								
Visualizing								
Connecting								
Deciding What Is Important								
Questioning								
Inferring								
Summarizing								
Comparing/Contrasting								
Giving an Opinion/Evaluating								

Comprehending the Cereal Box 42

GRETCHEN OWOCKI
AND CAMILLE CAMMACK

MEET THE AUTHORS

GRETCHEN OWOCKI *is a researcher and teacher-educator at Saginaw Valley State University in University Center, Michigan, where she teaches courses in literacy, teacher research, and early childhood education. She is the author of several Heinemann books including:* Comprehension: Strategic Instruction for Young Children (2003).

CAMILLE CAMMACK *is an Associate Professor of Teacher Education at Saginaw Valley State University. Her areas of specialization include discourse analysis, gender in education, and preservice teacher education.*

FOCUS QUOTE

When teachers encourage children to draw on the literacies from their broader community and cultural lives, children are able to deepen reading comprehension.

We often hear that the ultimate goal of reading instruction is *comprehension*. As educators, we'll go along with that—as long as *comprehension* is broadly defined to include a wide range of strategies for constructing meaning in the real world. If comprehension instruction leads only to school-based literacies, such as answering teachers' questions, performing retellings, and filling out graphic organizers, then we believe the ultimate goal of reading instruction is lost.

Going Beyond School-Based Literacies

Effective reading instruction draws from and expands children's real-life literacies. It uses children's knowledge—both from home and school experiences—as a foundation for supporting their construction of new literacies. Not only do children learn to read and write, they also learn to ask questions, make inferences, read for a variety of purposes, and thoughtfully critique and evaluate text. The result of effective reading instruction is that children learn the specifics of decoding and comprehending *as* they learn to use written language in powerful and useful ways.

One way to support children's simultaneous development of school-based literacy practices and real-world literacies is to provide opportunities for them to use environmental print sources, such as printed advertisements, directions, toy packages, candy wrappers, and prepackaged mixes or cereal boxes as tools for developing their comprehension strategies. This practice brings together the literacy-related experiences children encounter in the world outside of school with more common pedagogical comprehension practices. As teachers engage children in such experiences, many find it helpful to have a specific set of comprehension strategies in mind. The strategies in the following figure are understood to facilitate comprehension (Owocki 2003) and can be used as a launching point for an environmental print inquiry.

Comprehension Strategies

Strategy:	What It Involves:
Predicting and Inferring	• Drawing on prior knowledge to make hypotheses (or predictions) and assumptions (or inferences) about content • Confirming and revising hypotheses and inferences
Purpose Setting	• Formulating goals • Overviewing and reading selectively to meet goals • Evaluating whether goals are achieved
Retelling	• Rethinking and reviewing • Summarizing and synthesizing
Questioning	• Wondering about text content • Considering where answers to questions can be found • Reading selectively to find answers to questions
Monitoring	• Tracking comprehension • Revising understandings as new information is encountered • Using fix-up strategies to clarify confusions
Visualizing	• Mentally representing book ideas using your senses
Connecting	• Activating prior knowledge • Making connections to self and connections between texts
Deciding What's Important	• Using reader purpose, text format, and text features to help make decisions about what is important
Evaluating	• Critiquing and establishing opinions • Considering author intents and viewpoints • Preparing to apply new information

To set the stage for a comprehension study using environmental print, you might want to start with a highly familiar print source, a cereal box. The following table lists a set of questions connected to cereal box inquiries. You could use these questions to help your students get started on their own inquiries, or as examples to help them write their own questions based on each of the core comprehension strategies.

Examples of Inquiry Questions for Cereal Boxes

Strategy:	Questions to Get Started:
Predicting and Inferring	• Do you think this cereal is made for children, adults, or both? How can you tell? • On which box do you think sugar will be listed as the first ingredient?
Purpose Setting	• When you read a cereal box, what are you looking for? If you want to analyze the ingredients, what parts of the box will you read? • Does the cereal box include games, contests, or prizes? Why do the authors/advertisers include these? Do you usually read them? Why or why not? What other parts of the box do you read?
Retelling	• Describe what stands out the most for you on this box. • What brand is this cereal (who makes this cereal)? How many times does the brand name appear on the box? • What information does the box have about nutrition? • Which cereals have a mascot or a particular character to represent the cereal? What is the character pictured doing? Why do you suppose the authors/advertisers chose this character?
Questioning	• What do you wonder about this cereal? What questions would you like to ask the cereal makers? The authors/advertisers?
Monitoring	• Which parts of the box are difficult for you to understand? What could you do to understand better?

Strategy:	Questions to Get Started:
Visualizing	• Find a place where the cereal is described. Based on the description, what smells, tastes, sounds, and images come to mind? • After tasting this cereal, how would you use the various senses to describe it?
Connecting	• What appeals to you about these boxes—what do you most like to read on them? • Which cereals are your favorites? • Where else do you see the symbols or characters you see on the boxes? • What kinds of pictures, packaging features, and advertising seem most typical on foods made for children?
Deciding What's Important	• When choosing a cereal what do you look for? Are you interested in taste, nutrition, or something else? Given your purpose, which part of the box should you focus on? • What do the authors/advertisers want children to notice on this box? How can you tell?
Evaluating	• Do you think the authors/advertisers who created the box have done a good job of selling their cereal? Why or why not? • What do the authors/advertisers think about kids? About adults? What do they have to say about what it means to be cool? • Are some cereals marketed to boys more than girls or girls more than boys? What makes you think so?

When teachers encourage children to draw on the literacies from their broader community and cultural lives, children are able to deepen reading comprehension. Through a process of *recontextualization,* children blend their knowledge of popular culture literacy materials and practices (as with cereal boxes) with school literacy materials and practices. By taking an active part in constructing meaningful paths into school literacies, children achieve growth that is meaningful within both home and school settings (Dyson 2003). Further, the use of environmental print and popular print media in reading comprehension instruction provide opportunities for children to develop the ability to evaluate, monitor, and critically reflect upon these texts while expanding their control over core comprehension strategies.

References

Dyson, A. 2003. *The Brothers and Sisters Learn to Write: Popular Literacies in Childhood and School Cultures.* New York: Teachers College Press.

Owocki, G. 2003. *Comprehension: Strategic Instruction for Young Children.* Portsmouth, NH: Heinemann.

KEY QUESTIONS

1. How might you engage learners in applying core comprehension strategies across a wide range of environmental print sources?

2. What kinds of environmental print would be relevant for your students' inquiries?

3. How might application of comprehension strategies in a study of environmental print affect your students' ability to think critically?

4. There is a lot of persuasive text in the world. Author bias and purpose is especially inherent in print resources designed to make sales. How might you elevate awareness of persuasive or biased environmental print?

Record-Keeping Grid: Environmental Print Sources

A grid such as this could be used:

- By students as they work with a variety of print sources to ensure that they attempt to apply each comprehension strategy on the target texts that they have selected.

- By teachers to monitor think alouds and demonstrations. Are you remembering to model the use of comprehension strategies across a wide and diverse range of environmental print sources?

List the Sources ⇨			
Predicting and Inferring			
Purpose Setting			
Retelling			
Questioning			
Monitoring			
Visualizing			
Connecting			
Deciding What's Important			
Evaluating			

Environmental Print Investigations

Researcher(s)_____ Date _____

We are focusing on the following comprehension strategies: _____

_____

_____

The environmental print sources we examined include: _____

_____

_____

We noticed that: _____

_____

_____

We learned that: _____

_____

_____

Advice we would give to others about understanding environmental print: _____

_____

_____

Evaluating Environmental Print: Noticing Persuasion and Bias

Researcher(s)_____ Date _____

As you review environmental print sources, watch for print that is trying to get you to buy something or to take a certain point of view. Look closely to notice how the writers try to affect your thinking.

Print Sources That Show Evidence of Bias and Persuasion	Print Sources That Are Without Bias
_____	_____
_____	_____
_____	_____
_____	_____
_____	_____
_____	_____
_____	_____

What did you learn about bias and persuasion? How do the writers attempt to affect your thinking? How might you be more aware of this when you watch television, read a book review, or go shopping?

43

Making Thinking Come Alive in the Early Childhood Classroom

CAROLE IMUS

MEET THE AUTHOR

CAROLE IMUS *has taught for 32 years and continues to grow as a learner. She has a master's in Early Childhood Education and received her National Board Certification as an Early Childhood Generalist. She is presently serving as an Early Childhood Facilitator at Cooper Elementary in Spokane, Washington.*

FOCUS QUOTE

When selecting a book for a read aloud, it must hold the child's interest, develop deeper thinking, and have the capacity to make a difference in how the young child sees the world.

"Oh look, it's Timothy!"

"He was in our book about Yoko!"

"Yeah and he ate her sushi, but not with the chopsticks, with his fingers."

"They became friends and made a restaurant together at the end of the book. Remember?"

"I think this book is by the same person who made *Yoko!*"

"I bet we see Yoko in this book!"

"Children, you are brilliant, I am always so amazed by your thinking," replies the teacher as she gently opens the book, *Timothy Goes to School*, by Rosemary Wells.

The first and foremost goal when reading to young children is embedding the love of reading into their hearts and minds. It is a pure delight to see how excited young children become when a book engages their thinking, becomes a part of who they are and how they respond to the world.

Selecting a Book for a Read Aloud

When selecting a book for a read aloud, it must hold the children's interest, develop deeper thinking, and have the capacity to make a difference in how young children see the world. There is no replacement for quality children's literature.

Two children's authors, Rosemary Wells and Bernard Waber, are extremely talented in focusing on the problems young children encounter in their everyday lives. These books often lead to meaningful conversations with and between children. The connections children make to such delightful stories allow them to become emotionally involved in the story, promoting deeper learning.

Engaging Children in Conversation

During repeated readings of the same text, the teacher should maintain a clear focus on what she wants the children to gain from the readings. They may be asked to make predictions, ask questions, search for answers, make connections, explore character traits, and/or examine themes. During the readings, the teacher shares her thinking as she makes her way through the text. The children become active participants, involved in lively discussions. The "talk" can look different throughout the reading of the story.

• When the conversation is between teacher and child, the goal is to know what the child is thinking and WHY. Delving deeper encourages the child to explain his/her thinking and helps him/her understand the story not just remember it.

• When a one- or two-word response is requested, sharing with an elbow partner allows the child to provide an answer quickly and efficiently.

• When longer conversations are needed, encouraging children to turn and talk with their knee-to-knee or eye-to-eye partner allows for more in-depth discussions.

Involving children in talking about their thoughts helps them clarify their thinking and allows them to feel more comfortable in sharing their ideas during a whole group discussion. It gives each child an opportunity to be heard. Kindergarteners are masters at this! Ardith Davis Cole's professional text, *Knee-to-Knee, Eye-to-Eye: Circling in on Comprehension*, goes into great detail on how conversation supports deeper thinking.

Through Wells' delightful books, the children learn they are not alone in the everyday problems they encounter. Children delight in making connections to "Noisy Nora" who felt her parents ignored her because they were too busy with the other children, "Timothy" who is bullied by a boy who does everything right, and "Yoko" who is teased about the sushi in her lunch.

It is so important when reading aloud that the teacher shares her own connections with the text. It is a marvelous modeling technique, which brings the story to life and helps support the young child in his/her quest for meaning.

TEXT-TO-SELF CONNECTIONS

During text-to-self connections, the child makes a parallel comparison to an event that happened in the story and an event that happened in his/her own life.

The following are examples of connections the children from Trudy's kindergarten class made with Rosemary Wells' book *Timothy Goes to School.*

- "Claude didn't say those mean things to Timothy by accident, he said them to be mean. I know." Semir
- "My sister said I was ugly and that hurt my feeling just like Claude did to Timothy." Savannah

FIGURE 43–1a, b Children in Trudy Lambert's kindergarten class are involved in knee-to-knee, eye-to-eye conversations discussing their connections they made with Timothy in Rosemary Wells' book *Timothy Goes to School.* Notice how they focus on the speaker with genuine attention and eye contact.

- "My friend didn't have a teddy bear and I did and she yelled at me. It really hurt my feelings." Amanda
- "My brother said I was watching a baby show and I wasn't. It really hurt my feelings." Johnny
- "When my sister tripped me, my feelings were hurt and then she laughed at me." Cyrus

After orally sharing their connections, the children were invited to illustrate and write how they had connected to the story. Time was then allowed for each child to share his/her written response to the story. The oral discussions that occurred before the writing helped the child clarify his/her thinking and respond with greater detail. The sharing component validated the child's work and allowed the teacher to assess the child's thinking and understanding of the story.

TEXT-TO-TEXT CONNECTIONS

During a text-to-text connection, a child makes a connection to an event in the story to a similar event in another story.

Many times during a read aloud a child may "pop-up" with a connection he/she has made with the book being highlighted to another text read weeks or months ago. The following are connections the children from Trudy's room made while hearing the story *Yoko* by Rosemary Wells:

- "This reminds me of that book we read about the boy who was going to spend the night with his friend and his sister was mean to him and teased him about his teddy bear." (*Yoko* and *Ira Sleeps Over* by Bernard Waber)
- "When the kids said 'ICK' and didn't taste Yoko's food, it is like the Sam I Am not wanting to taste green eggs and ham." (*Yoko* and *Green Eggs and Ham* by Dr. Seuss)

But it is not enough to make parallel or surface connections. The thoughtful discussions that follow such connections must help the young child make sense of his/her world. To go deeper, the teacher must lead the children in discussions to understand the characters, see how the problems are solved, and learn how this can help in their own lives when similar problems arise.

From the two stories, *Timothy Goes to School* and *Yoko*, the children in Trudy's room came up with ideas and reflections targeting the parallel themes. As you can see by their comments below, they truly had an understanding of the story and how it could help them make sense of their own world.

- When you say mean things it is rude.
- You should say nice things to each other.

- You should try a new food, you might like it.
- Give new things a chance.
- You should never make fun of someone's clothes.
- You should never tease someone about anything!
- Find a friend who is like you.
- Find a friend who wants to do what you want to do.

Developing Character Traits

Quality literature can lead the teacher and class to lively discussions regarding the traits of certain characters. When examining the main characters, the students recognize how the characters look, how they act, and what they say. Encouraging children to illustrate characters they meet in a story and brainstorm adjectives to describe each one helps them develop a deeper understanding of what each character brings to the story.

When reading Bernard Waber's book *Loveable Lyle,* the children in Mrs. Liere's classroom were enchanted by his kind and caring ways. They were appalled when Clover Sue Hipple hurt Lyle's feelings and wrote hate letters to him. They celebrated when Lyle saved Clover's life and they became friends. After reading and revisiting the story, the children in Mrs. Liere's classroom brainstormed adjectives that described Lyle and Clover Sue. After a list was made, they realized some of the adjectives described the characters at the beginning of the story and some were descriptive of the characters at the end of the story. So they decided to label the pictures "At the beginning of the story" and "At the end of the story" with the correct adjectives placed under each heading. Imagine the great discussions that were included during such in-depth thinking! The children really came to see how people could change their feelings about someone when they talked and tried to work things out in a kind and peaceful manner.

FIGURE 43–2a, b Children from Karen Liere's K/1 Multi-age class brainstormed adjectives to describe the main characters from *Loveable Lyle* by Bernard Waber.

Taking Thinking Deeper

Children love to talk about their favorite stories, and natural conversations often flow from one story to the next. Graph organizers are excellent tools to help children see the similarities and differences from text to text. The following organizer was used to compare *Timothy Goes to School* with *Yoko*. This was done on a large chart in front of the entire class.

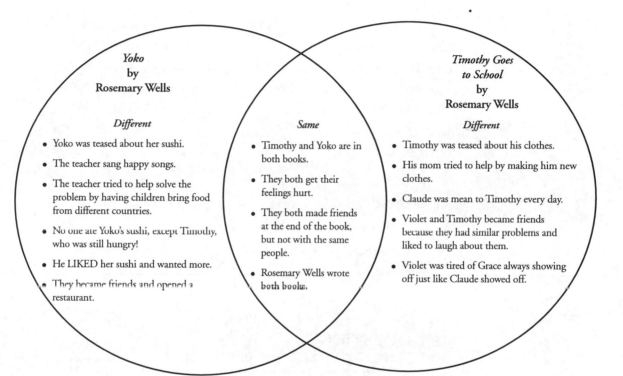

Yoko
by
Rosemary Wells

Different

- Yoko was teased about her sushi.
- The teacher sang happy songs.
- The teacher tried to help solve the problem by having children bring food from different countries.
- No one ate Yoko's sushi, except Timothy, who was still hungry!
- He LIKED her sushi and wanted more.
- They became friends and opened a restaurant.

Same

- Timothy and Yoko are in both books.
- They both get their feelings hurt.
- They both made friends at the end of the book, but not with the same people.
- Rosemary Wells wrote both books.

Timothy Goes to School
by
Rosemary Wells

Different

- Timothy was teased about his clothes.
- His mom tried to help by making him new clothes.
- Claude was mean to Timothy every day.
- Violet and Timothy became friends because they had similar problems and liked to laugh about them.
- Violet was tired of Grace always showing off just like Claude showed off.

The lessons our class learned were:

- We need to be nice and not be mean to others.
- When someone wants to play, let them.
- Don't make fun of other people, it hurts their feelings.

In a classroom where thinking is promoted, children are engaged in meaningful conversations with the teacher and each other. They respond to well-selected pieces of literature through paintings, drawings, and other creative expressions adults may never have envisioned! They are delighted by books and are not afraid to give an opinion or ask questions. Wondering is celebrated throughout the day. And when the teacher puts a new book on the easel, it is like a present waiting to be opened. The children can hardly wait to find out what adventures are hidden inside. They may meet a new friend or revisit an old acquaintance; either way they know the book will be an adventure, sure to bring new meaning to their lives.

Books by Rosemary Wells	Books by Bernard Waber
Ruby's Beauty Shop, 2003	*Evie and Margie,* 2004
Max Drives Away, 2003	*Courage,* 2003
Ruby's Tea for Two, 2003	*A Lion Named Shirley Williamson*
Shy Charles, 2001	*Gina,* 1996
Timothy Goes to School, 2000	*But Names Will Never Hurt Me,* 1994
Emily's First 100 Days of School, 2000	*Ira Says Goodbye,* 1988
Max Cleans Up, 2000	*Ira Sleeps Over,* 1973
Yoko, 1998	*Lovable Lyle,* 1994
Morris's Disappearing Bag, 1999	*The House on East 88th Street,* 1973
Noisy Nora, 1997	*Lyle, Lyle Crocodile,* 1973
Max's Dragon Shirt, 1996	

References

Website for Rosemary Wells: <*www.rosemarywells.com*>

Website for Bernard Waber: <*www.houghtonmifflinbooks.com/authors/waber/index.shtml*>

KEY QUESTIONS

1. Meaningful conversations between learners are important. What do you do to ensure that there is a lot of interaction between children that includes eye-to-eye contact and active listening?

2. What authors would you select for *your* classroom in order to promote deeper thinking? Why would you choose these authors?

3. How do you select literature to share with your students? Which books seem to have the power to take them to deeper levels of thinking?

4. What do you do to help take children's thinking deeper?

Discussion Observation and Reflection Form: Through the Eyes of the Teacher

(Use this form to guide your own reflections and inform future planning or save it so you can remember what worked really well with this book!)

Teacher_____ Date _____

Literature Selection used today _____author_____

I got the best conversations from my students when _____

_____

_____

The questions that brought about the deepest thinking included: _____

_____

_____

The part of the book that brought on the most reaction was _____

_____

_____

I stimulated child-to-child conversation by _____

_____

This book was a good ☐ poor ☐ discussion starter because _____

_____

_____

"You Are My Sunshine" Is Not About the Sun!

44

Teaching Comprehension to Young Children Through Song Lyrics

JILL HAUSER

MEET THE AUTHOR

JILL HAUSER *is a national presenter on early literacy and the award-winning author of numerous educational activity books. Her Enterprise Elementary School District kindergarten is in Redding, California.*

FOCUS QUOTE

Directing children to make pictures that match lyrics results in a lovely product, but a superficial interpretation. Grappling with lyrics to discover theme results in deeper understanding and a richer learning experience. What a profound difference in thinking this sort of approach promotes!

Why did I think to question my kindergartners' understanding of one of our favorite class songs? After all, we had sung "You Are My Sunshine" dozens of times. We had even made a class musical big book. I assigned Jordan the task of drawing the sunshine to match the lyrics, "You are my sunshine." Samantha drew the happy face for "You make me happy," and Dallas took care of the gray clouds to illustrate "when skies are gray." We would flip through the pages while singing and everyone felt proud of our art work and musical ability. Yet something was missing. We had never actually grappled with the beautiful metaphor at the heart of the song. So one fateful day, I decided to find out if they really understood the message. I asked the class simple, open-ended questions that transformed our interaction with the lyrics.

Bringing Deeper Thought to Our Learning

Mrs. Hauser: Hummm . . . The song says, "You are my sunshine." What's that all about? What do you make of it?

Nick: It's about a sunny day.

Ethan: The sun is hot.

Zach: I love a sunny day.

Kayla: I like to play outside.

Jen: I like to play at Kid's Kingdom *(local park)*

Zach: I've been to Kid's Kingdom. The waterslide is cool.

With great confidence and enthusiasm, the kindergartners continued to take their thinking in wrong directions, piggybacking on each other's limited comprehension. Astonished, I was about to ban the song forever from the classroom, when suddenly from the back of the carpet came Destiny's voice.

Destiny: The sunshine is me.

Mrs. Hauser: Whoa *(I couldn't contain my joy)*. Destiny, what makes you think so?

Destiny: My mom sings me the song every night *(proudly)*. I'm her sunshine.

Mrs. Hauser: Oh, I get it! *(walking among the children on the carpet and pointing to each child)* Nick, *you* are my sunshine. Kayla, *you* are my sunshine, Ethan *you* are my sunshine . . . So kids, the sunshine must be . . .

Class: Someone you love!

The Power of Experience

No wonder Destiny "got it." She was the only child with key background experience: a private serenade by one who loves her dearly. This does not mean only children with prior experience can comprehend. As a comprehension coach, I let every child be part of the song's language by creating an experience for each similar to Destiny's. They could then apply the song's message to their own lives.

Mrs. Hauser: Now think for a minute. Who is your sunshine? Share with the person next to you . . . who is your sunshine and why?

The classroom buzzed with excitement, then we shared:

Nick: My mom is my sunshine because she loves me.

Kayla: I love Cocoa, my kitten, because we cuddle.

Jen: My baby sister is my sunshine.

Ethan: Zach is my sunshine because he plays with me.

. . . and so the personal connections to the song abounded.

Wanting to keep the enthusiasm and deeper thinking alive, I structured a new class songbook during recess. I simply used a plate to trace a circle with a marking pen at the center of sheets of watercolor paper. When the children returned, I asked them to paint their "sunshine" in the center of the circle and sunrays on the outside of the circle. Children wrote what they had stated during our discussion, and pasted these written labels beneath their pictures. Because every picture now illustrated the big idea, lyrics could be sung with any picture and be meaningful. The class sang while I turned the pages of our new book, created to reinforce the true message of the song. Now the children were able to make an emotional connection to the last line, "Please don't take my sunshine away."

Illustrations Related to Word Recognition May Lead to Superficial Understanding

Directing children to make pictures that match lyrics results in a lovely product, but a superficial interpretation. Grappling with lyrics to discover theme results in deeper understanding and a richer learning experience. What a profound difference in thinking this sort of approach promotes!

Inferring Meaning and Grasping Theme

I have discovered that lyrics are an ideal form of text for helping young children infer meaning and grasp theme. Songs are generally concise with a clear, universal message described through rich, figurative language. Songs carry

FIGURE 44–1a, b Student writing shows connections to the theme of the song.

emotion, and when sung repeatedly, children become attached to the words. By connecting to their lives and building key background knowledge, children can be guided to appreciate poetic language and symbolism as well as unravel the song's greater meaning. An interpretive, hands-on experience, such as a painting, allows them to externalize their thinking and cement their understanding. But again, as comprehension coaches, we must be sure that they are considering deep rather than just surface understandings.

Comprehension lessons for songs focused on the author's message or theme should include the following elements:

- Familiarity with the song
- Building or stimulating background knowledge needed to access theme
- Personal connection to the theme
- Open-ended questioning to assess and deepen student understanding of the theme
- Engagement with the theme through discussion, art, writing, or drama

Accessing the Theme Before Discussing the Lyrics

Mrs. Hauser: There is something special about each of you. Maybe it's how you invite friends to come play. Maybe it's the way you share toys or how you love to learn. Think about the person sitting next to you. What do you think is special about them? Take turns telling what you like about each other. *(Wait several minutes.)* Now let's share. Pairs stand up and each of you tell what makes your friend special.

Kayla: Talisha always lets me play with her.

Talisha: Kayla helps her mom.

Nick: Ethan shares Legos with me.

Ethan: Nick makes cool pictures.

(*. . . and so the kind words flowed.*)

Mrs. Hauser: Kids, you heard why your friends think you are special. Maybe there's a different way you think you are special. Write and draw a picture of your idea.

(*Later in the day*)

Mrs. Hauser: I remember when we talked about "You are my Sunshine." The author wasn't talking about the sun at all. Can you remember what that song was about?

Montana: Someone you love.

Mrs. Hauser: Yes. Words like sunshine or light, how do they make us feel?

Nathan: Like love.

Jesse: Happy.

Mrs. Hauser: What makes you think so?

Jesse: Because I like a sunny day better than a rainy day.

Kayla: It just makes me feel good. Like . . . yes! We can play outside today!

Mrs. Hauser: Okay. So, I'm thinking that your special-ness makes us happy. It's like a little light that shines from you. Here are the pictures you drew this morning. Draw a circle and rays around your picture to make your special-ness look like a shinning light.

FIGURE 44–2a, b Students extend their understanding of "This Little Light of Mine" by drawing and writing about the "lights" in their lives.

I assembled the pages into a book, and read to the children, "Kayla says, *I am special because I help my mom.* Montana says, *I can ride a two-wheeler . . .*" and so on. Although the children could sing, "This Little Light of Mine," we had never discussed its meaning. Now I asked them to sing the song while I quietly turned the pages of our class book.

Mrs. Hauser: So kids, what do you make of the words, *"this little light of mine."* Take turns sharing ideas with the person next to you. *(Within moments lots of hands shot up.)*

Jesse: It's about how we are special!

Zach: The light is how we are good.

Mrs. Hauser: Thumbs up if you agree with Jesse and Zach. *(Unanimous approval.)* I agree, too.

My Favorite Things

"My Favorite Things" provides rich text for visualizing, making personal connections, and inferring meaning. To help twenty-first century, urban, California kids visualize the favorite things of a WWII, rural, Austrian woman, I read the book, *Rodgers and Hammerstein's My Favorite Things,* illustrated by Renee Graef, as a poem. We visualized *brown paper packages tied up with string* as something quite different from a plastic Walmart shopping bag. We pushed beyond the literal meaning of *"grey geese that fly with the moon on their wing"* . . . "What's that about? How can the moon be on a bird's wing?" ". . . No, Mrs. Hauser, it's light on their wings. It's nighttime!" We then listened repeatedly to the CD of the song as children drew and wrote about their own favorite things (cool computer games, beautiful Barbies, Chuckie Cheese Pizzas . . .). These personal connections became pages of an innovative class songbook.

A hurdle to understanding was to get beyond the literal meaning of *"when the dog bites, when the bee stings."* I showed a video clip from *The Sound of Music.* Frightened Von Trapp children sneak into Maria's bed during a thunderstorm while she sings, "My Favorite Things."

Mrs. Hauser: I don't get it. *"When the dog bites, when the bee stings . . ."* I didn't see any dogs or bees in that scene. What do you make of that? (Some children insisted there was a dog or bee somewhere the viewer couldn't see. I focused their attention instead on how we *feel* when we are stung or bitten. So, I posed the question again.)

Samantha: No, Mrs. Hauser. It's when you're scared, like they were.

Ethan: Or when you're feeling sad like the song says.

Mrs. Hauser: O.K., so what's the scared, sad part in the movie?

Class: The thunder!

Mrs. Hauser: *(Singing)* When the dog bites. When the bee stings. So what might we feel bad about in our classroom?

Nick: When kids say, "You can't play."

Mrs. Hauser: Kids, sing with me: When the dog bites. When the bee stings.

Zach: Punching.

Mrs. Hauser and class: When the dog bites. When the bee stings.

Jen: Cutting in line.

Mrs. Hauser and class: When the dog bites. When the bee stings.

Mrs. Hauser: Alright, so what can we do when these bad things happen? What does the song say?

By offering targeted support through the figurative language, the author's message became transparent to the children: Thinking about favorite things can cheer us up during hard times.

Making Connections to Build Understanding
We recalled the *sunshine* of "You Are My Sunshine" to build understanding of *light* as a symbol for something positive in "This Little Light of Mine."

FIGURE 44–3a, b Kindergarteners think in terms of symbolism as they connect, "When the Dog Bites" to challenging moments in their own lives.

This was reinforced through similar art projects for both songs. We also made a connection between the metaphors, *when the dog bites, when the bee stings* to the words *when skies are grey* in "You Are my Sunshine." In revisiting the song, children's immediate response to the words was to say, "It's about rainy days." I prompted them to brainstorm tough situations just as we had done with "My Favorite Things." This time we sung, *when skies are gray* after each child's testimonial, solidly linking each child's personal experience to the language. Children could now add another rich phrase to their repertoire of metaphoric ways to express hard times.

To keep these literacy symbols alive, we applied the language to classroom routines. *Let it shine* became a reinforcement phrase in our classroom. "Awesome writing, Samantha, *Let it shine!*" "Zach let Nick stand in front of him in line, *Let it shine!*" Angry children could be coaxed to crack a smile by reminding them, "Sorry mom forgot to pack your snack, Justin. *Simply remember your favorite things and then you won't feel so bad!*" *You are my sunshine* was added to the list of greeting card messages at our writing center.

Sharing the books *You Are My Sunshine,* illustrated by Jill Dublin, and *This Little Light of Mine,* illustrated by Sylvia Walker, gave us insight on how professional illustrators interpret theme. The Greg and Steve CD, "Rockin' Down the Road," combines "You Are My Sunshine" and "This Little Light of Mine" into one song. It was fitting that we sung the *Sunshine Medley* for parents at our spring learning celebration with this introduction: "Parents, you are our sunshine. Thanks to you, our little lights of learning shine more brightly!"

Reflections

The ultimate text for developing comprehension in young children uses rich language to communicate a universal message. Text that's concise and familiar is perfect for young learners. Songs provide all this and something more: music and emotion to keep the message alive in our hearts and minds.

Young children tend to think literally and miss major ideas we assume they understand. Asking open-ended questions such as, "What do you think of it? What makes you think so?" gives us a window into their thinking and an instant assessment of their depth of comprehension. Guiding children through figurative language to access theme not only helps them understand the lyrics; it builds awareness that words can be used flexibly to create powerful images and messages. It also plants the seeds for them to use this technique in their own speech and writing.

Because songs are sung again and again, we can seize the opportunity to repeatedly engage children's minds in deeper thinking. Rather than recite a jumble of words, children think of the song's language and its message, if we have taken the time to make it comprehensible. In my classroom, songs that have served as text for interpretation are those most requested by children and sung with greatest passion.

When the focus changes from a teacher-assembled product to a child-centered process of accessing and connecting to a song's poignant theme, thinking deeply becomes the heart of the experience. Talisha summed up why grappling with meaning is worth the effort. One day during recess she pointed to the sky and said, "Look Mrs. Hauser, those birds have the sun on their wings. That makes me happy!"

References

Rodgers and Hammerstein's My Favorite Things, illustrated by Renee Graef, Harper Collins, 2001.

This Little Light of Mine adapted by Rachel Lisberg, illustrated by Sylvia Walker, Scholastic, 2003.

You Are My Sunshine, adapted by Steve Metzger, illustrated by Jill Dublin, Scholastic, 2001.

KEY QUESTIONS

1. What other songs can I use for rigorous student interpretation? Look for depth of message or richness of language. Consider using Broadway tunes ("Somewhere Over the Rainbow"), patriotic songs ("America the Beautiful"), children's songs ("We All Sing with the Same Voice"), popular songs ("We Are Family").

2. What obstacles to understanding are in the text that I will need to help children clarify and overcome? (metaphors, similes, idioms, imagery, figurative language)

3. What sort of interaction can best help children cement their thinking while encouraging connections and questions about this song? (art, dramatic skit, an innovation of the song)

Assessing Deep Understanding in Young Children

As young children develop deeper ways of thinking about text (songs, poems, stories, nonfiction), they may show their understanding in their comments, drawing, writing, or personal conversations. Observe closely to determine which learners are beginning to think more deeply and which kinds of experiences elicit deeper comprehension.

Learner _____ Teacher _____

Title of Text/Song/ Unit of Study	Surface Understanding (Recall of information)	Deeper Understanding (Connections, inferences, theme, evaluation, opinion, synthesis)
"There Was a Little Turtle," Poem	3/2 good retell	3/2 T-T connection
Mrs. Wishy Washy	3/11 characters, events, problem	Question: Why didn't Mrs. Wishy Washy remember they are animals and like to be dirty?
Blueberries for Sal	Sequenced events	Opinion! "Her mom should have watched her."

Title of Text/Song/ Unit of Study	Surface Understanding (Recall of information)	Deeper Understanding (Connections, inferences, theme, evaluation, opinion, synthesis)

Read Alouds and Retells

Building Early Text Comprehension

45

CATE HILL

MEET THE AUTHOR

CATE HILL *has enjoyed teaching in early childhood and primary classrooms for over 20 years. She currently works as a program developer for Title 1, a kindergarten teacher for the Bend-La Pine School District, and as an early childhood instructor for Central Oregon Community College.*

She loves horses, the outdoors, and bringing young children into the world of literacy.

FOCUS QUOTE

When I first started using retells as a means of assessing comprehension and language development, I became overwhelmed with the amount of information I was getting on each student and how to keep track of it all.

I t's early in the kindergarten year and twenty-some children are gathered together for storytime. Watching intently as the pages turn and the story unfolds, even the wiggly ones are spellbound as their teacher reads *Yoko* by Rosemary Wells.

In the story, Yoko is a little kitten who represents a young girl from a Japanese family who loves the Japanese foods prepared by her mother in her cold lunch. Yoko's classmates make fun of her when she brings things such as sushi and green tea ice cream for lunch. Her teacher attempts to develop acceptance and tolerance by initiating a foods-from-around-the-world activity where everyone brings traditional foods from home to share. In spite of the teacher's good intentions, Yoko is still ostracized by her peers for the unusual nature of her food. However, at the end, one boy who is still hungry ventures over to try some of Yoko's sushi and finds that he likes it. The two classmates become friends and begin a play restaurant where they serve courses from each of their lunches.

As the story comes to an end, the teacher looks around the room and asks, "Is there anyone who would like to come up and tell us everything they remember about the story?" A bright-eyed girl named Mariah eagerly raises her hand and jumps to her feet when her name is called. "It was about a guy who liked chopsticks. He used them like a drum. I do'd that at the restaurant with my mom sometimes," she said.

The teacher smiles and thanks Mariah as she returns to her seat, making a mental note of the inconsistencies in grammar and lack of detail in her retelling of the story. A few minutes later as the class moves onto morning centers, the teacher quietly pulls a boy named Devin aside and invites him to retell the same story.

> Well, first, Yoko said to her mother, "Pack all my favorite things
> in my lunch." Then she went to school and they laughed at her
> food and said it was wiggling. Then she was sad. She went home
> and the next day at school everyone had to try something new
> but no one tried Yoko's yummy food except Timothy. She heard
> these little tapping chopsticks and it was Timothy. Then they
> went on the school bus. They went and decided to make a restau-
> rant. That was the end.

Retells Enhance Awareness of Story Elements

The stark difference in the amount of detail given in the two retellings is representative of the different levels of listening comprehension found in many kindergarten classrooms. While the first child is only able to articulate one seemingly unimportant event, the retelling by the second child includes the characters, setting, and main events from the beginning, middle, and end of the story. Why such a disparity in listening comprehension at this age? I find that children come to kindergarten with a vast discrepancy in experience with literacy and language. Children who have been read to regularly tend to have a more intuitive sense of how a story fits together and are better able to follow along and remember events and details in the stories they hear. The good news is that children who lack such experience can acquire these skills by enhancing their read aloud experiences with retell activities that guide their awareness, helping them focus on the critical elements of a story.

A Window into Comprehension and Language Development

When I first started using retells as a means of assessing comprehension and language development, I became overwhelmed with the amount of information I was getting on each student and how to keep track of it all. I developed a retell checklist that I use to monitor progress and plan from. I put a checklist for each child in my assessment notebook (each child has a tab), which I keep right next to our class meeting area on the rug (see form on page 432). Using the checklist enables me to easily view progress and plan appropriate activities to boost student growth in language and literacy competence.

Retelling Personal Experience

Notice that in Mariah's retelling of the story, she made a personal connection with a minor event in the story, but the main character and events seem to have escaped her. For a student like Mariah, whose oral language skills need bolstering, a good place to start is with retelling stories from her personal experience. It might help Mariah if she could do a retell of going to recess, baking cookies, getting ready for bed, and so on. This would help build a better understanding of the elements of a retell before she transitions to retelling stories.

Illustrations Support Retells

A teacher might ask the students to draw a picture of a favorite part of the story, then use it as a prop to elicit a multi-event retell. In my own classroom, students from all levels of comprehension development do this in small, heterogeneous groups at a center they rotate to each week during writing centers. As they draw their pictures, they keep in mind that they will be sharing a story to go with their picture. Afterwards, as each student from the group shares, the rest of the class carefully listens, knowing they will get a chance to be called upon by the author to identify who the story was about, where the story took place, and what happened in the beginning, middle, and end of the story. As they gain proficiency, they might be asked to illustrate the beginning and the end of the story.

Peer Models Scaffold Success

The diversity of achievement levels in the group translates into pictures and stories of varying detail, providing peer models to scaffold the students with less-developed language and literacy proficiency. In addition to being a very popular activity with young children, it helps them develop the underlying structure of story, characters, and sequencing. These are all important skills that will support reading comprehension as they become readers.

As children begin to connect with and comprehend the stories they hear read aloud, you might try some of the following activities to strengthen their understanding and develop their skills:

Picture story maps: While introducing the story to be read aloud, let the students know they will be choosing an event from either the beginning, middle, or end of the story to illustrate. After reading, review the story (and illustrations if necessary), discussing which events were at the beginning, middle, and end. Next, have the students choose an event to illustrate and either write or dictate a brief description to go with their picture. When first introducing this activity, you may choose to seat all the students who are drawing events from the beginning of the story together at one table, middle together, etc., to help them stay focused on the part of the story they chose to illustrate.

After the pictures are finished, students share them briefly in front of the class and place their illustrations on a timeline to create a story map. For younger or less experienced students, the timeline can be outlined on a bulletin board in the form of a story map with sections labeled beginning, middle, and end. For more skilled students, a clothesline or wire with clothespins works well, with each student having to decide where on the timeline to place their picture.

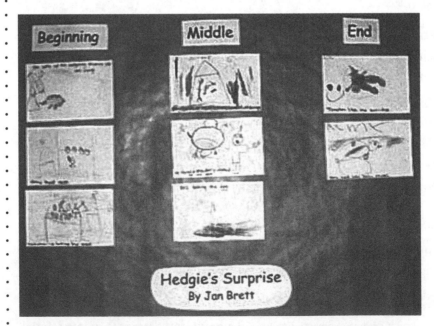

FIGURE 45–1 A story map done by kindergartners, highlighting the concepts of beginning, middle, and end of a story.

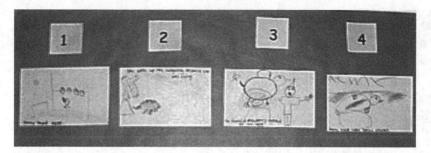

FIGURE 45–2 Select pictures from the story map are used for students to practice sequencing events.

If your students are having difficulty sequencing events, you can take three or four pictures of significant events from the timeline and ask them to practice by putting just those few pictures in sequence as they retell what happened.

Student-led book recommendations: One way to help foster the home-school connection is to send home an assignment where family members are asked to read a story to the student and the student draws a picture of their favorite part to bring back and share. For families who have hectic schedules or who have other reasons that make this difficult to accomplish, I send home a book on tape with a compact tape player and headphone set so the student can still fulfill the task.

The sharing of this assignment takes place in the form of an oral sharing, where students summarize the main idea of the book, what they liked about it, what it reminds them of, and whether or not they think other children would like to read the story, too. This helps develop the ability to identify main ideas as well as enhancing connections between literature and self, the world, and other texts.

Story retells: Whenever a story is read aloud, there exists an opportunity for a retell. It only takes a minute and is a great way to collect ongoing data on student progress. Early in the year when the concept of a retell is still new, I prefer to do whole class retells, where all students have the opportunity to contribute information. Sometimes I write down their words, while other times we just discuss them. As the year progresses and the class becomes more familiar with the retelling format, I find props are helpful to aid students in including all the critical elements of the story in their retelling. Using cue cards (who, where, beginning, middle, end) is one way for students to self-check whether or not their retell is complete.

Storytelling glove: Using a variation of a storytelling glove (Hoyt 1999) is another good prop. In this case, the storytelling glove is a glove with the words for the main components: characters, setting, beginning, middle, and

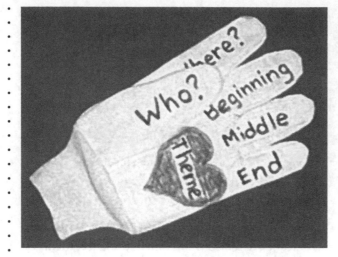

FIGURE 45–3 Linda Hoyt's version of the storytelling glove lists story elements such as problem, solution, characters, setting, and so on. This modified version focuses kindergarten children on beginning, middle, and ending events.

end, written on each finger and a heart drawn on the palm for plot, or the heart of the story. The student wears the glove and can tick off each finger as they cover the element it stands for.

Create a Genuine Audience

To create a more genuine atmosphere for the retell, where the student is actually telling the story to someone who has not heard it before, try inviting a guest into the classroom. Performing a retell to guests (students from another class, secretaries, principals, etc.) requires the student to go into more detail

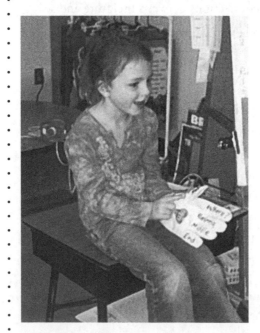

FIGURE 45–4 The storytelling glove supports learners as they practice their retells.

and allows for more authentic questions to be asked by the listener. Lacking a real visitor, try having students tell it to a puppet that "hasn't heard the story." Young children have no problem pretending the puppet is a real person and are often observed practicing their skills in this manner during free choice time and at home.

References

Brett, Jan. 2001. *Hedgie's Surprise*. New York: Scholastic.

Hoyt, Linda. 1999. *Revisit, Reflect, Retell: Strategies for Improving Reading Comprehension*. Portsmouth, NH: Heinemann.

Wells, Rosemary. 1998. *Yoko*. New York: Scholastic.

KEY QUESTIONS

1. How do retells fit into your comprehension instruction? What are your favorite retelling strategies?

2. Which retell strategies work best for read aloud, shared reading, guided reading, and independent reading?

3. What are you doing for retells with informational texts?

4. How do you assess retells?

5. How do you keep track of the data you gather during retells?

Student Retell Record

Student: _____

Year: _____

	+ = tells independently
	P = tells with prompting
	P- = prompted but still can't retell

Date	Story or Retell Activity	Used Props	Characters	Identifies Main character	Setting	Summarizes Plot	# Independent	# w/prompt	Beginning	Middle	End	Personal Connection T → S = Text to Self T → T = Text to Text T → W = Text to World

| | Describes Events | | | |

Story Retell Directions: Tell about this book; pretend you are telling a friend about it who has never seen or heard it before. Did the story remind you of anything?

Contributed by C. Hill © 2005 by Linda Hoyt from *Spotlight on Comprehension*. Portsmouth, NH: Heinemann.

Illustrating the Story

Have the reader illustrate the beginning, middle, and end of a story then use the pictures to support a retell. The retelling checklist at the bottom can be either folded back or torn off and saved as an assessment of progress.

Reader _____ Date _____ Book _____

The Beginning	The Middle	The End

During the oral retell of the story, this reader included:

	Great job!	Almost there	Oops
All main characters	☐	☐	☐
Secondary characters	☐	☐	☐
The setting	☐	☐	☐
The beginning	☐	☐	☐
The middle	☐	☐	☐
The end	☐	☐	☐
The problem	☐	☐	☐
The events were in the correct order	☐	☐	☐
The solution	☐	☐	☐
The author's message	☐	☐	☐

Higher-level response:
(opinion, connection, visualization, other) _____

Notes about the retell/Implications for instruction: _____

46

Searching for a Comprehension Game-Plan? . . . Just Follow the Yellow Brick Road!

KAREN LOKTING

MEET THE AUTHOR

KAREN LOKTING *has been an elementary-level classroom teacher for 16 years. She has also worked as a reading specialist and a staff development presenter. Karen is currently an educational consultant, focusing on math staff development and curriculum design.*

FOCUS QUOTE

As we strive to develop comprehension skills in our learners, it is critical that we know our standards well and make critical decisions about time, rigor, and substance. If this was just an art activity or a way to fill time, it would not be justifiable. However, with a clear focus on deep thinking, state standards, and long-term understanding, this Comprehension game has a well-deserved place in my comprehension instruction.

The Students Led the Way

"I'd turn back if I were you . . ."

Some people would say I was young and naïve to start such a big project with only six weeks left in the schoolyear. It was Friday night and I was exhausted. Our first-grade team spent the day celebrating Cinco de Mayo, and now a group of teachers, parents, and children were laying out sleeping bags for a sleepover at school, the culmination of a schoolwide reading program. Looming in my mind, however, was the task of setting up a unit on the Wizard of Oz. Although I had big plans of creating a yellow brick road leading to my classroom with its door serving as the entrance to the Emerald City, I was tired and overwhelmed and beginning to have second thoughts. Should I file the idea away for next year, or could I put it off another week and still get the unit done before the end of the year? The answer became clear when Katie, one of my first graders, crawled into the sleeping bag next to mine with a copy of the *The Wonderful Wizard of Oz*. She had no idea about my plans, yet chatted nonstop about the book.

There was no turning back.

My emphasis for the unit was to compare and contrast the book and the movie and interweave an understanding of story structure. As the unit progressed, I was astounded by my first graders' ability to recognize subtle details in both the movie and the book. I was also impressed with the comparisons they made between the two. However, the real lesson took place unexpectedly. Alicia, one of my students, created a Wizard of Oz comprehension game complete with game board and game cards. In her work, I could clearly see the integration of character, setting, and plot. Since story elements are a first grade literary focus, Alicia gave me a whole new comprehension "game-plan."

Getting Started

The next afternoon, our class looked at Alicia's game, discussed her inclusion of literary elements, and brainstormed other ways to incorporate our understanding of the story into a game. The children paired up with blank paper and I gave them the time to create their own Wizard of Oz games. Their in-

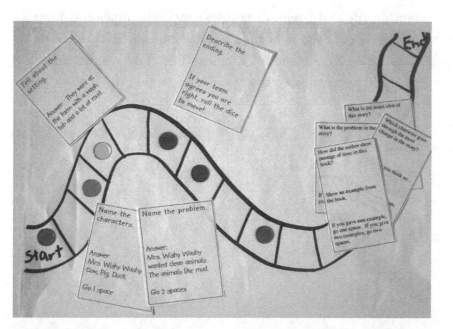

FIGURE 46–1 The comprehension stretches both the designer of the game and the teams of players as they review, reflect, and retell their understandings to move through the game.

tegration of story elements was amazing, but I could not overlook the creativity, problem solving, and negotiation that took place. The thinking was deep and rigorous with plentiful returns to the storyline to confirm opinions and argue for personal points of interest.

Expanding the Comprehension Game to Other Selections

The experience was so powerful that the literary game became a core experience whether I was teaching first, second, or third grade . . . designing a unit for *Charolette's Web, The Lion, the Witch, and the Wardrobe,* or *Willie Wonka and the Chocolate Factory.* Best of all, students were very likely to reflect on our read aloud, guided reading, and independent reading with statements like: "If I were to create a game about this, I would be sure to. . . ."

Integrating Standards

Our state has a strong emphasis on performance-based assessments such as projects, oral reading assessments, and writing samples. As I looked closely at the experiences provided during development of the games, I realized that I could support a wide range of standards and assessments within the context of these comprehension games. To develop a game around a book, students refined summarization skills, applied expository writing skills, expanded their oral language bank, developed deeper understanding of story grammar, and looked closely at character development . . . all within the context of planning and developing their game.

More Than an Activity

On the outside this might look like an "activity." As we strive to develop comprehension skills in our learners, it is critical that we know our standards well and make critical decisions about time, rigor, and substance. If this was just an art activity or a way to fill time, it would not be justifiable. However, with a clear focus on deep thinking, state standards, and long-term understanding, this Comprehension game has a well-deserved place in my comprehension instruction.

Sample Project Task—Comprehension Game

The Game Division of Literary Games Association is looking for games that represent the story of the _____.

Contracts will be offered for games that:

- Clearly represent characters, settings, and plot (problem, main events, and solution).
- Are challenging, yet fun, to play.
- Encourage players to use reading strategies to think about the text: (visualize, question, summarize, make connections, infer, evaluate, and so on).
- Provide a way for players to offer opinions and cite evidence for their statements about the text.

Please submit a plan for your game, complete with the information listed above and a supply list to your teacher for prior approval.

Reference

The Dreamer of Oz: The L. Frank Baum Story. Script: Richard Matheson. USA—Television Broadcast. 10 December 1990. Portrayal of L. Frank Baum's life-experiences that were instrumental in the development and revision of ideas for *The Wonderful Wizard of Oz.*

KEY QUESTIONS

1. The author completed this comprehension experience in primary classes. How could this be adapted to the level of your student? Could it be altered to other content areas?

2. Which of your state standards could be addressed through development of a comprehension game?

3. Think of ways you can provide your students time to work on a project such as this, without infringing on time you need for other lessons? What strategies might you use to ensure that the art work doesn't consume too much time?

4. What assessments could be woven into this experience?

5. Would you have students develop the rubric? How would you go about doing this?

Planning Sheet—Comprehension Game

Questions to Consider:

- What kind of game will you make?
- How will you incorporate the characters?
- How will you incorporate the settings?
- How will you incorporate the plot?

Problem:

Events:

Solution:

- How will players give their opinion of the story?
- How will the game help players to think about strategies?
- How will you demonstrate pride in your work?
- What supplies will you need from me?

My game board will look like:
(make a rough sketch)

One sample game card

Planning Sheet for Writing: Rules for My Comprehension Game

Name of Game Designers: _____

Name of the Game: _____

Based on: _____ by_____
(title of the book and author)

Object of the game:

    How to win:

    Number of players:

    Materials needed to play the game:

Important rules:

The steps you follow to play the game

1. _____

2. _____

3. _____

4. _____

5. _____

Assessment Tool for Comprehension Game

Game Designer_____ Book Read_____

Date _____

Review the work of the student to determine the level of his/her understanding.
Look for evidence of comprehension in the oral retell, in the game board, the game
cards, and rules. As you complete the form below, indicate to the right the source
of information that supports your assessment of understanding. Circle the numbers
that apply for the assessment based on: (a) oral retell, (b) written retell, (c) game
board, (d) game cards, (e) rules

	Clearly identified				Not apparent	Based on a,b,c,d,e
Main idea	5	4	3	2	1	_____
Important events	5	4	3	2	1	_____
All characters are present	5	4	3	2	1	_____
Reflects knowledge of character	5	4	3	2	1	_____
Development						_____
The setting	5	4	3	2	1	_____
The problem	5	4	3	2	1	_____
The solution	5	4	3	2	1	_____
Opinions about the story	5	4	3	2	1	_____
Evidence from the story	5	4	3	2	1	_____
Use/awareness of comprehension strategies	5	4	3	2	1	_____

Examples of the Comprehension Game Cards

Version I: Primary Example

Name the characters. Answer: Mrs. Wishy Washy Cow, Pig, Duck Go 1 space.	**Name the problem.** Answer: Mrs. Wishy Washy wanted clean animals. The animals like mud. Go 2 spaces.
Tell about the setting. Answer: They were at the farm with a wash tub and a lot of mud. Go 1 space.	**Describe the ending.** If your team agrees you are right, roll the dice to move!

Game Cards

Which character goes through the most change in the story?

Tell why you think so . . .

Check with your team. Do they agree? Go forward 1 space.

How did the author show passage of time in this book?

Show an example from the book.

If you gave 1 example, go 1 space. If you gave 2 examples, go 2 spaces.

What is the main idea of this story?

Tell why you think so . . .

If your team agrees you are correct, move 1 space.

What is the problem in the story?

How was it resolved?

If you get a thumbs up from your team, move 2 spaces.

Part Eight

Supporting Comprehension for English Language Learners (ELL's)

Frontloading for ELL's

47

Building Concepts and Vocabulary Before Reading

JAN MCCALL

MEET THE AUTHOR

Jan McCall *has taught for many years in elementary classrooms where her combined love of children and reading has provided impetus for powerful innovations in literacy education. She currently works as a Reading Specialist and a Guided Language Acquisition Design (GLAD) trainer in Beaverton, Oregon.*

FOCUS QUOTE

The importance of accessing and building background for all learners has been well documented. Taking a few minutes to jump-start students' schema, finding out what they know or have experienced about a topic, and linking their knowledge directly to the lesson's objective, will result in greater understanding for English learners.

English language learners (ELL's) encounter many challenges when faced with new, unfamiliar text. To help ensure that the text is comprehensible, it is important learners are given scaffolds before reading to help them set a purpose for reading, to spend time accessing and building background knowledge, to make connections from the known to the new, and to emphasize key vocabulary.

This process naturally brings prior knowledge to a level where it is ready to apply, stimulates questions on the topic, builds interest, and most of all, builds the content language that will support the reading (Hoyt 2002).

There are a variety of ways to frontload information to maximize success for English language learners.

Realia

Bring in the real thing! For example: when reading a text about the life cycles of fruits, bring in the fruits, seeds, branches, and buds and allow students time to observe, touch, and have discussions prior to encountering the new vocabulary in the text.

FIGURE 47–1 Bringing in real objects helps English language learners to build content knowledge and the english vocabulary to use in describing what they know.

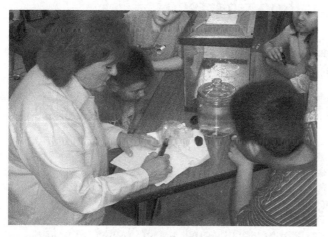

FIGURE 47–2 Real objects stimulate conversation, questions, and set strong purposes for reading.

Video

Provide rich visual imagery through video, with the sound on or off, to help students understand concepts from a text before they read. Establish a focus for viewing so students look for key points. Pause often to clarify, or have students turn to a partner and discuss what they just saw. For example: when reading a text about extreme weather, view video clips of a variety of forms of weather so students have a context before reading.

Field Trips

Why wait until the end of a unit or reading to take a field trip? You can frontload key concepts and vocabulary by going on a field trip prior to

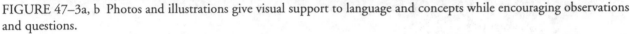

FIGURE 47–3a, b Photos and illustrations give visual support to language and concepts while encouraging observations and questions.

embarking on your study. Take photographs, then discuss and write about the experience when you return to the classroom. The information you study in a related text will be much more meaningful when it can be connected to shared real-life experiences.

Picture Observation Charts

Collect a variety of pictures that connect to the text to be read. Post them on chart paper around the classroom and have students move from poster to poster, observing and discussing the pictures with a partner. Encourage students to write their questions, connections, and observations on the posters. Students will begin thinking about the topic and you will have information to assess prior knowledge and plan for instruction.

Text Bits

Using pictures from the text to be read, or related pictures, pass one picture to each student and ask them to face one other person. Students describe their picture, predict what the book may be about, and listen to the same from their partner. They then move to another student and repeat the process. When pictures have been shared, students write a quick prediction of the book's content, based on the pictures. A whole class discussion follows.

Text Bits can also occur with actual text from the book to be read. Select key sentences or phrases from the text and write each on a strip of paper. Pass one to each student. Students move around the room reading their strip and listening to each partner. Again you may wish to have them write what they remember or predict the content of the book to be read.

As they gain proficiency with this scaffold, they can carry a book or newsmagazine around as they engage in partner conversations about possible content.

FIGURE 47–4a, b Students work in partners to generate predictions about the text and about vocabulary they expect to see and relate their prior knowledge on the topic.

Read Aloud and Shared Reading

Prior to having students read a selection independently, read aloud a book with related content and use a think aloud strategy to discuss the concepts and vocabulary that are common to both texts. This helps the learners pull background knowledge forward and activate content vocabulary that is likely to appear in their own reading.

You might also consider a big book on the same topic, because the students will be reading individually and the large illustrations and photographs may assist the ELL in solidifying the concepts and language.

KW . . . E Focus on Questions

Use the familiar KWL format, but consider changing the *K* to "what I *think* I know" and *W* to "what I wonder." The last column could be *E* for "what ELSE do you want to know now, after reading?" This keeps the learners focused on questions before, during, and after reading which stimulates language and conversation.

Word Sorts

Identify key vocabulary from the text to be read. Provide a list of words to students to sort into categories determined by either the teacher or the students. Encourage metacognition by asking them to provide the rationale for placing words in certain categories. If the selection to be read is a narrative, students can sequence the words in a way that makes sense and use the words to tell the story, based on their prediction of what the story will be about.

FIGURE 47–5 Read alouds and big books, when partnered by topic with the books students will read individually, provide strong levels of support for concepts and language development.

The words can be re-sorted to reflect the actual story as the reading occurs, and can be sorted again at the end of the reading to aid in retelling.

Cloze

Select a paragraph from the text to be read. Delete some of the words that provide multiple possibilities for substitutions. Ask students to read through the passage and insert words that make sense. When finished, ask students to share with a partner and then with the whole group. By interacting with the cloze activity prior to reading the text, students are introduced to key vocabulary, they have a chance to negotiate meaning with a partner, and their interest in the reading is piqued. Then, as they enter the author's version of the text, they have strong personal purposes for reading.

Expert/Guest Speaker

Invite an expert to your class to present information on the topic of study. Encourage the expert to bring the "tools of the trade." For example, invite a meteorologist to bring weather instruments and present information about forecasting the weather. Students will read texts about the weather with a new understanding after their experience with an expert.

Partner Preview: I Notice

When introducing new nonfiction, ask students to turn to a partner with their text in hand and begin to preview the text by saying "I notice . . ." Have them take turns as they page through the book noticing text features, structures, or key vocabulary. When they have finished, debrief with the whole class. You can create a visual roadmap of the text on chart paper as they share what they have noticed.

The importance of accessing and building background for all learners has been well documented. Taking a few minutes to jump-start students' schema, finding out what they know or have experienced about a topic, and linking their knowledge directly to the lesson's objective, will result in greater understanding for English learners.

References

Brechtel, M. 2001. *Bringing It All Together: Language and Literacy in the Multilingual Classroom.* Carlsbad, CA: Dominie Press.

Hoyt, L. 2002. *Make It Real: Strategies for Success with Informational Texts.* Portsmouth, NH: Heinemann.

KEY QUESTIONS

1. The traditional sequence of reading instruction started with the text and moved to connections and construction of meaning after reading. Knowing the importance of emphasizing before reading experience with ELL's, how might ELL's get before reading support in math, science, health, read alouds, and so on?

2. Many before-reading strategies involve partner work prior to sharing whole group. What are the advantages to ELL of chatting with a partner before sharing whole group?

3. Are there genres that might need more scaffolding than others for English language learners?

4. Which genres might provide the most support?

5. How could you use before reading strategies to encourage cultural respect in your classroom?

KW . . . E

Student _____ Date _____

Before Reading	Before *and* During Reading	After Reading
I think I *Know:* ..	I *Wonder* about...	What *Else* Do I Want to Know About this Topic?

The topic is _____

Passage Predictions

Reader _____ Text _____ Date _____

As I preview this text, I think it will mostly be about _____

_____

_____

I think there will also be information on _____

_____

_____

Some words I predict will be used: _____

_____

_____

Connections I can make to this topic:

Text-to-self   Text-to-world   Text-to-text

_____

_____

_____

_____

Think and Sketch

Reader_____ Date _____

Before Reading

Take a moment to preview the book you are about to read . . . glance at the pictures, skim the titles and headings. Make a quick sketch of one or two things you believe will be important in this passage. You might want to jot a few key words that will help you think about this topic.

During Reading

As you read, think about what you are learning. As you come across ideas that you think are important make a quick sketch below and add key words that will help you remember.

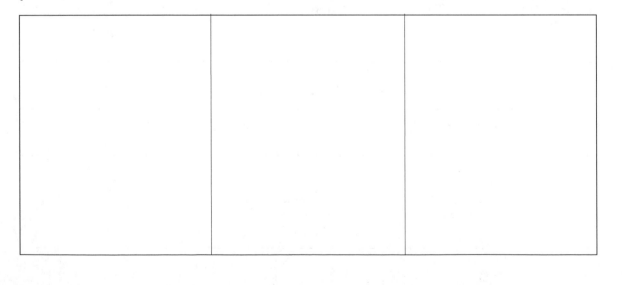

Preview, View, Review

Giving Multilingual Learners Access to the Curriculum

48

YVONNE AND
DAVID FREEMAN

Imagine yourself in a classroom where Lithuanian, Greek, Thai, or Punjabi was the language of instruction, and you did not speak or understand that language very well or at all.

MEET THE AUTHORS

YVONNE FREEMAN *is a professor of bilingual education and* **DAVID FREEMAN** *is a professor of reading at the University of Texas Pan American in Edinburg, Texas. The Freemans have published seven books on second language acquisition, ESL methods, bilingual education, linguistics, and reading with Heinemann, and their newest book,* Dual Language Essentials for Teachers and Administrators, *will come out in the fall of 2004. They present regularly at local, state, and national conferences and consult in the United States, South America, Spain, and Lithuania.*

FOCUS QUOTE

If students enter school speaking languages other than English, and if English is the only language of instruction, then the students may simply not understand enough English to acquire English or to learn any subjects taught in English.

Over 4.7 million children in U.S. schools are English Language Learners (ELL's) and need to comprehend the English instruction in our classrooms (OELA 2002). Becoming proficient in a second language takes time. Research has consistently shown that it takes English learners four to nine years to acquire the academic language they need for school success. Primary language support is crucial for multilingual students during the time they are acquiring English (Collier and Thomas 2004, Cummins 2000).

To learn a second language, students need to have an understanding of what they hear or read. Krashen tells us that people acquire language when they receive comprehensible input, messages that they understand (Krashen 2003). For second language students, the use of the primary language can help make input comprehensible. If students enter school speaking languages other than English, and if English is the only language of instruction, then the students may simply not understand enough English to acquire English or to learn any subjects taught in English.

Preview, View, Review

One excellent strategy for working with second language learners at any grade level, is Preview, View, Review (Freeman and Freeman 2002). This strategy can work in classes with English learners from different primary language backgrounds, and it can work whether or not the teacher speaks the students' languages.

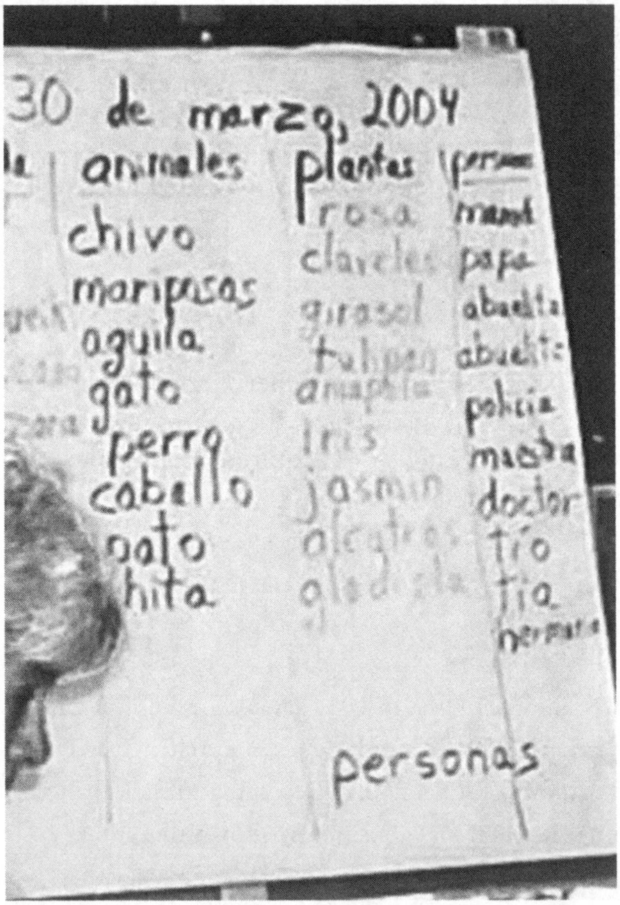

FIGURE 48–1 The preview is provided in the learner's native language to ensure concepts are clearly understood.

The Preview

If the teacher, a bilingual peer, a bilingual cross-age tutor, a bilingual aide, or a parent can simply tell the English learners in their native language what the upcoming lesson is about, the students are provided with a Preview. This Preview might be simply a few sentences explaining what is going to happen in the class that day or that period, or it could be more complex. So, for example, the class is going to study seeds and classify them and the teacher wants the ELL's to have a Preview. The Preview could be given by a fellow student who would explain in the students' native language, "Today we are going to look at different kinds of seeds. We are going to sort them and then describe them." A more complete Preview might be the reading of a book or two in the students' native language(s) about seeds and their characteristics.

The View

During the View the teacher conducts the lesson using strategies to make the content comprehensible. Teachers make the content comprehensible in various ways including using visuals, incorporating hands-on activities, organizing students in groups, using charts and graphs, making frequent comprehension checks, and using gestures.

In the seed lesson suggested above, the teacher might read a large-sized book about seeds in English that has limited text and lots of pictures. During the reading, the teacher points to the pictures and the key words. Then students work in groups to sort a bag of seeds, and together they complete a chart on which students identify the seeds and list characteristics such as color, texture, and shape. With the help of the Preview, the students can follow the English better during the View and acquire both English and academic content.

Review

Finally, it is good to have a short time of Review during which students again use their native language. In the seed lesson example, the teacher or a peer could read another book about seeds in English and the students could discuss it or they could be allowed to clarify what they did not understand during the reading and classification in English.

When no first language resource people are available, students who speak the same first language can meet in groups to Review the main ideas of the lesson and then report back in English. Students who are literate in their first language might read books in their native language that support the concepts and summarize in English or further investigate their topic on the Internet in their first language. Teachers should try to use any first language resources they can find. The following chart outlines the Preview, View, Review technique.

> **Preview/ View/ Review**
>
> **Preview:**
>
> **First language**
>
> The teacher, a classmate, a parent volunteer, or a paraprofessional gives an overview of the lesson or activity in the students' first language (this could be giving an oral summary, reading a book, showing a film, asking a key question, etc.)
>
> **View:**
>
> **Second or target language (English)**
>
> The teacher teaches the lesson or directs the activity in the students' second language making the input comprehensible by using different techniques. These may include reading and hands-on learning.
>
> **Review:**
>
> **First language**
>
> The teacher, a paraprofessional, or the students summarize key ideas and raise questions about the lesson in their first language or further investigate the topic.

The Preview, View, Review technique provides a structured way to alternate English and native-language instruction. Students are given access to the academic concepts they need to know and, at the same time, acquire English.

Concurrent Translation Not Productive for Language Learning

Simply translating everything into a student's first language is not productive because the student will tune out English, the language that is harder to understand. This concurrent translation method does not lead to either concept or language acquisition. Using Preview, View, Review can help teachers avoid concurrent translation and can also motivate students to stay engaged during the English part of the lesson.

When lessons are well taught, the concepts presented in the primary languages transfer to English. Teachers of multilingual students need to find ways to help them access the curriculum and learn both English and school content. Using the Preview, View, Review technique can help any teacher to reach this goal.

References

Collier, V., and W. Thomas. 2004. "The Astounding Effectiveness of Dual Language Education for All." *NABE Journal of Research and Practice* 2 (1): 1–19.

Cummins, J. 2000. *Language, Power and Pedagogy: Bilingual Children in the Crossfire.* Tonawanda, NY: Multilingual Matters.

Freeman, Y. S., and D. E. Freeman. 2002. *Closing the Achievement Gap: How to Reach Limited Formal Schooling and Long-Term English Learners.* Portsmouth, NH: Heinemann.

Krashen, S. 2003. *Explorations In Language Acquisition and Use.* Portsmouth, NH: Heinemann.

OELA. 2002. *The Growing Number of Limited English Proficient Students 1991–2002.* Retrieved 10/17/02.

KEY QUESTIONS

1. How might Preview, View, Review work with the ELL's you support?

2. What would a Preview, View, Review lesson look like using your math curriculum, science, health, and so on?

3. What activities can you use with pairs or groups of students who speak the same first language?

4. Hands-on learning is essential for language learners during the View. What strategies have you found for **organizing small group** activities that include hands-on instruction?

5. How does Preview, View, Review help teachers avoid concurrent translation?

Assessment of Language Learner Understanding

Subject Area _____ Topic Being Studied_____

Name of Learner_____Grade _____

	Date Observed:	Date Observed:	Suggestions for further instruction:
During the native language Preview, did the learner: • attend to the introduction • appear to understand in the native language • ask any questions or attempt to clarify • make connections to prior knowledge			
During the View in English, did the learner: • appear to be engaged • attempt to use English • ask a question • make a connection • read the text • relate the hands on learning to the text • express an opinion • use vocabulary related to the topic			
During the native language Review, did the learner: • summarize the learning • write in response • ask extending questions • draw to support long-term memory • attempt to use English vocabulary related to the topic after the review in the native language was complete			

Preview, View, Review

If possible, translate this form into the students' native language(s) and encourage them to write in the language they find most comfortable.

Student _____ Date _____

The Topic: _____

_____

_____

During the Preview, I learned: _____

_____

_____

_____

During the View, I also learned that: _____

_____

_____

Key points I want to think about in the Review are: _____

_____

_____

Preview: native language
View: English
Review: native language
Group Sharing: English

49 Three for the Road
Strategies for Success with Bilingual Learners!

ALICIA J. BOLT

MEET THE AUTHOR

ALICIA J. BOLT *is a Mexican teacher currently working for the Mercedes ISD in South Texas. She's doing her master's in Bilingual Education with Principalship Certification at UTPA in Edinburg, Texas.*

FOCUS QUOTE

What I like the most about these kinds of strategies is that they are fun. Children can be working in a specific skill without even noticing it at all, because they consider what they are doing to be a fun thing to do.

Being a teacher is an amazing experience. For starters, you need to care about children, put in a lot of work and time, be willing to take classes, and read professionally. And, I have learned that being a bilingual teacher demands even more. . . . Children who are learning English as an additional language need *more* support than their peers who are native speakers of English. That is why bilingual teachers are always searching for instructional strategies that can be useful for our bilingual children, offering them substantial support while making the learning feel like fun.

When children learn to read and write, especially when learning in a new language, they must focus on meaning to ensure that they develop the internal support systems that support language and literacy at the same time. So as educators for bilingual learners, we must focus on children's comprehension, rather than just decoding and fluency. We must be sure that they are using language as a tool for making meaning rather than being satisfied with simply naming words. We must provide them with tools for making

FIGURE 49–1 Students use sticky notes to record their thinking during Once Is Not Enough.

FIGURE 49–2 Previewing the Text Through Questioning engages students in asking questions before and after reading.

meaning across the curriculum to ensure that they are acquiring content knowledge while they are learning English.

　　With that focus in mind, I am always watching for instructional supports that will be flexible enough to use with many books, focus my learners on meaning, and empower them with strategies they can use over time. I selected the following three strategies because they can be easily adapted to any student's need and have been very useful for my ELL's. I especially like the way these strategies fit into a thematic curriculum, support state standards, and teach processes that are helpful on standardized tests. With so many reasons to use these strategies, I decided they were perfect for my bilingual students. The original formats are found in *Make It Real* by Linda Hoyt (2002). I have translated them into Spanish (see the reproducibles at the end of this chapter) to support strategic thinking in both languages and in all learners.

Once Is Not Enough

This strategy helped my students by making their reading comprehension easier. This strategy takes them step by step, scaffolding their comprehension, and building knowledge from their previous experience. There's even a part where students can come up with their own questions, which reaffirms their newly acquired knowledge. (See the strategy from Hoyt 2002, 187.)

Previewing the Text Through Questioning

What I like the most about these kind of strategies is that they are fun as well as rigorous. Children can be working in a specific skill without even noticing it at all, because they consider what they are doing, a fun thing to do. I chose this strategy because I firmly believe that teachers can do a lot for our students by designing classes based on the students' inquiries. We need to keep this in mind, because if what we are trying to teach our students is not relevant for them, we can lose our students' interest. (See the strategy from Hoyt 2002, p. 125.)

After reading about the impact pictures have as part of a text, I decided to try Investigating Visual Supports.

FIGURE 49–3 Students review visual supports to compare and contrast resources.

Investigating Visual Supports

Before starting with the strategy, I explained to my children what this strategy was about. I told them that I wanted to know which books they really like and which ones they don't. I could tell their self-esteem was rising, just by knowing I was taking their opinion into consideration to choose future literature. They were very excited and didn't even want to stop sharing. This strategy can help teachers know more about the kind of books that their children consider interesting. (See the strategy in Hoyt 2002, p. 138.)

Reflections

Once Isn't Enough, Previewing the Text Through Questioning, and Investigating Visual Supports all provide stimulation for language learning and long-term understanding. When you provide strategic supports like this in multilingual environments, you increase the likelihood that language, content, and strategy use will grow in powerful harmony. I hope your students enjoy my translations of these strategies.

Reference

Hoyt, Linda. 2002. *Make It Real: Strategies for Success with Informational Texts.* Portsmouth, NH: Heinemann.

KEY QUESTIONS

1. How might we ensure that English language Learners maintain their focus on meaning during reading?

2. What are the benefits of strategies that stimulate rigorous thinking and feel like fun?

3. Bilingual teachers need to support language and culture while working on content. Do any of the strategies in this article capture your interest? Are there others that you think are particularly successful with English language learners?

4. If you support bilingual learners and do not speak their native language, how might you get key resources translated?

¡UNA VEZ NO ES SUFICIENTE!

La primera vez: Hojeando solamente . . .

¿Qué notas? _____

¿Cuáles crees que podrían ser los puntos más importantes en la lectura? _____

_____

¿Qué palabras predices?_____

La segunda vez: Explorando . . .

Lee con detenimiento . . . (¡¡Saca las lupas!!) _____

Identifica las palabras claves e ideas _____

Usa las notitas pegajosas para marcar los puntos claves _____

_____

Discute con un compañero. Lleguen a un acuerdo en los puntos importantes_____

_____

La tercera vez: Sintetiza/Resume . . .

Cuestionate a tí mismo_____

Elabora preguntas que podrían estar en un examen. ¿Si tu estuvieras escribiendo un

examen, que preguntarías? _____

Piensa y habla. ¿Por qué crees que esta información es importante? _____

_____

Once Isn't Enough!

First time around: Skim . . .

What do you notice?_____

What do you think the key points might be?_____

What words do you predict? _____

Second Time Around: Scan

Read slowly . . . (bring out the magnifying glass!) _____

Identify key words and ideas _____

Use sticky notes to mark key points _____

TALK to a partner. Reach agreement on the important points_____

Third Time Around: Synthesize/Summarize . . .

Quiz yourself _____

Write questions that could be on a test. If you were writing a test, what

would you ask? _____

Think and talk. Why is this information important?_____

PREGUNTAS INCIALES AL REVISAR EL TEXTO

Nombre:_____ Libro: _____

Paginas revisadas: _____ Fecha: _____

Preguntas al revisar
Mientras le daba un vistazo a las
ilustraciones, mis preguntas son: Las respuestas posibles podrían ser:

_____   _____

_____   _____

_____   _____

_____   _____

Reflexiones Después De La Lectura
Las respuestas que respondí correctamente durante el vistazo fueron:_____

_____

_____

Pude contestar las preguntas antes de leer porque:_____

_____

_____

Durante la lectura, descubrí las respuestas de:_____

_____

_____

Previewing the Text Through Questioning

Name _____ Book _____

Pages Previewed _____ Date _____

Previewing Questions
As I previewed the illustrations
my questions are   Possible answers could include

_____   _____

_____   _____

_____   _____

_____   _____

After-Reading Reflections
The questions I answered correctly during the preview were about _____

_____

_____

I was able to answer them before reading because _____

_____

_____

During reading I discovered answers to _____

_____

_____

_____

ANALIZANDO LAS IMAGENES QUE APOYAN EL TEXTO

Nombre del equipo: _____

Nombre de los integrantes: _____

Su trabajo es revisar por lo menos diez libros informativos y pensar cuidadosamente acerca de las imagenes en los libros. ¿Cómo te ayudan estas imagenes? ¿Son ejemplos cuidadosamente seleccionados? ¿Se ven interesantes las páginas? ¿Te invitan a la lectura? ¿Porque? Revisa los encabezados u otras características que sabemos apoyan la lectura.

Libro revisado: **Evaluación de las imagenes**

1. _____   5   4   3   2   1

¿Por qué le diste esta evaluación? _____

2. _____   5   4   3   2   1

¿Por qué le diste esta evaluación? _____

3. _____   5   4   3   2   1

¿Por qué le diste esta evaluación? _____

4. _____   5   4   3   2   1

¿Por qué le diste esta evaluación? _____

5. _____   5   4   3   2   1

¿Por qué le diste esta evaluación? _____

¿Qué aprendiste acerca de las imagenes y sus preferencias?_____

_____

_____

Translated from *Make It Real* (2002) by Linda Hoyt.

Investigating Visual Supports

Review Team _____

Your job is to review at least ten informational books and think carefully about the visuals in the books. How do the visuals help you? Are these examples well chosen? Do the pages look inviting? Do they draw you into the reading? Why? Check for captions and other features we know support reading.

Book Reviewed   **Rating of the Visuals**

1. _____   5   4   3   2   1

Why did you give it this rating? _____

2. _____   5   4   3   2   1

Why did you give it this rating? _____

3. _____   5   4   3   2   1

Why did you give it this rating? _____

4. _____   5   4   3   2   1

Why did you give it this rating? _____

5. _____   5   4   3   2   1

Why did you give it this rating? _____

What did you learn about visuals and your own preferences?

_____

_____

_____

50

Scaffolding and Contextualizing
Reading for Real with English Learners

DENISE REA

AND SANDRA MERCURI

MEET THE AUTHORS

SANDRA MERCURI *is currently on the faculty in the Language, Literacy and Culture Department at Fresno Pacific University. She was the coordinator of the Excell program at Fresno Pacific University and has co-authored books such as* Closing the Achievement Gap *and* Dual Language Essential.

DENISE REA *is currently the Director of Multiple Subjects for the Graduate School of Education at Fresno Pacific University. She has extensive curriculum development experience and has been a staff developer, literacy coach, and bilingual teacher.*

FOCUS QUOTE

Contextualizing by the addition of visuals to a reading lesson can have a tremendous impact on reading comprehension.

I have been in classrooms where some students don't speak any English. They seem totally lost. They don't understand what is being said. There is no special instruction for them either. They just kind of follow along and do what they see the other students doing. One student I know just puts his head down on the desk and cries sometimes . . . It's hard to watch. The teacher just ignores the student. Is this the right thing to do?

Debbie—student teacher

"Is this the right thing to do?" is the question the authors were asked recently by a student teacher in a university education course. It raises an issue that many teachers face on a daily basis but ignore, not because they do not care about English learners, but because they do not know how to engage an English learner's active participation in their learning activities and classroom community.

Every year there are more and more English learners in our schools. Many teachers feel these are the students they have the most difficulty reaching. There is growing evidence that schools are not meeting the needs of linguistically and culturally diverse students, and federal and state governments are calling for all students to meet higher-level standards in addition to new graduation requirements and exit exams. There is more pressure on teachers to see academic growth with all learners, but there is a special emphasis on groups such as English learners. Teachers we have talked with state that teaching their English learners to read and write in English is their primary, although sometimes elusive, goal. It is the intent of this article to promote the use of instructional scaffolds as an effective way to reach English learners. By the simple inclusion of scaffolds in their instruction, teachers can make a significant difference in the academic success of English learners.

Scaffolds for English Learners

A scaffold is a temporary support that helps learners achieve at a higher level than they could reach on their own. Through scaffolds, teachers increase learner understanding of the lessons they teach, help students learn new vocabulary and skills, and support the development of concepts as students become literate in English. A scaffold helps clarify the purpose of a lesson, keeps students on task, and creates a momentum that engages students in new learning.

A scaffold can be as simple as giving students time to draw pictures of the beginning, middle, and end of a story or bringing in a real frog before reading a selection about frogs and amphibians. In secondary classrooms teachers may scaffold by giving students an outline of their lecture notes before they start to lecture. In the early part of the year, the teacher offers a

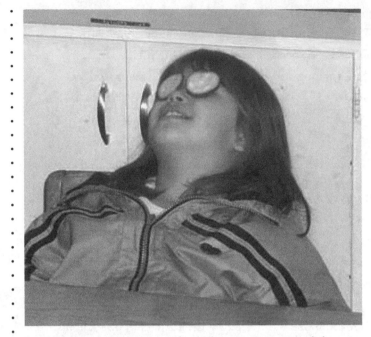

FIGURE 50–1 In a unit on foods, learners experienced the benefits of cucumbers as eye compresses before reading about it in their foods unit.

fairly detailed outline of the lecture, encouraging students to follow along and providing pauses for note-taking. As the year progresses, the scaffolding can be reduced and teacher-made outlines become increasingly skeletal until students are note-taking on their own. What is essential about a scaffold is that it allows English learners to complete assignments they may not otherwise be able to do and, therefore, supports their full inclusion in classroom learning activities.

Contextualizing

These scaffolds provide a context for the learning, giving learners an opportunity to make connections to prior knowledge, experience English vocabulary that surrounds the concept, and to think in terms of relationships between the content of the reading and their own understandings. When a learner has little or no prior knowledge on a topic, the scaffolds must be stronger and include hands-on real experience to create adequate context for the learning.

A common learning task is to ask students to read from a textbook and answer comprehension questions based on the reading. The result is often frustration for the students because they do not understand. Prereading experiences related to the content help learners understand the concepts and activates related vocabulary. A prereading scaffold could be photographs, a dramatization, or an experience with manipulatives. These scaffolds contextualize the learning and improve understanding.

Reading for Real Boxes

Reading for Real Boxes (adapted from Literature-Based Theme Packets, Lakeshore Learning) bring real things into prereading conversations. These real items provide clues about the content and help learners to develop understandings before they begin to read. Reading for Real Boxes can be used for literacy as well as content-area instruction.

To build your own Reading for Real Box, you would simply gather an array of real items related to the topic in the reading passage, then spend time talking with students about the items, how they might relate to one another, what they might have to do with this reading passage, and so on. To add additional scaffolding, you might provide 3 × 5-inch cards with the English words for each item as a visual link between the item and the English text.

A great addition is to take digital photos of students in the school engaged in activities that relate to the story or the content-area study. This provides another rich context and encourages learners to make connections between their school experiences and the literature selection.

Reading for Real Boxes can be created and saved in a central location where staff members can easily locate them. This allows all staff members to

FIGURE 50–2 In this Reading for Real Box for *Sadako,* the real items stimulate vocabulary, conversation, and discussion to help ELL's prepare for reading.

share the resources as well as share the work in gathering the items for the boxes. Making a Reading for Real Box requires some thinking and work ahead of time, but once a teacher has made it, it can be used again and again.

Scaffolds and Real Experiences Support Language Learners

When reading experiences are contextualized, linked to real things and real experiences, English learners understand more and learn English more rapidly. Contextualized communication that is enhanced through props, real things, and related visuals does take time to prepare, but it is worth it. Learners whose teachers scaffold their understanding through real things are learners who will develop positive attitudes about English and the content they are learning (TESOL 2004). These are English learners who have the benefit of comprehension to assist their language-learning efforts.

The following chart summarizes the importance of contextualizing:

Contextualizing—Organizing Visual and Physical Information in a Way That Enables All Students, Including English Learners, to Make Sense of a Lesson.

What is it?	It is a strategy where teachers use photographs, drawings, pictures, big books, picture books, children's art work, videos, models, artifacts, and/or realia (real objects) to add informational clues to lessons. Students hear English language and connect it to the visual images.
Why is it important to do or learn?	The use of props and visuals builds English language skills, background knowledge, increases understanding, and helps students access knowledge and experiences they already have. It engages students in learning because the lesson becomes more interesting and enjoyable.
How do you do it?	Teachers look for visuals in magazines, on the Internet, or in videos. Teachers make or purchase models and artifacts that relate to the subject matter of the lesson.

References

Coerr, E. 1986. *Sadako.* New York: G. P. Putnam's Sons.

Cummins, J. 1989. *Empowering Minority Students.* Sacramento: California Association For Bilingual Education.

Lakeshore Learning Materials. 1993. Literature-Based Theme Packets. Carson, California.

Reading/Language Arts Framework for California Public Schools. Kindergarten Through Grade Twelve. 1999. Adopted by the California State Board of Education. Sacramento, CA: California Department of Education.

TESOL. 2004. Advancing the Profession: ESL Standards for Pre-K–12 Students. *www.tesol.org/assoc/k12standards/it/01.html.* (April).

Van der Werff, J. 2003. *Using Pictures from Magazines.* The Internet TESL Journal. Vol IX, No. 7, July, *iteslj.org/Techniques/Werff-Pictures. html.*

Walqui, A. 2003. *From Apprenticeship to Appropriation: Scaffolding the Development of Academic Language by English Learners.* 2003. Iowa Culture and Language Conference: Land of Promise, Harvest of Hope.

KEY QUESTIONS

1. Chat with a colleague about the scaffolds he/she uses with English language learners. What scaffolds seem to best help English learners become more effective readers?

2. How might you contextualize instruction in science, social studies, math, health, and so on?

3. Is there a picture file in your school that could help you scaffold content studies? If so, what is it like? If not, how might you get one started?

4. Think about ways to lessen the load of creating Reading for Real Boxes. A suggestion might be to have older students create them as a new type of book report, then share with and/or donate them to lower-grade students. How else might that work at your school?

Reading for Real Box: *Sadako*

Objectives:

    To help build background knowledge and vocabulary before reading the book *Sadako* (Coerr 1986). To help students practice using prediction and confirmation as a reading comprehension strategy.

Comprehension Strategy: Prediction

Possible resources for the Reading for Real Box

1. multiple copies of *Sadako*
2. rice paper lantern
3. origami cranes of various sizes
4. a pair of chopsticks
5. a track jersey
6. a Japanese tea cup
7. stethoscope from a child's toy doctor kit
8. photograph of a Japanese man, preferably in WWII uniform

Scaffold/Contextualize

1. The teacher talks briefly about the book, presenting the title, author, genre, topic, cultural background of the setting, and a short summary of the book.
2. Each prop is shown to students and passed around the group. Each object is named and the relevance of each object to the story and the culture is explained. Students share personal connections they make to the objects.
3. Students read the selection silently or in partner-pairs, stopping occasionally to make predictions about the text and about the items in the box. When they come to a place where they think an item in the box is about to appear in the story, they mark it with a sticky note and tell why they think that item is related to this portion of the story.

Assessment: The teacher takes notes to record the quality of the predictions being made and the ability of the learner to use English to relate understanding of the real items and the story line.

 Contributed by S. Mercuri and D. Rea © 2005 by Linda Hoyt from *Spotlight on Comprehension*. Portsmouth, NH: Heinemann.

Scaffolding and Contextualizing Learning: Supporting English Language Learners

Topic to Teach	Texts at the Learners' Level	Scaffolds I Will Use	Real Things to Create Context
Example: Weather	*Weather All Around* *Severe Storms* *Thunderstorms* Textbook	• Sketch weather experiences • Observe/chart weather	• Rain gauge • Video on weather • Pictures

Teaching Learners to Contextualize

Student Partners_____   _____

Date _____

We have been learning about _____.

We are going to share our learning and want our learning partners to know that:

_____

_____

(list important facts and ideas)

Planning:
To help others understand, we will include: _____

Visuals: What visuals (pictures, drawings, Internet graphs, a book) will you use to

extend the learning for your partners? List them here: _____

_____

Real Things: Are there any real things that you could show your partners that will

help them understand? List them here: _____

Writing: What could you write that would help your partners understand what

you have learned? _____

_____

Reflections:
After sharing with your partners, think. What did they learn? What helped them

the most? _____

_____

     © 2005 by Linda Hoyt from *Spotlight on Comprehension*. Portsmouth, NH: Heinemann.

Expanding the World Through Read Alouds

Unlocking Comprehension for English Language Learners

51

LESLIE MARICLE-BARKLEY

MEET THE AUTHOR

Leslie Maricle-Barkley *lives and teaches in the small, rural northern California town of Hopland. She provides training in portfolio assessment and literacy development, but her greatest joy is working with bilingual, multiage students in her primary classroom. Leslie has taught since 1979.*

FOCUS QUOTE

Student questions teach me a lot. I have learned to make no assumptions when it comes to comprehension. I have been surprised more than once by student requests for clarification of vocabulary that I thought was easily understood by all!

In the late 1970s, Dr. Berman, my reading theory professor, opened every class with a poem, a short story, or a passage from a book. By netting us with words, he demonstrated the power of enticing readers with read alouds. His passion was reading, and he felt that the most powerful tool teachers could employ to inspire students to read was reading to the class every day. So, I have always read stories to my class daily with the goal that I, like Dr. Berman, could ignite a passionate love of reading in my students.

My English language learners (ELL's) love this time and I consciously include fiction and informational selections with explicit illustrations, knowing the illustrations are often the key to unlocking the story for the students. As positive as this experience has been, my knowledge of facilitating language development has helped me to realize that my read alouds are also powerful tools for developing and assessing language.

FIGURE 51–1

I hold the book up, I pause, I glance at the expectant faces of my class. Eyes glued to the illustration, every student freezes with anticipation, hanging on the words: "This is a fine, fine school . . ." Suddenly, they all chime in and soon we're chanting away in unison. Is this the first time I've read Sharon Creech's hilarious, yet pointed, tale about a principal who loves school so much he does away with all holidays? No, it is not. In fact, I've read this book at least 10 times this year. Are the students tired of hearing the story? Bored with the repetition? Absolutely not! They choose this book during independent reading time and beg to hear it again and again. We've made a class mural, written ideas in our learning logs about why our school is a fine, fine school, and still they can't get enough of this book. And A Fine, Fine School is just one of many read-aloud books that appeal to the students in my class.

FIGURE 51–2

Once again, I'm reading a story to my class. "That's curious," I say, "I won-der what the prince will do next?" Amarilis, who's been closely following the story, looks puzzled. "Curious?" she asks with a slight frown. "What does curious mean?" I'm stunned at the question, because, in my opinion, Amarilis is one of the most proficient English language learners in my class. She converses freely on the playground and in the classroom, reads English books at grade level, and gen-erally participates fully in all discussions. I would expect the word curious to be part of her vocabulary.

FIGURE 51–3

Finally, it is nonfiction read-aloud time. I reread a short piece about the life cycle of a butterfly, taking time to point to the illustrations, read the captions, and highlight some of the key vocabulary using highlighter tape. I then list the key vo-cabulary on a whiteboard I keep by my chair. "Who can describe the stages in the development of a butterfly?" I ask. "Quick, use the keywords on the whiteboard and share with a partner!" I give the students a few minutes to discuss the life cy-cle of a butterfly, eavesdropping on the discussion while I prominently display the whiteboard, encouraging students to use the pertinent vocabulary. Is this new vocabulary to the English language learners in the group? No, it is not. In fact, during English Language Development time the students have already had oppor-tunities to listen to this and other books about butterflies. More importantly, they've drawn the life cycle of the butterfly, labeled the illustration, and described the life cycle to partners in that group. This read aloud merely reinforces their de-veloping grasp of the vocabulary.

These vignettes underscore the versatility of read alouds as a tool for working with English language learners. Read alouds:

- Provide a body of common literature in the classroom
- Present many opportunities to model and practice comprehension strategies
- Supply context for rich vocabulary expansion
- Create community in the classroom

- Deepen knowledge about the world
- Offer students opportunities to connect to their own experiences and build on previous knowledge
- Fill students with the sounds and rhythms of the language
- Model language structures and develop a sense of the language
- Offer a springboard for partner sharing/discussions/written responses
- Illustrate conventions of print

Frontload Vocabulary and Concepts

Before a read aloud, I often share topic-related realia and guide prereading discussions to scaffold concepts and content. This works well and ensures that the ELL's have had some prereading exposure, which ensures their comprehension of the selection.

Gathering a Small Group Before Read Alouds

At times, I pull a small group of ELL's together *before* the read aloud. My goal, in this small group setting, is to frontload vocabulary and concepts for those who most need it. Because we are in a small group, I can give them more opportunity to talk and to discuss the concepts in the book. They can get close to the pictures and spend time looking and thinking in a way that is not possible when they are sitting at the back of the story circle. I can also assess their level of prior knowledge on the topic and their grasp of the English vocabulary that relates to this text.

These pre-read aloud, small group experiences give ELL's a chance to become the class "experts," instead of merely struggling to understand what is being discussed. This "expert" status boosts the students' self-confidence, lowers their anxiety (affective filters), and increases the students' participation in whole class oral language activities.

The Importance of Interactive Talk

Read alouds used to be a time when children sat silently. Conversations were saved for after-reading discussions where the teacher was the center of the conversation and learners got to speak one at a time.

We now know that engagement and oral-language use support the development of vocabulary and concepts, so I take frequent breaks in the reading to insert think alouds or invite the children to go knee-to-knee with a partner and share their thoughts. This gives ELL's time to process their understanding and an opportunity to use English to explain their thinking.

Encouraging discussions during reading allows children to clarify meanings and apply comprehension strategies. While many may be reluctant to speak in front of the class, especially ELL's, partner discussions provide a safe, supportive environment to explore the concepts and vocabulary of the read aloud. By listening to partner conversations, I can gauge the depth of specific students' comprehension and assess language use.

Encourage Questions

We know children are naturally curious. In a one-to-one setting, they punctuate a read aloud with questions and comments about the selection. They want to know "why" and "how" and to make personal connections. To encourage this natural curiosity, I consciously build in time for partners to generate questions about a reading selection before, during, and after the reading. I want them to understand that questions help us to make sense of our world, rather than to assume that a question will spotlight a deficit in understanding.

The questions students pose provide me with important assessment information. Their questions help me understand their grasp of the vocabulary and concepts, and to clearly see which learners are operating at a literal level of understanding and which are thinking more deeply.

Student questions teach me a lot. I have learned to make no assumptions when it comes to comprehension. I have been surprised more than once by student requests for clarification of vocabulary that I thought was easily understood by all!

Multiple Readings

Multiple readings of favorite books immerse ELL's in key vocabulary, story elements, and concepts. Through hearing and using vocabulary over time, the language becomes internalized and the student's vocabulary expands. Through multiple readings, learners become familiar with the language so they can relax and enjoy the story. Their confidence builds and they have the opportunity to become absorbed in a book, participating as fully as native speakers in the enjoyment and discussions.

Related Books

Reading books that are related by topic, by author, or by theme assists learners in making connections and having repeated exposure to vocabulary, text structures, and language features. As in the vignette about the butterfly book earlier in this chapter, we read a wide range of books on butterflies and soon the vocabulary was comfortable to all students so they could focus on the way this author presented information, noticing the author's craft in a way they could never do if they were experiencing a first exposure to the topic.

Similarly, reading series books where the same characters come back in book after book brings that same sense of familiarity and predictability to the reading. This is comforting to ELL's who spend so much of their day working hard to make meaning and grasp the linguistic elements they need to express themselves.

KEY QUESTIONS TO CONSIDER WHEN CHOOSING READ ALOUD BOOKS FOR ELL's:

- Is the language of the book particularly melodic, repetitive, and engaging?
- What are the challenges to comprehension? How could they be addressed?
- How can ELL's be frontloaded with vocabulary, concepts, and information before a whole class lesson?
- Can the selection connect to previous learning or experience?
- What is the key vocabulary?

Assessment During Read Alouds

It is important to have a notepad, spiral notebook, or clipboard at hand during read alouds because the opportunities for assessment are so rich and varied. I try to write down learner statements that document moments of growth, take notes about language use and vocabulary development, or jot my observations about a learner's use of a comprehension strategy that may be revealed during our discussions. Depending on the student and the focus of the instruction, I might record a phrase or a sentence, or paraphrase a longer statement. Here are some of the things I look for when recording observations.

CONFIDENCE:

Does the student ask questions for clarification of vocabulary or concepts?

Does the student participate fully in whole group discussions or does he/she prefer to share with a partner? Who does he/she choose?

GRAMMATICAL STRUCTURES:

Does the student speak in words, phrases, or sentences?

Does the student use proper pronoun/subject agreement (he/she)?

Does the student follow verb usage (past tense forms, correct verb form)?

Does the student use correct word order (especially when posing questions)?

Is the student aware of sentence structures?

VOCABULARY:

Does the student understand/use key vocabulary independently?

Can the student explain key vocabulary?

Does the student use basic vocabulary or more complex words?

Does the student understand and use idiomatic expressions?

COMPREHENSION:

Does the student understand the story on a literal or inferential level?

Has the student grasped the main concepts being taught?

Is the student able to retell the story with sequence and detail?

Can the student list the main points using their own words?

Is the student able to generate questions about the text?

Can this learner make connections (text-to-text, text-to-world, text-to-self)?

Is the child able to create visual images of the content of the selection?

But, most importantly, read alouds provide opportunities to extend, assess, enrich and develop English in a safe, supportive atmosphere for English language learners.

Favorite Books:

*Creech, Sharon. 2003. *A Fine, Fine School.* Pine Plains, NY: Live Oak Media. ISBN: 159112221X.

Garland, Michael. 2003. *Miss Smith's Incredible Storybook.* New York: Dutton Books. ISBN: 0525471332

James, Simon. 1996. *Dear Mr. Blueberry.* Aladdin Library. ISBN: 0689807686.

*O'Neill, Alexis. 2002. *The Recess Queen.* New York: Scholastic. ISBN: 0439206375.

Ryan, Pam Munoz. 2001. *Rice and Beans.* New York: Scholastic. ISBN: 0439183030.

Teague, Mark. 2002. *Dear Mrs. La Rue: Letters from Obedience School.* New York: Scholastic. ISBN: 0439206634.

Yep, Laurence. 1999. *The Dragon Prince.* Madison, WI: Demco Media. ISBN: 0606158456.

*By far the most requested books for read aloud this year.

References

Freeman, D. E., and Y. S. Freeman. 2001. *Between Worlds: Access to Second Language Acquisition, 2nd edition.* Portsmouth, NH: Heinemann.

Garcia, G. G., ed., 2003. *English Leaners: Reaching the Highest Level of English Literacy.* Newark, DE: International Reading Association.

Routman, R. 2003. *Reading Essentials: The Specifics You Need to Teach Reading Well.* Portsmouth, NH: Heinemann.

KEY QUESTIONS

1. Have you tried multiple rereadings of a selection with your students? What do you see as the benefits? How have your ELL's responded?

2. Pulling together English language learners for small group work before reading a specific text to the entire class works in read aloud, science, math, and so on. How might you use this strategy in your classroom to recast ELL's as experts?

3. How many read alouds do you provide each day? What is the balance between fiction and informational read alouds?

4. Which comprehension strategies lend themselves to modeling during read aloud times? Which ones seem to best support your ELL's?

Observation Log for Language Learners During Read Aloud

Learner _____ Date of Observations _____

Confidence—Does the student: #1   #2   #3   #4

Ask questions for clarification of vocabulary or concepts?   ☐   ☐   ☐   ☐

Participate fully in whole group discussions?   ☐   ☐   ☐   ☐

Prefer to share with a partner?   ☐   ☐   ☐   ☐

Use English or native language to respond?   ☐   ☐   ☐   ☐

Grammatical Structures—Does the student:

Speak in words, phrases, or sentences?   ☐   ☐   ☐   ☐

Show pronoun/subject agreement (he/she)?   ☐   ☐   ☐   ☐

Have correct verb usage (past tense forms, correct verb form)? ☐   ☐   ☐   ☐

Use English word order (especially when posing questions)?   ☐   ☐   ☐   ☐

Vocabulary—Does the student:

Understand/use key vocabulary independently?   ☐   ☐   ☐   ☐

Explain key vocabulary?   ☐   ☐   ☐   ☐

Use basic vocabulary or more complex words?   ☐   ☐   ☐   ☐

Understand and use idiomatic expressions?   ☐   ☐   ☐   ☐

Comprehension—Does the student:

Understand the story on a literal level?   ☐   ☐   ☐   ☐

Make inferences?   ☐   ☐   ☐   ☐

Grasp the main concepts being taught?   ☐   ☐   ☐   ☐

Retell the story with sequence and detail?   ☐   ☐   ☐   ☐

List the main points using his own words?   ☐   ☐   ☐   ☐

Generate questions about the text?   ☐   ☐   ☐   ☐

Make connections (text-to-text, text-to-world, text-to-self)? ☐   ☐   ☐   ☐

Create visual images of the content of the selection?   ☐   ☐   ☐   ☐

Read-Aloud Reflections

Student_____ Date _____

My favorite read-aloud books are: _____

_____

_____

I like them because: _____

_____

_____

I understand our read alouds best when _____

_____

_____

When we talk with a partner, I try to _____

_____

_____

During the read aloud, I try to_____

_____

_____

I am improving at _____

_____

Part Nine

Considering Instruction That Works

52

A Veteran Teacher Reflects on Comprehension

TERESA THERRIAULT

MEET THE AUTHOR

TERESA THERRIAULT *has been involved in education for over 30 years working as a classroom teacher, a talented and gifted specialist, Title 1 reading specialist, and special needs educator. She has worked as a district-level literacy facilitator and as a district language arts specialist. Teresa and her husband live in San Diego where she works as an independent literacy consultant.*

Teresa loves to exercise and be out of doors. She loves to read and to share her joy in literacy with the students and teachers she serves.

FOCUS QUOTE

Strategy instruction is ever present. At times it's positioned on a front burner on high, other times it's simmering on a back burner. But it's always there. My purpose is no longer to teach the text, but to grow strategic readers.

It's been more than 30 years since I began teaching. Some things have remained the same. I still enjoy kids. I still feel passionate about teaching and I still feel a responsibility to be a better teacher tomorrow than I am today.

A lot has changed . . . There is more emphasis on accountability and standards, kids with a wider range of life experiences, and what drives my thinking about the teaching of reading.

Thirty some years ago, I believed that *first you learn to read and then you read to learn.* My personal knowledge of the reading process was limited. I could leave that to the experts. The teacher's edition of my reading adoption made decisions for me. I followed the guide with little deviation. Whole group instruction ruled the day. Round robin reading was pervasive in all my instruction. Instruction? I suppose we called it that, but looking back, it was more telling students what to do then asking questions, usually requiring literal answers. I taught the story. Fiction dominated.

Comprehension was about questions—my questions to the students. I asked questions, they answered them . . . pretty simple.

Reading instruction was taught during reading time. Teaching reading during a science lesson wasn't considered, as that was science time. We didn't write during reading. In fact, we didn't write much at all. When it came to writing, I taught subsets of writing: nouns, verbs, writing to prompts.

What I called assessment was really evaluation. It was a test or a grade focused on an end product. It wasn't about finding learner strengths, it was about putting labels on their products. It didn't drive my instruction.

Now this past may sound bleak. I'm a bit embarrassed, but I'm also amazed at how I've evolved as a teacher. It's really quite amazing. If I only knew then, what I know now about teaching students to be active readers . . .

I can't go back, but I am going forward and doing a much better job of helping students to become readers, thinkers, and comprehenders. Here are a few of my ah-ha's as a veteran teacher.

- **The "learning to read, then reading to learn"** ditty no longer runs through my head. Now I know that from the most emergent reader through the most skilled reader, all readers benefit from strategy instruction. All readers who are making meaning read to learn, to enjoy, and to make connections from the beginning. It's my responsibility to ensure that both strategy learning and "story" or content learning take place concurrently. This is true for kindergarten as much as for high school.

- **I'm making the teaching decisions.** I no longer leave that to a teacher's edition. A teacher's edition is just a resource to assist my decisions. So what guides my decisionmaking? Knowledge in at least four areas:

  - *The reading process:* The cueing systems and the strategies used to make meaning are now firmly embedded in my teaching psyche.
  - *The students:* Their understandings about the reasons for reading, strategy use, layout, and features of text; approximate reading and fluency levels; vocabulary and comprehension skills; and their

attitudes about reading. I'm looking for a **collection of assessment information** that gives me the fullest picture of the student, rather than a single snapshot of a reader.

• *The texts:* Fiction no longer rules the day—it's a part of the day. Informational texts abound from the earliest grades on up. I'm aware of the supports and challenges provided in different kinds of texts so that I can expose students to the genres they will experience in life outside the classroom walls. I try to take into account interests of students as I select texts.

• *The standards:* We must be knowledgeable of our district and state standards. Standards-based teaching has made me a more focused teacher. But while keeping an eye on the goal, we can never lose sight of the individual readers we are guiding. We must begin where they are and move them toward the standard.

• **Assessment** is a big part of my teaching. How can I know how to scaffold a student, make a decision about strategy use, or select a guided reading text if I don't have current information on individual students? "On-the-run assessment" that I conduct daily within the natural contexts of the learning day enable me to arrive at a student's "zone of proximal development" (Vygotsky 1978). That is, the range where a learner can only perform a task with the help of a teacher. The learning experience is not too hard, not too easy. Rather like the bowl of porridge in Goldilocks . . . just right.

• **Strategy Instruction** is ever present. At times it's positioned on a front burner on high; other times, it's simmering on a back burner. But it's always there. My purpose is no longer to teach the text, but to grow strategic readers. We still celebrate a great book, but it's not the only focus of my teaching or my students' learning. *Snapshots: Literacy Minilessons Up Close* (Hoyt 2000) continues to offer me fresh ideas on how to keep strategy instruction front and center.

• **Show, don't tell!** The gradual release of responsibility model (Pearson and Gallagher 1983) guides my teaching and rules the day! It's simple. It makes sense. It's not another thing. It's the thing that makes the difference. It includes the following steps:

• *Introduce the strategy by modeling and thinking aloud:* Explain the what, how, when, and why of a strategy. Make your thinking transparent. Students observe.

• Provide *guided practice:* Invite participation while you support.

• *Independent practice:* Students work independently to apply the target strategy.

- *Self-Reflection:* Students consider what they learned, how, where, and why a strategy is used. Self-regulation is modeled, reinforced and monitored. (Adapted from Linda Hoyt. *Snapshots: Literacy Minilessons Up Close.*)

- **Engagement** is a critical component in learning to read. I'm vigilant about keeping engagement in reading high for both my students and me. If I'm not passionate about something I'm presenting, how can I build passion in my students? For comprehension to occur, students must engage with meaningful text. Rote completion of assignments is just not the same.

So if instruction is not hitting the mark, what helps me analyze the situation? *Cambourne's Conditions of Learning* (Cambourne 1988) have provided me with that guide. Dr. Cambourne speaks not only to the importance of engagement (it's like the umbrella over all the other conditions), but to those conditions that will support, in this case, the learning of reading (and writing). I used to hear myself say with much frustration, again shared with some embarrassment, "I already taught this to them. Why don't they have it?" Dr. Cambourne made it transparent to me that it's not them and it's not even me. It's that the following conditions may not be in place:

- *Immersion* must be long and deep and permeate my planning. There needs to be opportunity to be immersed in the strategy over time and within many texts.
- *Demonstrations* abound. Students need *multiple opportunities* to **see** things modeled. This is where thinking aloud plays such a crucial piece, and that thinking aloud must occur across the full range of the curriculum. Thinking aloud in fiction is not enough.
- *Expectations* convey to students that they *can* learn and that we believe it. Here is another reason to engage in ongoing assessment: I need to get to know my students so that my expectations for individuals are valid.
- *Taking responsibility* means that a student actively and consciously takes responsibility to apply the learning in some meaningful way. When expert teams research a topic and then share their learning with another group, they take responsibility for the learning of the other group. When buddy readers plan their stories and think ahead about points to share in the book, they are taking responsibility for their own thinking as well as for the experience of their partner. When a reader practices visualizing independently during silent reading, he is taking responsibility for the learning. Giving responsibility doesn't mean that students can

choose not to learn or that teachers just stand back; it does mean that I need to be prepared to provide similar demonstrations over and over again.

• *Approximations* speak to the idea that we recognize the attempts students make toward an end goal. If we expect error-free application of reading strategies from the beginning, we will be setting up the student and ourselves for frustration. As Cambourne (1988) stated, "Freedom to approximate (make mistakes) is an essential ingredient of all successful learning."

• *Use,* succinctly stated, is that students need plenty of opportunities and time to practice. This has implications for my classroom. If lesson time is taken up with teacher talk and demonstrations and little time is available for students to apply or practice strategies in authentic pieces of reading, then a very important piece of learning has been neglected. This also relates to the importance of the volume of reading our students experience. They simply must read *a lot* to get better at reading and comprehending.

• *Response* provides relevant, timely, and appropriate feedback to learners. While general feedback to a whole group can be useful, there is no substitution for creating time to work with small groups and to conference with pairs and individuals.

Being conscious of the Conditions of Learning influences my planning as I work to ensure that all conditions are met. It also helps me to adjust my lessons instead of pointing fingers when things don't go well. The Conditions of Learning help me provide an optimum environment in which to support learners.

Other key elements of my classroom include:

• **Read alouds with picture books:** They're present for all grade levels, not just in primary classrooms. Where I used to use only fiction, now nonfiction/informational books hold equal favor. There are times when I share a book just for the love of the book or to introduce a new author, but now I consistently use my read-aloud time to model and think aloud what active readers do. Many read alouds become "interactive read alouds," where students have the opportunity to practice the modeled strategy. Here is another opportunity to hand over the learning in scaffolded steps.

• **Anchor Activities:** When I read Harvey and Goudvis' beliefs about best practices in *Strategies That Work* (2000), a huge smile crossed my face when I read about providing anchor experiences. It's the idea of carefully selecting a book or activity when first introducing a strategy. We anchor strategy instruction to a book worth referring back to, so students can activate their prior knowledge independently at a later date. I had been using this practice for a long time and was so gratified to see that I wasn't alone.

• **Round robin reading** has been replaced by partner reading, silent reading, choral reading, and readers' theater, even in small group instruction. I try to be very conscious of time with text issues. When readers take turns reading out loud, only one learner is reading, so I need to select strategies that ensure that all learners read as much as possible. *Good-Bye Round Robin,* (Opitz and Rasinski 1998) has been a key source for effective oral reading strategies. I don't know about you, but to this very day, if I had to read a portion of an unfamiliar text out loud to my peers, I'd be skimming ahead, finding my part, and practicing. Saving face by not making mistakes jumps to the head of my priorities, and comprehension goes out the window! I don't want to set up this kind of environment for my students.

• **Reading conferences** and an emphasis on blocks of time for uninterrupted independent reading have a carefully preserved place in each day. Time on task, actually reading for meaning, and density of instruction have increased . . . Each independent reading session opens with a minilesson on a comprehension strategy and learners understand that their task is to apply the strategy while they are reading on their own. I am not correcting papers or doing emails. I sit side by side with students conferring about their reading, assessing, and giving feedback in the special way you an only achieve when working one-on-one.

• Readers use **writing** to record questions, comments, and connections, to clarify thinking and then, when appropriate, to respond to text when reading is complete. We don't ever read without access to a pen and notebook. Empowering students to capture their own thoughts is a critical piece to becoming active, reflective readers and thinkers.

• **Integration of reading and writing across curriculum is intentional.** Where I used to segregate subjects, now reading and writing strategy-talk are embedded within math and science. Providing demonstrations and guidance on how to navigate science and math textbooks, how to write-up a science experiment and decipher explanations for a math story problem, are integral components of science and math. An observer seeing a portion of a math lesson wouldn't always be able to decide if this is reading time or math time. That's good! It needs to be both. It should have always been that way. I now know better.

• **Literature and Information Circles** are one component of my comprehensive reading program. Simply stated, they are book clubs that focus on actively reading, i.e., preparing for discussion by taking notes, flagging Very Important Points, VIP's, (Hoyt 2000) and using both fiction and informational texts in order to deepen comprehension through active reading and group discussion. Daniels (2002) and Peterson and Eeds (1990) got me started on my journey into book clubs; Johnson and Schlick Noe (1995, 1999, 2000) have helped me continue my exploration. Time and effort go into building successful circles. They are worth it. Remember: It's important for teachers to be readers outside the classroom, too. Join an adult book club . . . for the conversation and bonding . . . for the fun of it.

• The **classroom library** looks different now. It reflects my belief that students need exposure to a rich array of both informational materials and great pieces of fiction. A range of books from easier to more challenging is now available. My old classroom library was not as supportive of students who were not at grade level or who were passionate about informational texts. Students take an active part in organizing "our" library. They provide feedback on book selection, sort and resort the books, and I modify some of my ordering based on their ideas.

• **Wall space** looks different. Wall space, which has always been at a premium, was filled with bulletin boards that were prepared by me and often consisted of purchased posters and student work. Now these same areas have become depositories of growing lists of strategies, genres studies, author studies and class-generated think alouds: tools the students use in their work as learners and comprehenders.

• **Professional reading** keeps us thinking and growing. We must continue to read, reflect, and align our current practices with new information that rings true. *Belonging to a professional book club* not only makes for good conversation, but it often is the catalyst that keeps us reading.

• **Joining professional organizations,** like IRA or NCTE, keeps us connected to other educators who thrive on learning. If we are to grow comprehenders in our classroom, we must ensure that we are comprehenders of best practices ourselves.

My list is still growing; I'm still growing. Pretty nice after all these years.

References

Cambourne, B. 1988. *Whole Story: Learning and the Acquisition Literacy in the Classroom.* New York: Scholastic.

Daniels, H. 2002. *Literature Circles: Voice and Choice in Book Clubs and Reading Groups.* Portland, ME: Stenhouse Publishers.

Harvey, S., and A. Goudvis. 2000. *Strategies That Work: Teaching Comprehension to Enhance Understanding.* Portland, ME: Stenhouse Publishers.

Hill, B., K. Schlick Noe, and N. Johnson. 2001. *Literature Circles Resource Guide.* Norwood, MA: Christopher-Gordon.

———. 1999. *Literature Circles and Responses.* Norwood, MA: Christopher-Gordon.

Hoyt, L. 2000. *Snapshots: Literacy Minilessons Up Close.* Portsmouth, NH: Heinemann.

———. 1998. *Revisit, Reflect, Retell: Strategies to Improve Reading Comprehension.* Portsmouth, NH: Heinemann.

Opitz, M., and T. Rasinski. 1998. *Good-bye Round Robin: 25 Effective Oral Reading Strategies.* Portsmouth, NH: Heinemann.

Peterson, R., and M. Eeds. 1990. *Grand Conversations.* New York: Scholastic.

Routman, R. 2000. *Conversations: Strategies for Teaching, Learning, and Evaluating.* Portsmouth, NH: Heinemann.

Schlick Noe, K., and N. Johnson. 1999. *Getting Started with Literature Circles.* Norwood, MA: Christopher-Gordon.

Vygotsky, L. 1978. *Mind in Society: The Development of Higher Psychological Processes.* Cambridge, MA: Harvard.

KEY QUESTIONS

1. If you were to create a list of "ahha's" or non-negotiables about comprehension instruction, what would you list?

2. If you think of Teresa's list as affirmations and invitations, what would you identify as an affirmation of your current practice? What invitation did you notice?

3. What do you think separates the teacher who continues to grow, learn, and change over 30 years from one that does not? What can you do to ensure that you continue to grow and understand best practices?

4. What are the strengths of your comprehension instruction? What areas do you want to work on?

Focus on Comprehension—A Checklist to Ponder

☐ Are you teaching reading and content in the same lessons, helping children to understand that we read to learn from the beginning?

☐ What guides instruction in your classroom? Knowledge of the reading process? Ongoing assessments?

☐ Is there a clear balance between fiction and nonfiction in all elements of the day: read aloud, shared reading, guided reading, independent reading?

☐ Are the genres of the real world evident in your classroom?

☐ Do the comprehension standards inform your instruction and become part of your thinking or are they separate and treated as an add-on to the day?

☐ How do you integrate assessments into the heartbeat of daily teaching?

☐ How do you record and save what you learn about students?

☐ Is strategy instruction clearly present in every lesson of the day?

☐ Are you growing strategic readers or teaching the book?

☐ Are you implementing all four stages of the gradual release model? (modeling/thinking aloud, guided practice, independent practice, self-reflection?)

☐ How would you describe the engagement of your students? Are they excited and passionate about their learning?

☐ Consider a lesson in light of Cambourne's conditions. How many conditions were in place?

☐ Do you revisit picture books over and over again to see them with new eyes?

☐ How are anchor experiences used over time to ensure that they are not written and forgotten?

☐ What alternatives to round robin reading do you employ?

☐ How is writing used as a tool for learning in your classroom? Do students write all day long?

☐ Are literature circles and information circles part of your reading program?

☐ If you analyze your classroom library, are there invitations for deep comprehension with a range of fiction and nonfiction selections arranged in interesting, appealing ways?

☐ Are your walls a mirror of learning, showing content and the tools students use as learners?

☐ Are you a professional reader, striving to stay on top of the ever-changing landscape in education?

☐ Do you belong to a professional organization?

☐ How have you changed since your first year of teaching?

Aligning Strategy Instruction Across Classrooms

The Middle School High Five

53

AMY GOODMAN

MEET THE AUTHOR

AMY GOODMAN *started her teaching career in Evanston, Illinois, where she grew up. She then headed north to Alaska for a new challenge and stayed for the next 23 years. She participated in a year-long teacher exchange to Melbourne, Australia, in 1987. She has taught grades 4–8 and has a passion for teaching reading and writing. Currently, she is the Middle School Literacy Teacher Expert for the Anchorage School District.*

FOCUS QUOTE

By focusing closely on a few key strategies, students will see a unified approach to instruction across grade levels and content areas.

S trategies. Everywhere I look I uncover new strategies for teaching more effectively. I love the clever names, the acronyms, and the unique approaches. I am a collector of these strategies and never hesitate to try out new ones with my students. My file cabinets are loaded with them and so are my computer files. Recently, my struggle has been finding the one I want to use for tomorrow. Did I file that under spelling, word study, or vocabulary? My favorite days are the ones where I rediscover a strategy that I haven't used in years, a strategy that somehow went forgotten.

If I feel somewhat scattered with all of these great teaching ideas, I can imagine how a seventh grader feels on the receiving end. Our middle school students typically have seven classes a day. Even with the team approach to teaching, students are bombarded with content information, various classroom structures, and a wide array of teaching styles in every 45-minute class that they attend. Should we really be surprised that students forget homework assignments, don't see connections between classes, and have difficulty learning the curriculum? How can we help our students successfully navigate this sea of stimulation?

I am the literacy teacher expert for middle schools in Anchorage, Alaska. Supporting the literacy programs in our schools has been a challenge for me because our district embraces site-based management. Each building has its own unique literacy plan. Our teachers love the academic freedom that is associated with this model, but still crave specific direction in trying to make sense of the reading, writing, speaking, and listening curriculum. How do we put it all together and make sure that students become proficient in the standards along the way?

Our teachers recognize the need to be efficient with our limited instruction time, so reading and writing across the curriculum is understood and expected in our district. I know that our math teachers are dabbling in learning logs, our science teachers are experimenting with nonfiction read-alouds, and our social studies teachers are incorporating cooperative learning techniques. Individually we are all trying our hardest, but collectively we are all going about it in different directions.

We are now launching a districtwide effort to align our teaching strategies. We have chosen five strategies that we know will help with student comprehension in all of their content-area classes. We specifically chose strategies that support students before, during, and after reading. Rather than hope students get a few teachers along the way who use strategies for effective instruction, the Middle School High Five (our acronym for the collection of strategies) ensures that teachers who use such practices are the norm, not the exception. By focusing closely on a few key strategies, students will see a unified approach to instruction across grade levels and content areas. Teachers who are new to strategy instruction will be able to rely on five excellent tools. Teachers who already rely on a plethora of strategies will continue to do so, but will also be encouraged to join in on this systematic approach to instruction.

All teachers receive a stapled, layered brochure with the five strategies outlined and explained. Students generate their own strategy brochure by creating one page for each strategy in a blank book. This step helps the students to gain ownership of each strategy when they write it in their own words, draw their own visuals, and put in examples from each of their content-area studies.

The core strategies include:

1. **Read Around the Text:** A previewing strategy that focuses students on setting a purpose for reading, making connections, and asking questions before reading. (Melvina Prichett Phillips 2004)

2. **K.I.D. Vocabulary:** A strategy focusing on vocabulary that integrates word recognition with important information related to the word and a visual to make it memorable.

3. **Two-Column Notes:** A strategy that helps pull the main ideas out of reading material. The left-hand column is for main ideas. The right-hand column is for details. (Santa, Havens, and Maycumber 1988)

4. **Reciprocal Teaching:** A cooperative reading strategy that engages teams of students in predicting, questioning, clarifying and then summarizing passages. (Palincsar and Brown 1984)

5. **Sum It Up:** A combination of VIP and A+B+C Summaries.

   • **VIP:** Students use a limited number of sticky notes strips to identify important points (VIPs) then share and compare points with a learning partner. (Hoyt 2002)

   • **A+B+C Topic Sentence:** Students identify the topic, select a strong verb, and ensure they have hit the main idea when writing their topic sentence. Then it is easy to use the VIP points to add content to their summary. (Auman 2002)

Our students find the A+B+C formula a powerful tool. It gives them a place to start (no excuse for writer's block) and puts a word bank at their

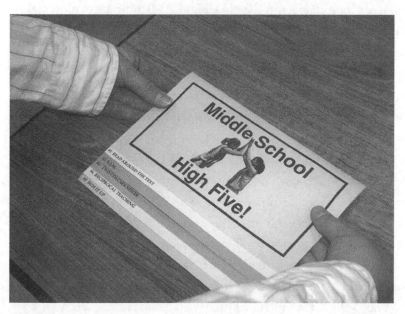

FIGURE 53–1 Each teacher is given a colorful brochure featuring the strategies and examples of how to use each one. Students create their own brochure paraphrasing the steps in each strategy.

fingertips. Once they get started, they find it easy to use their VIPs to elaborate the body of the summary. Here is an A+B+C topic sentence based on this article.

> The article, Middle School High Five, by Amy Goodman, outlines how to unify comprehension strategy instruction in a school or a district.

Each school agreed to use these five strategies in the designated weeks during first quarter. For example, the week of September 20 will focus on Read Around the Text, the week of September 27 will focus on K.I.D. Vocabulary, etc.

The structure of each week looks the same in all our schools. On Monday of the High Five week, language arts teachers provide explicit, direct instruction about the strategy. Language arts teachers typically have the most experience in this area and can accept the bulk of responsibility for introducing them effectively. The rest of the week, all content-area and elective teachers are required to use the strategy within their lesson plans. Now, let's imagine this from a seventh grader's point of view.

On Monday our seventh grade student learns about Read Around the Text in language arts class and is told that it will be one of five anchor strategies that will be used in all classes throughout the year. On Tuesday, she notices that her math teacher uses the exact same process while previewing the next unit in algebra. In physical education, she discovers that her PE teacher is using Read Around the Text on a flyer being distributed about after-school volleyball. Wednesday, the principal talks about a letter she received from the superintendent citing changes in the No Child Left Behind legislation and how she Read Around the Text in order to preview it. The rest of the week unfolds in much the same way, with our student Reading Around the Text in four additional classes. By the end of the week, she has used this strategy seven times in seven different settings. The student has seen how flexible the strategy is, how it can be easily used in many contexts . . . and a foundation is laid for long-term use.

For five weeks at the start of the new school year, we come together as a middle-level division. We agree to organize ourselves as a collective group of educators and use strategy instruction in an explicit, sequenced way. What will be our results? Students will master five reading strategies used across all content areas and comprehension will improve. Teachers will master five reading strategies used across all content areas and their instruction will improve. And together, students and teachers can rely on these strategies for the rest of the year. Valuable instructional time is saved since there has been a schoolwide, systematic approach to teaching these strategies.

In March, a health teacher can use Reciprocal Teaching to coach a difficult chapter on the circulatory system without having to reteach the strategy. Students already know it. They have used it repeatedly in various classes over the last few months and have internalized the strategy to the degree that they even apply it to their own independent reading.

The Middle School High Five is a simple way to organize a teacher, unify an instructional team, bring together an entire staff, or align an entire district. The end result in all of these situations is students reading and comprehending with success.

References

Cover clip art for Middle School High Five

University of Minnesota, Crookston. Retrieved March 2004, from *www.crk.umn.edu/people/athletics/womensBB/Roster/captains.htm*

Read Around the Text

Phillips, M. P. *National Association of Secondary School Principals.* Retrieved March 2004, from *www.nassp.org/schoolimprove/read_around.cfm*

Two-Column Notes

Santa, C., L. Havens, and E. Maycumber. 1988. *Project CRISS—Creating Independence Through Student-Owned Strategies.* Kalispell, MT: Kendall/Hunt Publishing.

Reciprocal Teaching

Palincsar, A., and A. Brown. 1984. "Reciprocal Teaching of Comprehension-Fostering and Comprehension-Monitoring Activities." *Cognition and Instruction* 1 (2): 117–75.

VIP Strategy

Hoyt, L. 2002. *Make It Real: Strategies for Success with Informational Texts.* Portsmouth, NH: Heinemann.

A+B+C Topic Sentences

Auman, M. 2002. *Step Up to Writing.* Longmont, CO: Sopris West.

KEY QUESTIONS

1. If your school decided to use the High Five approach, what five comprehension strategies would you use to best meet the needs of your students? Would the emphasis look different at each grade level?

2. Could an elementary school implement a focus like this? What would be the advantage to learners if specialists, classroom teachers, and parents emphasized the same strategies?

3. Do you think too much repetition of selected strategies can backfire and cause motivational issues? If so, how would you supplement the procedure in order to ensure that motivation stays high?

4. How would you keep the momentum going through year 1? Year 2? And so on?

Read Around the Text

The Steps:

1. Look at any pictures that are provided. What ideas are being presented?
2. Read the captions.
3. Look at the maps, charts, and graphs. Discuss the information they present.
4. Look at the titles and headings. What is the big idea?
5. Read the first and last lines of each paragraph for more information.
6. Ask questions. What do you wonder about? Give yourself a reason to read.

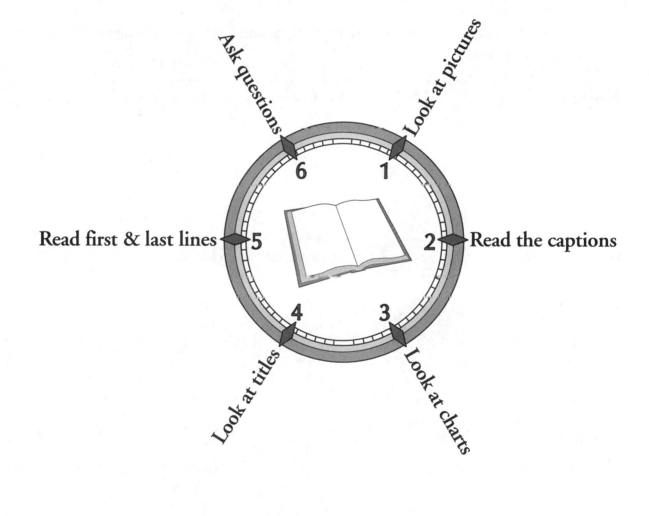

Adapted from M. P. Phillips, *National Association of Secondary School Principals.*

K.I.D. Vocabulary

Key Word + **I**mportant Information + **D**raw to remember

The Steps:

1. Record a key word. Focus on one that is really important.
2. Write down important information about it. What do you know? What connections can you make?
3. Create a visual or memory device to help you remember. (Draw an illustration or a symbol.)
4. Use the word in a sentence. Be sure that the meaning does not change in the sentence you create.

Key Word	**I**mportant Information	**D**raw to remember

Use the word in a sentence . . . Be careful not to change the meaning.

Social Studies		
Key Word	**I**nformation	**D**raw
Latitute	East/west	_____
	Lines	_____
Anchorage is 61 degrees north latitude.		

Math		
Key Word	**I**nformation	**D**raw
equilateral	3 equal angles 3 equal sides	
	_____	
The equilateral triangle has 60-degree angles.		

Two-Column Notes

The Steps:

1. A student pulls the main ideas from a reading selection, placing the main ideas in the left-hand column.
2. Details/elaboration that relate to the main idea are placed in the right-hand column.
3. Students study by folding the grid in half and then looking at main ideas while quizzing themselves on the details.

Extension: Power Notes
4. On the detail side of the grid, items can be numbered by importance. The most important detail would get a number 1, the least important detail would get a number 4.

Math Example: Triangles	
Right triangle	90-degree angle
Scalene triangle	no sides congruent
	No angles congruent

Science Example: Geology	
Igneous rock	fire rock
	cooled magma
Sedimentary Rock	wind/water erosion
	layers
	sediment
	pressure

Social Studies Example: Underground Railroad		Power Notes
Freedom for slaves	1. Moved slaves from South to North	
	2. Path taught through songs, quilt patterns, symbols	
	2. Harriet Tubman	
Conductors	1. Provide safe shelter and transportation	
	2. Former slaves, antislave activitists	

Adapted from Project CRISS—*Creating Independence Through Student-Owned Strategies* by C. Santa, L. Havens, and E. Maycumber.,

Reciprocal Teaching

The Goal: Work in Collaborative Small Groups Using the Following Processes:

Predict: Survey the text. Think about the probable content.

Read: Read silently or in unison. Avoid round robin reading.

Question: Pose questions for the group to discuss.

Clarify: Talk about points that were confusing and discuss unknown words.

Summarize: Work together to create a well-crafted summary.

Preparing the Students:

1. It is important to model each of the four steps very clearly. You can model them as part of a read aloud or as a guided whole class experience with a text.
2. Provide visuals in the classroom or a set of cards to ensure that the students have visual access to the four recurring steps in the process.

Getting Started:

Format 1: It works well to have one discussion director who guides the group through all four processes on a short passage (from one bold heading to the next). The next discussion leader then guides the group through the next short passage, again ensuring that all four processes are utilized before passing the leadership role to the next person.

Format 2: You might want to organize your reciprocal groups in a cooperative learning format with role cards. In this format, students are gathered in teams of four with one student being responsible for each element of the process, 1. Predictor 2. Clarifier 3. Questioner 4. Summarizer.

Adapted from "Reciprocal Teaching of Comprehension—Fostering and Comprehension Monitoring" by Palincsar and Brown in *Cognition and Instruction*.

Reciprocal Teaching *continued*

Predict:
Preview the section. Think about the main ideas. Consider topics you think will be covered and key vocabulary you might expect to encounter.

Clarify:
Consciously think about the passage. Were there any words you found to be confusing or did not know? Were there any ideas that you were confused about? Talk to your team. This is a good time to focus on making connections to help yourselves understrand.

Question:
During reading, jot down "I Wonder" questions that come to mind. Share your questions with your team.

Summarize:
Think about the main idea(s) and the most important details. Use the headings and boldface print to help you create a strong summary for this passage.

Sum It Up

A Two-Step Process

1. VIP (Hoyt 2002). Students cut sticky notes into "fringe" ensuring that each piece of fringe has a bit of the adhesive material on it. Encourage them to read and place sticky note pieces next to the *most important ideas* that they read. It is helpful to assign a limited number of VIPs they can mark on each page. This forces readers to separate most important ideas from those which are not so vital to the content. Provide an opportunity for partners to discuss their selections and tell why they chose the points they did.

2. A+B+C Summary Strategy (Auman 2002). Students use their VIP points to generate a topic sentence. They need to be sure their sentence includes:

A Identifies the topic with a title and author
B Uses strong verbs
C Attaches the big idea from the passage

3. Add VIP points to create a paragraph

> Here is an A+B+C topic sentence based on this article.
>
> The article, Middle School High Five, by Amy Goodman outlines how to unify comprehension strategy instruction in a school or a district.

VIP

Cut fringe from sticky notes then use the pieces to mark the MOST important ideas in a passage.

Meet with a partner to discuss your selections and tell why you selected the ones you did.

A+B+C Topic Sentence

A. Identify what you are summarizing. Be sure to include a title and the author.
B. Use a strong verb. Consider verbs like demonstrates, explains, or describes
C. Attach the big idea to the end of the sentence.
Then, use your VIP points to add to your summary.

Adapted from *Make It Real* by Linda Hoyt (2002) and *Step Up to Writing* by M. Auman (2002).

"Can I Tell You A Secret?"

Lessons From a Resistant Middle School Reader

54

KELLI KESLER

MEET THE AUTHOR

KELLI KESLER *is a middle school teacher from Lake Stevens, Washington. She says, "I've enjoyed working in education for 22 years as a teacher, principal, and parent of three wonderful kids. My husband also teaches."*

FOCUS QUOTE

Thus began our journey of learning how to pick a good book from the library and knowing if it's the RIGHT Book. Easy as it sounds, to students like mine, it's often the biggest obstacle to reading comprehension.

The tiny closet of a classroom had cleared at the sound of the bell and Alex hung back, waiting until the door clicked shut after the other students rushed off to their next class. You might recognize Alex as the school bully: Bleached bangs hanging to his chin and low-slung jeans shuffling along the carpet. Alex's appearance betrayed his background. His uncle's girlfriend took him in after his mom's drug use broke up their family. When Alex's baby sister came along a year ago, the girlfriend took the baby in as well to ensure Alex had a family.

"Mrs. Kesler, can I tell you a secret?" Alex almost whispered in the empty classroom.

"Sure!" I said, making sure to stay out of his established personal space, but close enough to hear the revelation his flushed, bowed face told me was coming.

"I've never read a whole book before, until today. *Holes* was a really cool book!"

"Tell me what was cool about the book?" I asked, attempting to be low-key about the whole thing, but realizing this was a defining moment for both Alex and me.

Finding the Key

Alex began telling me how he always pretended to read books because they were so boring, just a bunch of words. But *Holes* was like "a movie inside his head." Alex knows kids like those characters. (The movie version wasn't out yet.) I asked him if he'd like to start another book. He said he might keep reading, but the book had to be good. He asked if he could just read *Holes* again instead of starting a new book that might be boring. Thus began our journey of learning how to pick a good book from the library and knowing if it's the RIGHT Book. Easy as it sounds, to students like mine, it's often the biggest obstacle to reading comprehension.

"So you like books about stuff you know about?" I asked moving toward my classroom library.

"Yah, real-life stuff. Not stupid stories about wimpy kids."

"Here's one called *A Child Called It*. To be honest, I didn't like it. It's a true story about a boy whose mom abuses him. Try reading 10 pages tonight. See if you can get that movie going in your head."

He came back the next day, having read not 10 but 20 pages and said, "It's an okay book." He finished it the next week and then read the next book by Dave Pelzer. (He hooked into several more series of books like the *Cirque de Freak* series, *The Series of Unfortunate Events* by Lemony Snicket, and *Among the Hidden* series by Margaret Peterson Haddix.)

A Defining Moment

For me, this was one of those "This is why I teach!" moments that define my calling to serve as an educator. Because of Alex, I know that teaching reading to middle school students who hate to read is my gift; a gift both to me and to the students. Alex told me his secret. He chose to share his shortcoming with me, but only after he successfully addressed his comprehension problem. That moment validated all the work I had been doing with resistant readers. For Alex to actually **think** while he read, rather than just recite the words on the page, was the goal of six months of teaching! But the best part was that Alex believed he had figured out that trick on his own; he was able to maintain his "tough guy" status, thoroughly believing himself responsible for his improved reading comprehension.

Believing

Alex now comes to my class as a guest. He's not served in the reading assistance program, but he comes to my class every day because he likes how he feels in there. You see, Alex is struggling in every other academic area of school. He's headed to high school next year and hopefully he'll find another arena to be successful in, thanks to his faith in his ability to read. I always tell my students, "If you can read, you can do anything and go anywhere!" I wonder where Alex will go?

IMPROVING COMPREHENSION FOR RESISTANT MIDDLE SCHOOL READERS:

1. **Watch for "Fake Reading"**—Call it what it is and don't let it continue!

2. **Get the RIGHT Book**—Students have to be interested in the story or book. Get Richard Allington's book, *What Really Matters for Struggling Readers* for advice on reading material.

3. **Set the Hook!**—Use books from a series so students learn to trust an author that meets their reading interest. They get lots of reading practice when they have familiar characters and connected plots.

4. **Be Specific**—I work with six specific strategies in every lesson, every day: Ask Questions, Make Connections, Draw Inferences, Determine Important vs. Less Important, Synthesize, and Repair Faulty Comprehension. See *Strategies That Work* by Stephanie Harvey and Anne Goudvis.

5. **Do It 100 times!**—Those six strategies have to be modeled, practiced, discussed, and assessed constantly. Once is never enough!

6. **Make It Count**—Reading at home every night is required, checked every day, and part of the grade. Get parents on board because it often makes all the difference.

7. **Listen to Kids**—They are telling you what they need to know but they've resisted it for so long, they want you to make them do it. Really, they will thank you later. Cris Tovani's *I Read It, But I Don't Get It* is a great tool and inspiration to get inside the heads of resistant middle school readers.

8. **Make sure they read every night and link the reading to your strategy instruction.** Notice the following at-home reading record sheets and the way the strategy focus changes . . . The at-home reading strategy is linked to the strategies we are working on in class.

References

Allington, Richard. 2001. *What Really Matters for Struggling Readers: Designing Research-Based Programs.* New York: Addison-Wesley.

Harvey, Stephanie, and Anne Goudvis. 2000. *Strategies That Work: Teaching Comprehension to Enhance Understanding.* Portland, ME: Stenhouse Publishers.

Pelzer, Dave. 1995. *A Child Called It.* Deerfield Beach, FL: Health Communications.

Peterson Haddix, Margaret. 2000. *Among the Hidden.* New York: Aladdin Paperbacks.

Shan, Darren. 2000. *Cirque du Freak.* Boston, MA: Little, Brown & Co.

Snicket, Lemony. 2001. *Series of Unfortunate Events.* New York: Scholastic.

Tovani, Cris. 2000. *I Read It, But I Don't Get It: Comprehension Strategies for Adolescent Readers.* Portland, ME: Stenhouse Publishers.

KEY QUESTIONS

1. Do kids like Alex really think no one knows their secret?

2. Where does denial about reading ability begin?

3. Some kids hate to read. How does that happen?

4. What one thing can I do tomorrow to help a resistant reader?

5. What started me reading?

6. How has reading changed my life?

At-Home Reading Log

Focus on the strategy we have been learning.

Date_____
Title_____
Main Idea: _____
_____
Minutes Read:_____ Pages:_____
Evidence from the text to support the main idea you listed:

1._____ 2._____

3._____ 4._____

Date_____
Title_____
Main Idea: _____
_____
Minutes Read:_____ Pages:_____
Evidence from the text to support the main idea you listed:

1._____ 2._____

3._____ 4._____

Date_____
Title_____
Main Idea: _____
_____
Minutes Read:_____ Pages:_____
Evidence from the text to support the main idea you listed:

1._____ 2._____

3._____ 4._____

At-Home Reading Log

Focus on the strategy we have been learning.

Date_____
Book Title _____
Pages Read _____ Time _____
Summary:

Parent Signature _____

Date_____
Book Title _____
Pages Read _____ Time _____
Summary:

Parent Signature _____

Date_____
Book Title _____
Pages Read _____ Time _____
Summary:

Parent Signature _____

Date_____
Book Title _____
Pages Read _____ Time _____
Summary:

Parent Signature _____

Understanding Our Reading Preferences

Reader _____

As readers, we need to constantly think about our level of enjoyment in our reading and to wonder if the book we have chosen is a good match for us . . .

    For the next few days, think closely about your feelings about the book you are reading. Wonder why you like it and want to continue or why you don't. You will be asked to jot down your thinking every day.

Date	Title of Book	How are you feeling about this book?	Why?	What are you learning about your preferences as a reader?

Focus on Book Selection

Reader _____ Date _____

Name a book you have enjoyed listening to or reading yourself_____

_____

Why did you like it? Try to list five specific things you liked about the book.

- _____

- _____

- _____

Using this list of reasons, think about choosing another book. How might this list

help you find another book you will really like? _____

_____

If you were to give someone else advise about book selection, what would tell

them? _____

Have you ever read books that are part of a series, like *Harry Potter,* or read two

books by the same author? What were the advantages of choosing books with

familiar characters and/or writing styles? _____

_____

Interview another student about book selection. Find out how that person chooses

books. Jot down what you learned._____

_____

Sticky Note Reviews

Many newspapers carry reviews of popular books to help readers use the opinions of others to assist their personal book choices. Some bookstores place book reviews written by staff members on the shelf right under the books to assist their customers.

Your task is to write a review of the book you are reading on a sticky note. (Keep it short!) Include your name and some thoughts about the book. You might also give the book a rating. On a scale of 1–5.

Would this book be a 1: Pretty boring, or 5: Really exciting!

Would this book earn a 🙂 because you liked it a lot or a frown because it wasn't very good?

Place your sticky note review in the back of the book for the next reader to enjoy.

Hatchet by Gary Paulson
Review by Roana

I rate this book a 5. There is a lot of action and there are times when I felt my heart pound faster as Brian fought to stay alive. This book is filled with not only excitement and challenge but also wonderful descriptions that helped me create visual images.

Mrs. Wishy Washy
From Alana

Mrs. Wishy washy has funny animals and a lot of mud.

Finding Our Way Through Diverse Perspectives
55
Comprehending Points of View and Language

ADRIA F. KLEIN

MEET THE AUTHOR

ADRIA F. KLEIN, *PhD, is professor emeritus of reading education at CSU San Bernardino. She is a visiting professor at Saint Mary's College in Moraga, California. She completed her PhD at the University of New Mexico in the areas of reading and English as a Second Language. She is the Coordinator and Trainer for the Extended Literacy Learning and Second Chance programs for the Foundation for Comprehensive Early Literacy Learning. She is the author of a number of professional books from Dominie Press, Inc., and Heinemann, as well as many children's books for various publishers.*

FOCUS QUOTE

We do not work together by finding our differences; we grow by being open to other ideas and finding ways so that we speak a common language.

College courses, professional development, specialized credentials—all these opportunities for further learning are part of a teacher's training and experiences. One of the challenges teachers face is to add new information and perspectives within the scope of what is already known, understood, and practiced. How does an educator consider and incorporate various theories and new ideas into their current understanding?

Understanding Diverse Perspectives

One example of this challenge is in special education where teachers study a variety of approaches to working with students in a resource setting. Conflicts are inherent in the theories underlying these various approaches. Full inclusion, pull-out, push-in, collaborative curriculum, and separate and parallel curriculums are approaches that are all used in schools for special education instruction, but all these methods are not compatible. Teachers work within a school district and must follow the guidelines and mandates for their district. Perhaps a teacher in a particular district with a pull-out program is working on a graduate degree at a local university with a respected special education program. The university faculty endorses a collaborative curriculum approach with push-in resource instruction. How does a teacher reconcile these differences?

This example may seem extreme, but another familiar conflict of long standing revolves around the area termed "The Reading Wars." Philosophies of teaching reading and research in the field ranges from whole language to scripted basal approaches to phonics-based programs, and everything in between. A teacher's philosophy and approach, developed over time and based on experience, training, research in the field, and professional readings, may well be in conflict with the prevailing mandates. Again, how does a teacher reconcile these differences? Trying to describe the range of these conflicts would take the length of this book and several others.

Looking for Shared Beliefs: A Foundation for Communication

How can a teacher examine different approaches and fit aspects of these methods into her current perspective? The term eclectic will quickly come to mind, but that is not my intent or philosophy. I want to suggest that all theories have aspects of compatibility. Searching for those commonalities is the task that challenges all of us. Finding common areas of agreement allows teachers to understand theories and develop a clear perspective on the aspects of the approaches or methodologies that may be different. Too often we start with the differences, the incompatible issues we disagree with, and vigorously defend our position. Even if we don't take this defensive posture, what is our strategy for learning and incorporating new ideas?

In education, as in any field, success is often built on finding ways to work with others even when we do not believe the same things. How might looking for commonalities and points of agreement provide a foundation for working together?

Finding Commonalities in Theories

An example from the various research and theories of comprehension that might best illustrate this issue involves understandings of both Reciprocal

Teaching and KWL. Palincsar and Brown (1984; 1986) developed and did the research for the Reciprocal Teaching method, which focuses on helping students to comprehend challenging text. The four comprehension strategies identified by the researchers are Predict, Clarify, Question, and Summarize.

This approach to improving comprehension was originally researched with seventh and eighth grade special education students. The majority of texts used were expository. Over the last twenty years, Reciprocal Teaching studies have produced improved comprehension scores on a standardized measure with students as young as third grade. As a small group intervention, it is designed to be implemented for 21–28 days. Many models of comprehension instruction have been developed from the original design created by Palincsar and Brown.

At about the same time, in 1986, Donna Ogle wrote about the KWL strategy for improving comprehension. This activity usually focused on expository text. Using a set of three organizing questions (What I KNOW about a topic, What I WANT to know, and What I LEARNED), Ogle helped teachers have access to another powerful comprehension strategy. The strategy is used regularly in a whole class instructional setting and most often includes presenting the key concepts in a graphic organizer.

On the surface, these approaches seem quite different. The terminology varies in the two methods as does the suggested group size, frequency of use, and many other variables. How can a teacher understand the two approaches and make choices of what to use, when, how, and with which students? If we look for commonalities, it makes both approaches more useful to us.

In a simplistic way, "Prediction" in Reciprocal Teaching is similar to the "What do I KNOW" step in KWL. Students are asked to probe background knowledge for the information they know that is related to the material. Both approaches begin with the known material that is within the student's grasp, establishing a platform for further learning. By looking for these commonalities, this underlying theory of reading instruction is seen in both approaches.

Similarly, the Clarify and Question strategies in Reciprocal Teaching are like the "What do I WANT to know" step in KWL. Students approach the new material looking for vocabulary and concepts to clarify and to create questions that would help them learn more about the subject. Theories of vocabulary instruction that recommend putting words in meaningful context underscore both strategies. The concept of the students' posing questions to better comprehend reading materials is also common to both strategies.

The "Summarize" component of Reciprocal Teaching is like "What I LEARNED" in KWL. Encouraging and promoting the summarizing step after reading a selection is a key aspect of learning new concepts.

While we may not find these approaches in conflict per se, we need to look for the commonalities in theory and practice. In a school setting, the discussion between teachers could easily be that these are distinct and separate entities. Preferences for Reciprocal Teaching or KWL could produce conflicts among educators. It is critical that these strategies be examined to find the underlying theoretical foundation and their commonalities. This would lead to embracing both strategies in a strong program of comprehension instruction.

Finding Commonalities: The Impact on Metacognition

What is the advantage of looking for the common elements in different theories and approaches? How can we work toward an inclusive theory of reading instruction? For the students in these teachers' classrooms, the development of metacognition depends, in part, on the teacher's helping the students make these links across instructional practices. The teacher can look for aspects of different approaches that are compatible and the students will benefit by developing a deeper understanding of similar strategies and common terminology in reading and writing. Even the simple idea of demonstrating how different teaching approaches are used to teach the same concepts is important to point out to students.

Common Terms

Common terms need to be developed for strategies that help align curriculum in a school or district. In the early grades, one teacher may use the term "talking marks" while another uses the term "quotation marks." In the intermediate grades, one teacher may use the term "question" and another the term "interrogatory." As simple as these differences are to the adult learner, the connection needs to be obvious, visible, and directly taught to the students.

Common Language

I started with some questions about the conflicts in the field of education, and in reading in particular. I end with a challenge to all teachers to embrace new theories and approaches by finding commonalities and teaching these ideas and terminology so students make the connections along with the teacher. We do not work together by finding our differences; we grow by being open to other ideas and finding ways to speak a common language.

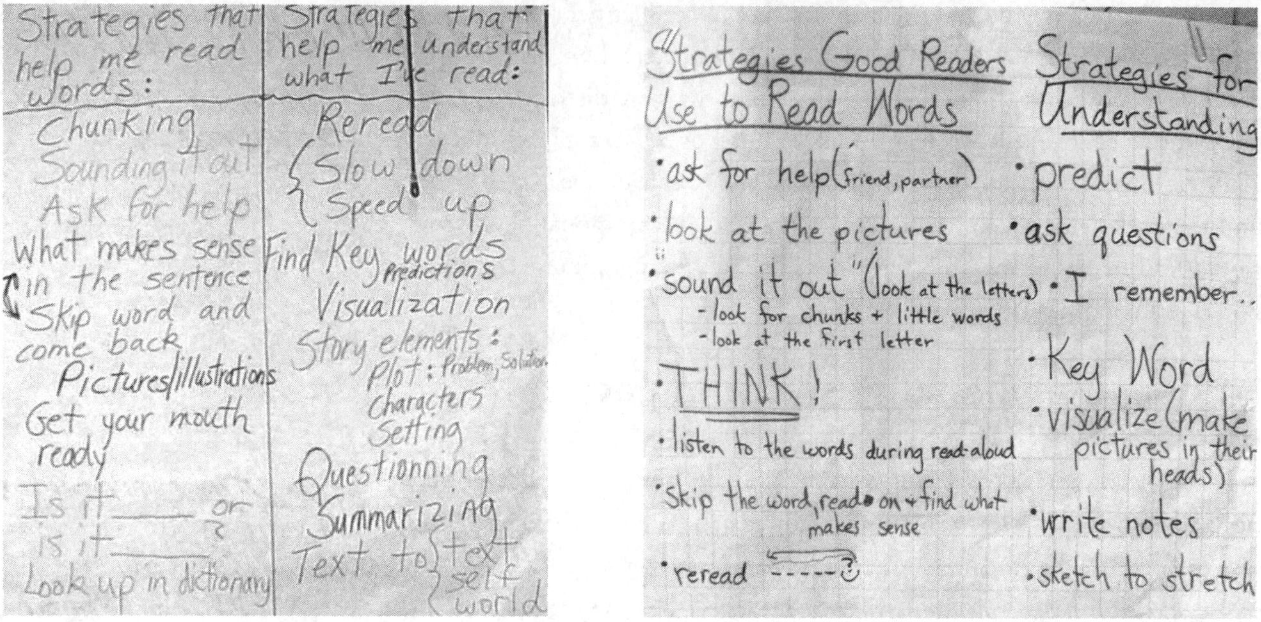

Strategies that help me read words:
- Chunking
- Sounding it out
- Ask for help
- What makes sense in the sentence
- Skip word and come back
- Pictures/illustrations
- Get your mouth ready
- Is it ____ or is it ____?
- Look up in dictionary

Strategies that help me understand what I've read:
- Reread { Slow down / Speed up
- Find Key words / Predictions
- Visualization
- Story elements:
  - Plot: Problem, Solution
  - Characters
  - Setting
- Questionning
- Summarizing
- Text to { text / self / world

Strategies Good Readers Use to Read Words
- ask for help (friend, partner)
- look at the pictures
- "sound it out" (look at the letters)
  - look for chunks + little words
  - look at the first letter
- THINK!
  - listen to the words during read-aloud
  - skip the word, read on + find what makes sense
  - reread

Strategies for Understanding
- predict
- ask questions
- I remember...
- Key Word
- visualize (make pictures in their heads)
- write notes
- sketch to stretch

FIGURE 55–1a, b Finding common ways to describe processes and strategies may assist learners in understanding and generalizing comprehension strategies.

References

Ogle, D. 1986. "K-W-L: A Teaching Model that Develops Active Reading of Expository Text." *The Reading Teacher,* 39: 564–70.

Palincsar, A. S., and A. L. Brown. 1986. "Interactive Teaching to Promote Independent Learning from Text." *The Reading Teacher,* 39: 771–7.

———. 1984. "Reciprocal Teaching of Comprehension-Fostering and Comprehension-Monitoring Activities." *Cognition and Instruction,* 2: 117–75.

KEY QUESTIONS

1. Having a belief system about reading development is important in helping educators to make conscious and thoughtful decisions about instruction. What do you believe about reading development? What do your colleagues believe? What are the commonalities in your thinking?

2. The article starts with a question in the first paragraph: How does an educator consider and incorporate various theories and new ideas into their current understanding? Consider this question in terms of your current teaching situation.

3. How can we avoid polarization to ensure open communication with those whose theory of reading is different?

4. How might you handle a situation where prevailing mandates suggests you engage in practices that you do not believe in? How might you look for commonalities in thinking? How might this affect comprehension instruction?

Finding Commonalities

Reflections on our practices and the language that surrounds our learners:

When you ask students to gather on the rug for storytime, how do you describe the way they sit?

What do you call the time when students read by themselves in books of their own choosing?

If you say a learner is an emergent reader, what exactly does that mean?

What does "shared reading" mean to you? Be specific.

When you have a colleague who believes in a different style of instruction than you do, what do you do? How can you find commonalities in forging conversations, establishing a working relationship, and ensuring that children do not receive conflicting messages?

What is "writer's workshop" in your classroom? Be specific.

What is "reader's workshop" in your classroom?

When you talk about conferring with a reader or writer, what exactly do you mean? What happens during this time?

Contributed by A. Klein © 2005 by Linda Hoyt from *Spotlight on Comprehension*. Portsmouth, NH: Heinemann.

Boys Will Be Boys 56

BRUCE MORGAN

MEET THE AUTHOR

BRUCE MORGAN *has been teaching for 24 years in Douglas County Schools in Colorado, grades 3–6. He has also worked as a Reading Specialist. Currently, he is involved with the Public Education Business Coalition demonstration lab classroom and works as a Cornerstone Literacy Consultant for the national literacy reform initiative at the University of Pennsylvania.*

FOCUS QUOTE

I began to actively model my own reading, my real-life reading, and I began to use these various texts to model my reading comprehension strategies: *This Old House, National Geographic, Motor Trend,* the *Denver Post* newspaper, and emails all made appearances in minilessons and think alouds.

The statistics stared at me from the page. I groaned. Why, why oh why did I read this book tonight? Why didn't I pick up some trashy novel that I could read and then, bored, fall asleep? I glanced over at the clock and groaned again. Midnight . . . midnight, a school night. A big day tomorrow. I set the alarm and *tried* to sleep.

I lay, thinking about the book, horrified by the numbers, horrified that I was part of the reason those numbers were so high. Finally, giving up on sleep, I shuffled off to sort out my thinking. I have been concerned about the boys in my room. They have made a lot of progress over the course of the year, but not as much as I would have liked. I had already read Smith and Wilhelm's book *Reading Don't Fix No Chevys* and tonight, the book keeping me awake was Tom Newkirk's *Misreading Masculinity* (2002).

I reopened the book to the part about the gender gap in literacy between boys and girls where Newkirk states, "The gap between females and males is comparable to that between whites and racial/ethnic groups that have suffered systematic social and economic discrimination in this country" (35).

To make matters worse, Wilhelm writes about the results of the 1996 National Assessments of Education Progress (NAEPs) when he says, "The lowest performing boys performed at a considerably lower level than they had on the 1992 assessment and the gap between girls and boys in Grade 12 continues to widen."

I wasn't really shocked by the results. I identified with these findings on two levels: personally and professionally. First, I related because I am one of those boys, only all grown up. For me, school was a disaster. *I* was an academic disaster. I remember all too well the dreaded reading groups: the Robins or the Bluebirds being pulled to the front and the warm smiles of the teacher. And then, my group: *The Buzzards*. I was the honorary spokesperson for this ragtag group of boys—the nonreaders. After-school phonics tutoring to help improve my reading ranked up there with my piano lessons. I'd quietly do the time, waiting for freedom. My poor parents.

I witness this literacy gap on a daily basis in my own classroom, and must constantly reflect on my practices so that I can maximize my role in helping all students, especially the boys, reach their potential. My classroom is made up of 18 boys and five girls. Sixteen of the boys read and write substantially below grade level and are on individual learning plans. Those boys are just like I was in school. At the beginning of the year, the literacy block more resembled Dr. Dodgeball in P.E. than an academic experience. The boys got more exercise wandering around the room avoiding reading than they did in the school fun run. The only standard these guys had mastered was the art of avoidance! I had a classroom full of kids just like me.

Building from Their Passions

There is much evidence to suggest that boys may be disadvantaged in academic literacy as a result of current curricular emphases, teacher text and topic choices, and lack of availability of texts that match their interests and needs (Smith and Wilhelm 2002). So our challenge as teachers may be:

1. To get know the field of contemporary children's and young adult literature and
2. To get to know our students so that we can help them choose appropriate books and learning projects.

Nick was a prime example, a classic underachiever. He rarely read, and when he did, it was an easy text like *The Magic Treehouse* books. My running records indicated those books were way too easy for him, but there was no motivation on his part to read harder text. I wanted him in text that fit his actual level of development, but didn't know what to do to get him engaged.

One night his parents couldn't pick him up from our after-school tutoring program. I took him to his apartment where he led me on a tour of his bedroom—which was more like a Star Wars museum than a bedroom. He had everything: Star Wars games, books, action figures, and posters. I picked up an adult-level *Star Wars* book on the nightstand and asked, "Are your parents reading this to you?"

In reply, he picked it up and read to me, then accurately synthesized what he had read. "Why don't you read this at school?" I questioned.

"This isn't school reading! It's fantasy and we haven't studied that yet," he declared.

Because I did not know his passions, because I didn't have him in text that was engaging to him personally, I misjudged his range of reading. The next day, Nick brought in his *Star Wars* book for his free reading book. He looked at me as he pulled it out; waiting to be busted, and then began to read. He didn't wander that day.

Broadening Horizons

The experience I had with Nick when he told me that *Star Wars* wasn't school reading pushed me to rethink what I classified as "quality literature." Newkirk argues for a broadening of what we consider good literature.

> In the end, a broadening of the literacy spectrum will not only benefit boys, it will benefit any student whose primary affiliation is to the "low status" popular narratives of television, movies, comics, humor, sports pages, and plot-driven fiction. (p. 170)

When we work with narrow definitions of literacy and the restrictive rules about what constitutes reading, more students are left out. If we open the scope of what we consider quality reading to allow more kids in, we can hook them with intrinsic motivation, teach the strategies and skills they need within a topic they care about . . . then lead them into a broader range of texts.

Modeling Comprehension Strategies in a Variety of Everyday Texts

Because of Nick, I began to actively model my own reading, my real-life reading, and I began to use these various texts to model my reading comprehension strategies: *This Old House, National Geographic, Motor Trend,* the *Denver Post* newspaper, and emails all made appearances in minilessons and think alouds. I bought classroom subscriptions to *Time for Kids* and *Sports*

Illustrated for Kids. I triumphed over my disdain for *Goosebumps.* I was broadening *my* reading horizons.

I constantly try to find ways to demonstrate my love of learning, of being amazed at life events. When I read in the *Denver Post* about the Civil War submarine, I was astounded. Submarine? Civil War? I pulled Internet articles about it and introduced it to the class. For a week, a tight group of kids marveled at the technology, the inventions, the daring, and shared their contagious energy. My amazement fueled their reading and helped them find passion in inquiry.

Now, I've even conceded to a comic book study, something I thought I'd never do. Because of Newkirk and Wilhelm, I thought back to my *Mad Magazine* and comics collections, and conceded that I actually read when I was a kid, actually read passionately. I shelled out lots of money from my paper route for those magazines, and knew every story line. That was reading for me.

I do push for a balance during the reading period. If the kids are reading a magazine, I want them to balance that with other quality literature from our classroom library. I can't and won't give that up. I'm the teacher. It is my job to expose and build prior knowledge in different genres. Kids don't know what they're passionate about until they experience it, so we read in a variety of genres. It's my job to help them discover their next passion.

In the End

My sleepless night was well worth it. I have taken time to rethink what I allowed in the classroom; what I accepted as reading. I have begun to accept obsession on the part of my kids, because many times, obsession results in passion, and passion creates engagement. Now, instead of trying to force kids from a topic they love, I push for new research and a different perspective on the topic. In return, when it's time to study a new genre, I expect the class to return the favor and oblige my need to lead them into a new territory.

The research seems as valid for girls as it does for boys; it's good teaching. Period. Tapping into student passion, knowing them as individuals, and establishing a safe place for risk-taking and learning is good instruction for all.

At the heart of this research is the student. In this test-crazed, assessment-obsessed culture, it is refreshing to hear that the student is the center of the learning, not the testing. It is gratifying to read of the need to establish a climate where students and student growth are valued over the numbers on the standardized print-out.

I'm the teacher in the room. It is up to me to draw them in, engage them in the reading and writing, and then use that engagement to push their limits and their learning. Suck them into the learning, and then blind-side them when they least suspect it!

Our job is amazingly hard. You never really know what is the best technique, the best curriculum, the best way to deal with a distraught child. I love our profession—love the sleepless nights and the times when I'm pushed into new learning. The sleepless night was worth it because it led to new understandings about kids and texts and comprehension.

References

Cambourne, Brian. 1988. *The Whole Story: Natural Learning and the Acquisition of Literacy in the Classroom.* London, England: Scholastic.

Conrad, Lori L. 2004. "Where the Boys Are(n't): Bringing Boys Back to School Literacies." Denver, CO: Public Education and Business Coalition.

Joseph, Oscar. 2004. *Boys of Color and Academic Achievement.* Denver, CO: Public Education and Business Coalition.

Keene, Ellin, and Susan Zimmerman. 1997. *Mosaic of Thought: Teaching Comprehension in a Reader's Workshop.* Portsmouth, NH: Heinemann.

Lyons, Carol A. 2003. *Teaching Struggling Readers: How to Use Brain-Based Research to Maximize Learning.* Portsmouth, NH: Heinemann.

Newkirk, Thomas. 2002. *Misreading Masculinity: Boys, Literacy, and Popular Culture.* Portsmouth, NH: Heinemann.

Smith, Michael W., and Jeffrey D. Wilhelm. 2002. *"Reading Don't Fix NO Chevys": Literacy in the Lives of Young Men.* Portsmouth, NH: Heinemann.

KEY QUESTIONS

1. How can you broaden your definition of classroom literature, taking into account your own personal teaching style?

2. How can you bring the passions of your students into the classroom so they feel valued as individuals?

3. How can you provide models of reading strategies in various genres and texts?

4. What teaching practices of yours hold kids back, and what will you do about that?

Student Profile

Reader_____ Date _____

What do you like to do in your free time? _____

_____

What else do you like to do? _____

_____

What do you like to read in school as well as away from school? _____

_____

List three things you have read recently and enjoyed. _____

_____

Do you like comic books, magazines, the TV guide, or ???? _____

_____

If you could learn more about a topic, what would you want to learn about? _____

_____

What is your favorite subject in school? _____

_____

Contributed by B. Morgan © 2005 by Linda Hoyt from *Spotlight on Comprehension*. Portsmouth, NH: Heinemann.

Key Points to Consider

In designing learning environments for learners, especially boys, you might consider:

- The importance of social interaction

- The need for physical movement

- Strategies for determining student interests and passions

- Ways to broaden the range of reading experiences and texts

- Modeling comprehension strategies in a broad range of sample texts

- Avoiding stereotypes

- Showing your own passion for reading and learning

- Helping students find a sense of ownership in the learning

- Wondering, objectively, what you might change in the environment to increase student engagement

Contributed by B. Morgan © 2005 by Linda Hoyt from *Spotlight on Comprehension*. Portsmouth, NH: Heinemann.

Closing Thoughts

The Comprehension Coach

Some coaches can tally the score of the game
Or take pride in a run that was fast
But for me with my books and my thoughts and my kids
It's a game that will last and will last

We analyze authors and features
Good books are what we love best
We consider our strategies daily
In every subject and text

Meaning is the core of our reading
We know it's the heart of our game
I'm proud to be coach of these winners
I know that they feel the same

—Linda Hoyt

Index

Aardema, Verna, 203
A+B+C strategy, 502
Abercrombie, Barbara, 202
Across AMERICA I Love You (Loomis), 230
action words, mentor texts for, 198
active listening, 69
active reading, 301, 302
adjectives
    for characters, 410–11
    descriptive, 187
Adkisson, Pat, 194
after-reading test strategies, 370–80, 378
"aha" moments, 26
Alexander and the Terrible, Horrible, No Good, Very Bad Day (Viorst), 201
algebra
    comprehension activities, 349–50
    vocabulary words, 180
Aliki, 203
Allen, Mary Beth, 118
All the Places to Love (Maclachlan), 191
alphabetic principle, 11
alphabet strips, 73
Alphabet Time activity, 350
Alphaboxes, 174–81
    form, 183
Alvin Ailey (Pinkney), 199
Amber on the Mountain (Johnston), 204
Amelia and Eleanor Go for a Ride (Ryan), 228
America the Beautiful (Bates), 230
Among the Hidden series (Haddix), 512
analogy, 48
Analyzing Poetry (form), 344
anchor activities, 494–95
anchor charts, 316–17
Animal Lives: The Frog (Tagholm), 231
animals hiding, companion collection, 251–52
Animals Nobody Loves (Simon), 233
Annandale, Kevlynn, 46
applying, in gradual release of responsibility model, 47, 54
approximations, 494
Arkansas Literacy Model, 67
Art of Teaching Reading (Calkins), 135
Asking Questions (form), 34
Assessing Deep Understanding in Young Children (form), 424
assessment
    building into lessons, 315–16
    of comprehension games (form), 440
    of deep understanding, 424
    of English Language Learner Understanding (form), 458
    ongoing, 75
    during read alouds, 484–85
    with retelling, 425–31
    of science notebooks, 332
    of student comprehension of nonfiction texts, 266–67
    traditional views of, 491

Assessment of Language Learner Understanding (form), 458
Assessment of Science Notebook (form), 332
Assessment Tool for Comprehension Game (form), 440
At-Home Reading Log (form), 515–16
audience, genuine, for retelling, 431
Aunt Harriet's Underground Railroad in the Sky (Ringgold), 229
Australian Reading Association, 108
authentic conversation, 80–81
authentic literacy events, 15–16
authors. *See also* writers
    comprehension strategies of, 194–205
    questioning, 119–20

background knowledge
    activating, for standardized tests, 376
    deep thinking and, 416
    English language learners and, 447
    guided reading and, 244
    inferences and, 139
    inquiry curriculum and, 360
    scaffolding and, 472
    targeted discussion of, 389
    using, 33
    word sorts and, 166
Baylor, Byrd, 187, 191, 203
Beat the Teacher activity, 369–70
Because You're Lucky (Smalls), 79–80
Beck, Isabel, 166, 390
Beers, Kylene, 131–32
before-reading test strategies, 378
Bennett-Armistead, V. Susan, 97
Bernhard, Cathy, 347
bias, in environmental print, 405
bilingual partners. *See also* English language learners (ELL's)
    partner think-alouds for, 127
birds, companion collection, 252–53
birthday read alouds, 135
Blos, Joan, 140
Blume, Judy, 199
Bolt, Alicia J., 460
book buddies program, 100
book clubs, 77, 495–96
book-lending programs, 100, 101
bookmarks
    Read, Cover, Remember, Reread, 313
    Read, Cover, Remember, Retell, 313
book recommendations
    student book reviews, 518
    student-led, 429
books. *See also* informational texts; picture books; text selection
    classroom display of, 67–68, 74
    comparing (form), 207
    informational, 15, 142
    language-rich, 191
    leveled, 244
    mentor texts, 196–207
    organized by writing attributes, 196

organizing by strategy, 196
    related, 483–84
    for teaching strategies, 112
    vocabulary-rich, 182
book selection. *See* text selection
Boy on Fairfield Street, The: How Ted Geisel Grew Up to Become Dr. Seuss (Krull), 229
boys
    learning environments for (form), 526
    motivation of, 529
    reading interests of, 528–31
    reading progress of, 527–31
    text selection for, 528–31
Brand, Max, 163
Brave Irene (Steig), 191, 204
Brown, Ruth, 187, 191
Browne, Anthony, 132
Bryson, Jill, 300, 304
buddy reading, cross-age, 127
Bullfrog at Magnolia Circle (Dennard), 232
Bunting, Eve, 205

Calkins, Lucy, 135, 365, 374
Cambourne, B., 493
Cambourne's Conditions of Learning (Cambourne), 493
Cammack, Camille, 397
Carl Sandburg: Adventures of a Poet (Niven), 237
cause and effect relationships, 140
celebrations, personal, 187–88
Chandra, Debra, 191
characters
    adjectives for, 411–12
    analysis of, 292, 296
    connecting with, 408–9
    descriptions of, 204
    discussion of, 292, 296
    inferences about, 140, 147
    mentor texts for, 204–5
    traits of, 410–12
Charlie Anderson (Abercrombie), 202
charts
    anchor, 316–17
    comparing texts with, 411
    for data collection, 328, 330
    picture observation, 446
    reading, 351
    strategy, 287
    T-charts, for algebra, 350
Checklist for Vocabulary Instruction (form), 170
Child Called It, A (Pelzer), 512
choral reading, 75
chunking
    defined, 48
    with movie-making software, 337
Cinder-elly (Minters), 201
Cirque de Freak series (Shan), 512
classical music, 61
classroom climate of inquiry, 314–15

classroom environment. *See* learning
   environments
classroom library
   book displays, 67–68, 74
   informational texts for, 315, 321
   text selection for, 496
Clay, Marie, 76, 264
Cleary, Beverly, 199
"Click and Clunk" strategy, 15
clips, paragraphs as, 337
cloze procedures
   for English language learners, 448
   in guided reading, 153–54
   oral cloze, 152–53
   using overhead projector, 153
clues, textual, inferences from, 140
coaching
   achievement and, 151
   defined, 112
   reading partnerships, 298–300
   self-coaching, 157
   student-directed questioning, 112–13
   for word-level comprehension, 151–56
"co-empowerment," 99
Cole, Ardith Davis, 408
Cole, Johanna, 201
Coleman, Barbara, 340, 374
Coleman, Evelyn, 182
Coles, Robert, 182, 230
collaboration. *See also* cooperative groups;
   groups
   desk arrangement and, 74
   interactive paragraphs, 211–14
Collaborative Strategic Reading, 15
Collecting Great Words and Phrases
   (form), 192
Collins, Marge, 92
comic books, 530
community, sense of
   comprehension strategy instruction
     and, 41–42, 44
   rereading and, 135
   teacher self-assessment of, 45
companion collections
   building content knowledge with,
     245–46
   for guided reading, 243–63
   for independent reading, 247–49
   multilevel, 248–49
   read alouds and, 247, 249
   shared reading and, 247
   suggestions for, 246, 251–52
   vocabulary development with, 245–46
Comparing Texts on My Own (form),
   207
comparisons
   of books, 207
   defined, 48
   graphic organizers for, 411
comprehension. *See also* deep understanding
   author strategies and, 194–205
   background knowledge and, 244, 360
   checklists for, 92–95, 498
   consistent language for, 28
   defining, 22–29
   discussion and, 13–14

engagement and, 12
by English language learners, 485
of environmental print, 397–401,
   403–5
factors affecting, 27–29
importance of, 2, 491–92
inquiry curriculum and, 359–60
listening and, 236–39
many ways of knowing, 58–63
monitoring, 2, 35–36, 157–58
of nonfiction, 266–67, 272
parents and, 105
picture books and, 226–34
questioning and, 113–14
rereading for, 309
retelling and, 425–31
skills needed for, 11–12
of song lyrics, 414–22
of standardized tests, 363–70
student-created games for, 434–37
student problems with, 3–5
student roles in, 93–94
teacher reflections on, 490–96
teacher roles in, 93
traditional views of, 491
vocabulary and, 11–12, 161
volume reading and, 12–13
word-level, 150–55, 186
comprehension classroom, 85–90
   intermediate, 88–89
   primary, 86–87
   teacher assessment of, 86–90
"Comprehension Coach" (Hoyt), 534
comprehension coaching. *See* coaching
Comprehension Equation (form), 159
comprehension research, 9–17
   authenticity, 15–16
   characteristics of effective readers, 10–11
   comprehension skills, 11–12
   discussion, 13–14
   engagement, 12
   explicit instruction, 14
   multiple strategy instruction, 15–17
   volume reading, 12–13
comprehension strategies. *See also specific*
   strategies
   applying across the curriculum, 5
   assessment and, 315–16
   commonalities in, 521–23
   confusion caused by, 499–500
   demonstrating during rereading, 227–
     28
   for emergent readers, 386–91, 393–96
   for English language learners, 460–63
   for environmental print, 397–401,
     403–5
   explicit instruction in, 2, 14
   of good readers, 10–11, 21
   learning to use together, 47
   for mathematics, 347–52
   modeling for emergent readers, 391
   modeling with everyday texts, 529–30
   multiple, 5–6, 15–17
   for nonfiction guided reading lesson,
     269–70
   reflecting on (form), 339
   sharing circles on, 283–86

for standardized tests, 364–70, 372,
   373, 374–80, 381–82
strategy charts, 287
student awareness of, 58–59
types of, 14, 48
comprehension strategy instruction
   alignment across grade level, 499–
     503
   components of, 15
   context for, 41–43
   deep conversations and, 43, 44
   explicit, 2, 14, 46–54
   gradual release of responsibility model
     for, 15, 41, 44, 47, 49
   in guided reading, 275–78
   for independent reading, 283–87
   minilessons prior to independent
     reading, 283–86
   movie-making software for, 334–38
   self-reflection and awareness and,
     42–43, 44
   sense of community and, 41–42, 44
   with a sense of urgency, 5–6
   strategic reading tips, 142
   traditional, 24–25
   value of, 491
concentration, 27
Concept-Oriented Reading Instruction
   (CORI), 16
concepts of print, 11
conceptual learning themes, 16
conclusions, forming, 140, 329–30
concurrent translation method,
   456
Condra, Estelle, 197
conferencing
   in independent reading, 299
   on informational texts, 315
   reading log for (form), 289
   value of, 495
connected discourse, 14
connections
   companion collections and, 243–63
   deep thinking about, 408–10
   defined, 48
   encouraging, in discussion, 13–14
   for environmental print, 399, 401
   home-school, 429
   personal, to vocabulary, 164
   to song lyrics, 416, 420–22
   technology and, 339
   text-to-self, 408–9
   text-to-text, 409–10
   to vocabulary, 164
   Word Sorts and, 168
content areas. *See also* curriculum
   Alphaboxes for, 179–81
   building knowledge with companion
     collections, 245–46
   classroom environment for, 74
   comprehension in, 25
   strategies for English language learners,
     444–49, 453–56
   Two-Word Strategy for, 179–81
   vocabulary for English language
     learners, 447–49
   vocabulary strategies, 179–81

contextualizing
    defined, 474
    for English language learners, 470–74
    forms, 476–78
    process, 474
conversation. *See* deep conversation;
    discussion
Cooney, Barbara, 205
cooperative groups, 15. *See also* collabora-
    tion; groups
    poetry discussion in, 340–43
    teaching standardized test strategies in,
    376–80
counting books, 348
Counting is for the Birds (Mazzola), 348
Cowley, Joy, 231
Creech, Sharon, 480
Crimi, Carolyn, 191
Crockett, Alicia, 298–99
cross-age buddy reading, 127
cue cards
    for retelling, 429
    about strategies, 15
curiosity, 483. *See also* questioning
curriculum. *See also* content areas
    comprehension strategies across, 5, 28
    language consistency across, 28
    planning across, 29
    reading across, 495
    thinking strategies across, 28
    writing across, 75, 495

Darian, Shea, 202
data analysis
    comprehension activities, 351
    in science notebooks, 329–30
data collection
    charts and, 328, 330
    for science notebooks, 328
Davidson, Sue, 233
decisionmaking, 121
Deedy, Carmen Agra, 231
deep conversation, 5, 43, 44. *See also*
    discussion
deep thinking. *See also* thinking
    background knowledge and, 416
    classroom environment and, 71
    discussing, 407–8, 411–12
    by emergent readers, 387–88
    in independent reading, 293
    interactive paragraph revision and,
    212–14
    language of, 387–88
    read aloud books and, 407–12
    reading as a writer and, 196
    rereading for, 309
    about song lyrics, 415–22
    teacher notes and, 70
    about text-to-self connections, 408–9
    about text-to-text connections, 409–10
    about themes, 410–11
deep understanding. *See also* comprehen-
    sion
    assessment of, 424
    guided reading and, 248–49
    in independent reading, 301
    reading partnerships and, 291–304

rereading and, 131, 135
demonstration, 493. *See also* modeling
description text form, 325
descriptive language
    mentor texts for, 197
    nonfiction, 268
Designing Interactive Paragraphs: The
    Steps (form), 216
desk arrangement, 74
details, listening for, 237
determining importance. *See* importance,
    determining
Determining What is Important in Text
    (form), 31
Developing Quality Questions (form),
    124
dialogue, mentor texts for, 203
dice, for probability analysis, 352
dictionaries, 321
digital photos, of students, 473
diPaola, Tomie, 203
Directed Listening and Thinking activity
    (DLTA), 389
Directed Reading and Thinking activity
    (DRTA), 389
discussion
    authentic, 80–82
    challenging each other in, 80
    of characters, 292
    comprehension and, 13–14, 28
    deep conversation, 5, 43, 44
    deep thinking and, 407–8, 411–12
    by English language learners, 482
    fishbowls, 69
    of informational texts, 269, 315
    inspiration through, 80–81
    instructional conversations, 13–14
    learning and, 59–60
    learning environment and, 60–70, 73
    partner, 68–70, 284, 285, 292, 407–8
    piggybacking on statements, 70, 415
    planning, 13–14
    of poetry, 340–43
    for questioning the author, 120
    of read alouds, 407–12
    responsive, 69–70
    risk-taking in, 79–80
    rules for, 77–79
    stages in, 302
    teacher notes on, 70
    teacher role in, 45, 68, 73
    thoughtful, 80–82
    trusting relationships and, 77–81
    value of, 482
Discussion Observation and Reflection
    Form: Through the Eyes of the
    Teacher (form), 413
Doctor DeSoto (Steig), 205
documentary video, 390
Dogteam (Paulsen), 191
Dr. Seuss, 409
drama, mentor texts for, 200–201
dramatization, 60–61, 63
drawing
    favorite parts of book, 335, 429
    learning through, 59, 61
    as scaffolding, 471

visualization and, 335
drawing conclusions, 140, 329–30
Drawing Inferences (form), 32
Dream Weaver (London), 198, 199
Dublin, Jill, 421
Duke, Nell K., 9, 16, 264
during-reading test strategies, 377–78

Earth from Above (Arthus-Bertrand), 231
eavesdropping, in independent reading,
    299
Edwards, Pamela Duncan, 187, 191
elbow partners, 69, 407–8. *See also* knee-
    to-knee conversations
emergent readers
    comprehension strategies for, 386–91,
    393–96
    deep thinking by, 387–88
    nonfiction for, 320–22
    questions for readers, 332
    questions for teachers, 332
Emma's Rug (Say), 132
emotional environment. *See also* learning
    environments
    creating, 83
    rules for, 77–79
    teacher assessment of, 84
    for thoughtful literacy, 76–82
emotional images, 39
emotions, mentor texts for, 201–2
End-of-the-Year Read Aloud (form), 137
energy, companion collection, 262–63
engagement
    comprehension and, 12
    conditions for, 493–94
    deep thinking and, 411–12
    of English language learners, 471, 482
    importance of, 493–94
    questioning and, 110–14, 117, 122
    in read alouds, 481–82
    in reading partnerships, 297
    stages in, 302
English language learners (ELL's)
    assessment of understanding by (form),
    458
    challenges for, 444
    as class "experts," 482
    companion collections for, 257
    comprehension strategies, 460–63
    concurrent translation method for, 456
    content area strategies, 444–49, 453–
    56
    contextualizing for, 472–74
    discussion by, 482
    engagement of, 471, 482
    frontloading for, 444–49, 482
    language acquisition by, 453–54
    language banks for, 186
    needs of, 460–62
    nonfiction for, 320–21
    primary language use by, 453–54
    read alouds for, 447–49, 479–85, 487
    reading partnerships and, 303
    rereading by, 483
    scaffolding for, 471–74
    shared reading for, 447–49
    using real objects with, 445, 473–74

environmental print
   comprehension of, 397–401, 403–5
   recontextualization of, 401
Environmental Print Investigations
   (form), 404
Epstein, Joyce, 98
Erandi's Braids (diPaola), 203
Esbensen, Barbara, 191
Evaluating Environmental Print: Noticing
   Persuasion and Bias (form), 405
evaluation. *See also* assessment
   of environmental print, 399, 401
Event and Picture Sort activity, 389
events
   inferences about, 140
   main, mentor texts for, 202–3
expectations, 493
expert speakers
   for English language learners, 448
   English language learners as, 482
explanations, encouraging, 13–14
explanatory text, 268, 326
explicit instruction. *See also* comprehension strategy instruction
   coaching and, 112–13
   of comprehension strategies, 2, 14
   of multiple comprehension strategies,
      46–54
   for questioning, 120–22
   reading partnerships and, 295
   value of, 46
expository writing, in science notebooks,
   327–30

Fables (Lobel), 203
Fact/Fib sheets, 370
"fake reading," 513
family literacy nights, 98, 100, 101
Feathers and Fools (Fox), 182
feelings, mentor texts for, 201–2. *See also*
   emotions
field trips, for English language learners,
   445–46
figurative language, 187, 420
Finding Commonalities (form), 526
Fine, Fine School, A (Creech), 480
fishbowl discussions, 69
fix-up strategies, 37
flashback, movie-making software and,
   337–38
Fleischman, Sid, 201
Florian, Douglas, 191
flowers and plants, companion collection,
   257–58
Focus on Comprehension—A Checklist
   to Ponder (form), 498
Follow the Drinking Gourd (Winter), 230
follow-up activities
   for nonfiction guided reading, 270
   for questioning the author, 120
food, companion collection, 258–59
Fox, Mem, 182, 191, 198, 202
Francescani, Kathleen, 76
Frederick Douglas, the Last Days of Slavery
   (Miller), 229
Freeman, David, 453
Freeman, Yvonne, 453

frogs, companion collection, 253
frontloading, for English language learners, 444–49, 482
"Funds of Knowledge," 98

Galway, Timothy, 112
games, student-created, 434–37
genres
   good readers' approaches to, 11
   in nonfiction writing, 324
   standardized tests as, 363–70, 375–80
geometry
   comprehension activities, 350
   vocabulary words, 180
Get the Gist strategy, 15
Ghost-Eye Tree, The (Martin), 199
Giff, Patricia Reilly, 202
G is for Googol (Schwartz), 350
Give Me Five strategy, 238–39
   form, 241
goals, of good readers, 10
Gogh, Vincent Van, 22–24, 25, 29
Good-Bye Round Robin (Opitz and
   Rasvinski), 495
Goodman, Amy, 499
good readers, strategies of, 10–11, 21
Goudvis, Anne, 117, 494
gradual release of responsibility model
   applying, 49, 54
   comprehension strategy instruction
      and, 15, 41, 44
   guiding, 49, 53–54
   for independent reading, 300–301
   for inferences, 139–40
   modeling, 49–52
   for questioning, 116
   for reading partnerships, 300–301
   sharing, 49, 52–53
   steps in, 492–93
   student roles in, 49
   teacher roles in, 49
   teacher self-assessment of, 45
   using, 47, 49
Graef, Renee, 419
Graham-Yooll, Liz, 187–88, 191
grammatical structure, English language
   learners and, 484
Grandpa's Garden (Darian), 202
graphic organizers, comparing texts with,
   410–11
graphophonic knowledge, 11
graphs, 351
Green Eggs and Ham (Dr. Seuss), 409
Greenfield, Eloise, 80
groups. *See also* collaboration
   cooperative, 15
   modeling questioning in, 112
   patterns of, 74
   poetry discussion in, 340–43
   teaching standardized test strategies in,
      376–80
guest speakers, for English language
   learners, 448
Guided Comprehension: A Teaching Model
   (McLaughlin and Allen), 118
guided reading
   background knowledge and, 244

cloze procedures in, 153–54
companion collections for, 243–63
comprehension strategy instruction in,
   275–78
deepening understanding with, 248–49
inferencing lesson in, 277–78
lesson planning, 267–71, 273
making inferences in, 142
of nonfiction, 264–71
nonfiction record (form), 274
text selection for, 266
Guided Reading Strategy Log (form),
   280
Guided Reading with a Strategy Focus
   (form), 280
guided retelling, 388
guiding, in gradual release of responsibility model, 49, 53–54
Guthrie, John, 12

Haddix, Margaret Peterson, 512
Hahn, Mary Lee, 135, 333
hands-on experiences, 73
Harvey, Stephanie, 117, 495
Harwayne, Shelley, 66, 71
Hauser, Jill, 414
"have-a-go," during sharing sessions, 52
Heads-Up Vocabulary (form), 173
hearing, listening *vs.*, 237
Helpful Test Taking Strategies (form), 373
Henny Penny (Wattenberg), 191
Hill, Cate, 425
Holes (Sachar), 512
home reading
   drawing favorite parts of book, 429
   importance of, 513
   linking to class inference strategies, 146
   log for (form), 515–16
home-school connections. *See* parental
   involvement
home visits, 99, 101
House, Molly, 174
Houston, Gloria, 205
How to Help Emergent Readers (form),
   332
Hoyt, Linda, 2, 58, 66, 105, 125, 150,
   161, 209, 243, 284, 308, 326, 363,
   377, 386, 462, 534
Human Body Revealed (Davidson and
   Morgan), 233
humor, mentor texts for, 200–201

illustrations
   of beginning, middle, and end of story
      (form), 433
   inferencing lesson on, 277
   retelling and, 427
   student review of, 463
I Love My Hair (Tarpley), 202
image creation, 48
I'm in Charge of Celebrations (Baylor),
   187, 191
immersion, 493
iMovie, 333–38
   chunking with, 337
   for comprehension strategy instruc-
      tion, 333–38

features of, 334
flashback with, 337–38
point of view and, 338
sequencing with, 336–37
tutorial, 334–38
visualization with, 335–36
importance, determining, 58
defined, 47
for environmental print, 399, 401
by mathematicians, 31
by readers, 31
by researchers, 31
by writers, 31
Imus, Carole, 406
independent reading
book selection for, 293
classroom environment for, 74
companion books for, 247–49
deep thinking in, 293
deep understanding in, 300–301,
301
nonfiction for, 270–71
strategy instruction for, 283–87
student behavior during, 293
Inference Equation, 139, 144
inferences, 138–47
about characters, 140, 147
defined, 48, 141
determining importance in text, 32
about environmental print, 399, 400
about events, 140
guided reading lesson on, 277–78
home reading and (form), 146
in informational texts, 142
minilessons, 139–42
modeling, 138, 142
in poetry, 141
prior knowledge and, 139
recording, form for, 145
from song lyrics, 416–18
sources of, 139, 141
teaching tips for, 142
technology and, 339
from text clues, 140
about themes, 141
types of, 139, 141
understanding, 140
vocabulary development and, 166
information, transmediation of, 59
Informational Text Forms (form), 326
informational texts
assessing student comprehension of,
266–67
authentic reading and writing of, 16
for classroom library, 315, 321
comprehension rubric, 272
comprehension strategies for, 267–70,
269–70
discussing, 315
for emergent readers, 320–22
features of, 321
forms of, 326
guided reading of, 264–71
guided reading record (form), 274
for independent reading, 270–71
inferences about, 142
reading aloud from, 315

rereading, 308–11
selecting for students, 266
student problems with, 265
text feature strategies, 269
time for, 265–66, 315, 324
types and purposes of, 268
value of, 492
variety of, 268
writing, 324
information circles, 495–96
initiating queries, for questioning the
author, 120
In November (Rylant), 198
In/Out Game, 349–50
inquiry
classroom climate of, 314–15
questions, for environmental print,
399, 400
inquiry curriculum, 356–60
background knowledge and, 360
comprehension and, 359–60
defined, 358–59
motivation and, 357
perspectives and, 359
planning sheet (form), 362
processes, 358–59
writing and, 356–60
Inquiry Planning Sheet (form), 362
Insectlopedia, Poems and Paintings
(Florian), 191
insects and bugs, companion collection,
254–55
inspiration, discussion and, 80–81
instructional nonfiction, 268. *See also*
informational texts
interactive paragraphs, 209–14
collaboration on, 211–14
multiple paragraph essays, 214
process, 211–14, 216
proofreading, 212
revising, 212–14
topic sentences for, 211
interactive read alouds, 494
interests
book selection and, 512–13, 517
of boys, 528–31
inquiry and, 357
Student Profile (form), 532
intermediate grades, 88–89
Investigating Visual Supports strategy,
463
form in English, 469
form in Spanish, 468
Ira Says Goodbye (Waber), 202
Ira Sleeps Over (Waber), 202, 409
I Read It But I Don't Get It (Tovani), 513
I-R-E (Initiation-Response-Evaluation)
pattern, 14

Jemma's Journey (Romain), 176, 182
Jenkins, Steve, 233
Jensen, Eric, 62
jigsaw puzzle metaphor, 375–77
Johnson, Angela, 182
Johnson, N., 496
Johnston, Tony, 204
Jordan, Rachel, 326

"Junie B. Jones" books, 292
Just Like Josh Gibson (Johnson), 182
"Just My Size" activity, 351

Kaur Khalsa, Dayal, 191
Keene, Ellin Oliver, 22, 138
Keeping Quilt, The (Pollaco), 140
Kesler, Kelli, 511
Key Points to Consider (form), 534
Key Word Strategy (form), 129
K.I.D. vocabulary, 165, 501, 502
form, 506
kindergarten
comprehension checklist, 94
vocabulary development in, 163–64
kinesthetic response, 62
Klein, Adria F., 520
Knauf, Michael, 303–4
*Knee-to-Knee, Eye-to-Eye, Circling in on
Comprehension* (Cole), 408
knee-to-knee conversations, 69
about favorite parts of books, 284, 285
in read alouds, 407–8
Koi and the Kola Nuts (Aardema), 203
Krull, Kathleen, 228, 229
KW. . . . E, 447
form, 450
K-W-L strategy, 522–23

Lambert, Trudy, 408
language
acquisition by English language
learners, 453–54
consistency across curriculum, 28
of deep thinking, 387–88
test style, 365–66, 367
theoretical approaches and, 523
language banks, 185–89
figurative language, 187
personal language, 187–88
poetry with imagery, 188
powerful verbs, 186–87
similes, 187
learning
characteristics of, 26–27
conditions for, 493–94
purpose in, 73
learning environments
attractiveness of, 67
boys and (form), 534
characteristics of, 73–74
classroom climate of inquiry, 314–15
comprehension checklist, 92–95
comprehension classroom, 85–90
considerations for (form), 534
discussion in, 68–70, 73
organization of, 66, 67, 75
partner-to-partner conversation in,
68–70
for reading and writing, 194–95
retail stores as models for, 67–68
teacher assessment of, 86–90, 96
time use in, 70–71
trusting relationships in, 77–81
wall displays, 73
learning logs, 15
learning partners. *See* partner learning

Lesser, Carolyn, 191
Lesson Plan, A: Focus on Whales (form), 319
lesson planning
    building assessment into, 315–16, 319
    for guided reading, 267–71, 273
leveled books, background knowledge and, 244
Linking At-Home Reading to Our Class Strategy Lessons (form), 146
Listen! Hear! (Opitz and Zbaracki), 238
listening
    comprehension and, 236–39
    defined, 237
    guided experiences in, 237–39
    observing listening behaviors, 242
    timeline activity, 237
    trusting relationships and, 79–80
Literacy Eco Maps, 100
"literary landscapes," 66
literature circles, 121, 495–96
Literature Log (form), 56
literature webbing, 389
Little Red Cowboy Hat (Lowell), 201
Lives of the Musicians, Good Times, Bad Times (and What the Neighbors Thought), 229
Lobel, Arnold, 203
Locker, Thomas, 198, 232
Lokting, Karen, 434
London, Jonathan, 198, 203
Loomis, Christine, 230
Love, Ruby Lavender (Wiles), 335
Loveable Lyle (Waber), 410–11
Lowell, Susan, 201
Luba the Angel of Bergen-Belsen (McCann), 231

MacLachlan, Patricia, 191
Magic School Bus, The (Cole), 201
magnets, companion collection, 250
main events, mentor texts for, 202–3
Make It Real (Hoyt), 389, 462
Making Inferences about Characters, 147
Maloney, Alison, 108
Maricle-Barkley, Leslie, 479
Martha Calling (Meddaugh), 203
Martha Speaks (Meddaugh), 203, 204
Martin, Bill, Jr., 199
Martin's BIG WORDS, The Life of Dr. Martin Luther King, Jr. (Rappaport), 229
mathematics
    algebra, 349–50
    Alphaboxes for, 179–81
    comprehension strategies for, 347–52, 355
    counting books, 348
    data analysis, 351
    determining importance in text, 31
    drawing inferences, 32
    fix-up strategies, 37
    geometry, 350
    measurement, 350–51
    monitoring meaning and comprehension, 36
    prior knowledge and, 33

probability, 351–52
    questions about, 34
    selecting books for (form), 354
    sensory and emotional images and, 39
    synthesis in, 38
    Two-Word Strategy for, 179–81
McBroom's and the Big Wind (Fleischman), 201
McBroom's Ear (Fleischman), 201
McBroom Tells the Truth (Fleischman), 201
McCall, Jan, 444
McIlvain, Dona, 40
McKeown, Margaret, 166, 390
McLaughlin, Maureen, 118
meaning
    good readers and, 10
    monitoring, 35–36
    natural search for, 387
    of poetry, 340–43
    searching for, while reading, 118
    word-level comprehension, 150–51
measurement, comprehension activities, 350–51
Measuring Penny (Leedy), 350–51
Meddaugh, Susan, 203, 204
mentor texts
    for action words, 198
    for author comprehension strategies, 196–207
    for characters, 204–5
    for descriptive language, 197
    for dialogue, 203
    for drama, 200–201
    for feelings and emotions, 201–2
    for humor, 200–201
    for main events, 202–3
    for monologue, 203
    for "show, don't tell" strategy, 199
    for suspense, 200–201
    for vivid language, 198
Mercuri, Sandra, 470
metacognition
    common language in, 523
    comprehension strategy instruction and, 42–43, 44
metaphors, 421
Middle School High Five, 499–503
Miller, William, 229
minilessons
    on comprehension strategy, 283–86
    on inferences, 139–42
    on rereading, 132–33
Minters, Frances, 201
M is for Music (Krull), 228
Misreading Masculinity (Newkirk), 527–28
Mississippi Mud (Turner), 198
Miss Rumphius (Cooney), 205
mistakes, 494
Miz Berlin Walks (Yolen), 187, 191
modeling. *See also* gradual release of responsibility model
    comprehension strategies for emergent readers, 391
    comprehension strategies with everyday texts, 529–30
    in gradual release of responsibility model, 49–52

inferences, 138, 142
    language of standardized tests, 365–66
    peer, for retelling, 427–28
    peer, for scaffolding, 427–28
    questioning, 111
    standardized test strategies, 365–66
    use of science notebooks, 327–30
monitoring
    comprehension, 3, 35–36, 157–58
    environmental print, 399, 400
    meaning, 35–36
    of nonfiction guided reading, 270
    Reader Self-Monitoring (form), 157–58
Monitoring Meaning and Comprehension (form), 35–36
monologue, mentor texts for, 203
Monreal, Staci, 291
Monroe, Mary, 185
Morgan, Ben, 233
Mosaic of Thought (Zimmerman and Keene), 28
motivation
    of boys, 529
    inquiry curriculum and, 357
movie-making software, 334–38
multilevel companion collections, 248–49, 249
multiple paragraph essays, 214
multiple strategy instruction
    explicit, 46–54
    value of, 5–6, 15–17
music. *See also* song lyrics
    deep thinking and, 62, 64
    learning through, 60
    song writing, 63, 217–20
My Dream of Martin Luther King (Ringgold), 229
"My Favorite Things," 419–20
My Great-Aunt Arizona (Houston), 205
My Reading Strategies (form), 393

narratives
    nonfiction, 268
    of personal celebrations, 187–88
    queries, for questioning the author, 119–20
    text form, 326
National Assessment of Education Progress (NAEP), 528
National Council of Teachers of Mathematics (NCTM), 348
natural disasters, companion collection, 263
Naylor, Reynolds, 199
"Neighborhood Street" (Greenfield), 80–81
New Improved Santa, A (Wolff), 197
Newkirk, Tom, 527–28, 529, 530
newsletters, parent involvement and, 100
night creatures, companion collection, 257
Night Noises (Fox), 198
nonfiction. *See* informational texts
Nonfiction Guided Reading Record (form), 274
nonfiction writing, 324
nonsense words, 4

"No Put Downs" rule, 71
notebooks
    science, 326–30, 332
    writer's, 186
nouns, 186
novels, vocabulary strategies for, 175–79

Observation Guide: Focus on Test Taking
    Strategies (form), 372
Observation Log for Language Learners
    During Read Aloud (form), 487
Observation of Comprehension Strategies
    (form), 396
Observation rubric for tracking compre-
    hension of nonfiction (form), 272
ocean
    companion collection for, 260–
        62
    student songs about, 217–20
Ocean Songs CD samples, 221–22
Ochoa, Marissa, 217
Odell, Marion, 92
Old Henry (Blos), 140
Once is Not Enough strategy, 462, 463
    form in English, 465
    form in Spanish, 464
Once Upon a Starry Night (Mitton and
    Balit), 232
One in the Middle is a Green Kangaroo,
    The (Blume), 199
open-ended questions
    about author strategies, 197–207
    coaching and, 113
    defined, 118
    for emergent readers, 388–89
Opitz, Michael F., 236
oral cloze, 152–53
organization, in learning environments,
    66, 67, 75
original thinking, 26
Other Side, The (Woodson), 132–33
Owl Moon (Yolen), 198
Owocki, Gretchen, 397

Page, Robin, 233
Painted Words/Spoken Memories (Aliki),
    203
paint pots of poetry, 341–43
    materials, 342
    process, 341–43
    questions for, 342–43
paragraphs
    interactive, 209–14
    movie-making software and, 337
paraphrasing, 48
parental involvement, 97–101
    barriers to, 99
    book buddies program, 100
    book-lending programs, 100, 101
    drawing favorite parts of book, 429
    family literacy nights, 98, 100
    goals for, 100–101
    home reading, 146, 429, 513, 515–16
    home visits, 99, 101
    Literacy Eco Maps, 100
    newsletters, 100
    on-going teacher consultation, 100

parent education nights, 99
Parent Educator/Community Early
    Literacy Specialist, 98
    tips for nurturing readers, 104
    value of, 98–99
    Williamston Community Schools
        projects, 98–101
Parent Educator/Community Early Liter-
    acy Specialist, 98
Parent Project, 101
Park, Barbara, 201
Park, Sue, 122
Park Beat (London), 232
partner discussion, 68–70, 284, 285,
    286, 292, 407–8
partner learning
    for comprehension instruction, 6
    deep thinking and, 408
    interactive paragraphs, 211–14
    reading partnerships, 75, 291–304
    sharing comprehension strategies in in-
        dependent reading, 283–86
    song writing with, 217–20
    value of, 69
Partner Preview: "I Notice" activity
    for English language learners, 448–49
Partnership Observations (form), 306
partner think-alouds, 125–27
    planning form, 128
passage of time, in poetry (form), 346
Passage Predictions (form), 451
Paulsen, Gary, 191
peer models, for retelling, 427–28
Pelzer, Dave, 512
personal connections. See connections
personal experiences, retelling, 427
Personal Reading Strategy Log (form),
    289
perspectives. See points of view
persuasive nonfiction, 268
    environmental print, 405
    text form, 326
Pfister, Marcus, 197, 203
phonemic awareness, 11
phonics, 73
photographs, of students, 473
physical sensation, 62
picture books
    building comprehension with, 226–
        34
    read alouds with, 494
    rereading, 227–28, 235
    value of, 226
picture observation charts, 446
picture story maps, 428–29
piggybacking statements, 70, 415
Pink and Say (Polacco), 182
Pinkney, Andrea Davis, 199
planning
    across the curriculum, 29
    discussion, 13–14
    guided reading, 267–71, 273
    inquiry curriculum, 362
    nonfiction guided reading, 273
    partner think-alouds, 128
    for queries to author, 118
    questioning the author, 118

student-created games, 438–39
    writing, 208
Planning for Nonfiction Guided Reading
    Lesson (form), 273
Planning My Writing (form), 208
Planning Sheet—Comprehension (form),
    438
Planning Sheet for Writing: Rules for
    My Comprehension Game (form),
    439
poetry
    analyzing (form), 344
    cooperative discussion of, 340–43
    imagery in, 188
    inferences about, 141
    passage of time in (form), 346
    visualization of, 343, 345
    writing, 63, 188
points of view
    inquiry curriculum and, 359
    multiple, 359
    teacher evaluation of, 520–23
    understanding with movie-making
        software, 337–38
Polacco, Patricia, 140, 182
popular culture materials, 401. See also
    environmental print
Possum Magic (Fox), 191
practice, learning and, 494
precious pearl metaphor, 71
predictions
    comprehension and, 28
    defined, 48
    for environmental print, 399, 400
    by good readers, 10
    inferences and, 140
    about standardized tests, 376
prefixes, 166–67
prereading scaffolds, 472
Preview, View, Review strategy, 453–54
    form, 459
previewing, 15, 501, 502
    questioning, 462, 463
    standardized tests, 376, 377, 378
Previewing the Text Through Question-
    ing strategy, 462, 481
    form in English, 467
    form in Spanish, 466
Price, Joyce, 194
prior knowledge. See background knowl-
    edge
probability, comprehension activities,
    351–52
Probably Pistachio (Murphy), 351–52
problem solving, 121
procedure text form, 326
professional organizations, 496
professional reading, 496
proofreading, 212
Public Education & Business Coalition,
    28
Pumpkin Circle: The Story of a Garden
    (Levenson), 233
purpose
    in learning, 73
    in reading, inquiry curriculum and,
        359–60

purpose *continued*
  of reading, 359–60
  setting, for environmental print, 399, 400

question answer relationships (QAR), 388–89
questioning
  assessing comprehension with, 109
  coaching stance in, 113
  comprehension and, 25, 109
  connections and explanations encouraged by, 13–14
  engagement and, 110–14, 117, 122
  environmental print, 399, 400
  explicit instruction in, 120–22
  first readings, 227
  functions of, 58, 111–12
  gradual release of responsibility model for, 112
  inquiry curriculum and, 356–60
  by mathematicians, 34
  modeling, 111
  natural curiosity and, 109–10, 118, 483
  previewing the text, 462, 463
  by readers, 34
  rereading and, 133, 309
  by researchers, 34
  role of, 108–14
  standardized tests, 376
  strategies, 117–22
  student directed, 109–14
  teacher-directed, 109, 112–13
  teachers and, 116, 483
  technology and, 339
questioning the author, 119–20
  discussion, 120
  planning, 119
  query development, 119–20
  segmenting, 119
Questioning the Author (Beck), 119
questions
  authentic, 110–11
  categorizing, 389
  developing, 119–20, 124
  for emergent readers, 332
  follow-up, 120
  inference, 278
  initiating, 120
  narrative, 120
  open-ended, 113, 118–19, 389
  for paint pots of poetry activity, 342–43
  recording, 115
  on standardized tests, 366, 368, 381
  for teachers of emergent readers, 332
  test-style, 366, 368
  thick, 118–19
  thin, 118–19
  true-false, 370
  types of, 110–11
  for word-level understanding, 151
  by writers, 34
Quick as a Cricket (Wood), 187, 191
Quick Draw, 61

Rainbow Fish, The (Pfister), 197
rainforest, companion collection, 256
Rain Talk (Serfozo), 197
Rambo, Jane, 85, 275
Ramona Forever (Cleary), 199
Ramona the Brave (Cleary), 199
Rea, Denise, 470
Read, Cover, Remember Reread strategy, 311, 313
Read, Cover, Remember Retell strategy, 311, 313
Read Aloud Reflections (form), 488
read alouds
  assessment during, 484–85
  benefits of, 481–82
  birthday, 135
  book selection for, 407, 484
  character analysis and, 410–11
  companion books for, 247, 249
  comprehension and, 226–34
  deep thinking in, 407–12
  deep understanding in, 301
  drawing favorite parts of book, 335, 429
  end-of-year (form), 137
  engagement in, 481–82
  for English-language learners, 447–49, 479–85, 487
  informational texts for, 315
  interactive, 494
  inviting conversation about, 407–8
  observation log for (form), 487
  partner-to-partner conversation during, 69
  with picture books, 494
  reflections on (form), 488
  rereading, 133
  retelling, 425–31
  teacher's connections in, 408
  text-to-self connections in, 408–9
  text-to-text connections in, 409–10
Read Around the Text strategy, 501, 502
  form, 505
reader engagement. *See* engagement
Reader Self-Monitoring (form), 157–58
Reader's Theater, 63, 75
Reading Don't Fix No Chevys (Smith and Wilhelm), 527–28
Reading Essentials (Routman), 309
Reading for Real Boxes strategy, 473–74
  form, 476
Reading Like a Writer (form), 193
Reading Log (form), 160
Reading Log for Conferencing During Independent Reading (form), 289
reading partnerships, 75. *See also* partner learning
  assessing, 298–300
  benefits of, 303–4
  book selection for, 294
  book sharing in, 295
  coaching, 298–300
  deep thinking in, 296
  deep understanding in, 291–304
  engagement in, 297
  English language learners and, 303

explicit teaching and, 295
  forming, 294
  gradual release of responsibility for, 300–301
  observing, 298–300
  Partnership Observations (form), 306
  rubrics for evaluating, 300
  self-evaluation of, 299–300
  supporting, 298–99
reading rate adjustment, 48
Reading Response Sheet (form), 280
reading theory, 522
"Reading Wars, The," 521
real objects, for English language learners, 445, 473–74
reciprocal reading, 15
Reciprocal Teaching, 389, 501, 503
  forms, 508–9
  K-W-L and, 522–23
Recommended Books (form), 182
Reconsidering Read Aloud (Hahn), 135
recontextualization, 401
Recording My Inferences (form), 145
Recording My Questions (form), 115
Record-Keeping Grid: Environmental Print Sources (form), 403
recount text form, 326
Red-Eyed Tree Frogs (Cowley), 231
RED LEGS: A Drummer Boy of the Civil War (Lewin), 230
references, 48
Reflecting on My Comprehension Strategies (form), 339
Reflecting on Your Practice chart, 22
reflection
  classical music and, 62
  on comprehension strategies (form), 339
  on comprehension strategy instruction, 42–43, 44
  on discussion (form), 413
  learning through, 62
  on read alouds (form), 488
  on retelling (form), 394
  self-reflection, 42–43, 44, 493
  on teacher practices, 22
Relatives Came, The (Rylant), 198
rereading, 130–35
  communities of readers and, 135
  deep understanding and, 131, 133
  defined, 48, 131
  by English language learners, 483
  importance of, 130
  informational texts, 308–11
  minilessons for, 133
  picture books, 227–28, 235
  purposes of, 132, 309
  for questioning, 309
  read alouds, 133
  in reading workshop, 131
  strategies for, 309–10
  student research on, 310
  for thinking, 309
  for understanding, 309
  for wondering, 309
Rereading for Information (form), 312
Rereading Picture Books (form), 235

Rereading—Reading Again, Reading Differently (form), 134
research. *See* comprehension research
researchers
   determining importance in text, 31
   drawing inferences, 32
   fix-up strategies, 37
   monitoring meaning and comprehension, 36
   prior knowledge and, 34
   questions and, 34
   sensory and emotional images and, 39
   synthesis by, 38
resistant readers, 511–13
respect
   between parents and teachers, 98–99
   trusting relationships and, 77–81
response, learning and, 494
responsibility for learning. *See also* gradual release of responsibility model
   anchor charts and, 316–17
   defined, 493–94
   resistant readers and, 513
responsive conversation, 69–70
retail stores, 67–68
retelling
   assessing comprehension with, 425–31
   checklist for, 427, 432
   comprehension and, 25
   cue cards for, 429
   environmental print, 399, 400
   format for, 429–30
   genuine audience for, 431
   illustrations and, 427
   nonfiction, 268
   peer models for, 427–28
   personal experiences, 427
   with picture story maps, 428–29
   with storytelling glove, 429–30, 432
   student-led book recommendations, 429
   Student Retell Record (form), 432
Retell Reflections (form), 394
revision
   of interactive paragraphs, 212–14
   of sentences, 212–14
Revisit, Reflect, Retell (Hoyt), 378
Reynolds, Julia Moorhead, 9
Rich Lizard and other Poems (Chandra), 191
Ringgold, Faith, 229
risk-taking, in discussion, 78–79
Rodgers and Hammerstein's My Favorite Things (Graef), 419
Romain, Trevor, 176, 182
rote memorization, 161–62
Roucher, Nancy, 229
round robin reading, 491, 495
Routman, Regie, 6, 309
Rylant, Cynthia, 131, 141, 198

Sadako (Coerr), 476
Sadeghian, Lili, 296, 299
Sample Passage for Puzzle Lessons (form), 382
Sample Questions for Puzzle Lessons (form), 381

Say, Allen, 132
scaffolding
   anchor charts for, 316–17
   defined, 471
   for English language learners, 470–74
   forms, 476–78
   peer models and, 427–28
Scaffolding and Contextualizing Learning: Supporting English Language Learners (form), 477
scanning, 48
Schools That Beat the Odds studies, 151
science
   Alphaboxes for, 179–81
   Concept-Oriented Reading Instruction (CORI) of, 16
   inquiry curriculum for, 356–60
   Two-Word Strategy for, 179–81
science notebooks, 326–30
   assessment of, 332
   determining data to record in, 327–28
   forming conclusions, 329–30
   modeling strategies for recording in, 327–30
   tables of contents, 329
   titles, 38–329
Scott, Susanne C., 92
Scurlock, Joy, 117
Searching for Balance (form), 324
Seashore Book, The (Zolotow), 197
See the Ocean (Condra), 197
segmenting the text, for queries to author, 119
Selecting Books to Match Math Standards (form), 354
self-assessment, by teachers
   classroom community, 45
   classroom discussion, 45
   gradual release of responsibility, 45
   student self-awareness, 45
self-assessment, of reading partnerships, 299–300
self-awareness, of students, 45
self-coaching, 157
self-correction, 151
self-questioning, 48
self-reflection. *See* reflection
sensory images, 28, 39
sentences, 211–14, 212–14
sequencing, with movie-making software, 336–37
Serfozo, Mary, 197
series books, 483
Series of Unfortunate Events, The (Snicket), 512
Seven Blind Mice (Young), 140
Shaggy (Pfister), 203
shared reading
   companion books for, 247
   deep understanding in, 301
   for English-language learners, 447–49
   making inferences in, 142
sharing, in gradual release of responsibility model, 49, 52–53
sharing circle, 283–86

Sharing Our Visualizations (form), 345
Shiloh (Naylor), 199
"show, don't tell" strategy, mentor texts for, 199
Shrek (Steig), 203
Sibberson, Franki, 130
similes, 187
Simon, Seymour, 233
Single Shard, A (Park), 122
Sketch Around the Text, 61
Sketch a Word, 165–66
sketching. *See* drawing
Sketch to Stretch, 61
skimming, 48
Skinnybones (Park), 201
Sky Tree (Locker), 232
Smalls, Irene, 79
Smith, Michael W., 527–28
Snapshots: Literacy Minilessons Up Close (Hoyt), 492
Snicket, Lemony, 512
Snyder, Jodi, 314
solar system, companion collection, 251–52
Some Smug Slug (Edwards), 191, 194
song lyrics. *See also* music
   background knowledge and, 416
   comprehension instruction through, 414–22
   connections to, 416, 420–22
   deep thinking about, 415–22
   figurative language in, 420
   finding theme in, 416–18
   Ocean Songs CD samples, 221–22
   visualizing, 419–20
   writing, 63, 217–20
sounding out, 48
special education, 521–23
spinners, for probability analysis, 352
standardized tests
   after-reading test strategies, 378, 379–80
   asking questions about, 376
   before-reading test strategies, 378
   comprehension of, 363–70
   during-reading test strategies, 377
   jigsaw puzzle metaphor for, 375–77
   modeling language of, 366
   modeling strategies for, 365–66
   predictions about, 376
   previewing, 376, 377, 378
   prior knowledge and, 376
   question analysis for, 366, 368
   stamina for, 365
   strategies for, 364–70, 373, 374–80, 381–82
   student-written questions, 368–69
   teaching as genre, 363–70, 375–80
   test practice *vs.* test preparation, 363, 364
   true/false questions for, 370
standards, integration of, 74
Stauffer, Russell, 389
Stead, Tony, 264, 326
Steig, William, 191, 203, 205
Steptoe, John, 202
Stevie (Steptoe), 203

Sticky Note Reviews (form), 518
sticky notes
    for book reviews, 518
    for cloze procedures, 153
    for marking favorite parts, 284, 285
Stolz, Mary, 203
Storm in the Night (Stolz), 203
story elements
    enhancing with retelling, 426–27
    illustrating (form), 433
story maps
    for emergent readers, 389
    picture, retelling with, 428–29
Story of Ruby Bridges, The (Coles), 182,
    230
storytelling glove, 429–30, 432
Stranger, The (Van Allsburg), 132
Stranger in the Mirror (Say), 132
Strategies That Work (Harvey and
    Goudvis), 117, 494
Strategy Demonstration Plan (form), 56
Strategy Demonstration Plan format,
    50
Strategy Log for Primary Readers (form),
    395
student-created games, 434–37
    assessment tool, 440
    game card examples, 441–42
    planning sheets, 438–39
student-led book recommendations, 429
Student Profile (form), 532
Student Retell Record (form), 432
suffixes, 166–67
Sum It Up strategy, 501
    form, 510
summarizing, 48
Sunshine Medley (Greg and Steve), 421
suspense, mentor texts for, 200–201
synthesis, 26, 38, 48

tables of contents, for science notebooks,
    329
Table Where Rich People Site, The
    (Baylor), 203
Tagholm, Sally, 231
Taking an Active Stance as a Listener
    (form), 242
Tales of a Gambling Grandma (Kaur
    Khalsa), 191
Talking to Faith Ringgold (Ringgold and
    Roucher), 229
tape-recorded books, reading with, 75
targeted discussion of background
    knowledge, 389
Tarpley, Natasha Anastasia, 202
T-charts, for algebra, 350
"teachable moments," 321
Teacher Observation (form), 116
teachers
    approaches over time, 491–92
    as coaches, 112–13
    evaluation of diverse perspectives by,
        520–23
    explicit strategy instruction by, 2
    on-going consultation with parents,
        100
    personal reading shared by, 74

questions generated by, 109, 112–13,
    389
    roles of, 73, 93
teacher's guides, 109, 491
*Teacher's Guide to Standardized Reading
    Tests, A* (Calkins), 374
Teaching Learners to Contextualize
    (form), 478
Tenth Good Thing About Barney, The
    (Viorst), 202
terminology, 523
Tessa's Tip-Tapping Toes (Crimi), 191
test practice, 363, 364
test preparation, 363, 364–70
tests, standardized. *See* standardized tests
test-style questions
    on standardized tests, 366, 368
    student-written, 368–69
Text Bits, for English language learners,
    446
text features, 269
text selection
    broadening choices in, 528–31
    for classroom library, 496
    for guided reading, 266
    helping students with, 512–13
    for independent reading, 293
    interests and, 517
    for mathematics, 354
    nonfiction, 266
    for read alouds, 407, 484
    for reading partnerships, 294
    student book reviews for, 518
    student problems with, 512
    for teaching strategies, 112
text structure, 12–13
Text Talk activity, 390
text-to-self connections, 408–9
text-to-text connections, 409–10
thematic units, 243
themes
    deep thinking about, 411–12
    inferences about, 141
    in song lyrics, 416–18
Therriault, Teresa, 226, 490
thick questions, 118–19
think alouds
    comprehension and, 13
    partner, 125–27, 128
    during sharing sessions, 52
    teaching inferences through, 139–40
    for test strategies, 365–66, 376
Think and Sketch (form), 452
thinking. *See also* deep thinking
    discussion and, 59
    dramatization and, 60–61, 63
    with music, 60, 62, 64
    physical activity and, 62
    strategies, across the curriculum, 28
    visual arts and, 59, 61
Thinking About Words (form), 171–72
thin questions, 118–19
"This Little Light of Mine," 419, 421–22
This Little Light of Mine (Walker), 421–
    22
thoughtful literacy. *See also* comprehen-
    sion; deep thinking; thinking

classroom environment for, 66–71,
    73–75
creating, 8
emotional environment for, 76–82
requirements for, 2–3
Tiger Math (Nagda and Rickel), 351
Tiger Rising, The (DiCamillo), 130
time
    effective use of, 70–71
    for nonfiction books, 315
    passage of, in poetry (form), 346
    for reading, 59, 71, 75
    for writing, 75
timelines, as listening guides, 237
Timothy Goes to School (Wells), 407, 409–
    10, 411
Timothy Tib (Graham-Yooll), 191, 194
titles, for science notebooks, 328–29
Toad (Brown), 187, 191
Today Was a Terrible Day (Giff), 202
To Kill a Mockingbird (Lee), 175, 179
Tolan, Kathleen, 374
topic sentences, 211
Tovani, Cris, 513
Tower, Cathy, 356
Transactional Strategy Instruction (TSI),
    390–91
transitions, movie-making software and,
    337
transmediation, 59
transportation, companion collection,
    259–60
Trelease, Jim, 228
true-false questions, 370
trusting relationships
    in classroom, 73, 77–81
    defined, 77
    encouraging, 83
Turner, Ann, 198
Two-Column Notes strategy, 501–2, 503
    form, 506
Two of Everything (Hong), 349
Two-Word Strategy, 174–81
    form, 184

Ulbricht, Susan, 66
Una Vez No es Suficiente! (form), 464
Understanding Our Reading Preferences
    (form), 517
Understanding Passage of Time (form),
    346
Updegraff, Carol, 283
Using Prior Knowledge—Schema (form),
    33

Van Allsburg, Chris, 132
Van Gogh Café, The (Rylant), 130–31
Velveteen Rabbit, The (Williams), 197
verbs
    descriptive, 188
    powerful, 186–87, 186–87, 198
Very Important Points (VIPs), 496
video activities
    for emergent readers, 390
    for English language learners, 446
Viorst, Judith, 201, 202
VIP strategy, 501, 503

visual arts, 61
visual imagery, 389–90
visualization
   awareness of, 58
   demonstrating with picture books, 227
   by emergent readers, 390
   of environmental print, 399,
     401
   with movie-making software, 335–36
   of poetry, 342–43, 345
   sequencing and, 336–37
   sharing (form), 345
   of song lyrics, 419–20
   technology and, 339
vivid language, mentor texts for, 198
vocabulary
   language banks, 185–89
vocabulary development
   Alphaboxes, 174–81
   assessment, for English language
     learners, 484–85
   book selection for, 182
   building with companion collections,
     245–46
   checklist for (form), 170
   comprehension and, 11, 25, 161
   concept-related, 162
   for content areas, 179–81
   effective, 11–12, 161
   frontloading, for English language
     learners, 482
   in grades one and two, 94
   in grades three to five, 94
   inferences and, 166
   interesting words, 171–72
   K.I.D. Vocabulary, 165
   in kindergarten, 163–64
   for novels, 175–79
   personalizing vocabulary, 164
   prefixes and suffixes, 166 67
   Sketch a Word, 165–66
   strategies for, 161–68
   strategies of good readers, 10
   Two-Word Strategy, 174–81
   unrelated word lists for, 161–62
   Vocabulary Mapping, 165
   Vocabulary Teams, 164
   word collecting forms, 173, 192
   Word Replacement, 165
   Word Sorts, 167–68
   Word Theater, 165
   word use and, 162
   Word Wizards, 165
Vocabulary Mapping, 165

Vocabulary Teams, 164
Voices in the Park (Browne), 132
volume reading, 12–13

Waber, Bernard, 202, 407, 412
Walker, Sylva, 421
wall displays, 73, 496
Wallis, Judy, 138–52
Watch Me Grow Frog (Magloff), 232
water, companion collection on, 253
Water Dance (Locker), 198, 233
Watterberg, Jane, 191
weather, companion collection on, 255–
   56
Wednesday Surprise, The (Bunting), 205
Wells, Rosemary, 407, 409, 411, 412,
   425
What a Wonderful Day to Be a Cow
   (Lesser), 191
What Do You Do with a Tail Like This?
   (Jenkins and Page), 233
What Good Readers Do (form), 20
wheels, companion collection on, 250
When I Was Young in the Mountains
   (Rylant), 141, 198
When Kids Can't Read (Beers), 131–32
When Marian Sang (Ryan), 228
When the Wind Stops (Zolotow), 191
Where the Big Fish Are (London), 203
White, Jennifer, 291
White Socks Only (Coleman), 182
whole-class inquiry, 356
Wigfield, Allan, 12
Wilfrid Gordon McDonald Partridge
   (Fox), 202
Wilhelm, Jeffrey D., 527–28, 530
Williams, Margery, 197
Williamston Community Schools, 98–
   101
Wills, Jesse, 294
*Wilma Unlimited: How Wilma Rudolph
   Became the World's Fastest Woman*
   (Krull), 228
Winter, Jeanette, 230
Wolff, Patricia Rae, 197
Wombat Divine (Fox), 204
Wonderful Wizard of Oz, The (Baum),
   435
wondering, rereading for, 309
Wood, Audrey, 187, 191
Woodson, Jacqueline, 132–33
word-level comprehension, 150–55, 186
Word-Level Comprehension Equation,
   152–53

Word Replacement, 165
Word Sorts, 167–68, 447–48
word study lessons, 73, 386–87
word substitution activities, 154–55
Words with Wrinkled Knees (Esbensen),
   191
Word Theater, 165
Word Wizards, 165
worms, companion collection on, 259
Wrap-up strategy, 15
Wright, Marlee, 320
writers. *See also* authors
   comprehension strategies of, 194–205
   determining importance in text, 31
   drawing inferences, 32
   fix-up strategies, 37
   monitoring meaning and comprehen-
     sion, 35
   prior knowledge and, 33
   questions by, 34
   reading as, 186, 188, 193
   sensory and emotional images and, 39
   synthesis by, 38
writer's notebooks, 186
writing
   across curriculum, 75, 495
   in grades one and two, 94
   in grades three to five, 94
   inquiry curriculum and, 357–58
   nonfiction forms, 324
   planning (form), 208
   by readers, 495
   in science notebooks, 327–30
   songs, 217–20
Writing Songs to Share Our Learning
   (form), 223

*Yellow House, The, Vincent van Gogh &
   Paul Gaugin Side by Side* (Rubin),
   231
*Yellow Star, The: The Legend of King
   Christian X of Denmark* (Deedy),
   231
Yoko (Wells), 409–10, 411, 425–26
Yolen, Jane, 187, 191, 198
"You Are My Sunshine," 415–17, 421
You Are My Sunshine (Dublin), 421
Young, Ed, 140

Zbaracki, Matthew D., 236
Zimmerman, Susan, 138
Zolotow, Charlotte, 191, 197
zone of proximal development, 492
Zoo Books, 188